Vintage Vicksburg

Featuring

More than 900 tested Recipes
Historical Color Photographs
Miss Mississippi's Favorites
Cooking for Children
Menus
Garnishes
Cooking Tips

Compiled by

Junior Auxiliary of Vicksburg, Mississippi

Editor
Mrs. Robert R. Bailess

Co-Editors
Mrs. Joseph P. Harris
Mrs. Jerry M. Hall

Since 1936 the members of the Vicksburg Jr. Auxiliary, Inc., have been improving the quality of life in this community. Through the efforts of trained volunteers and the profits realized from the sale of *Vintage Vicksburg*, programs concerning child advocacy, the elderly, family development and public education have become a reality in Warren County.

Additional copies of *Vintage Vicksburg* may be obtained by contacting:

Vintage Vicksburg
P.O. Box 86
Vicksburg, Mississippi 39181
(601) 634-1084

First Printing	October 1985	10,000 copies
Second Printing	July 1986	10,000 copies
Third Printing	June 1988	10,000 copies
Fourth Printing	December 1990	10,000 copies
Fifth Printing	July 1992	10,000 copies
Sixth Printing	June 1995	10,000 copies
Seventh Printing	October 2000	5,000 copies
Eighth Printing	July 2002	7,000 copies
Ninth Printing	September 2008	3,000 copies

ISBN 978-0-9614988-0-1

WIMMER
COOKBOOKS
ConsolidatedGraphics
1-800-548-2537

COMMITTEES

Testing:

Mrs. Robert M. Abraham

Editing:

Mrs. Frank Campbell
Mrs. Gordon Carr, Jr.
Mrs. Kenneth Grogan, III
Mrs. Jed Mihalyka
Mrs. Bobby Miller
Mrs. Robert Moss

Index:

Mrs. O. E. Bradway, III
Mrs. Gordon Carr, Jr.
Mrs. Hays Latham
Mrs. Jerry Mayfield
Mrs. Robert Sadler
Mrs. David Sessums

Proofreading:

Miss Mary Louise Cashman
Mrs. Robert F. Evans, III
Mrs. Kenneth Grogan, III
Mrs. Russell Hawkins
Mrs. Jack Stamm, Jr.

Photographs:

Mrs. Robert M. Abraham
Nick Cassino - Floral Design
Bob L. Pickett
Mrs. Bob Pickett

Art:

Mrs. Harold Blue

Typing:

Mrs. Gordon Carr, Jr.
Mrs. Shouphie Habeeb
Mrs. Dan Waring

Patrons:

Mrs. Sammy Ashley
Mrs. Albert Dornbusch
Mrs. George Jabour, Jr.
Mrs. Mark Prewitt
Mrs. Ken Rector
Mrs. Larry Rocconi

Marketing and Promotion:

Mrs. Oren Bailess, Jr.
Mrs. James W. Cook
Mrs. Larry Rocconi

Special Sections:

Mrs. Robert M. Abraham
Mrs. Briggs Hopson
Mrs. Jerry Mayfield
Mrs. David Sessums

Literary Introduction:

Gordon Cotton

Photographic Descriptions:

Charles J. Faulk

Recipe Compiling:

Mrs. Jack Stamm, Jr.

COOKBOOK CHAIRMEN

Mrs. Robert R. Bailess - *1986*
Mrs. Jerry Mayfield - *1987*
Mrs. Raymond Abraham - *1988*
Mrs. Chester Redditt - *1989*
Mrs. Kurt Schrock - *1990*
Mrs. John Farr - *1991*
Mrs. Howard Waring - *1992*
Mrs. Bruce Ebersole - *1993*

Mrs. Mark Mazzanti - *1994*
Mrs. Stuart Green - *1995*
Mrs. Denise Broussard Sassone - *1996*
Mrs. Mille Goodwin Wolfe - *1997*
Mrs. Nancy Nelson Bullard - *1998*
Mrs. Debbie Haworth Rose - *1999*
Mrs. Mary Jane Gilmer Wooten - *2000*

Acknowledgments

We deeply appreciate the help of these people. Without their time, support and efforts *Vintage Vicksburg* would not have been possible.

Mrs. Harold Blue
Miss Mary Louise Cashman
Nick Cassino
Gordon Cotton
Charles J. Faulk, Jr.
First National Bank, Vicksburg, Mississippi
Mr. and Mrs. Bob Pickett
Mr. and Mrs. B. N. Simrall, III
Mrs. Jack Stamm, Jr.
Vicksburg Junior Auxiliary Active and Associate Members
Wheeless, Beanland, Shappley and Bailess
Mr. and Mrs. John Wayne Jabour - Lakemont
Mr. and Mrs. Ted Mackey - Cedar Grove
Mr. and Mrs. Martin White - Anchuca
Vicksburg Evening Post
Gold Patrons
Patrons

* * * * * * * * * * * * * * * * *

ROBERT L. "BOB" PICKETT

A picture tells the story, especially when Bob Pickett is the photographer. Pickett has a rare eye for form and beauty and an in-depth perception of his subject, which he combines with perfection in photographic technique. He's an artist.

Vicksburg... Born of the River

Vicksburg.

It's the most southern of cities in history and traditions—a name that stirs imaginations and memories of romance and intrigue, of shantyboats and columned mansions, of Catfish Row and 15 China Street, of a bustling, teeming waterfront and of the sounds of steel and steam in the sawmills and railroad yards, of roustabouts and elegantly dressed ladies, of a battle that sealed the fate of a struggling southern nation.

Vicksburg is the South.

Yet little more than a century ago a visitor to our city would seldom have heard a Dixie drawl, for Vicksburg was an Irish town. And German. And African—with a sprinkling of Italian, Swiss, French, Scot, English, Spanish, and even one family from Sweden. Later others would come—the Chinese and Lebanese, more Italians, people from Central Europe, from Russia. There were Protestants and Jews and Orthodox and Catholics, shantyboat Irish and lace curtain Irish, rich and poor and those in between, all mixing and mingling, all neighbors.

Though the Spanish discovered this land on the bluffs above the Mississippi where the Indians lived, it was the French who first settled it and the British who became the landlords before we became Americans in the late 1700's.

Vicksburg, when it was still called Walnut Hills before the Reverend Newit Vick came to establish the city in 1819, was a wilderness frontier that attracted the first settlers, those adventurers who came by horseback and on flatboats. Some built shanties along the streams; others carved farms from the forest.

A generation later others arrived, bringing with them some of the treasures and trappings of civilization. They traveled by steamboat, that marvelous contraption that looked like a floating wedding cake with its gingerbread trim.

Vicksburg's skyline began to change. Clapboard shacks gave way to more substantial buildings; modest mansions rose from the terraced hills and church steeples pierced the horizon. Vicksburg was coming of age, outgrowing its frontier beginning, but it wasn't without pain; rumblings of conflict and discontent like distant thunder erupted into open warfare on July 4, 1836, between the restless rowdies along the waterfront and the folks who lived on the bluffs. When it ended, a respected citizen was dead, shot by gamblers; six of the ruffians were hanged as a warning. A city was born, but it wasn't an easy birth.

The river—that great lifestream, that highway that flows through mid-America from Canada to the Gulf of Mexico—is the reason for Vicksburg's being. Its waters carved out a harbor, creating an ideal location for a city. By river came those who would populate our hills, and by the Mississippi came the tools it would take to create a civilization and treasures to satisfy the souls of the citizens.

It was by the river that Vicksburg would send out its raw materials, linking it to the rest of the world, even to the lands from whence its sons and daughters had originally come. That same river that brought life to Vicksburg would bring death and destruction, on another July 4, in 1863, when the city kept its date with destiny. A long siege ended on that date, and with it ended the hopes and dreams of the South. But Vicksburg began rebuilding, looking to the future, but remembering, honoring its past.

From an exciting heritage and a diversity of origins, our city became a melting pot where the best traditions—the vintage of each era, of every race and nationality—have blended to create a culture that is uniquely Vicksburg.

Gordon A. Cotton, Director
Old Court House Museum -
Eva W. Davis Memorial

Table of Contents

Menus

Wedding Party Brunch

Mimosas (pg. 59)
Cocktail Sesame Wafers (pg. 24)
Creole Eggs (pg. 122)
Cheese Pudding (pg. 126)
Cucumber Salad (pg. 103)
Company Carrot Bread (pg. 298)
Pecan Muffins (pg. 307)
Chocolate Eclairs (pg. 316)

Morning Bridge Brunch

Brandy Milk Punch (pg. 65)
Easy Egg Brunch (pg. 121)
Grits Soufflé (pg. 126)
Individual Frozen Fruit Salads (pg. 110)
Fresh Blueberry Muffins (pg. 308)
Story's Fudge Ripple Bars (pg. 382)

Soup and Salad Luncheon

Bloody Mary (pg. 59)
Chilled Cucumber Soup (pg. 79)
Ladies' Day Lunch (pg. 91)
Spinach Sandwiches (pg. 38)
Normandy Chocolate Mousse (pg. 326)
Coffee

Ladies' Day Luncheon

Betty's Strawberry Daiquiris (pg. 60)
Nancy's Crab and Shrimp Casserole (pg. 222)
Broccoli and Carrots Amandine (pg. 259)
Citrus-Avocado Salad (pg. 100)
Light-As-A-Feather Rolls (pg. 291)
Praline Cheese Cake (pg. 332)
Demitasse

Afternoon Tea

Almond Tea (pg. 67)   Tangy Catawba Juice (pg. 66)
Cucumber Sandwiches (Spread) (pg. 40)
Cheddy's Corned Beef Rolled Sandwiches (pg. 41)
Cheese Straws (pg. 24)
Orange-Glazed Pecans (pg. 27)
Hawaiian Cheese Ball (pg. 20)
Aspic Miniatures (pg. 34)
Cheese and Spinach Puffs (pg. 29)
Almond Date Rumaki (pg. 28)
Thumbprint Cookies (pg. 374)
Chocolate Fudge (pg. 394)
Pecan Tarts (pg. 380)

Candlelight Dinner for Two

Peach Fuzzy (pg. 60)
Homemade Herb Cheese with Crackers (pg. 23)
Shrimp Scampi II (pg. 210)
Confetti Rice (pg. 132)
Mr. B.'s Sesame Spinach Salad (pg. 98)
Crème de Menthe Parfait (pg. 389)
White Wine

Large Cocktail Party

Twenty-Four Hour Cocktail (pg. 60)   Favorite Mixed Drinks
Sesame Chicken (pg. 50)
Marinated Steak Bites (pg. 52)
Tangy Cocktail Meatballs (pg. 403)
Crabmeat au Gratin (pg. 15)
Marinated Shrimp (pg. 44)
Bacon-Onion Sandwiches (pg. 42)
Phyllo Pastry Triangles with Cheddar Chicken Filling (pg. 57)
Gouda Wellington (pg. 22)
Miniature Stuffed Potatoes (pg. 31)
Stuffed Cocktail Tomatoes (pg. 33)
O. C.'s (pg. 25)
Butter Creme Brownies (pg. 384)
Orange Balls (pg. 375)   Meringues (pg. 374)

Dinner Party

Cheese Krispies (pg. 23)
Betty's Shrimp Mousse (pg. 43)
French Onion Soup - page 75
Red Wine
Carpetbagger Steak (pg. 153)
Spinach-Artichoke Casserole (pg. 275)
Rockwood Scalloped Potatoes (pg. 273)
Fruit Francine (pg. 112)
Refrigerator Spoon Rolls (pg. 292)
Crêpes Fitzgerald (pg. 313)
Coffee Bourbon Punch (pg. 63)

After the Theatre Encore

Party Pepperoni Canapés (pg. 40)
Tomato Sandwiches (pg. 39)
Shrimp Party Sandwiches (pg. 39)
Fruit 'n Crackers (pg. 24)
Toasted Pecans (pg. 27)
Lemon Jelly Cake (pg. 339)
Coffee

Strictly Southern

Old Southern Mint Julep (pg. 59)
Civil War Chicken (pg. 184)
Fried Green Tomatoes (pg. 279)
Corn Pudding (pg. 260)
Mease's Mustard Greens (pg. 263)
Corn Bread (pg. 288)
Down in Dixie Bourbon Pie (pg. 368)

Mexican Dinner

Madrid Sangria (pg. 61)
Hot Sombrero Dip (pg. 19)
Shoe Peg Dip (pg. 19)
Chicken Enchiladas (pg. 202)
Mexican Wastebasket Stew (pg. 407)
Jalapeño Relish Dip with Tortilla Chips (pg. 19)
Taco Salad (pg. 100)
Fried Ice Cream (pg. 415)

Christmas Dinner

Farrell Holiday Egg Nog (pg. 62)
Sugared Pecans (pg. 27)
Bacon-Cheese Mold (pg. 21)
Roast Turkey (pg. 204)
Corn Bread Dressing with Giblet Gravy (pgs. 204 and 205)
Georgie's Sweet Potatoes in Orange Cups (pg. 272)
Squash Casserole (pg. 277)
Broccoli with Almonds (pg. 258)
Christmas Salad (pg. 109)
Viola's Biscuits (pg. 289)
Ambrosia (pg. 329)
Miriam's Fruit Cake (pg. 345)
Fluffy Gold Coconut Cake (pg. 341)
Southern Pecan Pie (pg. 355)

New Year's Day Buffet

Coca-Cola Ham (pg. 172)
Southern Black-Eyed Peas (pg. 267)
Fantastic Potato Salad (pg. 101)
Pineapple Cheese Casserole (pg. 283)
Cheesy Jalapeño Corn Bread (pg. 287)
Chocolate Buttermilk Sheet Cake (pg. 352)

Fourth of July Barbecue

Dilled Broccoli (pg. 32)
Shrimp Spread (pg. 44)
Bobby's Barbecue Ribs (pg. 178)
Tweety's Baked Beans (pg. 255)
Red Slaw Relish (pg. 95)
Macaroni Salad (pg. 101)
Herb Bread (pg. 298)
Fresh Strawberry Ice Cream (pg. 385)
Cream Cheese Pound Cake (pg. 334)
Summertime Tea (pg. 68)

Football Tailgate Picnic

Party Ham Sandwiches (pg. 41)
Oyster Loaf (pg. 46)
Cold Beef Platter (pg. 151)
Sliced Smoked Chicken (pg. 184)
Hot Mustard Sauce and Homemade Mayonnaise (pgs. 115 and 179)
Assorted Breads
Rice-A-Roni Salad (pg. 102)
Antipasto (pg. 38)
Great Keepsake Brownies (pg. 383)
Lemon Cookies (pg. 373)

River View

The mighty Mississippi River nuzzles close to the hills of Vicksburg, as it flows through the heartland of America to the sea. This city was a haven for early settlers, a mighty fortress in the Civil War, and then the chosen site for the first rail-highway bridge between Memphis and New Orleans.

Gala ceremonies marked the opening of the old bridge on May 20, 1930. It linked Mississippi with Louisiana, opening highway and rail connections sea to sea across America. Vicksburg was blessed by destiny. The river continued to dominate.

In rebuilding after the terrors of the Civil War in 1863, Vicksburg preserved the traditions and culture of the Old South as the New South emerged. The city on the hills retained the best of each. Another giant step forward was the new, four-lane Interstate 20 Bridge, dedicated February 15, 1973. It parallels the old structure.

A lonely Civil War cannon sits on an overlook near the crossing, still guarding the majestic stream below. Trains and cars speed across the bridges and mighty towboats push their barges up or down, according to their destinations.

The awesome power of the river is inescapable, as its currents and eddies flow toward the sea.

Appetizers and Beverages pictured:
Gouda Wellington, Mimosa, Peach Fuzzy, Bloody Mary, Stuffed Cocktail Tomatoes, Marinated Shrimp, Sweet Dip

Appetizers and Beverages

Crabmeat au Gratin

4 Tablespoons butter
1²/₃ cups chopped green onions
1 (7-ounce) jar mushrooms
9 Tablespoons flour
2 cups light cream
½ teaspoon salt

½ teaspoon cayenne pepper
1 pound crabmeat (well cleaned)
1 to 2 Tablespoons sherry
1 cup shredded American or Swiss
  cheese

Melt butter; sauté green onions and mushrooms. Add flour. Blend carefully with light cream. Cook slowly until thickened, stirring constantly. Add monosodium glutamate, salt, cayenne pepper, and crabmeat. Next add sherry and cheese. Cook slowly until well blended. Yield: 10 to 12 servings.

This can be served as a dip in a chafing dish or served in pastry shells as a main course.

Mrs. George R. Abraham
(Katherine Abraham)

Monterey Crabmeat Dip

2 slices bacon
1 small onion, finely chopped
2 medium tomatoes, peeled, seeded,
  and chopped
½ cup finely chopped celery
1 (7-ounce) can green chili salsa

¼ teaspoon salt
2 cups shredded Monterey Jack
  cheese
6 ounces lump crabmeat
Tortilla chips

Cook bacon in a skillet until crisp. Remove bacon and crumble. Set aside. Add onion, tomatoes, and celery to bacon drippings. Cook over medium heat until onions are tender. Add bacon, salsa, and salt. Over low heat, stir in cheese, a little at a time, until melted. Do not let the mixture boil. Fold in lump crabmeat. Pour into a bowl placed on a heated tray and surround with tortilla chips. Can be doubled for a chafing dish. Yield: 15 to 20 servings.

Mrs. Frank Maxwell
(Louise Middlebrook)

Oven-Baked Crab Dip

2 (8-ounce) packages cream cheese,
  softened
½ cup mayonnaise
1 Tablespoon powdered sugar
1 Tablespoon dry white wine
½ teaspoon onion juice
½ teaspoon prepared mustard

¼ teaspoon garlic powder
1 to 2 (6-ounce) cans white lump
  crabmeat
Salt and pepper
1 Tablespoon chopped parsley
Crackers

Combine first 8 ingredients. Salt and pepper to taste. Spoon mixture into lightly greased 1-quart baking dish. Bake at 375° for 15 minutes. Sprinkle with parsley. Serve warm with crackers of choice. Yield: 2¾ cups.

Mrs. Jimmy Keyes
Laurel, Mississippi

Hot Clam Dip

1 (8-ounce) package cream cheese
6 green onions (plus half of green
  tops), chopped
2 to 3 (8-ounce) cans minced clams,
  drained, reserving some liquid

1 teaspoon lemon juice
¼ teaspoon Worcestershire sauce
A few dashes of cayenne
Paprika to garnish

In a double boiler, melt cream cheese with onions. Add clams and spices, mixing well. If this mixture is too stiff, add a little liquid from clams. Serve in chafing dish with melba rounds. Top may be sprinkled with paprika to garnish. Yield: 2 to 3 cups.

Mrs. E. A. Buckner, Jr.
(Ruth Vicknair)

Hot and Spicy Shrimp Dip

2 pounds cream cheese
1 onion, diced
1 Tablespoon garlic juice
3 chili peppers

3 medium mild banana peppers
1 tomato, diced
1½ pounds canned or fresh shrimp

Mix all ingredients except tomato and shrimp. Heat in chafing dish. Add tomato and shrimp after the mixture is melted and mixed well. Yield: 12 servings.

Deanne Lipani
LaPlace, Louisiana

Creole Shrimp Dip

1 (8-ounce) package cream cheese, softened
Juice of 1 lemon
2 pounds boiled shrimp, coarsely ground
10 green onions, minced
⅔ cup mayonnaise

¼ teaspoon cayenne pepper
Dash Tony Chachere's Famous Creole Seasoning or salt and pepper to taste
TABASCO brand pepper sauce to taste
1 Tablespoon Worcestershire sauce

Soften cream cheese with lemon juice. Add shrimp and onions to mixture. Add enough mayonnaise to give a consistency for dipping with crackers or potato chips. Season with cayenne pepper and other seasonings to taste. Refrigerate. Best made 8 hours in advance. Yield: 4 cups.

Mrs. James W. Cook
(Naomi Paquette)

Curry Dip

1 quart mayonnaise
4 teaspoons Worcestershire sauce
2 teaspoons prepared horseradish
½ medium onion, grated
2 garlic cloves, grated
1 Tablespoon celery seed
¼ teaspoon curry powder

5 drops TABASCO brand pepper sauce
2 teaspoons mustard
½ teaspoon monosodium glutamate
½ teaspoon black pepper
¼ teaspoon salt

Combine all ingredients in a large container. Stir until blended together. Refrigerate until time to serve. Delicious with shrimp. Yield: 6 cups.

Mrs. W. H. Campbell
(Jane Fisher)

Sweet Dip

1 (18-ounce) jar marshmallow cream
2 (3-ounce) packages cream cheese

Fresh or canned fruit of choice, cut into bite-size pieces

Set marshmallow cream and cream cheese out at room temperature. Mix marshmallow cream and cream cheese in serving dish. Stir to mix thoroughly. Dip fruit into mixture. Yield: 4 cups.

Miss Mary Beth Grogan

Cold Mexican Dip

2 cans jalapeño bean dip (1 large
   and 1 small)
3 avocados
2 Tablespoons lemon juice
2 teaspoons salt
¼ teaspoon pepper
1 cup sour cream
½ cup mayonnaise

1 package taco seasoning
1 large bunch green onions with
   tops, chopped
3 medium tomatoes, chopped
1 (4-ounce) can chopped ripe olives
8 ounces Cheddar cheese, shredded
Tortilla chips

Spread jalapeño bean dip in the bottom of a 9 x 13 x 2-inch casserole. Blend avocado with lemon juice, salt, and pepper. Layer this on top of bean dip. Blend sour cream, mayonnaise, and taco seasoning. Put this mixture on next. Put chopped onions on top of mayonnaise mixture. Next place a layer of chopped tomatoes and then chopped olives. Top with cheese. Serve with tortilla chips. Yield: 1 quart.

Mrs. Dick Peterson
(Josephine Coker)

Guacamole Dip

1 large very ripe avocado
1 Tablespoon grated onion
2 Tablespoons squeezed lemon or
   lime juice
½ teaspoon salt

½ teaspoon chili powder
1 tomato, chopped
2 Tablespoons mayonnaise
1 (1-pound) bag corn chips or
   vegetables

Peel, pit, and mash pulp of avocado in the same dish in which it is to be served. Mix in the onion, lemon juice, salt, chili powder and tomato. Carefully spread mayonnaise over the top of the avocado to make the mixture airtight. Cover completely to prevent the avocado from darkening. Prior to serving, stir mayonnaise into avocado mixture. Serve with chips or vegetables. Yield: 1 pint.

Gail Guider Curry
Jackson, Mississippi

To ripen an avocado, place in a brown paper bag and store in a warm place.

Jalapeño Relish Dip

8 cherry tomatoes, quartered
1 (10-ounce) can green chilies and
  tomatoes
1 (4-ounce) can chopped ripe olives
1 (7-ounce) can hot jalapeño relish

4 green onions, chopped
3 Tablespoons vegetable oil
1½ Tablespoons vinegar
1 Tablespoon garlic salt
Tortilla chips for serving

Combine all ingredients. Let set overnight before serving. Serve with tortilla chips. Yield: 2 cups.

Becky S. Anderson
Fort Worth, Texas

Hot Sombrero Dip

2 cans bean dip
1 pound ground chuck, browned
1 can chopped green chilies
1 small jar picante sauce

1 cup shredded Cheddar cheese
2 fresh tomatoes, diced
2 large packages tortilla chips

Layer bean dip, browned ground chuck, chilies and picante sauce in 3-quart casserole dish. Top with shredded cheese. Heat in a 375° oven to melt cheese. Top with tomatoes and serve hot with tortilla chips. Yield: 3 quarts.

Mrs. Pam Sanders
(Pam Hughes)

Shoe Peg Dip

1 can shoe peg corn, drained
1 medium tomato, chopped
½ medium green pepper, chopped
3 green onions, chopped
1 jalapeño pepper, chopped

2 Tablespoons mayonnaise
Seasoned salt to taste
Lemon pepper
Whole wheat wafers

Drain corn and add remaining ingredients including a generous amount of lemon pepper. Let stand at least 1 hour before serving. Serve with whole wheat wafers. Yield: 10 servings.

This is also delicious served as a salad with beef. White corn may be substituted for shoe peg corn.

Mrs. Bill Pierce
(Pat Hand)

Duck Dip

4 wild ducks
1 slice bacon
6 Tablespoons butter
1 medium onion, chopped
1 large can mushrooms or 1 small
    package fresh mushrooms, sliced

1 (7-ounce) package wild rice,
    cooked according to package
    directions
Salt and pepper
Melba rounds

Cover ducks with bacon strip and cook at 350° for 4 to 5 hours or until tender. Remove meat from breast and legs and grind finely in food processor. Melt butter; sauté onions and mushrooms. Mix rice, meat, onions, and mushrooms together. Add more butter to desired consistency. Salt and pepper to taste. Serve in chafing dish with melba rounds. Yield: 10 to 12 servings.

Linda Rundell Dismuke
Germantown, Tennessee

Hawaiian Cheese Ball

2 (8-ounce) packages cream cheese,
    softened
1 (8½-ounce) can crushed
    pineapple, drained
1½ cups finely chopped almonds

¼ cup chopped green pepper
2 Tablespoons chopped onion
1 Tablespoon seasoned salt
1 cup chopped almonds

Combine first 6 ingredients and mix well. Shape into 1 large ball or 2 smaller balls and roll in 1 cup chopped almonds. Refrigerate until ready to use. Yield: 1 cheese ball.

Mrs. Robert R. Bailess
(Natalie Waring)

Ham Cheese Ball

2 (8-ounce) packages cream cheese,
    softened
2 Tablespoons horseradish
2 Tablespoons prepared mustard

2 teaspoons grated onion
2 cups finely chopped ham
1 cup finely chopped pecans

Blend cream cheese, horseradish, mustard, and onion. Add ham and mix well. Form into ball and chill. Roll in pecans before serving. Serve with assorted crackers.

Mrs. Walter Reynolds
(Pat Piazza)

Dried Beef Cheese Ball

2 (8-ounce) packages cream cheese
2 packages dried beef
6 to 8 green onions, chopped
2 teaspoons Worcestershire sauce
2 teaspoons monosodium
  glutamate
Paprika to garnish

Mix all ingredients and shape into ball. Sprinkle with paprika. Yield: 6 to 8 servings.

Mrs. Gene Parker
(Pat Hardy)

Joy's Cheese Ball

¼ pound bleu cheese
¼ pound Cheddar or 1 small jar
  garlic cheese
1 (3-ounce) package cream cheese
1 medium onion, grated
1 teaspoon steak sauce
1¼ cups chopped pecans, divided
2 Tablespoons chopped parsley

Mix softened cheeses, onion and steak sauce in mixer. Fold in ¾ cup pecans and refrigerate 1 hour. Remove and shape into ball. Roll in parsley and remaining pecans. Serve with your favorite crackers.

Mrs. Charles Moss
Meridian, Mississippi

Bacon-Cheese Mold

1 pound bacon
1 pound Cheddar cheese, shredded
1 bunch green onions and half of
  tops, sliced
1 (3-ounce) package slivered
  almonds
¼ to ⅓ cup mayonnaise
1 (10-ounce) jar strawberry
  preserves

Fry bacon crisply and crumble. Mix bacon with cheese, onions, almonds, and just enough mayonnaise to hold mixture together. Spray a ring mold with non-stick spray. Spread mixture in mold, cover, and refrigerate overnight. Loosen edge of cheese mold with knife and unmold. Spread strawberry preserves over top. Serve with butter crackers.

Mrs. Harold Blue
(Jean Johnson)

Gouda Wellington

1 box phyllo pastry
6 Tablespoons butter, melted
1 (8-ounce) round Gouda cheese

1 egg white
1 Tablespoon water
⅓ cup pepper jelly

Cut phyllo pastry into squares of about 10 inches per side to make a total of 16. With a pastry brush, lightly brush butter on 1 side of a phyllo square. Place another square on top and brush with butter. Repeat until 8 squares have been done. Remove rind from Gouda and place in center of pastry. Place a phyllo square on top of cheese molding around sides of cheese. Brush with butter. Repeat with remaining phyllo squares. Roll edges of pastry in toward center of cheese to resemble a turban. This may be easier if corners are trimmed. Slightly beat egg white with water. Brush this glaze over pastry. Bake at 450° for 10 to 15 minutes until golden brown. Remove from oven and spoon warmed jelly over pastry. Serve warm, but not hot, as cheese may be too runny.

Edam cheese may be substituted. There will be enough pastry left over to make another Gouda Wellington.

Mrs. Bob Coleman
(Cissy Wagner)

Hot Stuff

½ cup butter or margarine
10 eggs
½ cup flour
1 teaspoon baking powder
Dash of salt

1 (4-ounce) can chopped chilies
1 pint small curd cottage cheese
1 pound jalapeño Monterey Jack
  cheese, shredded

Melt butter in a 9 x 12-inch casserole. Beat eggs lightly. Add flour, baking powder, and salt to eggs. Add butter from casserole dish, chilies, cottage cheese, and shredded cheese. Blend with spoon. Pour into casserole. Bake at 400° for 15 minutes. Turn oven to 350° and bake for 30 to 40 minutes or until lightly browned. Cut into squares. This may be made ahead. Cover with foil and rewarm at 350°. Yield: 60 to 80 squares.

Kathleen Hand Carter
Rolling Fork, Mississippi

 Shred Cheddar or Swiss cheese and freeze; whenever you need some for cooking, just measure.

Homemade Herb Cheese

12 ounces cream cheese, softened
½ cup butter, softened
3 large cloves garlic, crushed
1 Tablespoon minced chives
1½ teaspoons dried chervil,
  crumbled

1½ teaspoons dried tarragon,
  crumbled
1 teaspoon dried parsley, crumbled
½ teaspoon thyme
¼ teaspoon white pepper
Crackers

Combine all ingredients in medium bowl and mix until smooth. Spoon into crock. Cover and chill. Serve with crackers. Yield: 2 cups.

Mrs. Steve Rodman
Rockford, Illinois

Cheese Strips

1 loaf thin-sliced bread
½ pound sharp Cheddar cheese,
  shredded
6 slices bacon, fried, drained, and
  coarsely broken

1 small onion, finely minced
3 ounces slivered almonds, toasted
1 cup mayonnaise
Salt and pepper to taste

Remove crust from bread. Mix next 6 ingredients well. Spread filling over slices and cut into 3 strips. Place on cookie sheet and bake 10 minutes at 400°. This freezes well. If frozen, thaw slightly prior to cooking. Yield: 5 dozen strips.

Miss Martha Wise
Greenville, Mississippi

Cheese Krispies

1 cup margarine, softened
8 ounces sharp Cheddar cheese,
  shredded
2 cups flour

½ teaspoon salt
¼ to ½ teaspoon red pepper
2 cups puffed rice cereal

Cream margarine and cheese. Add flour, salt, and pepper. Mix well. Add rice cereal and mix with hands as dough is very stiff. Roll into walnut-size balls and flatten into cookie with fork. Bake on ungreased cookie sheet at 325° for 20 to 25 minutes. Yield: 7 to 8 dozen.

Mrs. Johnny Mims
(Susan Bailess)

Cheese Straws

½ cup butter or margarine
1 jar Old English cheese
1½ cups sifted flour

½ teaspoon salt
½ teaspoon cayenne pepper

In mixing bowl, cream butter or margarine and cheese. Mix well. Add sifted flour, salt, and cayenne pepper. Stir well. Press through cookie press onto cookie sheet. Bake at 375° for 15 minutes. Yield: Approximately 4 dozen.

Mrs. Stan Terry, Jr.
(Sallie Bingham)

Cocktail Sesame Wafers

1 cup margarine
½ pound sharp Cheddar cheese,
  shredded
2 scant cups flour
½ teaspoon salt

1 to 2 teaspoons red pepper
2 teaspoons caraway or sesame
  seed
1 cup very finely chopped nuts

Let margarine and cheese soften. Then add the remaining ingredients and mix well. Drop by teaspoonfuls onto a cookie sheet or roll into 3 logs and refrigerate until firm. Slice and bake at 350° for 15 to 20 minutes or until lightly browned. Yield: 6 dozen.

Mrs. Walter T. Scott
Tallulah, Louisiana

Fruit 'n Crackers

1 (8-ounce) package cream cheese,
  softened
2 Tablespoons orange juice
1 teaspoon grated orange rind
1½ teaspoons Triple Sec

4 dozen multi-shaped crackers
5 to 6 cups assorted fresh and/or
  canned fruits (grapes, kiwi,
  strawberries, etc.)

Mix cream cheese with orange juice, orange rind, and Triple Sec. Lightly toast crackers in 350° oven. Spread crackers with cream cheese mixture. Cut fruits into various shapes. Decorate tops of crackers with fruit. Yield: 4 dozen.

Mrs. Mark Prewitt
(Susie Harmon)

Onion Toasties

4 to 5 large onion rolls
½ cup margarine or butter, softened
2 cloves garlic, mashed

1 scant teaspoon salt
2 teaspoons McCormick® Salad
Supreme® with Bleu Cheese

Freeze rolls. Working with 1 roll at a time, slice thinly with bread knife. There should be 14 to 16 slices per roll. Mix butter, garlic, salt, and Salad Supreme. Spread mixture on one side of bread slices. Place unbuttered side on ungreased cookie sheet and bake at 350° for 8 to 10 minutes or until golden brown and crisp. This spread will do about 4 to 5 onion rolls.

Mrs. Charles Scanlon
Highland Beach, Florida

O.C.'s

1 (10-ounce) package small oyster
crackers
1 package HIDDEN VALLEY
RANCH® salad dressing

½ teaspoon garlic powder
½ teaspoon dill weed
½ teaspoon lemon pepper
¾ cup vegetable oil

Mix all in a bowl until ingredients are absorbed into crackers.

Mrs. Pam Sanders
(Pam Hughes)

Party Toast Cups

Fresh white bread

Butter or margarine

Using a biscuit cutter, cut slices of fresh white bread into rounds. 2 inches in diameter is about the right size for a small muffin tin. Roll rounds flat with rolling pin. Melt butter or margarine and brush inside of small muffin tin. Fit bread rounds into cups, handling carefully to avoid tearing. Brush inside of bread cups with butter. Bake at 375° for about 15 minutes or just until lightly and evenly browned. Remove from muffin tins immediately. Yield: 4 dozen toast cups will serve 20.

Serve with chicken salad, chicken à la king, or crabmeat mornay.

Mrs. Jack Stamm, Jr.
(Laurin Fields)

Gold'n Nut Crunch

1 (12-ounce) can mixed nuts
¼ cup butter, melted
¼ cup grated Parmesan cheese
¼ teaspoon garlic powder

¼ teaspoon ground oregano
¼ teaspoon celery salt
5 cups graham cracker cereal

Heat oven to 300°. Mix nuts and butter together thoroughly. Add cheese, garlic powder, oregano, and celery salt. Mix well. Spread mixture on ungreased cookie sheet. Bake for 15 minutes, stirring occasionally. Stir in cereal; cool. Store in airtight container. Yield: 7 cups.

Mrs. John Kamman
(Betty Blackburn)

TV Snacks

1 (12-ounce) box rounded oat cereal
1 (12-ounce) box Wheat Chex
1 (12-ounce) box Corn Chex
1 (9-ounce) box pretzel sticks
1 (5-ounce) box cheese Tidbits

2 cups peanuts
1 cup pecans
1 (8-ounce) bag small corn chips
   (optional)

Put all dry ingredients together in a large roaster. Toss gently to mix.

Sauce

2 cups margarine
1½ cups bacon drippings
6 Tablespoons Worcestershire sauce
6 Tablespoons TABASCO brand
   pepper sauce

3 teaspoons garlic salt
3 teaspoons seasoned salt
2 teaspoons salt

Melt margarine in saucepan; add bacon drippings. Add seasonings and let simmer about 10 minutes. Spoon sauce over dry mix, stirring gently. Preheat oven to 275°. Bake snacks uncovered 1 hour, stirring and lifting from bottom every 15 minutes. Remove from oven and stir every 10 to 15 minutes while cooling. Store in airtight containers. Yield: 4 to 5 quarts.

Mrs. Bruce Ebersole
(Story Stamm)

Toasted Pecans

½ cup margarine
4 cups shelled pecan halves

1 teaspoon salt

Preheat oven to 400°. Melt margarine in a 9 x 12-inch baking pan. Remove from oven; pour in pecans. Coat pecans evenly with melted margarine. Sprinkle salt over pecans and mix well. Place pecans in single layer. Return pan of pecans to oven and turn off the heat. Leave in the oven for 25 minutes. Do not open oven door. Yield: 20 to 30 servings.

Mrs. R. Crofton Sloan
(Mary Bayer)

Orange-Glazed Pecans

1 egg white
½ teaspoon salt
½ teaspoon cinnamon

1 Tablespoon orange juice
½ cup sugar
3 cups pecans

Beat egg white until foamy. Add salt, cinnamon and orange juice. Fold in sugar and mix well. Add pecans. Bake on a well-greased cookie sheet at 250° for 45 to 60 minutes. Turn pecans every 15 minutes. Store in airtight container. Yield: 3 cups.

Mrs. Delbert Hosemann
(Patricia Faherty)

Sugared Pecans

1 cup sugar
¼ teaspoon salt
½ teaspoon cinnamon

6 Tablespoons milk
1 teaspoon vanilla extract
3 cups pecans

In a 2-quart saucepan, combine sugar, salt, cinnamon and milk. Bring to a boil and cook to soft ball stage. Remove from heat and add vanilla. Add pecans. Stir until all pecans are coated and turn white and grainy. Spoon out onto waxed paper. When cool, break up any clusters of pecans. Keep in well-sealed tin. Yield: 3 cups.

Mrs. Warner Biedenharn
(Jowilla Shaw)

Almond Date Rumaki

12 slices bacon
1 (8-ounce) package pitted dates

1 (2-ounce) package slivered
almonds

Cut each slice bacon into 3 pieces. Stuff each date with 2 or 3 almond slivers. Wrap each date with a piece of bacon and secure with toothpick. Place on a broiling tray and bake at 350° for 15 to 18 minutes or until bacon is crisp. Drain on paper towels. Serve hot. For other variations wrap bacon around dates or prunes stuffed with pineapple, smoked or fresh oysters, water chestnuts marinated in brown sugar and soy sauce, pickled onions, sautéed chicken livers, large stuffed olives, pineapple chunks, or grapefruit sections. Yield: 3 dozen.

Mrs. Mark Prewitt
(Susie Harmon)

Hot Artichoke Spread

1 (14-ounce) can artichoke hearts,
   drained and finely chopped
1 cup mayonnaise
1 cup grated Parmesan cheese

1 package Italian salad dressing
   mix
Crackers

In a medium mixing bowl or a food processor, place finely chopped artichoke hearts, mayonnaise, cheese and Italian dressing mix. Mix together thoroughly. Pour into a ramekin and bake at 350° for 20 minutes. Serve as an appetizer with assorted crackers. Yield: 30 servings.

Mrs. William Dawson
Muskogee, Oklahoma

Stuffed Artichokes

4 artichokes
2 cups bread crumbs
2 cloves pressed garlic

½ cup Romano cheese, grated
Salt and pepper
Olive oil

Wash and trim artichokes; turn upside down on paper towel to drain. Mix bread crumbs, garlic, and cheese together. Separate leaves just enough to fill with mixture. Salt and pepper artichokes; spoon mixture between leaves. Drizzle olive oil generously over the stuffing. Place in a heavy pot, standing upright, with a small amount of water. Cover and steam until leaves pull off easily, about 30 minutes.

Miss Mattie Canizaro

Melezanai Geonese
(Eggplant Squares)

3 medium eggplants
4 slices stale bread
3 eggs
1 pound Cheddar cheese, shredded
1 cup chopped yellow onions
1 bunch green onions, finely
    chopped
3 ribs celery and leaves, chopped
    finely

3 cloves garlic, chopped finely
½ cup chopped parsley
½ cup olive oil
1 wedge Romano cheese, grated
2 stacks Ritz crackers
Salt and pepper
1 teaspoon Greek seasoning
Paprika

Peel eggplant, cube, and boil until tender. Drain well. (This can be done a day ahead and refrigerated.) Remove crust from bread, soak in water, and squeeze dry. Place in large mixing bowl. Add eggs and mix well. Add Cheddar cheese and mix. Sauté onions, celery, garlic, and parsley in olive oil until clear. Add hot vegetable mixture to bread mixture. Mix well and then add grated Romano cheese. Add drained eggplant. Roll crackers until fine or crush in food processor. Add to mixture with salt, pepper, and Greek seasoning. Mixture should be fine. Bake in 9 x 13 x 2-inch pan at 350° for 30 minutes. Top with paprika. This can be served as a casserole if only 1 stack of crackers is used. Yield: 10 servings.

Mrs. Louis L. Patterson
(Theodocia Perry)

Cheese and Spinach Puffs

½ cup chopped onion
1 (10-ounce) package chopped,
    frozen spinach
2 eggs, slightly beaten
½ cup grated Parmesan cheese
½ cup shredded Cheddar cheese
½ cup bleu cheese salad dressing

¼ cup margarine, melted
⅛ teaspoon garlic powder
1 teaspoon black pepper
½ teaspoon red pepper
Worcestershire sauce to taste
1 (8½-ounce) package corn muffin
    mix

In saucepan, cook onions and spinach according to directions on box. Drain well and press out liquid. Combine all ingredients except muffin mix in bowl. Combine spinach mixture and muffin mix; cover and chill. Shape into 1-inch balls. Refrigerate or freeze. Bake 10 to 15 minutes at 350°. Yield: 5 dozen.

Mrs. Albert Dornbusch
(Gloria Abraham)

Spinach Pies

Spinach Pie Dough

1 package yeast
1½ cups lukewarm water
4 cups flour

½ cup cooking oil
1 Tablespoon salt

Dissolve yeast in water and add to all ingredients. Knead for 5 minutes. Cover and let rest in warm place about 1½ hours. When the dough rises, cut into small sections 3 inches in diameter. Cover again and allow to rise for ½ hour. Then flatten each section with hand to thinness of pie dough. Fill and fold over like a turnover.

Spinach Pie Filling

2 pounds fresh spinach
1 Tablespoon salt
3 finely chopped medium yellow or
   white onions

Juice of 3 lemons
Pepper and cinnamon to taste
1 cup cooking oil

Wash spinach thoroughly and cut into small pieces. Sprinkle with salt. Squeeze until all water is removed. Add onions, lemon juice, and spices. Mix well. Add oil and mix well again. Place 1 to 2 heaping Tablespoons on each circle and fold edges over to meet. Brush oil on baking tray and arrange pies in rows. Bake at 350° for 15 minutes or until bottoms are lightly browned. Place under broiler until tops of pies are lightly browned. Serve hot or cold. Yield: 36 servings.

Can also be used as an appetizer by reducing size of dough.

Mrs. Freddy Abraham
(Sara Stevenson)

Marinated Brussels Sprouts

2 quarts water
2 boxes fresh or frozen brussels
   sprouts

1 cup commercial Italian dressing

Bring to boil 2 quarts water. Drop in brussels sprouts and cook until barely tender, about 6 to 8 minutes. Drain and while hot, cover with Italian dressing. Let marinate at least 24 hours. Drain and serve cold. Yield: 4 servings.

Mrs. Robert Ivy
(Susan Hynam)

Spinach and Oyster Madeleine

2 (10-ounce) packages frozen
  chopped spinach
4 Tablespoons butter or margarine
2 Tablespoons flour
2 Tablespoons chopped onion
½ cup evaporated milk
½ cup vegetable liquor

1 (6-ounce) roll jalapeño cheese
½ teaspoon black pepper
¾ teaspoon celery salt
¾ teaspoon garlic salt
Salt to taste
1 teaspoon Worcestershire sauce
1 (12-ounce) jar raw oysters

Cook spinach according to package directions. Drain liquid, reserving ½ cup. Melt butter in saucepan over low heat. Add flour, stirring until smooth. Do not brown. Add onion and cook until soft, but not browned. Add evaporated milk and vegetable liquor slowly, stirring constantly to avoid lumps. Cook until smooth and thick, stirring constantly. Cut cheese into small pieces and add. Stir until all cheese is melted. Add seasonings. Pour cheese mixture over spinach and mix well. Heat oysters and their juice in a skillet. Simmer until edges begin to curl. Drain oysters in a colander. Chop oysters into small pieces and add to spinach. Mix well. Serve hot in a chafing dish with assorted crackers. This recipe is best if made a day ahead. Add oysters just before serving. Yield: 1 quart.

Mrs. Dan Waring
(Janice Gerache)

Miniature Stuffed Potatoes

1½ dozen small potatoes (A little
  larger than bite size is preferable.
  Medium potatoes, halved, will
  also work.)
1 (16-ounce) carton sour cream

2 Tablespoons very finely chopped
  onion
5 to 6 strips bacon, crisply fried
  and crumbled

Boil potatoes with peel for 30 minutes or until medium-tender. Do not overcook. Scoop out a portion of each to make a well, leaving surrounding skin intact. A melon scoop works well. Discard potato pulp. Mix sour cream and onion. Fill each potato with 1 or more teaspoons of this mixture. Top with crumbled bacon and reheat at 350° until warm. Shredded Cheddar cheese, black caviar or chopped chives may be substituted for crumbled bacon. Do not add other toppings except cheese before reheating.

To accompany a meal, use larger potatoes.

Mrs. Mike Engle
(Melanie Campbell)

Dilled Broccoli

1 cup cider or white vinegar
½ cup vegetable oil
1 Tablespoon dill weed
1 Tablespoon salt
1 Tablespoon garlic salt

1 Tablespoon black pepper
1 Tablespoon sugar
1 Tablespoon monosodium
 glutamate
1 bunch fresh broccoli florets

Mix vinegar, oil and spices together. Pour over broccoli florets. Toss until coated and marinate in refrigerator no more than 3 to 4 hours before serving. Serve as an appetizer or as a vegetable with dinner.

Cauliflower, fresh mushrooms, and carrots may be added for variety.

Mrs. Danny Massie
(Tita Morrison)

Spinach Balls with Mustard Sauce

2 (10-ounce) packages frozen,
 chopped spinach, thawed and
 squeezed dry
2 cups herb stuffing mix, crushed
1 cup firmly packed, freshly grated
 Parmesan cheese

½ cup butter, melted
4 small green onions,
 finely chopped
3 eggs
Dash of nutmeg, freshly grated

In a large mixing bowl, combine all ingredients and mix well. Shape into 1-inch balls. Cover and refrigerate or freeze until ready to bake. Preheat oven to 350°. Bake on ungreased baking sheet for 10 to 15 minutes or until golden brown. Serve with Mustard Sauce. Yield: 70 balls.

Mustard Sauce

½ cup dry mustard
½ cup white vinegar

¼ cup sugar
1 egg yolk

In a small bowl, combine mustard and vinegar. Cover and let stand at room temperature for 4 hours. In a small saucepan, mix sugar and egg yolk. Add mustard and vinegar mixture and cook over low heat, stirring constantly until slightly thickened. Cover and chill. Serve at room temperature with baked spinach balls.

Mrs. Jimmy F. Vessell
(Ann Duncan)

Miniature Cabbage Rolls

2 medium heads cabbage
1½ cups raw rice, rinsed with cold
    water
2 pounds ground beef
2 Tablespoons lemon juice
1½ teaspoons cinnamon or allspice

1½ teaspoons salt, divided
Pinch of black pepper
½ cup water
4 to 5 cloves of garlic
1 (8-ounce) can tomato sauce
½ cup lemon juice

Place cabbage in boiling water for several minutes until leaves separate. Mix together rice, beef, lemon juice, cinnamon, 1 teaspoon salt, pepper and ½ cup water. Cut each leaf in half and cut away hard white part. Fill each leaf with approximately 1½ teaspoons meat-rice mixture. Beginning with longer side, roll leaf while tucking in ends. Arrange rolled cabbage in pan; place cloves of garlic on top. Mix together tomato sauce with 2 cans water, ½ teaspoon salt, and ½ cup lemon juice; pour over cabbage. Cook on top of stove 1½ hours. Serve hot in chafing dish with toothpicks. Yield: 50 to 60 rolls.

Mrs. George Baladi
(Layla Zeino)

Stuffed Cocktail Tomatoes

Cocktail tomatoes, cored, seeded,
    and drained
1 (8-ounce) package cream cheese
1 small bell pepper, finely chopped
3 to 4 Tablespoons mayonnaise
Juice of ½ lemon

1 teaspoon finely minced onion
1 dash of Worcestershire sauce
2 dashes of TABASCO brand pepper
    sauce
Salt and pepper to taste
Paprika to garnish

Wash tomatoes. Soften cream cheese. Add rest of the ingredients and mix well. Stuff mixture in tomatoes and sprinkle with paprika. Delicious on brown bread and also makes a pretty and tasty open-faced sandwich for entertaining; Spread may be used to stuff a rib of crisp celery. Soften the spread with sour cream and serve as a dip with crackers or chips. Also good in tomato aspic.

Mrs. Jack Stamm, Jr.
(Laurin Fields)

 When cooking cabbage, place a small tin cup of vinegar on the stove near the cabbage to absorb the odor.

Aspic Miniatures

2 envelopes unflavored gelatin
½ cup cold water
1 (10¾-ounce) can tomato soup,
   undiluted
2 (3-ounce) packages cream cheese,
   cubed and softened
½ cup finely chopped celery
½ cup finely chopped bell pepper
¼ cup stuffed olives, sliced

1 Tablespoon grated onion
2 Tablespoons lemon juice
1 cup mayonnaise
1 teaspoon TABASCO brand pepper
   sauce
1 teaspoon Worcestershire sauce
Crackers
6 empty egg cartons used for molds

Dissolve gelatin in cold water. Place soup and cheese in top of double boiler; heat until blended. Add gelatin and all other ingredients except crackers. Mix well and remove from heat. Lightly grease egg carton pockets or tart pans with vegetable oil. Measure a slightly rounded Tablespoon of aspic mixture into each pocket. Chill until aspic has firmly set. Unmold with a regular table knife and serve on crackers. Yield: 60 to 70 aspic miniatures.

Small shrimp may be substituted for olives.

Mrs. James McAdams
Greenwood, Mississippi

Carnival Mushrooms

½ cup flour
⅛ teaspoon salt
1 egg, slightly beaten
⅓ cup milk
¾ pound fresh mushrooms

1½ cups dry bread crumbs
Vegetable oil for frying
1 cup mayonnaise
1 Tablespoon capers
Fresh lemon juice to taste

Sift flour with salt and whisk in egg and milk. Strain batter into another bowl and let it stand for 30 minutes. Pat mushrooms clean with damp cloth. Dip mushrooms into the batter. Coat them with the bread crumbs and fry in batches in hot oil at 375°, turning them once, for 2 minutes or until browned. Transfer mushrooms to paper towels to drain. Sprinkle lightly with salt. Combine mayonnaise with minced capers in a dipping sauce bowl. Add fresh lemon juice to taste and surround with mushrooms. Yield: 4 to 6 servings.

Mrs. Frank Maxwell
(Louise Middlebrook)

Mushrooms La Admiralty

16 ounces canned button
  mushrooms
1 Tablespoon Worcestershire sauce

2 jiggers brandy, divided
½ jigger Grand Marnier liqueur
2 jiggers cooking sherry

Drain mushrooms and reserve a small amount of juice. Add mushroom juice, Worcestershire, 1 jigger brandy, Grand Marnier, and cooking sherry to mushrooms. Simmer 30 minutes, but do not boil. Stir several times making sure juice covers all mushrooms. Serve hot in chafing dish, adding 1 jigger brandy at serving. Yield: 10 to 12 servings.

Mrs. Briggs Hopson
(Patricia Spearman)

Jean's Sausage Mushrooms

1 pound medium to large
  mushrooms
¾ pound good quality bulk
  sausage
⅔ cup finely chopped onion
⅔ cup finely chopped mushroom
  stems

1 (8-ounce) package cream cheese
⅛ teaspoon pepper (optional)
⅛ teaspoon salt (optional)
Grated Parmesan or Romano cheese
  (optional)
Italian bread crumbs (optional)

Pat mushrooms with a damp cloth. Remove stems and place caps on microwave cooking rack for microwave cooking or a large non-stick cooking sheet for regular oven. Brown sausage on medium heat, stirring to break into small pieces. While sausage is browning, chop onions and stems. Add to sausage and cook until onion is transparent. Drain well in colander. Add cream cheese to hot skillet and stir in sausage mixture until cheese is melted. Remove from heat and add salt and pepper if needed. Stuff caps just to edge. Do not mound. At this point caps may be refrigerated for up to 24 hours. Add optional toppings just prior to baking. Bake 7 to 9 minutes at full power in microwave oven or 18 to 25 minutes at 400° in conventional oven. If mushrooms are refrigerated before baking, cover with plastic wrap or waxed paper. Serve hot. Yield: 8 to 10 servings.

We also like to finish cooking these on the grill and serve with barbecue or steak as a side dish instead of potatoes. Use aluminum baking pan and cover with foil.

Mrs. Charles J. Lewis
(Jean Towne)

Mushrooms Marbu

1 pound large fresh mushrooms
1 bunch green onions, chopped
½ cup butter, no substitute
¾ cup Italian-style bread crumbs
½ cup dry white wine
1 (4¼-ounce) can shrimp, drained

1 (4¼-ounce) can crabmeat,
  drained
Lemon pepper marinade
Garlic salt
Juice of 1 lemon

Clean and stem mushrooms. Chop stems and reserve caps. Sauté chopped mushroom stems and green onions in butter. Add bread crumbs slowly and mix well. Add wine; mix well and remove from heat. Stir in shrimp and crabmeat. Season with lemon pepper and garlic salt to taste. Return to heat and mix well. Stuff mushroom caps with mixture and place on ungreased cookie sheet. Bake at 325° until topping is crisp (about 10 minutes). Top with fresh lemon juice prior to serving. Yield: 4 to 6 servings.

Stuffing mixture combines well with eggs for a basic quiche filling. Can be served in pastry shells for a luncheon dish.

Mrs. Jerry Nations
Brookhaven, Mississippi

Creamed Mushrooms

2 pounds fresh mushrooms
6 Tablespoons butter
6 Tablespoons sherry
2 cups sour cream

1½ cups grated Parmesan cheese
1 teaspoon salt
1 teaspoon freshly ground pepper
1 teaspoon monosodium glutamate

Leave mushroom caps whole, but chop stems. Sauté in butter for 2 minutes. Add sherry and cook 1 minute. Blend in sour cream, cheese, salt, pepper and monosodium glutamate. Cook over low heat until thickened. Serve in chafing dish. Yield: Serves cocktail party of 20.

May be served on toast points or as a side dish with beef.

Mrs. Sam Davis
(Mary Stockton)

 Do not wash fresh mushrooms before storing them. Gently clean them by wiping with a damp cloth or paper towel just before using.

Almond-Stuffed Mushrooms

18 medium-size fresh mushrooms
¼ cup finely chopped purple onion
2 garlic cloves, crushed
3 Tablespoons butter, divided
3 Tablespoons vegetable oil, divided
¼ cup sliced almonds, toasted
1½ teaspoons dried parsley flakes

1½ teaspoons Worcestershire sauce
½ teaspoon dried basil
½ teaspoon paprika
4 to 6 Tablespoons bread crumbs
Parmesan cheese
Pepper, freshly ground

Clean mushrooms by wiping with damp cloth. Remove stems from mushrooms and set caps aside. Combine stems, onion, and garlic in food processor and chop finely. Heat ½ butter and ½ oil in small saucepan. Add mushroom stem mixture and sauté 4 to 5 minutes, adding more oil and butter if needed. Add almonds, parsley, Worcestershire, basil, and paprika and bring to simmer. Remove from heat; add bread crumbs, and toss lightly. Preheat oven to 400°. Heat remaining oil and butter in saucepan and sauté mushroom caps over high heat 1 to 2 minutes. Place caps rounded side down. Spoon crumb mixture into each mushroom cap. Dust with Parmesan cheese; dot with butter, and sprinkle with pepper. Turn oven to 350° and bake 15 to 20 minutes. Yield: 6 to 8 servings.

Mrs. Robert M. Abraham
(Billie Patterson)

Party Pizzas

2 Tablespoons minced onion
2 cups shredded sharp Cheddar
    cheese
1 (4-ounce) can chopped ripe olives
1 cup mayonnaise

1 cup bacon bits
1 or 2 jalapeño peppers, chopped
    (optional)
1 loaf party rye bread

Mix onion well with cheese, olives, and mayonnaise. Add bacon bits and jalapeño peppers if desired. Stir well. Spread mixture on bread. Bake 10 to 15 minutes at 350°. Serve hot. Yield: 24 appetizers.

For a variation, butter English muffins and toast. Spread with topping and quarter. Bake as directed.

Mrs. Larry Rocconi
(Nina Dottley)

Antipasto

2 (4-ounce) cans sliced mushrooms,
   drained
1 (14-ounce) can artichoke hearts,
   cut up
1 (5-ounce) jar stuffed olives,
   chopped

1 (2-ounce) jar pimento
¼ cup diced bell pepper
½ cup diced celery

Mix above ingredients in gallon jar. Combine the following ingredients in saucepan and bring to a boil. Cool and pour over the ingredients in the jar. Cover and refrigerate at least 24 hours before serving. Serve with crackers. Yield: 14 to 20 servings.

⅔ cup white vinegar
⅔ cup vegetable oil
¼ cup minced dry onion
2½ teaspoons Italian seasoning
1 teaspoon salt
1 teaspoon garlic salt

1 teaspoon onion salt
1 teaspoon seasoned salt
½ teaspoon seasoned pepper
1 teaspoon sugar
1 teaspoon monosodium glutamate

This is also great served on lettuce as a salad.

Mrs. B. B. Hosch
(Patty Ronan)

Spinach Dip or Spinach Sandwiches

1 (10-ounce) package chopped
   spinach
1 cup mayonnaise
1 cup sour cream
1 very small onion, chopped

1 (8-ounce) can water chestnuts,
   minced
1 envelope Knorr's dry vegetable
   soup mix

Thaw spinach. Press all water out of spinach. Add remaining ingredients and mix well. Refrigerate 2 hours before serving. Spinach can be put into large, round, hollowed bread. Use bread pieces to dip. Can also be used on thin wheat bread for spinach sandwiches. Yield: 1 pint dip or 3 dozen sandwiches.

Mrs. Robert R. Bailess
(Natalie Waring)

Shrimp Party Sandwiches

1 (8-ounce) package cream cheese,
  softened
½ cup mayonnaise
2 (5-ounce) cans shrimp, drained
  and chopped
1 Tablespoon grated onion

1 teaspoon fresh lemon juice
Dash of TABASCO brand pepper
  sauce
3 to 4 dozen white bread rounds
Paprika
Sliced olives

Mix well cream cheese and mayonnaise. Add shrimp and mix. Add onion, lemon juice, and TABASCO. Mix well and refrigerate. Spread should be made the day before serving. Allow mixture to soften and spread on bread rounds. Sprinkle with paprika and top with a slice of olive. This will keep 1 week in refrigerator. Yield: 3 to 4 dozen.

Mrs. Scooter Havard
Gloster, Mississippi

Tomato Sandwiches

4 loaves day-old bread
6 to 8 medium tomatoes, peeled
Homemade mayonnaise (see Index)

1 grated onion with juice
Salt to taste
Red pepper to taste

Cut bread with biscuit cutter into 72 rounds. Slice tomatoes thinly and place on double sheets of paper towels to drain. Salt and pepper tomato slices. Spread mayonnaise on bread rounds. Place well drained tomato slices on ½ rounds and sprinkle again with salt and pepper. Sprinkle ½ teaspoon onion with juice over each tomato and top with remaining bread rounds. To store until serving time, place on cookie sheet; put waxed paper between layers. Cover tightly and store in refrigerator. Yield: 36 sandwiches.

Mrs. Hugh Johnston
(Hazel Pond)

A hot knife makes slicing fresh bread easier.

To keep finger sandwiches from becoming dry, cover each layer with a damp dishtowel or damp paper towels and refrigerate.

Cucumber Sandwich Spread

1 large cucumber
3 Tablespoons vinegar
1 Tablespoon lemon juice
1 Tablespoon sugar
¼ teaspoon salt

¼ teaspoon pepper
1 teaspoon grated onion
4 (3-ounce) packages cream cheese,
softened

Peel and grate cucumber. Mix vinegar, lemon juice, sugar, salt, pepper and onion together. Soak cucumber pulp in vinegar mixture for 15 minutes; drain. Mix cream cheese with cucumber and put in refrigerator until ready to use. Yield: 1½ cups.

Mrs. William T. Harris
(Teresa Vaughn)

Party Pepperoni Canapés

2 (3-ounce) packages cream cheese,
softened
½ cup mayonnaise
1 cup medium Cheddar cheese,
shredded
⅛ teaspoon red pepper
2 pinches of salt
½ teaspoon paprika
½ teaspoon grated onion

1½ to 2 dozen slices thin-sliced
bread
2 to 3 Tablespoons margarine at
room temperature
1 (4-ounce) package sliced
pepperoni
Paprika to garnish
1 to 2 sprigs parsley to garnish

In food processor or blender put cream cheese, mayonnaise, Cheddar cheese, red pepper, salt, paprika, and onion. Blend until smooth. Cut bread slices into rounds about 1¾ inches in diameter or about diameter of pepperoni. (Each bread slice should make 3 or 4 rounds.) Spread each bread round with a very little bit of margarine, about ¼ teaspoon. Top each with a slice of pepperoni. Using a pastry bag, pipe about 1 teaspoon cheese mixture in center of each pepperoni slice. (If a pastry bag is not available, place a mound of cheese mixture on top of each.) Sprinkle with paprika. Place 1 tiny leaf from parsley in center of each canapé. Serve immediately or refrigerate until time to serve. Cheese mixture can be prepared ahead, but let come to room temperature before using. Bread rounds can be cut several days ahead and frozen if spread with butter and wrapped well in airtight container. Yield: 5 to 5½ dozen.

Mrs. Jerry M. Hall
(Carolyn Buckner)

Cheddy's Corned Beef Rolled Sandwiches

1 (12-ounce) can corned beef
1 pound Cheddar cheese, shredded
1 large white onion, grated
1 small jar mustard with
  horseradish
¼ teaspoon salt

Dash of Worcestershire sauce
Dash of TABASCO brand pepper
  sauce
½ cup mayonnaise
1 loaf thin-sliced bread

Shred corned beef with fork. Add shredded cheese, grated onion, mustard, salt, Worcestershire, TABASCO and mayonnaise. Mix thoroughly. Blend to a consistency for spreading on bread. Trim crusts from bread. Spread mixture on a slice and roll carefully. Continue for entire loaf. Toast slowly in 325° oven for 20 to 30 minutes or until brown. Yield: 3 dozen.

Mike Martinson
Jackson, Mississippi

Party Ham Sandwiches

1 cup margarine
2 teaspoons Creole mustard
¼ teaspoon grated onion

24 small sesame seed rolls
1 (12-ounce) package sliced ham
8 ounces Monterey Jack cheese

Melt margarine. Mix margarine, mustard, and onion. Remove tops of rolls with an electric knife. Spread tops and bottoms of rolls with margarine mixture. Place ham and cheese on each roll. Replace top. Wrap tightly in foil. Bake at 350° for 30 minutes. Yield: 24 sandwiches.

These may be made the day before and baked when ready to serve. Men love them!

Mrs. Bill Pierce
(Pat Hand)

To keep party sandwiches or other food hot for a picnic, wrap in foil then in several sheets newspaper. Store in insulated ice chest.

When making rolled sandwiches, steam bread a minute over boiling water. The slightly moist bread will roll better and won't crack.

Bacon-Onion Sandwiches

1 pound bacon
1 cup mayonnaise
6 green onions with 3 tops, chopped

Black pepper
1 loaf bread

Sauté bacon until crisp; drain and crumble. Mix together mayonnaise, onions, black pepper to taste, and bacon. Cut bread into rounds and toast on both sides. Spread mixture on bread rounds and serve open-faced. Mixture may be prepared ahead and refrigerated. Yield: 12 servings.

Mrs. Frank Campbell
(Carole Blackledge)

Dressing Squares

1 (10-inch) skillet cooked corn bread
4 eggs, slightly beaten
1 onion, chopped
1 bell pepper, chopped
2 ribs celery, chopped

1 cup dry bread crumbs
1 quart chicken broth
1 teaspoon sage
Salt and pepper to taste

Crumble corn bread and mix all ingredients. Spread thinly on a baking sheet and bake at 350° for 15 to 20 minutes. Cut into bite-size pieces and serve at room temperature. Yield: 3 dozen squares.

Walnut Hills Restaurant
Vicksburg, Mississippi

Crabmeat Puffs

1 (6-ounce) can crabmeat
1 jar Old English Cheddar cheese
  spread
½ cup margarine, softened
½ teaspoon garlic salt

½ teaspoon seasoned salt
½ teaspoon lemon pepper
1 Tablespoon mayonnaise
1 package English muffins

Mix first 7 ingredients. Spread on split muffins and freeze at least 15 minutes. Store in freezer until ready to use. Broil and serve quartered for appetizers. Yield: 48 pieces.

This may also be served whole for a luncheon.

Mrs. Dean Norman
(Beth Jamison)

Betty's Shrimp Mousse

2 (10¾-ounce) cans tomato soup,
   undiluted
2 (8-ounce) packages cream cheese
3 envelopes unflavored gelatin
1 cup mayonnaise
2 pounds boiled, seasoned shrimp,
   peeled and chopped
1 to 1½ cups green onions with
   tops, chopped

½ cup chopped green pepper
½ cup chopped celery
2 teaspoons TABASCO Brand
   pepper sauce
Lemon pepper to taste
Garlic powder to taste
Lettuce bed
Ritz crackers

Heat soup over medium heat. Add cream cheese. Continue cooking until smooth, stirring often. Remove 1 cup soup mixture. To this, add gelatin and mix well. Stir into soup mixture and remove from heat. Fold in remaining ingredients until well blended. Spray a large mold (shrimp or fish-shaped is attractive) with a non-stick cooking spray or grease lightly. Fill mold and chill for 8 hours. Unmold on a bed of lettuce and garnish. Serve with Ritz crackers only. Yield: 50 servings.

Almonds may be used as scales on fish mold; sliced olive for the eye of fish.

Mrs. Jerry M. Hall
(Carolyn Buckner)

Chinese Shrimp Toasts

36 medium shrimp, boiled and
   peeled
36 (1-inch) cubes of deli-type white
   bread, unsliced
3 eggs, beaten
3 Tablespoons water
4 Tablespoons cornstarch
4 Tablespoons flour

1 Tablespoon soy sauce
1 teaspoon garlic salt
1 teaspoon salt
1 teaspoon monosodium glutamate
3 green onions including tops, finely
   minced
Vegetable oil for frying

With toothpicks, spear shrimp on bread cubes. Make batter of remaining ingredients except oil. Heat oil; test for proper temperature by dropping in plain bread cube. It should brown in 60 seconds if temperature is correct. Dip shrimp toasts in batter, coating thoroughly. Drop into deep fryer; fry until crisp and golden brown. Lift out with tongs; drain on paper towels. Serve hot with Sweet and Sour Sauce (see Index) for dipping. Yield: 3 dozen.

Mrs. Edley H. Jones, III
(Brenda Ware)

Marinated Shrimp

5 pounds raw shrimp in shell
1 (3-ounce) box shrimp boil
1½ cups vegetable oil
1 cup vinegar
2 teaspoons salt

1 (3½-ounce) bottle capers
3 purple onions, cut in rings
¼ teaspoon TABASCO brand
    pepper sauce
1 teaspoon celery seed

Boil shrimp in shrimp boil according to package directions. Do not over-cook. Drain and peel shrimp. Combine remaining ingredients. Add shrimp. Cover and let marinate in refrigerator overnight. Yield: 5 pounds.

Mrs. Jerry M. Hall
(Carolyn Buckner)

Shrimp Spread

1 pound shrimp, boiled and cleaned
3 Tablespoons cream cheese,
    softened
1 Tablespoon chili sauce
1 teaspoon Worcestershire sauce
2 teaspoons horseradish
¼ cup finely chopped celery
2 Tablespoons finely chopped green
    pepper

1 hard-cooked egg, chopped
1 Tablespoon grated onion
1 Tablespoon chopped parsley
¾ teaspoon salt
Black pepper
Cayenne pepper

Chill shrimp. Mash very fine with a fork. Add remaining ingredients. Chill. Serve with crackers. Yield: 2 to 3 cups.

Mrs. James W. Cook
(Naomi Paquette)

Caviar Mayonnaise

1 cup homemade mayonnaise
2 Tablespoons lemon juice

1 can black caviar (red can be used
    if black not available)

Mix ingredients together and refrigerate. Better if made a day ahead of time. Delicious with turkey.

Mrs. Louis P. Cashman, Jr.
(Frances Reid)

Caviar Pie

Whites of 3 hard-cooked eggs,
  chopped
Yolks of 3 hard-cooked eggs,
  chopped

3½ ounces black lumpfish caviar
1 large white onion, chopped
12 ounces sour cream

Put chopped whites in bottom of buttered pie plate. Place another pie plate on top and refrigerate overnight. The next day spread chopped yolks on top of whites. Next layer caviar, onion, and sour cream. Be careful to totally cover everything with sour cream. Do not leave anything exposed. Serve with toast rounds. Yield: 8 to 10 servings.

Mrs. Henry Faser
(Hester Flowers)

Marinated Oysters

4 quarts or 10 dozen jarred oysters
  or equivalent
3 cups vegetable oil
2 cups fresh lemon juice
1 Tablespoon lemon pepper
  marinade or seasoning
2 teaspoons garlic salt
3 cloves garlic, minced
1 Tablespoon dill seed or 2
  Tablespoons dried dill weed

10 drops TABASCO brand pepper
  sauce
2 Tablespoons salt
1 teaspoon black pepper
3 to 4 green onions, finely chopped
Fresh bunch of parsley, tops washed
  and snipped from stems
Soda crackers

Simmer oysters in large pot in own juices until edges curl but oysters are still very plump, approximately 10 minutes. Drain in colander and cool. Check for shell pieces, but do not rinse. Place oysters in glass dish in single layer. Mix all ingredients except crackers. Pour over oysters. Refrigerate 12 to 24 hours covered with plastic wrap. Turn oysters at least twice. At serving time place oysters in lettuce leaf-lined glass serving dish surrounded by soda crackers. Serving spoons work better than toothpicks since a spoon of marinade with oyster on the cracker is superb. Yield: 40 to 50.

Looks beautiful served in ice-filled punch bowl containing oysters submerged inside; let lettuce leaves fold outward on the ice.

Mrs. Barry W. Holcomb
(Pat Horne)

Naomi's Oyster Mosca

¼ cup butter
¼ cup olive oil
⅔ cup Italian bread crumbs
½ teaspoon salt
½ teaspoon black pepper
¼ teaspoon cayenne
½ teaspoon dried tarragon

½ teaspoon oregano
2 Tablespoons minced parsley
2 teaspoons minced garlic
2 Tablespoons chopped green onions
1½ pints fresh shucked oysters or
   2½ dozen canned oysters

In a heavy saucepan, melt butter over low heat. Mix in olive oil and heat a few minutes longer. Add other ingredients except oysters. Mix well; remove from heat. Place well-drained oysters in ramekins and pour equal portions of sauce over each. Bake at 450° for about 20 minutes. Serve immediately. Yield: 4 servings.

Doubles beautifully.

Mrs. James W. Cook
(Naomi Paquette)

Oyster Loaf

½ cup finely chopped toasted
   pecans
1 can smoked oysters, drained and
   chopped
1 (8-ounce) package cream cheese

2½ to 3 Tablespoons mayonnaise
Dash garlic salt
Chopped parsley
Paprika

Mix chopped pecans and oysters. Mix together cream cheese, mayonnaise, and garlic salt. Pat cream cheese mixture into a circle on top of a piece of plastic wrap. Put oyster mixture in center of cream cheese circle. Using plastic wrap, pull 1 side of cream cheese over oyster filling. Then do the same with the other side. Mold edges around into ball using wrap. Do not touch cream cheese with hands. Smooth ball where edges meet. Wrap and chill. Before serving, sprinkle with chopped parsley and paprika. Serve with plain butter crackers. Yield: 12 to 16 servings.

To toast pecans, sprinkle with melted butter and salt. Bake at 325° for 15 to 20 minutes. Stir once or twice during cooking.

Mrs. E. A. Buckner, Jr.
(Ruth Vicknair)

Salmon Cheese Spread

1 (8-ounce) package cream cheese,
 softened
1 (7¾-ounce) can pink salmon,
 drained and flaked
2 Tablespoons minced onion

1 teaspoon Worcestershire sauce
2 teaspoons fresh lemon juice
⅛ cup chopped stuffed olives
¼ cup chopped pecans (optional)

In a medium mixing bowl blend cream cheese and salmon until well blended. Add onion, Worcestershire, and lemon juice. Mix well. Stir in olives and pecans. Use as a sandwich filling for party sandwiches, as a spread for crackers, or shape into a log garnished with fresh parsley and serve with crackers. Yield: 12 servings.

This recipe won first place in a local recipe contest for appetizers.

G. Louis Rowles
Amory, Mississippi

Scallops with Herbed Butter

1 pound fresh bay scallops or ocean
 scallops
8 Tablespoons unsalted sweet
 butter
3 Tablespoons finely chopped
 yellow onions
3 Tablespoons scallions (white part
 only), finely chopped

Salt to taste
1 Tablespoon parsley, finely
 chopped
⅓ cup fine white bread crumbs
1 Tablespoon fresh lemon juice
2 Tablespoons pine nuts, toasted

Preheat oven to 475°. Rinse scallops, remove attached muscle, and pat dry. If using ocean scallops, cut into halves or quarters, depending upon size. Beat butter with a wooden spatula (or work with fingers) until soft. Add onions, scallions, salt, parsley, bread crumbs and lemon juice. Place equal amounts of scallops with equal portions of seasoned butter. Place on a baking sheet and bake 10 minutes or until piping hot and bubbling. Sprinkle with toasted pine nuts before serving. Yield: 6 to 8 servings.

May be served as a first course with French bread.

Mrs. Bob Coleman
(Cissy Wagner)

 Fresh oysters should be a natural gray in color and the liquor should be clear.

Ceviche

1 pound diced fillets (bass or
    crappie)
2 bay leaves
Salt and pepper

1 cup lemon juice
½ teaspoon oregano
⅓ teaspoon garlic salt

Mix all ingredients except fillets. Pour over fillets and cover in a glass or plastic container. Marinate overnight in refrigerator.

1 white onion, diced
1 bell pepper, diced
1 fresh ripe tomato, chopped

3 cups mild white vinegar
1 cup water
Salt

Cover onions, bell pepper, and tomatoes with vinegar and water. Marinate 2 to 3 hours. Drain liquids from fish mixture and vegetable mixture. Mix and serve on butter crackers. Add additional salt to taste.

Billy Joe Cross, author
Cooking Wild Game and Fish

Venison Appetizer

1 (5-pound) venison roast
5 to 6 cloves garlic, slivered
Cracked black pepper
3 slices bacon
1 or 2 beef bouillon cubes
2 large onions, thinly sliced

2 cups sour cream
Juice of 2 to 3 lemons
Lettuce leaves, torn in pieces
Lemon slices to garnish
Paprika
Parsley

Stud roast with slivers of garlic. Sprinkle heavily with pepper. Place in roasting pan and cover with bacon slices. Cook in 500° oven for 5 minutes per pound. Reduce oven heat to 350°. Dissolve 1 bouillon cube in 1 cup hot water. Pour around roast. Place sliced onions around roast. Cook roast an additional 5 minutes per pound, basting several times. Add more bouillon if needed. Turn off oven and let roast sit in oven until cool. Shred venison, removing any sinew. Mix 1 quart shredded venison with pan juices and onions, sour cream, and lemon juice. (If mixture is too runny, add more sour cream.) Refrigerate. Serve on torn lettuce leaves garnished with lemon slices, paprika, and parsley. Serve with homemade rolls. Yield: Approximately 1½ quarts.

Mrs. Grace Clark
Tupelo, Mississippi

Duck Fingers

3 wild duck breasts
½ cup rosé wine mixed with ½ cup
    Italian dressing
Salt and pepper to taste

1 egg, beaten
Italian bread crumbs
Cooking oil

Soak duck in rosé mixture for 2 or 3 hours. Drain. Cut each breast into 3 or 4 long strips. Sprinkle with salt and pepper; then dip into egg and roll in bread crumbs. Fry slowly in cooking oil until golden brown for approximately 10 to 15 minutes, turning often. Drain on paper towels and keep hot until served. Yield: 8 to 10 servings.

Sauce

¾ cup margarine
1 teaspoon instant onion
1 teaspoon garlic salt

Worcestershire sauce to taste
Lemon juice to taste

Melt margarine with onion and garlic salt. Add Worcestershire and lemon juice. Simmer this mixture for 5 to 6 minutes. Serve sauce in individual dishes with individual servings of duck.

Pete Stone

Red Hot Chicken Bits

3 pounds boned chicken breasts
⅛ teaspoon garlic salt
2 Tablespoons red pepper

½ teaspoon black pepper
1 cup flour
Vegetable oil

Cut chicken breasts lengthwise into 1-inch pieces. Sprinkle garlic salt freely over chicken, turning pieces so each is coated. Continue with red, then black pepper. Set aside for 1 hour to let chicken absorb flavor. Dust chicken with flour, then deep fry in vegetable oil at 375° for 3 minutes. Drain on paper towels. Serve warm or cold.

Linda Rundell Dismuke
Germantown, Tennessee

 To quickly coat chicken or small meat pieces, place flour or crumbs in a plastic or paper bag with a few pieces of meat and shake.

Sesame Chicken

2 cups boiled chicken, cut into
  pieces
½ cup plain bread crumbs
¼ heaping cup sesame seed

½ cup mayonnaise
1 teaspoon dry mustard
1 teaspoon minced onion

Boil chicken in seasoned water and cut into bite-size pieces. Mix bread crumbs and sesame seed. Mix mayonnaise, mustard, and onion. Coat chicken pieces in mayonnaise mixture and then roll in crumb mixture. Place on baking sheet and bake at 425° for 10 to 12 minutes. Serve with Honey Mayonnaise or hot, sweet mustard. Yield: 6 to 8 servings.

Honey Mayonnaise

1 cup mayonnaise

2 Tablespoons honey

Mix well and refrigerate.

Mrs. James W. Cook
(Naomi Paquette)

Dot Kiely's Yankee Meatballs

3 pounds hot sausage
1 pound mild sausage

4 eggs, beaten
1½ cups soft bread crumbs

Mix all ingredients. Shape into small balls. Brown meatballs in skillet. Drain well. Serve with sauce.

Sauce

3 cups ketchup
¾ cup brown sugar
½ cup wine vinegar

¼ cup strongly brewed coffee
½ cup soy sauce

Combine all sauce ingredients in a saucepan and simmer 15 minutes. Add meatballs. Bake in oven at 350° for 30 minutes or simmer on stove for 30 minutes. Yield: 6 to 7 dozen.

Mrs. W. F. McGehee
(Brownie Burton)

Polynesian Meatballs

1½ pounds ground chuck
¾ cup uncooked quick oatmeal
1 egg, slightly beaten
1 teaspoon monosodium glutamate
½ teaspoon onion salt
½ teaspoon garlic salt

1 Tablespoon soy sauce
3 to 4 dashes TABASCO brand
   pepper sauce
⅓ cup milk
1 (8-ounce) can water chestnuts,
   drained and minced

Mix all ingredients well. Roll into bite-size meatballs. Place on cookie sheet and bake at 350° for 15 to 20 minutes. Meatballs can be made ahead and frozen. Make the sauce when ready to serve. Yield: 75 small meatballs.

Sauce

1 (8½-ounce) can crushed
   pineapple, drained, reserving
   liquid
1 cup firmly packed brown sugar
2 Tablespoons cornstarch

1 cup beef bouillon
½ cup vinegar
2 teaspoons soy sauce
⅓ cup chopped bell pepper

Mix pineapple juice, sugar, and cornstarch in saucepan. Add bouillon, vinegar, and soy sauce. Bring to a boil stirring constantly. Boil for 1 minute. Add bell pepper and pineapple. Pour sauce over meatballs. Serve in chafing dish.

Mrs. Buddy Lewis
Gloster, Mississippi

Pâté en Gelée

1 (13½-ounce) can beef broth
1 envelope unflavored gelatin
5 ounces cream cheese
1 (8-ounce) package liverwurst

1 small onion, grated
Worcestershire sauce to taste
TABASCO brand pepper sauce to
   taste

Heat beef broth and dissolve gelatin in it. Pour ⅓ of it into the bottom of a 3-cup mold and refrigerate until set. Have cream cheese and liverwurst at room temperature. Place them in a mixing bowl. Add grated onion and seasonings and beat all together until smooth. Pile this mixture on top of the jellied broth leaving space all around the sides. Pour remaining broth around the sides of the pâté in the mold and chill until set. Unmold on lettuce leaves and serve with crackers or melba toast. Yield: 1 mold.

Mrs. William R. Ferris
(Shelby Flowers)

Marinated Steak Bites

1 cup vegetable oil
¾ cup soy sauce
½ cup fresh lemon juice
Grated rind of 1 lemon
¼ cup prepared mustard

1 Tablespoon black peppercorns
2 to 4 cloves garlic, minced
1½ pounds sirloin steak, cut in
  bite-size pieces

Mix first 7 ingredients. Place meat in glass dish. Pour marinade over meat. Refrigerate for 24 to 48 hours. Meat cooks in marinade. Serve cold. Yield: 10 to 12 servings.

Don't tell your guests this is not cooked until after they have eaten it!

Linda Rundell Dismuke
Germantown, Tennessee

Sausage Strudel

1 pound bulk hot sausage, cooked
  and drained
4 (3-ounce) packages cream cheese
  at room temperature
½ cup sliced almonds
½ cup coarsely chopped pecans
½ cup coarsely chopped walnuts

2 or 3 green onions, minced
¼ teaspoon dried thyme, crumbled
Pinch of salt and red pepper
18 phyllo sheets
1½ cups butter, melted
Fine dry bread crumbs
Cherry tomatoes (optional garnish)

Combine sausage, cream cheese, nuts, green onions, thyme, salt, and red pepper in large bowl. Divide into 18 equal portions, about ⅓ cup each. Preheat oven to 400°. Place 1 phyllo sheet on work surface with long edge nearest you. Cover remaining phyllo with plastic wrap to prevent drying. Brush right half of sheet with melted butter. Sprinkle with bread crumbs. Fold left side over to cover. Brush bottom half of folded phyllo sheet with butter; sprinkle with crumbs and fold top half over to cover. Brush entire surface of folded sheet with butter. Form 1 portion of filling into short, thick sausage shape. Place vertically on center of folded phyllo sheet. Fold over long edges of dough to cover ends of "sausage", then roll phyllo over short end to enclose filling. Brush outside of roll with melted butter. Transfer to baking sheet. Repeat with remaining phyllo and filling. It can be frozen at this point and placed in freezer bags. Bring to room temperature before baking. Bake until golden brown 30 to 35 minutes. Serve hot. Garnish with cherry tomatoes if desired. Yield: 18 strudel rolls.

Mrs. Bob Coleman
(Cissy Wagner)

Winner Wontons with Sweet and Sour Sauce

1 (8-ounce) can shrimp, drained
1 (8-ounce) package cream cheese, softened
½ teaspoon steak sauce
1 clove garlic, minced
2 green onions, minced
2 teaspoons lemon juice

3 to 4 shakes TABASCO brand pepper sauce
1½ (12-ounce) packages wonton wrappers
1 egg, beaten
½ teaspoon water
Vegetable oil for frying

Combine shrimp, cream cheese, steak sauce, garlic, onion, lemon juice and TABASCO. Stir to mix. Place scant teaspoon of mixture in center of wonton wrapper. Moisten edges of wrapper with small amount of water. Fold diagonally to form a triangle. Seal the edges. Holding the folded side of the triangle against your finger, bring the 2 bottom points of the triangle around your finger and pinch together to form a little cap. Combine egg and water. Brush with egg and water mixture. Fry in hot oil several minutes until golden. Drain and cool. Freeze. Reheat at 350° for 15 minutes or until heated through. Yield: 60.

Sweet and Sour Sauce

¼ cup brown sugar
¼ cup white wine vinegar
¼ cup ketchup
1 cup water
¼ cup soy sauce

2 Tablespoons cornstarch
2 Tablespoons water
1 small green pepper, chopped
¼ cup canned crushed pineapple, drained

In a small saucepan bring sugar, vinegar, ketchup, water, and soy sauce to a boil. In a small bowl mix cornstarch with water. Add to sauce; bring sauce to a boil, stirring until smooth and thick. Stir in green pepper and pineapple. Yield: 3 cups.

May also be served with Hot Mustard Sauce. (see Index)

Mrs. William W. Ramsey
(Carolyn Sasser)

Make fine bread crumbs in a blender from crackers or bread. Store in freezer for use in recipes when needed.

It's Fun to Fondue

Fondue parties were the vogue in Vicksburg in the late 1960's, and many hostesses still use this medium for entertainment with minimum effort and maximum fun. The cheese fondue, which originated in Switzerland, calls naturally for Emmentaler cheese or Gruyère blended with wine and a dash of liqueur. Crusty French bread is selected for dunking. A variety of fondue suggestions follow.

Beef Fondue

Buy a tender cut of meat, allowing ½ pound per person. Cut beef into ¾ to 1-inch cubes and serve raw to allow guests to cook their own. In the center of dining table place a fondue dish or deep chafing dish filled with peanut oil heated to a very high temperature over an alcoholic flame. Provide each guest with a long 2-tined fork used to spear meat and dip into oil to cook. This takes a minute or less. Let each guest dip meat into a variety of sauces.

Sour Cream and Bleu Cheese Sauce

1 cup dairy sour cream
¼ cup crumbled bleu cheese

Dash of Worcestershire sauce

Mix all ingredients.

Red Sauce

¾ cup ketchup
2 Tablespoons lemon juice

1 teaspoon horseradish
Dash of Worcestershire sauce

Mix all ingredients.

Bordelaise Sauce

½ cup fresh mushrooms
1 Tablespoon butter or margarine
3 Tablespoons cornstarch
2 cups beef broth

3 Tablespoons red wine
2 Tablespoons lemon juice
1 Tablespoon tarragon leaves
Dash of pepper

Simmer mushrooms in butter 4 minutes. Stir in cornstarch well; blend in beef broth. Cook, stirring, until mixture boils. Add wine, lemon juice, tarragon leaves, and pepper. Simmer 15 to 20 minutes.

Swiss Cheese Fondue

1 clove garlic
1½ Tablespoons cornstarch
⅓ cup Kirsch
1½ cups dry white wine
1½ pounds Swiss cheese, shredded

¼ teaspoon baking soda
Dash of white pepper
Dash of nutmeg
Dash of paprika
French bread, cubed

Rub inside of fondue pot with garlic. Mix cornstarch and Kirsch; set aside. Heat wine in fondue pot until bubbles start to rise on surface. Add cheese gradually, stirring until melted. When mixture starts to bubble, add cornstarch mixture, stirring until thick. Reduce heat; add baking soda and spices. Serve with French bread cubes. Yield: 8 to 10 servings.

Mrs. Jerry Hayes
(Cris Page)

Lahem Bi Jeen
(Meat Rolls)

1 large onion, chopped
2 Tablespoons butter
2 pounds lean ground chuck
2 teaspoons salt
1 teaspoon pepper

1 teaspoon cinnamon
½ cup pine nuts
4 Tablespoons white vinegar
1 (16-ounce) box phyllo dough
½ cup butter, melted

Sauté onions in butter until transparent. Add meat and brown. Add salt, pepper, cinnamon, and pine nuts. Cook 5 to 10 minutes. Add vinegar and cook 5 more minutes. Let meat mixture stand until cool. Remove phyllo pastry from box. With sheets still in plastic covering, cut crosswise into 3 equal parts (approximately 14 x 5⅔-inches in size). Separate sheets carefully. Work with 1 sheet at a time keeping others covered with a slightly damp towel to prevent drying. Fold short end of pastry sheet over ½ inch. Brush melted butter over pastry sheet. Place a teaspoon of meat evenly along folded side. Roll up like a cigar. Each roll should be about as thick as a cigarette. Place on buttered cookie sheet. Brush meat rolls with butter. Bake in 300° oven on top rack for 15 to 20 minutes or until lightly browned. After baking, rolls may be cut to desired size. Best if served warm. Freezes beautifully. Yield: 66 meatrolls.

Mrs. Michael Baroudy
(Adeaby Khalo)

Egg Rolls, Stamm-Style

½ teaspoon sugar
2 Tablespoons dry sherry
2 Tablespoons soy sauce
1 Tablespoon cornstarch
1 pound fresh pork, boned and cut
   in small pieces (about 3 end-cut
   pork chops)
3 Tablespoons vegetable oil

2 cups chopped celery
2 cups green onions
½ pound chopped mushrooms
1 can bean sprouts, rinsed and
   drained
Salt or soy sauce to taste
20 egg roll wrappers
Vegetable oil for deep frying

Mix sugar, sherry, soy sauce, and cornstarch together and pour over raw pork. Set aside while preparing vegetables. Heat oil in skillet or wok. Add meat and cook until pork loses its pink color. Remove from skillet. Add celery and onions and cook for 2 or 3 minutes. Add mushrooms and mix thoroughly. Add bean spouts and mix well. Then add pork back to vegetable mix and stir. Check seasonings and add salt and/or soy to taste. Cook until liquid clears and thickens. Let cool. Cut egg roll wrappers on the diagonal, making 2 triangles out of each wrapper. With base of the triangle toward you, put a heaping Tablespoon of filling in center of wrapper and fold bottom corners toward center until they overlap. Roll up and continue to roll until you reach top of triangle. With a little cool water, seal corner securely to roll. Heat frying oil to 375° and deep-fry egg rolls for 3 to 5 minutes until golden brown. Yield: 40 egg rolls.

Serve with soy sauce or a mixture of 1 part dry mustard to 1 part water. Also may be served with Sweet and Sour Sauce (see Index).

Mrs. Bruce Ebersole
(Story Stamm)

Phyllo Pastry Triangles

Phyllo pastry   *Melted butter*

Since phyllo pastry is very thin, it dries out very quickly. Work with a little at a time, keeping remaining dough covered with a slightly damp towel. Cut sheets of dough crosswise into strips 2 inches wide and 14 inches long. Working with 1 strip at a time, brush lightly with butter. Place a heaping teaspoon of filling at bottom of strip. Fold bottom left corner over to right side. Then fold bottom right corner over to left side. Continue folding flag-fashion the same way until all pastry is folded into a triangle shape. Brush with butter. Bake at 350° for 15 to 20 minutes or until golden brown. Pastries may also be brushed with egg white glaze before baking. A variety of fillings follow.

Parsley Cheese Filling

½ pound Monterey Jack cheese,   *1 Tablespoon dried parsley flakes or*
  shredded   *fresh parsley*
1 egg, beaten

Mix all ingredients well.

Brown Sugar and Nut Filling

¾ cup brown sugar   *¼ cup butter, melted*
½ teaspoon cinnamon   *2 cups pecans or walnuts, chopped*
¼ teaspoon allspice   *1 egg, beaten*

Mix together all ingredients. Yield: 25 to 30 servings.

Mrs. Larry Lambiotte
(Carolyn Walker)

Cheddar Chicken Filling

1 (3-pound) chicken, cooked and   *½ medium onion, minced*
  minced   *3 teaspoons tarragon*
1 cup Cheddar cheese, shredded   *1 teaspoon garlic powder*
¾ cup mayonnaise   *Salt and pepper to taste*
1 egg, beaten

Mix chicken with cheese, mayonnaise, egg, and seasonings. Yield: 4 dozen.

Mrs. Edley H. Jones, III
(Brenda Ware)

Quickie Appetizers

Mix cream cheese, onion juice, and chopped nuts. Stuff into precooked pitted prunes. Store in refrigerator.

Cover a package of cream cheese with soy sauce and let set for several hours. Sprinkle heavily with sesame seeds. Add more soy sauce. Serve with wheat thins.

Pour Worcestershire sauce in a jar of olives from which juice has been drained. Turn upside down and marinate overnight.

Remove stems from large fresh mushrooms. Fill with uncooked hot sausage and bake at 375° for 30 minutes.

Spread a bag of tortilla chips in baking dish. Place jalapeño cheese on top; microwave approximately 30 seconds or run under broiler.

Sprinkle 2 to 3 seeded and chopped jalapeño peppers in a well-greased 9-inch square pan. Cover with 1 pound shredded Cheddar cheese. Pour 6 beaten eggs over this and bake at 350° for 30 minutes. Cool and cut into 1-inch squares.

Melt 1 roll of garlic cheese in microwave or double boiler. Add 1 can chili without beans and 1 can hot tamales, chopped. Heat until bubbly. Dip with tortilla or corn chips.

Cut package of wieners into bite-size pieces. Combine ½ cup each of bourbon, chili sauce, and brown sugar. Simmer wieners in sauce for 30 minutes. Serve in chafing dish.

Add leftover peeled shrimp to a mixture of onions sautéed in butter and softened cream cheese for a great dip. Serve with melba rounds.

Marinate 1 can drained mushrooms in Italian dressing. The longer they marinate the better they taste.

Place 1 can crabmeat on top 1 package cream cheese. Pour cocktail sauce on top. Serve with favorite crackers.

 For fresh onion juice, squeeze half an onion with skin on, just as you would squeeze a lemon.

 When making party sandwiches, freeze bread before cutting into fancy shapes and spread with filling while bread is still stiff. This eliminates torn or mashed bread.

Old Southern Mint Julep

Fresh mint *Bourbon*
Powdered sugar *Crushed ice*

Put 2 sprigs of fresh mint in bottom of tall thin glass. Add 1 rounded teaspoon powdered sugar and a few drops of water. Use a wooden muddler
and bruise the mint with sugar and water thoroughly. Add a jigger of
bourbon whiskey. Pack the glass to brim with finely crushed ice. Add 1
jigger of whiskey. Let trickle to bottom of glass. Put sprig of fresh mint in
top of glass and serve with two straws. If desired, top sprig of mint may
be dipped in powdered sugar while damp. Yield: 1 serving.

Warren Asher

Mimosa

1 quart orange juice, chilled *1 fifth champagne, chilled*

Just before serving, mix orange juice and champagne in large pitcher.
Serve over ice. These may also be mixed individually. Yield: 2 quarts.

This is a good brunch beverage.

The Editors

Bloody Mary

6 ounces tomato juice or tomato and *1 teaspoon horseradish*
vegetable juice *¼ teaspoon lemon pepper*
2 ounces vodka *⅛ teaspoon Tony Chachere's*
1 to 2 dashes TABASCO brand *Famous Creole Seasoning or salt*
pepper sauce *⅛ teaspoon black pepper*
1 teaspoon lime juice *Celery or carrot to garnish*
1 dash Worcestershire sauce

Mix tomato juice and vodka. Add TABASCO, lime juice, Worcestershire
sauce, horseradish, lemon pepper, Tony's Seasoning and pepper. Stir
well. Serve over ice. Garnish with small celery stem or carrot stick, if desired. Yield: 2 servings.

Jack Stamm

Twenty-Four Hour Cocktail

½ cup water
1½ cups sugar
Juice and rind of 12 lemons

1 fifth bourbon
Crushed ice

Prepare a simple syrup by combining water and sugar. Boil until sugar is completely dissolved. Add lemon juice, along with rind, and bourbon. Let syrup set for 24 hours. Strain and serve over crushed ice in sherbet glasses. Yield: 10 to 12 servings.

Mrs. John G. Collins
(Anita Sheffield)

Betty's Strawberry Daiquiris

1 (6-ounce) can frozen limeade
6 ounces rum or vodka
1 (10-ounce) package frozen
  strawberries

8 to 10 fresh strawberries (optional)
Ice
Strawberries for garnish (optional)

In blender, pour limeade and 1 limeade can full of rum. Add frozen strawberries and fresh strawberries if desired. Fill blender almost to the top with ice. Blend at high speed until ice is finely crushed and all ingredients are well blended. Stop blender and stir once or twice. Garnish with fresh strawberries if desired. 3 fresh bananas or 2 to 3 fresh peaches, unpeeled and sliced, may be substituted for strawberries. Yield: 6 to 8 servings.

Betty Bailey

Peach Fuzzy

1 (16-ounce) package frozen peaches
1 (6-ounce) can pink lemonade
1 juice can vodka
1 jigger peach brandy

2 cups crushed ice
2 seeded, unpeeled peaches
  (optional)

Mix all ingredients in blender. When in season, 2 seeded, unpeeled peaches may be added. Yield: 8 servings.

Mrs. Mike Chaney
(Mary Thurman)

Madrid Sangria

1 bottle dry red wine
½ cup cognac
¼ cup Cointreau
2 lemons, sliced

2 oranges, sliced
1 dash sugar
1 (10-ounce) bottle club soda

Mix all ingredients in ½-gallon stoneware jug. Yield: Approximately ½ gallon.

Mrs. Charles C. Moss
Meridian, Mississippi

Sangria Slush

1 (16-ounce) can crushed pineapple
2½ cups red wine
1½ cups orange juice
½ cup lemon juice

½ cup sugar
2 Tablespoons grated lemon rind
Orange slices to garnish

Blend first 5 ingredients in blender on high. Add lemon rind to taste. Pour into 9 x 9-inch pan and freeze. Shortly before serving, remove and let soften. Break up with a spoon and put into glasses. Garnish with orange slices. Yield: 4 to 6 servings.

Mrs. Vaughn Fields
(Janie Selby)

Gluhwein
(Glowing Wine)

4 cups tea
½ to 1 cup brandy or bourbon
Peel of 1 lemon (not the white part
  of the peel)
Juice of ½ lemon

Sugar (start with 1 cup and add
  more to taste)
3 cinnamon sticks
1 fifth red wine

Prepare 4 cups of tea using 4 tea bags. Put tea in an enamel or stainless steel pot. Add remaining ingredients. Heat very slowly; do not boil. Serve hot. If too strong, add more water or wine. Cannot reheat. Yield: 8 to 10 servings.

Mrs. Howell Jones
(Marianne May)

Hawaiian Hammers

2 (46-ounce) cans unsweetened
   pineapple juice
1 (15-ounce) can cream of coconut
½ pint rum

½ pint vodka
½ pint gin
Cherry to garnish (optional)

Pour all ingredients into a gallon jug. Shake and refrigerate. Serve, as is, over ice. This may be put into blender with ice to serve a frothy drink. Garnish with a cherry, if desired. Yield: 1 gallon.

Mrs. Bubba Rainer
(Tricia Frey)

Farrell Holiday Eggnog

¾ cup sugar, divided
6 large eggs, separated
1 jigger rum

½ cup bourbon
1 cup heavy cream, whipped
1 pint milk

Add ½ cup sugar to egg yolks and beat until lemon-colored and thick. Slowly add rum and bourbon to yolks while beating. Set aside. Beat egg whites until foamy; then add ¼ cup sugar gradually while beating. Beat until stiff. Fold yolk-bourbon mixture and whipped cream into whites; then add milk. Chill. Mixture must be stirred before serving. Recipe may be doubled. Yield: 6 to 8 servings.

Mrs. Fred Farrell
(Kay McCorkle)

Jamoca Nog

1 pint dark rum
¼ cup coffee liqueur
1 quart dairy eggnog

1 pint chocolate ice cream, softened
1 pint coffee-flavored ice cream,
   softened

Mix rum, liqueur, and eggnog; chill. Just before serving pour ⅓ of mixture into a chilled pitcher or punch bowl. Add softened ice creams and blend until smooth. Add remaining mixture and stir well. Yield: 14 to 16 servings.

Mrs. Joseph P. Harris
(Susan Gunn)

Amaretto Freeze

1 cup amaretto liqueur   1 quart vanilla ice cream

Pour amaretto into blender. Add ice cream. Blend until smooth. Yield: 6 to 8 servings.

May be served in Jefferson cups with silver demitasse spoons for dessert.

Mrs. Johnny Gussio
(Shirley Nejam)

Praline Freeze

¼ cup white crème de cacao   1 quart vanilla ice cream
¾ cup praline liqueur   1 praline (optional)

Pour crème de cacao and praline liqueur in bottom of blender. Add ice cream. Blend until smooth. Pour into glasses. Crumble praline and sprinkle pieces on top of each drink, if desired. Yield: 6 to 8 servings.

The Editors

Coffee Bourbon Punch

1 quart strongly brewed coffee   5 teaspoons vanilla extract
1 pint heavy cream   ½ gallon vanilla ice cream
5 Tablespoons sugar   1 pint bourbon

Brew coffee; cool in refrigerator until serving time. Whip cream; cover and refrigerate until serving time. At serving time pour coffee, sugar and vanilla into punch bowl and stir. Scoop ice cream into bowl and pour in bourbon. Mix lightly until all is blended and ice cream floats on top. Place large mounds of whipped cream on top. The sugar and vanilla can be added to the brewed coffee before refrigerating to save time. Serve at once. Yield: 24 punch cups.

Mrs. Barry W. Holcomb
(Pat Horne)

Junior Auxiliary Punch

½ cup sugar
½ cup fresh lemon juice
2 fifths sauterne

1 fifth champagne
½ cup brandy

Mix sugar and lemon juice until sugar dissolves, heating juice if necessary. Add other ingredients. Serve chilled or with an ice ring.

Vicksburg Junior Auxiliary

Varina Davis Punch

Punch Base

1½ pints lemon juice
3½ pounds sugar dissolved in 2
  cups water
12 fifths hearty Burgundy

1½ fifths sherry
½ fifth brandy
¼ fifth rum
1 cup grenadine

Mix and refrigerate until needed. Makes a little more than 3 gallons. Add following ingredients to serve.

Approximately 10 ounces ginger ale
  to each gallon of base
Approximately 20 ounces soda
  water to each gallon of base

2 lemons, thinly sliced
½ cucumber, sliced with peel
1 orange, sliced
Ice

When ready to serve, add ginger ale and soda water. Garnish with lemon, cucumber and orange slices. Remove them before storing leftovers. Serve with plenty of ice. Best prepared 1 day in advance and may be kept weeks. Yield: 150 (4-ounce) servings.

Mrs. M. E. Hinman
(Connie Jenkins)

Her wit, her beauty, and her vivacious personality made Mrs. Jefferson Davis one of the most popular hostesses in the political and social circles of antebellum Washington, where her husband held the positions of congressman, senator, and cabinet official. Around her table were frequently gathered the leaders of the nation, and in addition to her own receptions, Varina Davis was often the unofficial White House hostess for her friends Mrs. Zachary Taylor and Mrs. Franklin Pierce. In Richmond, as First Lady of the Confederacy, she continued her popular entertainments until times became austere.

Brandy Milk Punch

⅔ cup brandy
2 cups light cream
6 Tablespoons powdered sugar

¼ teaspoon vanilla extract
3 to 4 ice cubes

Combine all ingredients in blender until well mixed. Yield: 6 servings.

Another ⅓ cup of brandy may be added for a stronger drink.

Mrs. William W. Ramsey
(Carolyn Sasser)

Coca-Cola Punch

1 dozen lemons, squeezed
Grated rind of 1 lemon
1 cup sugar

36 ounces COCA-COLA
Crushed ice

Squeeze lemons and add rind. Cover with sugar the night before serving. Just before serving, add COCA-COLA and pour over crushed ice. Yield: 8 servings.

"The trademark COCA-COLA is used with permission of The Coca-Cola Company."

Mrs. Clave E. Gill, III
New Orleans, Louisiana

Irish Cream Liqueur

1¾ cups Irish whiskey
1 (14-ounce) can sweetened
   condensed milk
1 cup heavy cream
4 eggs

2 Tablespoons chocolate syrup
2 teaspoons instant coffee
1 teaspoon vanilla extract
½ teaspoon almond extract

Combine all ingredients and mix in blender. Keeps refrigerated up to 1 month. Stir or shake before serving and serve over ice if desired. Yield: 5 cups.

Put in a fifth bottle. This makes a wonderful Christmas gift.

Linda Rundell Dismuke
Memphis, Tennessee

Old Hotel Vicksburg Punch

2 cups boiling water
1 cup sugar
½ to 1 cup lemon juice
3 (12-ounce) cans frozen orange
    juice, made according to
    directions

1 (46-ounce) can pineapple juice
1 (20-ounce) can crushed pineapple
1 (6-ounce) jar maraschino cherries
1 (32-ounce) bottle ginger ale

To boiling water add sugar and lemon juice. Boil for 5 minutes. Set aside to cool. When cooled, add orange juice, pineapple juice, pineapple, and cherries. Chill. Just before serving, add ginger ale. Yield: Approximately 1 gallon.

This recipe was passed down by word of mouth until 1946 when it was tasted by General Eisenhower at a reception in Vicksburg. He requested the recipe for Mamie because he enjoyed it so much.

Mrs. J. Stanford Terry, Sr.
(Mary Frances Dent)

Princess Ann Punch

11 cups Hawaiian Punch Fruit
    Punch (Fruit Juicy Red)
2 cups grenadine syrup

5 cups pineapple juice
2 cups light cream

Mix all ingredients together and chill before serving. Yield: 15 to 20 servings.

This makes a pretty punch for a shower.

Mrs. Betty Harbison
Memphis, Tennessee

Tangy Catawba Juice

1½ (46-ounce) cans pineapple juice
1 quart ginger ale
1½ (6-ounce) cans frozen lemonade

1 quart catawba white grape juice
1 pint fresh strawberries

Combine and chill first 4 ingredients. Serve in juice or wine glasses and garnish with strawberries. Yield: 24 servings.

Mrs. Charles Moss
Meridian, Mississippi

Hot Cranberry Punch

8 cups cranberry juice
8 cups pineapple juice
2½ cups water
¾ cup brown sugar

4 teaspoons cloves
4 sticks cinnamon, broken into
pieces
1 cup rum (optional)

Mix cranberry juice, pineapple juice, and water in a 30-cup coffee pot. Put brown sugar, cloves, and cinnamon in the basket of the pot. Perk as you would coffee. 1 cup rum may be added if desired just before serving. This recipe can be reduced to 10 cups. Divide all ingredients by ⅓. Yield: 30 cups.

Mrs. Bill Pierce
(Pat Hand)

Hot Spiced Tea

16 whole cloves
2 cinnamon sticks
4 cups water
2½ cups sugar

1 (12-ounce) can orange juice,
frozen
1 (12-ounce) can lemonade, frozen
12 cups weak tea

Boil cloves and cinnamon sticks in 4 cups water 5 to 10 minutes. Add additional cloves and cinnamon sticks for a spicier taste. Strain and add to the remaining ingredients. This may be heated in individual servings or for a large group. Yield: 25 to 30 cups.

Mrs. Kenneth F. Grogan, Jr.
(Inez McNeely)

Almond Tea

8 cups water, divided
1½ cups sugar
2 tea bags

Juice of 4 lemons
1 Tablespoon vanilla extract
1 Tablespoon almond extract

Boil 6 cups water and sugar for 10 minutes. In a separate pan combine an additional 2 cups boiling water with tea bags. Steep 5 minutes. Remove tea bags and mix with water-sugar mixture. Add the juice of lemons, vanilla and almond extract. Serve hot. Yield: 8 servings.

Mrs. John Frazier
(Lyn Runyon)

Fruit Tea

4 heaping Tablespoons loose tea
1 quart boiling water
3½ cups sugar
1 teaspoon mint extract or fresh
  mint

2 (12-ounce) cans frozen lemonade,
  mixed as directed
2 (12-ounce) cans frozen orange
  juice, mixed as directed

Make tea with water and add sugar, mixing it well. Strain. Add mint extract. After tea cools, add fruit juices. Yield: 2 gallons.

Mrs. Bill Harris
(Teresa Vaughn)

Summertime Tea

2 quarts strong tea
2 cups sugar
1 cup water

10 to 15 sprigs fresh mint
1 large bottle ginger ale, chilled

Brew 2 quarts strong tea. In separate saucepan make syrup by boiling water and dissolving sugar. Next add fresh mint to syrup and let simmer for 10 minutes. Discard mint. Chill tea. When ready to serve, mix chilled tea and chilled ginger ale. Yield: 10 servings.

Mrs. John Province
Paris, Tennessee

Vicksburg National Military Park

So serene now, so violent in 1863! The Vicksburg National Military Park, 1800 acres of the Civil War battlefield that was the Gibraltar of the Confederacy, is a memorial to the savage struggle that once divided the nation brother against brother.

Men fought and died here. The trench lines of opposing armies were within shouting distance for 47 tortuous days. Cannons, mortars, muskets, and brute strength were arrayed at close range in a semicircle around Vicksburg. The central ridge alongside old Jackson Road is now dominated by a marble temple erected to honor the soldiers from the state of Illinois.

On bronze tablets within its walls are listed the men from Illinois who fought here, ranging from U.S. Grant, the commander in chief, down to the lowest private. Other states that supplied men to the North or South have memorials along the roads that follow the former trench lines.

On other hillsides not far away lie the graves of men who fell in battle; one is the U.S. Cemetery where 17,000 were interred; the other is Soldiers' Rest where thousands of Confederates were buried in unmarked graves.

The memory of the struggle lives on hauntingly. The National Park whispers to the visitor, "Never again."

Soups and Salads pictured:

Split Pea Soup, Tomato Aspic, Chunky Gazpacho, Asparagus in Raspberry Vinaigrette, Taco Salad, Squash Bisque

Soups, Salads, Salad Dressings

Elegant Fresh Mushroom Soup

½ cup butter
4 cups green onions, finely chopped
1 teaspoon salt
½ teaspoon white pepper
2 Tablespoons flour

5 cups chicken stock
¾ to 1 pound mushrooms
1¼ cups light cream
1 cup heavy cream (optional)
Cayenne pepper (optional)

Melt butter; add onions, salt, and pepper. Cover and cook very slowly for 10 minutes, being careful not to let onions brown. Remove from heat and stir in flour. When smooth, add the stock. Return to heat and stir until soup boils. Let simmer for 10 minutes. Meanwhile, wash and dry mushrooms; set aside ¼ pound. Coarsely chop remaining mushrooms and add to soup. Place contents into blender and blend until nearly smooth. Return to pan and add light cream. Heat until hot, but not boiling. Before serving, add remaining mushrooms that have been thinly sliced. Top each serving with a dollop of whipped cream and sprinkle with cayenne pepper. Yield: 6 to 8 servings.

Mrs. Robert M. Abraham
(Billie Patterson)

Cheesy Asparagus Soup

1 (10½-ounce) can Cheddar cheese
  soup, undiluted
1 (10½-ounce) can cream of
  asparagus soup, undiluted
1 soup can light cream
½ can white wine

1 (15½-ounce) can asparagus tips
  and pieces with juice
½ teaspoon white pepper
⅛ teaspoon red pepper
½ teaspoon garlic powder
Dash of Worcestershire sauce

Blend cheese and asparagus soups until smooth. Slowly add cream and white wine. Stir until smooth. Add asparagus and juice. Add seasonings and heat until bubbly. Serve with crackers or French bread. Yield: 6 servings.

Mrs. Elmer Neill, Jr.
Tallulah, Louisiana

71

Split Pea Soup

1½ pounds dry split peas
1 to 1½ cups diced ham
1 medium onion, finely diced
2 to 3 diced carrots

2 teaspoons salt
2 teaspoons pepper
1 teaspoon TABASCO brand pepper
   sauce

Wash peas. Place peas, ham, onions, carrots, and seasonings in a pot with 3 quarts water. Bring to a boil, stirring occasionally. Cover and let simmer 1½ hours. Stir occasionally. Can be frozen. Yield: 10 to 12 servings.

Mrs. Hugh Johnston
(Hazel Pond)

Cream of Tomato Soup

3 strips bacon
1 small onion, chopped
1 (16-ounce) can tomatoes
1 teaspoon baking soda

1 (12-ounce) can evaporated milk
1 can water
Salt and pepper to taste
Fresh parsley, chopped

Fry bacon, drain, and crumble. Set aside. Sauté onion in bacon drippings until clear; do not brown. Add tomatoes, breaking up tomatoes as stirred. Cook over low heat, covered, until most of juice is cooked down. Add soda, stirring constantly. Add milk and water. Bring to boil, but do not boil or soup will curdle. If thicker soup is preferred, cut down on water, or try half water and half tomato juice. Add bacon bits and chopped parsley to serve. Yield: 6 to 8 servings.

Mrs. C. O. Ratelle

Cream of Zucchini Soup

2 Tablespoons finely chopped green
   onions
1 clove garlic, minced
1 pound young zucchini, cleaned
   and thinly sliced

2 Tablespoons butter
1 teaspoon curry powder
½ teaspoon salt
½ cup heavy cream
1¾ cups chicken broth

In a tightly covered pan simmer onions, garlic and zucchini in butter for about 10 minutes until barely tender. Shake pan occasionally. Place mixture and remaining ingredients in blender for ½ minute. Serve either hot or cold. Yield: 4 servings.

Mrs. J. D. Thames
(Susan Davis)

Squash Bisque

1 cup minced onion
¼ cup minced carrots
4 Tablespoons butter
2 medium white potatoes, peeled
and cubed
2 (16-ounce) packages frozen
summer squash

4 (14½-ounce) cans chicken
bouillon or fresh chicken broth
2 cups light cream
Salt and pepper to taste
Cayenne pepper

Cook onions and carrots slowly in butter in covered saucepan until vegetables are tender. Add potatoes, squash, and chicken stock. Simmer until tender. Purée all in blender and then return to saucepan. Add cream and salt and pepper to taste. Sprinkle with cayenne pepper. Better if made a day ahead. Yield: 8 servings.

Mrs. D. P. Waring, Jr.
(Betty Jeanne Williams)

Garfield's Broccoli and Almond Soup

1 gallon water
4 chicken bouillon cubes
2 pounds fresh broccoli
1 medium carrot, grated
2 teaspoons garlic powder
½ cup butter
½ cup margarine

1 cup flour
½ cup sherry
Salt and pepper to taste
1 cup blanched almonds
1 Tablespoon monosodium
glutamate

In a large pan, bring water to boil and dissolve chicken bouillon cubes in it. Add broccoli, carrot, and garlic. Cook for about 30 to 45 minutes. In a deep pan, melt butter and margarine and add flour to make a roux. Stir in broccoli mixture and cook until slightly thickened. Add sherry and salt and pepper to taste. Stir in almonds and monosodium glutamate. Yield: 12 bowls or 24 cups.

This recipe from Maxwell's Restaurant has been requested by many, but never revealed until now.

Maxwell's Restaurant
Vicksburg, Mississippi

To remove excessive salt from soup, drop in a sliced raw potato.

73

Cream of Cauliflower Soup

1 head cauliflower
2 cans chicken stock
1 bunch green onions, finely
  chopped
½ cup butter

1 quart milk
10 Tablespoons flour
Salt and pepper to taste
3 Tablespoons parsley

Break up cauliflower into small pieces and boil in chicken stock. Sauté onions slowly in butter over low heat. When cauliflower is barely tender, remove from heat and add milk. Combine flour with onions and mix well. Cook about 3 minutes, stirring constantly; turn off heat for 1 minute. Slowly pour cauliflower mixture into flour mixture, stirring constantly until well mixed. Add salt and pepper. Turn heat on and let simmer 10 to 15 minutes. Do not boil. Remove from heat and add parsley. Yield: 6 to 8 servings.

Mrs. George Stevens
(Sidney McLaurin)

Cream of Broccoli Soup

4 cups chopped fresh broccoli or 2
  packages frozen broccoli
¾ cup chopped onions
3 cups chicken stock
½ teaspoon salt
½ teaspoon thyme leaves
1 garlic clove, crushed

¼ cup melted butter
¼ cup flour
¾ teaspoon white pepper
2 cups light cream
¾ cup dry white wine
⅛ teaspoon cayenne pepper
Green onions to garnish (optional)

In a large saucepan simmer broccoli, onions, stock, salt, thyme, and garlic for 15 minutes or until the broccoli is tender. When tender, place ⅓ of mixture at a time into food processor or blender to process. Return each portion to saucepan. Make white sauce with butter to which has been added flour and white pepper. When blended, add cream and stir until thick. Add to broccoli mixture. Stir over low heat to blend. Add wine and cayenne pepper; heat slowly. Sliced green onions are a nice garnish. Tastes better the second day. Yield: 4 to 6 servings.

Mrs. Don S. Miller, Jr.
(Deanna Blanchard)

 Add a pinch of herb, such as rosemary, tarragon, basil, thyme, or dill to canned soups while heating.

French Onion Soup

1½ pounds or 5 cups thinly sliced
yellow onions
3 Tablespoons butter
1 Tablespoon vegetable oil
1 teaspoon salt
¼ teaspoon sugar
3 Tablespoons flour
2 quarts boiling brown stock,
canned beef bouillon, or 1 quart
boiling water and 1 quart of
stock or bouillon

½ cup dry white wine or dry white
vermouth
Salt and pepper to taste
3 Tablespoons cognac (optional)
Rounds of hard-toasted French
bread, cut ¾ to 1 inch thick (1
per serving)
1 to 2 cups shredded Swiss or
grated Parmesan cheese

Cook onions slowly with butter and oil in a covered heavy-bottomed 4-quart saucepan for 15 minutes. Uncover; raise the heat to moderate, and stir in salt and sugar. Cook for 30 to 40 minutes stirring frequently, until the onions have turned an even deep brown. Sprinkle in flour and stir for 3 minutes. Off the heat, blend in the boiling liquid. Add wine and season to taste. Simmer, partially covered, for 30 to 40 minutes or more, skimming occasionally. Correct seasonings. (If not serving immediately, set aside uncovered; then reheat to simmer before serving.) Just before serving, stir in cognac. Pour into a soup tureen or soup cups over rounds of bread and serve cheese separately. If using cups or bowls, assemble soup with cheese on top and run under broiler just long enough to melt cheese. To toast bread slices, place in a single layer in roasting pan or cookie sheet and bake in preheated 325° oven for about 30 minutes until it is thoroughly dried out and lightly browned. Yield: 6 to 8 servings.

Mrs. H. Donald Barnes
(Betty Haraway)

Quick French Onion Soup

5 large onions, thinly sliced
¼ cup butter
4 (10½-ounce) cans beef broth

1½ cups water
French bread, thinly sliced
Mozzarella or Swiss cheese

Sauté onions in butter for 15 minutes. Add beef broth to onions and butter; add water and simmer for 1 hour or longer. Put soup into ramekin or small cup. Place slice of French bread on top of serving. Add cheese slice. Brown under the broiler. Yield: Eight (6-ounce) servings.

Mrs. Steve Harris
(Linda Walker)

Black Bean Soup

2 cups dry black beans
Cold water
2 teaspoons baking soda, divided
3 medium onions, chopped
3 cloves garlic, minced
4 Tablespoons parsley
¼ cup butter
1 to 2 cups chopped ham

2 teaspoons salt
Pepper to taste
2 bay leaves
1 cup white wine
Grated cheese for topping
Chopped green onions for topping
Sour cream for topping

Place beans in enough water to cover entirely. Add 1 teaspoon baking soda to beans. Let soak 2 hours and rinse. Add water to cover and 1 teaspoon baking soda and soak overnight (soda reduces acid in beans). Rinse beans. Cook in water in large kettle until soft about 3 to 4 hours. Sauté onions, garlic, and parsley in butter. Add all other ingredients to kettle. Cook over medium to low heat, stirring occasionally for 3 more hours. Add water, if it gets too thick. Top with grated cheese, chopped green onions, and sour cream. Yield: 10 to 15 servings.

Mrs. Jim Davidson
(Tupper Jones)

Navy Bean Soup

2 pounds dried navy beans
1 cup chopped onion
1 cup thinly sliced green onions
1 small green pepper, chopped
¼ cup chopped celery
2 Tablespoons chopped parsley
2 cloves garlic, minced
1 ham bone with ham on it
½ pound smoked sausage, chopped

4 quarts water
2 teaspoons salt
½ teaspoon black pepper
¼ teaspoon red pepper (more if
   desired)
¼ teaspoon thyme
2 whole bay leaves, crushed
¼ teaspoon dried basil

Soak beans overnight in cold water. When ready to cook, drain beans in colander and put in a heavy 8 to 10-quart pot with all other ingredients. Bring to a boil over high heat; then lower the heat and simmer for 4 to 5 hours or until beans are soft and the soup very thick. Stir often from the bottom. Remove ham bone and cut meat off. Return meat to soup and adjust seasonings. Serve with plenty of bread and butter. Yield: 8 servings.

Mrs. Vaughn Fields
(Lucy McLaurin)

Lentil Soup

¼ cup olive oil
2 large onions, chopped
1 meat hock or several cups diced,
  cooked ham
½ pound Polish sausage, cut into
  ½-inch slices
1 clove garlic, chopped
2 cups chopped celery with leaves

1 pound lentils, washed
½ teaspoon TABASCO brand
  pepper sauce
1½ teaspoons salt (more, if desired)
Black pepper to taste
1 package frozen leaf spinach,
  thawed and chopped

In a large pot, heat oil. Sauté onions until golden brown. Add ham, sausage and garlic; cook 5 minutes. Add celery, lentils, TABASCO, salt and pepper and water to cover (about 2 quarts). Cover and cook over low heat for 2 hours. Add spinach and cook an additional 10 minutes. Serve with hot bread. Yield: 8 servings.

Mrs. Dewey Purser
(Jean Nicola)

Mynastry

3 quarts water
2 Tablespoons salt
2 garlic cloves, minced
3 ribs celery, chopped
½ cup butter
½ cup olive oil

2 Tablespoons parlsey flakes
1 teaspoon pepper
1 (1-pound) package vermicelli
3 eggs
¾ pound American cheese, shredded
Romano cheese, grated (optional)

Bring first 8 ingredients to boil and cook on medium heat for 30 minutes. Add spaghetti to liquid and cook until tender. Beat eggs in separate bowl. Add ½ cup liquid to eggs and stir. Pour egg mixture into spaghetti. Add cheese to spaghetti and stir until melted. Sprinkle each serving with Romano cheese, if desired. Freezes well. Yield: 8 to 10 servings.

Mrs. Harry Meyer
(Louise Angelo)

 For tastier soup or stew, rub the inside of a soup pot with a cut garlic clove.

Peg's Cheese Soup

½ cup margarine
⅓ cup minced green onions
⅓ cup minced celery
⅓ cup minced bell pepper
½ cup flour

1 quart rich chicken broth
3 cups milk
1 pound processed cheese, cubed
4 ounces shredded Cheddar cheese
Dash of red pepper

In a double boiler melt margarine; sauté vegetables until tender. Stir in flour and blend well. Slowly add chicken broth and milk. Add cheeses and cook until melted. Add a dash of red pepper. The success of this recipe depends on a good rich chicken broth. Yield: 6 to 8 servings.

Mrs. William W. Ramsey
(Carolyn Sasser)

Chunky Gazpacho

3 medium tomatoes
1 large cucumber
1 green pepper
1 large onion
24 ounces canned tomato juice
⅓ cup olive oil

⅓ cup red wine vinegar
¼ teaspoon TABASCO brand
   pepper sauce
1½ teaspoons salt
⅛ teaspoon pepper

Dip each tomato into boiling water for 1 minute; lift out with slotted spoon. Peel and cut up 2 tomatoes into large bowl. Chop remaining tomato and set aside. Chop cucumber, putting ½ into large bowl and set ½ aside. Remove seeds from green pepper; chop; put ½ in large bowl and set ½ aside. Chop onion; put ½ into large bowl and set ½ aside. Add to large bowl ½ cup tomato juice and toss. Place these vegetables into blender a little at a time. Purée until smooth; pour into large bowl. Add remaining tomato juice, olive oil, vinegar, TABASCO, salt and pepper and mix well. Refrigerate, covered, until well chilled. Store remaining vegetables in separate dishes in refrigerator. As soup, serve in chilled bowls. Extra vegetables may be added as desired for a chunky texture. Serve with a chilled spoon. As beverage, serve in chilled mugs. Sprinkle a small amount of each chilled vegetable on top. Serve with a chilled spoon. Yield: 6 servings.

Prepare several hours ahead for better taste. Use glass or wooden bowls for refrigerating gazpacho.

Mrs. Jerry Yelverton
(Suzanne Smith)

Chilled Cucumber Soup

4 cups peeled, seeded, chopped
  cucumber
2 cups water
2 cups plain yogurt
1 clove garlic
Several fresh mint leaves

1 Tablespoon honey
1½ to 2 teaspoons salt
¼ teaspoon dill weed
Chopped green onions or chives to
  garnish

Put all ingredients except green onions or chives into blender and purée.
Serve very cold. Garnish with chopped green onions or chives. Yield: 4 to
6 servings.

Mrs. Hal Colisch
Monroe, Louisiana

Vichyssoise

2 cups cubed raw potatoes
1 cup chopped onions
2 cups water
3 chicken bouillon cubes
2 Tablespoons butter

¾ cup milk
¼ teaspoon pepper
2 Tablespoons parsley clusters
2 Tablespoons green onion tops
½ cup heavy cream

Combine potatoes, onions, water and bouillon cubes in saucepan. Cook,
covered, until just tender, approximately 15 minutes. Do not drain. Pour
into blender. Add remaining ingredients except cream. Blend on high for
approximately 30 seconds. Pour into bowls and add cream. Chill or serve
hot. Yield: 6 servings.

Mrs. William W. Ramsey
(Carolyn Sasser)

Cold Strawberry Soup

2 cups strawberries, washed
⅓ cup sugar
½ cup sour cream

½ cup heavy cream
1½ cups water
½ cup light red wine

Put strawberries and sugar into a blender and purée. Pour into a pitcher
and stir in creams; blend well. Add water and wine; stir and chill. Yield: 4
servings.

Mrs. Shouphie Habeeb
(Norma Daquilla)

Mama's Vegetable Soup

1 small chuck roast or 1 to 2
    pounds stew meat or boiling beef
    or round steak
3 to 4 quarts water
2 onions, quartered
2 ribs celery, cut in ½-inch pieces
2 bay leaves
2 beef bouillon cubes

Salt and pepper to taste
1 (16-ounce) can tomatoes, mashed
6 or 8 fresh carrots, sliced
3 or 4 potatoes, cubed
6 to 8 pods fresh okra
1 cup fresh grated corn or 1 (17-
    ounce) can whole kernel corn
1 (17-ounce) can English peas

Put meat, water, onions, celery, bay leaves, bouillon cubes, salt and pepper in soup pot. Bring to a boil and let boil gently for several hours. Skim foam off top periodically. Remove bones from roast as they separate. Remove stock from heat; refrigerate overnight or long enough for grease to harden on top. Remove grease layer from broth. Add tomatoes, carrots, potatoes, and okra. Continue cooking for about 1 hour. Break up meat with a fork. Add corn and peas and continue cooking until vegetables are completely done. Yield: 10 to 12 servings.

Miss Lauri Stamm

Creole Corn Soup

2 Tablespoons flour
4 Tablespoons vegetable oil
½ cup chopped onion
½ cup chopped bell pepper
¾ cup chopped celery
1 (17-ounce) can creamed corn
1 (12-ounce) can whole kernel corn
1 large potato, cut in pieces

1 small can cut green beans
    (optional)
5 cups hot water
3 Tablespoons tomato paste
Salt and pepper to taste
1 pound raw shrimp, peeled and
    deveined

Mix flour and oil. Cook over low heat, stirring often, to make a golden brown roux. Add onions, bell pepper, and celery. Cook 10 minutes. Add corn, potatoes, green beans, water, tomato paste and salt and pepper to taste. Simmer 30 minutes. Add shrimp. Cook 15 minutes. Yield: 4 to 6 servings or 1½ quarts.

Mrs. Kermit Hymel
Metairie, Louisiana

Soup of Soups

1 (10-ounce) package frozen
  Japanese-style crispy textured
  vegetables with seasoning
1 (11-ounce) can Cheddar cheese
  soup, undiluted
1 (10¾-ounce) can New England
  clam chowder soup, undiluted
2 soup cans light cream or milk

3 Tablespoons dry sherry
1 teaspoon Worcestershire sauce
½ pound fresh crabmeat
1 medium tomato, peeled and diced
1 Tablespoon butter
⅛ teaspoon white pepper
Chopped parsley to garnish

Prepare Japanese-style vegetables according to package directions. In a 4-quart saucepan, combine soup, chowder, cream, sherry, and Worcestershire; simmer a few minutes. Add cooked vegetables, crabmeat, tomato, butter, and pepper; heat. Garnish with chopped parsley. Yield: 8 servings.

Mrs. Bob Coleman
(Cissy Wagner)

Elaine's Shrimp and Corn Chowder

2 pounds small fresh shrimp or
  larger shrimp cut in half,
  deveined
Tony Chachere's Famous Creole
  Seasoning
¼ to ½ cup butter
2 medium red potatoes, diced
3 strips bacon, diced
½ cup minced white onion
½ cup chopped green onions (Do
  not put in food processor)

1 (20-ounce) can Delmonte cream-
  style corn (no substitution)
1 cup chicken stock
1 large can evaporated milk
2 cups light cream
1 clove garlic, minced
1 Tablespoon salted whipped butter
Salt to taste
1 generous pinch freshly ground
  nutmeg
Chopped parsley (optional)

Very gently sauté shrimp in Cajun seasoning and butter. Set aside and reserve liquid. Boil potatoes in small amount of water until they are soft and all water is almost gone. Do not drain. Fry bacon very slowly and when brown and crisp, remove from pan and crumble. Sauté onions in bacon fat until light brown; drain. Add bacon and onions to potatoes; blend in corn, stock, milk, and cream. Add garlic, butter, salt and nutmeg. Simmer 5 to 10 minutes. Just before serving, add shrimp. Garnish with parsley and more butter if desired. Yield: 6 servings.

Mrs. G. T. Dubose
New Orleans, Louisiana

Black-Eyed Oyster Soup

½ pound dry black-eyed peas　　*9 Tablespoons butter, divided*
3 quarts chicken broth　　　　 *Salt and pepper to taste*
1 smoked ham hock　　　　　　*2 dozen freshly opened oysters*
½ onion, finely chopped

Soak peas in cold water for about two hours. Drain and add broth and ham hock. Sauté onion in 1 Tablespoon butter and add to peas. Cook over low heat and simmer gently for about 2 hours. When done, force through a fine sieve and add salt and pepper to taste. Put back on stove and add remaining butter. Bring to boiling point and remove from stove immediately. Chop oysters coarsely and add to soup. Yield: 12 cups.

Mrs. Frank Maxwell
(Louise Middlebrook)

Oyster Soup

1 pint oysters　　　　　　　　　*5 Tablespoons flour*
3 cups oyster liquor and water or　*2 cups milk*
　clam juice　　　　　　　　　　*Dash of ketchup*
½ cup chopped green onions　　　*½ teaspoon salt*
1½ cups chopped celery　　　　　*¼ teaspoon white pepper*
½ package dried onion soup　　　 *TABASCO brand pepper sauce to*
5 Tablespoons butter　　　　　　　*taste*

Drain oysters and reserve juice. Boil green onions and celery in oyster liquor. Add dried onion soup. Simmer for 45 minutes. Melt butter; add flour. Add enough milk to make a cream sauce. Then add rest of milk. Combine the milk and oyster juice gradually. Season to taste with remaining ingredients. Add oysters. Cook gently until oysters curl. If heat is too high, oysters will be tough. Yield: 6 servings.

Oyster juice may be frozen until desired amount has been obtained.

Mrs. George Martin
(Barbara Gilmore)

 A leaf of lettuce dropped in a pot of soup absorbs the grease from the top.

Oyster Stew

6 dozen oysters with liquor
8 green onions, finely chopped
2 ribs celery, finely chopped
2 Tablespoons fresh parsley, minced
1 quart light cream

½ cup butter
Salt and pepper
1½ Tablespoons Worcestershire
   sauce

Strain oyster liquor and save. Remove any shells from oysters. Cook chopped vegetables and whole oysters in 1 to 2 cups oyster liquor until oysters are plump and edges begin to curl. Do not overcook. While oysters are cooking, simmer cream and butter in saucepan. Do not boil. Add oyster mixture to milk and butter. Add salt, pepper, and Worcestershire. Be careful when heating. It is best heated in a double boiler. Doubles easily. Yield: 6 to 8 servings.

Mrs. William Patterson
Union City, Tennessee

Fish Chowder

1½ cups diced raw fish of choice
2 cups sliced potatoes
1 cup finely chopped onions
¼ pound salt pork

½ Tablespoon salt
2 cups boiling water
1 cup milk
Pepper to taste

Add diced fish, potatoes, and onions to pork. Add salt and water. Simmer for 30 minutes. Add milk and simmer 8 minutes. Pepper to taste.

Mrs. Joel Horton
(Leslie Bell)

She-Crab Soup

1 cup butter
4 Tablespoons flour.
2½ cups milk
¼ teaspoon salt
¼ teaspoon pepper
¼ teaspoon nutmeg

½ teaspoon Worcestershire sauce
2 drops TABASCO brand pepper
   sauce
1 pound lump crabmeat
Sherry wine to taste

Melt butter; add flour and stir until creamy. Add milk, seasonings, and crabmeat. Bring to slow boil. Add sherry wine. Simmer. Yield: 10 to 12 (½-cup) servings.

Velchoff's Corner
Vicksburg, Mississippi

Cape Fear She-Crab Soup

1 (10½-ounce) can Harris American
   She-Crab Soup, undiluted
2 (10¾-ounce) cans cream of celery
   soup, undiluted
1 (10¾-ounce) can tomato soup,
   undiluted
4 soup cans milk
1 pound lump crabmeat
1 (8-ounce) tub whipped cream
   cheese with chives
½ teaspoon monosodium glutamate
1 cup sherry

Heat all ingredients, except sherry, in double boiler until creamy and hot. Add sherry just before serving. Yield: 6 to 8 servings.

Mrs. Joseph R. Compton
(Emily Raworth)

Chicken and Okra Gumbo

5 Tablespoons vegetable oil
5 Tablespoons flour
1 (4-pound) chicken, cut up or 4
   large chicken breasts
1 large onion, chopped
2 ribs celery with leaves, chopped
2 or 3 green onions and tops,
   chopped
2 garlic cloves, minced
4 cups fresh or frozen okra, thinly
   sliced
6 cups hot water
1 (16-ounce) can tomatoes
1 can chicken broth
3 bay leaves
½ teaspoon thyme
2 teaspoons salt
1½ teaspoons pepper
2 sprigs of parsley, chopped

In a large, heavy pot combine vegetable oil and flour. To make roux, cook over low heat, stirring often, until golden brown. Place chicken pieces in roux and brown over low heat. Remove chicken. Add onion, celery, green onions, garlic, and chopped okra to pot. (Okra slices well in food processor.) Cook, stirring often, about 15 to 20 minutes. Add hot water and stir well. Mash tomatoes and add to pot. Add chicken broth. Return chicken to pot. Break bay leaves in half to release flavor and add to soup. Add thyme, salt and pepper. Simmer 1 to 1½ hours. Remove chicken pieces and cool enough to remove bones. Cut into bite-size pieces and return to pot. Add chopped parsley. Simmer 10 minutes. Stir occasionally to prevent sticking. If roux is too thin, add 1 to 2 teaspoons chicken bouillon to broth. Remember, a good roux may take up to an hour to brown if done slowly. Yield: 2 to 3 quarts.

Mrs. Jerry M. Hall
(Carolyn Buckner)

Shrimp Bisque

¼ cup butter
1 cup sliced mushrooms
¼ cup chopped green onions
1 clove garlic, minced
3 Tablespoons flour
1½ cups chicken broth
1 pound medium or small shrimp,
    shelled and deveined

½ cup heavy cream
½ cup dry white wine
1 Tablespoon chopped parsley
1 Tablespoon chopped chives for
    garnish

In saucepan over medium heat, melt butter. Cook mushrooms, green onions, and garlic until tender, stirring occasionally. Stir in flour until smooth. Gradually stir in chicken broth. Heat to boiling, stirring constantly. Add shrimp. Reduce to low heat. Cover; simmer about 5 minutes or until seafood is done. Do not overcook. Stir in cream, white wine, and parsley; heat through. Ladle into bowls and top with chives. Yield: 6 servings.

Mrs. Eddy Sorey
(Boo McAdams)

Seafood Gumbo

2 cloves garlic, minced
1 rib celery, chopped
2 white onions, chopped
2 pounds okra, chopped
4 Tablespoons bacon drippings
1 Tablespoon flour
3 cans tomatoes
1 can tomato paste
1 ham hock

2 pounds or more shrimp
1 pound crabmeat
1 Tablespoon Worcestershire sauce
1 bay leaf
¼ bunch parsley, chopped
Dash of TABASCO brand pepper
    sauce
¼ teaspoon crushed red pepper
Salt and pepper to taste

Cook garlic, celery, onion and okra in bacon drippings. Add flour to drippings and then pour in tomatoes and tomato paste. Fill cans with water and add to mixture. Put in ham hock and ½ shrimp and crabmeat. Add Worcestershire, bay leaf, parsley, TABASCO, red pepper, salt and pepper. Cook 1 hour. Add rest of shrimp and crabmeat and cook 30 minutes longer. Yield: 6 to 8 servings.

This recipe is better the second day. Add bouillon to thin.

Mrs. George Martin
(Barbara Gilmore)

Creole Seafood Gumbo

Stock

5 quarts water
2 dozen boiled crabs
3 pounds raw shrimp in shell with heads

1 carrot
1 onion, quartered
½ cup coarsely chopped celery

Fill a large pot with water. Pull off back shells of crabs, adding shells to pot. Discard inedible spongy fingers; break crabs in half and set aside. Peel shrimp, adding heads and shells to pot. Set shrimp aside. Add carrot, onion and celery to pot. Cover and simmer for 2 hours. Strain and return to pot.

Gumbo

3 cloves garlic, finely chopped
3 cups finely chopped onion
1½ cups finely chopped celery
1 cup finely chopped green pepper
1 cup salad oil, divided
3 pounds okra, cut into ¼-inch pieces
1 Tablespoon bacon grease or salad oil
2 Tablespoons flour
1 (16-ounce) can tomatoes, drained
½ cup diced ham or sausage
1 teaspoon thyme

1 teaspoon basil
4 bay leaves
1 (10-ounce) can ROTEL Tomatoes and Green Chilies
¼ cup chopped parsley
Salt and pepper to taste
1 teaspoon TABASCO brand pepper sauce
1 Tablespoon Worcestershire sauce
Toney Chachere's Famous Creole Seasoning to taste (optional)
2 cups cooked rice

Sauté garlic, onion, celery, and green pepper in ¼ cup oil. Fry okra separately in ¾ cup oil for 40 to 50 minutes until soft and ropy texture is gone. Stir often. In separate pan make a roux with bacon grease and flour by cooking over low heat, stirring often, until brown. Add tomato pulp and cook into a paste. Add ham, thyme, basil, and bay leaves. Cook for 5 to 10 minutes. Add sautéed mixture, ROTEL Tomatoes and Green Chilies, and okra to stock. Gradually add seasoned roux mixture to stock. Simmer for 1½ to 2 hours. Add peeled shrimp, crab halves, and parsley. Season with salt, pepper, TABASCO, Worcestershire, and Tony Chachere's Creole Seasoning. Cook an additional ½ hour. Freezes beautifully. Serve over rice. Yield: 5 quarts.

Mrs. James W. Cook
(Naomi Paquette)

Vegetable Gumbo

2½ quarts water
1 ham bone with pieces of ham
2 onions, chopped
1 (32-ounce) can whole tomatoes, chopped
2 (16-ounce) cans sliced okra or 2 boxes frozen okra

2 (16-ounce) cans mixed vegetables, diced
1 (16-ounce) can tomato paste
¾ cup broken vermicelli
1 (16-ounce) can white creamed corn
Salt and pepper to taste

Put water into a large soup boiler. Bring water to a boil and add ham, onions, chopped tomatoes with juice, and the okra with its liquid. Simmer for 1½ hours. Add mixed vegetables, tomato paste, and spaghetti. Simmer for another 30 minutes. At this point check often to prevent sticking. Before serving, heat and add corn. Adjust seasonings. Serve with 1-inch square toasties or corn bread. Yield: 18 to 20 servings.

Mrs. Ernest Lipscomb
(Betty McCabe)

Turtle Soup

1 pound turtle meat, cut in 1-inch cubes
1 cup shortening
1 cup diced onions
1 cup diced celery
7 cloves garlic, chopped
1 cup flour
½ teaspoon TABASCO brand pepper sauce
3 to 4 quarts water
¼ cup beef stock concentrate
2 teaspoons celery salt

4 bay leaves
12 whole cloves
1 (16-ounce) can tomato sauce
1 teaspoon thyme
½ cup chopped parsley
½ cup Worcestershire sauce
Salt and pepper to taste
Sherry (optional)
Lemons, thinly sliced (optional)
Hard-cooked eggs, chopped (optional)

Sauté turtle meat in shortening until very brown. Add onions, celery, and garlic. Cook for 10 minutes; blend in flour, and cook 5 minutes. Add TABASCO, water, beef stock and then all other ingredients. Simmer 2 to 3 hours or until meat is tender. Garnish each serving with 1 Tablespoon sherry, hard-cooked eggs, or lemon slices, if desired. Better made ahead of time. Freezes well. Yield: 1 gallon.

Mrs. James W. Cook
(Naomi Paquette)

Chandler Chili

3 Tablespoons butter or margarine
1½ cups thin strips onion
1 cup chopped green pepper
2 pounds lean beef, cut in ½-inch
   cubes
1 (28-ounce) can tomatoes,
   undrained
½ cup dry red wine
1 clove garlic, crushed

2 Tablespoons salt
½ teaspoon pepper
½ teaspoon cumin
1 teaspoon dried oregano
1 teaspoon paprika
4 Tablespoons chili powder
1 (21-ounce) can red kidney beans,
   undrained

In a large wide saucepan melt butter; add onion and green pepper and cook gently until wilted. Add beef and brown. Add remaining ingredients except beans. Simmer, covered, until beef is tender, about 2 hours. Add beans and reheat. Yield: 6 servings.

Mrs. George Guider
(Annie Lee Faulk)

Chili

1 pound dry pinto beans or 1
   (15-ounce) can red kidney beans
5 cups tomatoes
1 pound bell pepper, chopped
1½ pounds onion, chopped
2 cloves garlic, minced
½ cup chopped parsley
⅓ cup vegetable oil
¼ cup butter

2½ pounds ground chuck
1 pound ground lean pork
⅓ cup chili powder
1 to 2 Tablespoons salt
1½ teaspoons pepper
1½ teaspoons cumin seed
1½ teaspoons monosodium
   glutamate

Wash beans. Soak overnight in water 2 inches above beans. Simmer, covered, in same water until tender. (Eliminate this step if using canned beans.) Add tomatoes to beans and simmer 5 minutes. Sauté green peppers in oil 5 minutes. Add onion and cook until tender, stirring often. Add garlic and parsley. Sauté meat in butter for 15 minutes. Add meat to onion mixture. Stir in chili powder. Cook for 10 minutes. Add this to beans and add spices. Simmer, covered, 1 hour. Cook uncovered 1 to 1½ hours, stirring occasionally. Cool and skim fat from top. Yield: 15 servings.

Mrs. John Prewitt
(Betty Marsalis)

 Soup can be topped with a variety of garnishes such as crisp bacon bits, grated cheese, sliced stuffed olives, thin lemon slices, chopped parsley or green onions, or fresh chopped tomatoes.

West Indies Salad

1 medium onion, finely chopped
1 pound fresh white lump crabmeat
Salt and pepper to taste
4 ounces vegetable oil
3 ounces cider vinegar (no
  substitute)

4 ounces ice water
Shredded lettuce
Tomato wedges, egg slices, parsley
  or capers (optional)

Place ½ onion in bottom of a small glass dish. Check crabmeat to be sure all shell has been removed. Spread all crabmeat over onion. Cover with remaining onion. Add salt and pepper to taste. Pour oil over crab mixture followed by vinegar and water. Do not stir. Cover and place in refrigerator for at least 2 hours before serving. At serving time toss lightly and serve on shredded lettuce. Garnish with tomato wedges, egg slices, parsley, or capers. Yield: 6 to 8 servings.

Use as seafood cocktail or hors d'oeuvres served with whole wheat or plain crackers.

Mrs. David May
(Martha Johnston)

Shrimp Arnaud

1 cup olive oil
⅓ cup tarragon vinegar
2 teaspoons paprika
¼ teaspoon salt
1 teaspoon sugar
1 jar Creole mustard

1 dozen large boiled shrimp per
  person
Lettuce, shredded
Tomatoes, quartered
Hard-cooked eggs

Mix first 5 ingredients well for sauce. Fold mustard into mixture. This requires a lot of mixing and must be mixed again if allowed to stand. Allow 1 dozen large boiled shrimp for each serving. Place shrimp on a bed of finely shredded crisp lettuce leaves. Garnish with quarters of ripe tomatoes and slices of hard-cooked eggs. Pour generous serving of sauce over all. Serve with hot buttered French bread which may be dunked in the sauce. Yield: 2 cups sauce.

Mrs. John G. Schaffer
(Margaret Patterson)

Shrimp Salad

3 cups cooked shrimp, diced (2
    pounds)
1 cup diced celery
4 hard-cooked eggs, chopped
½ cup sliced stuffed olives
¼ cup sliced green onion

¼ cup chopped dill pickle
1 cup mayonnaise
2 Tablespoons chili sauce
2 teaspoons horseradish
1 teaspoon salt

Combine shrimp, celery, and eggs. Blend other ingredients and add to shrimp mixture. Toss lightly and serve chilled. Yield: 6 servings.

Ann Carlson
Mt. Juliet, Tennessee

Curried Chicken Salad

2 cups diced cooked chicken
1 cup green grapes, halved
1 cup mayonnaise
1 Tablespoon curry

2 Tablespoons chopped chutney
½ cup heavy cream
Cantaloupe rings

Mix all ingredients thoroughly. Serve in cantaloupe rings. Yield: 6 to 8 servings.

Mrs. John T. Bottom
(Gloria Thames)

Exotic Chicken Salad

4 cups cooked, chopped chicken
    breasts
Salt, pepper, onion, and celery if
    desired
1 (8-ounce) can water chestnuts,
    chopped
2 cups chopped celery

1 cup slivered almonds
2 cups mayonnaise
½ to 1 teaspoon curry powder
1 Tablespoon soy sauce
1 (5¼-ounce) can pineapple chunks,
    drained

Boil chicken with salt, pepper, onion, and celery. Let chicken cool and chop for salad. Add chicken to remaining ingredients. Chill before serving. Yield: 6 to 8 servings.

Mrs. Rita Allison
Oxford, Mississippi

Ladies' Day Lunch

2 Tablespoons chopped green
  pepper
2 Tablespoons pimento
1 Tablespoon onion juice
1 hard-cooked egg, finely chopped
1 Tablespoon Worcestershire sauce

2 Tablespoons ketchup
2 Tablespoons chili sauce
1 cup mayonnaise
1 cup whipped heavy cream

Combine all ingredients. Store in refrigerator until ready to serve.

Salad

6 leaves lettuce
6 slices bread, buttered and toasted
6 slices chicken

6 slices tomato
6 slices bacon, fried
6 hard-cooked eggs, quartered

Assemble salad by placing lettuce leaf on each plate. Top with slice of toast, chicken, tomato, bacon, and quartered egg. Serve with dressing. Yield: 6 servings.

Mrs. Hugh Johnston
(Hazel Pond)

Chicken Mousse

1 (10¾-ounce) can cream of
  mushroom soup
2 (3-ounce) packages cream cheese
1 cup mayonnaise
1 Tablespoon Worcestershire sauce
½ teaspoon salt

2 envelopes unflavored gelatin
½ cup cold water
2 or 3 cups chopped chicken
1 cup finely diced celery
Cranberry jelly
Lettuce

Combine soup and cream cheese in top of double boiler. Heat and stir until well blended and creamy. Add mayonnaise, Worcestershire sauce and salt. Mix well. Soften gelatin in cold water. Add gelatin and stir until melted. Add chicken and celery. Put into dampened unfluted individual muffin tins. Chill until set. Turn onto waxed paper. Serve on top of ½-inch slice of cranberry jelly on lettuce leaf. Yield: 12 molds.

Substitute crabmeat for chicken and serve on slice of tomato aspic.

Mrs. Harris Bell, Jr.
(Sybil Holloway)

91

Congealed Tuna Salad

1 (3-ounce) package lemon gelatin
¾ cup hot water
2 cups white tuna, flaked
1 teaspoon salt
1 Tablespoon onion juice

½ cup mayonnaise
1 (2-ounce) can chopped pimento
1 cup diced celery
1 cup chopped pecans

Dissolve gelatin in ¾ cup hot water. Add other ingredients and mix; pour into an 8-inch square dish. Congeal in refrigerator. Cut into squares and serve on lettuce leaf. Yield: 6 servings.

Mrs. David A. McIntosh
(Rosemary Thigpen)

Asparagus in Raspberry Vinaigrette

30 young spinach leaves
30 fresh asparagus spears
4 quarts water
2 Tablespoons salt
1 (10-ounce) package frozen
    raspberries in syrup, drained
    until completely dry
6 Tablespoons olive oil

¼ cup heavy cream
2 Tablespoons sherry vinegar or any
    salad vinegar
Salt and freshly ground pepper to
    taste
1 teaspoon chopped chives for
    garnish
Coarsely cracked pepper

Wash spinach and remove stems. Roll in paper towels and keep cool. Trim asparagus to 4½ inches. Tie evenly into 6 bundles. Bring water to boil with salt in large saucepan over medium-high heat. Add asparagus and cook, uncovered, until tender, about 10 to 12 minutes. Rinse under cold running water and drain well. Untie and pat dry. Purée raspberries in processor or blender. Strain into small bowl, discarding seeds. Combine olive oil, cream, vinegar, salt, and pepper in processor or blender and mix well. Add to raspberry purée. Taste and adjust flavoring as desired. To serve, place spinach on salad plates. Arrange 5 asparagus spears over top. Spoon ribbon of dressing across center. Garnish with chives and dot with pepper. Accompany with additional raspberry vinaigrette. Yield: 6 servings.

Mrs. Harold Blue
(Jean Johnson)

 Never use metal bowls when mixing salads.

Asparagus Salad

1 bunch fresh asparagus
1 teaspoon salt
½ head lettuce, washed and torn
1⅓ cups commercial cucumber
   dressing

5 pieces bacon, fried and crumbled
1 (4.25-ounce) can chopped, ripe
   olives

Rinse asparagus and remove tough ends. Steam in 1 inch of salted water. Drain and chill. On each salad plate, place bed of lettuce and top with asparagus spears. Top with cucumber dressing, crumbled bacon, and olives. Serve cold. Yield: 4 servings.

Mrs. Joseph P. Harris
(Susan Gunn)

Broccoli Salad

1 bunch fresh broccoli, cut into
   florets
1 (6-ounce) can ripe olives, sliced
1 (5-ounce) jar stuffed green olives,
   sliced

1 small onion, chopped
4 hard-cooked eggs, chopped
¼ cup sweet pickle relish
⅔ cup mayonnaise
1 teaspoon lemon juice

Mix broccoli, olives, onion, and eggs. Add relish, mayonnaise, and lemon juice. Mix all very well. Put into covered bowl and refrigerate overnight. Stir well and serve. Yield: 4 to 6 servings.

Rebecca Jacobs
Gastonia, North Carolina

Old-Fashioned Coleslaw

½ cup mayonnaise
2 Tablespoons lemon juice
1 Tablespoon water
¾ teaspoon salt
½ teaspoon sugar

¼ teaspoon paprika
½ head cabbage, shredded
1 cup chopped celery
¼ cup green pepper
2 green onions, thinly sliced

In a large bowl, combine mayonnaise, lemon juice, water, salt, sugar, and paprika. Add cabbage and remaining ingredients. Toss well. Refrigerate to blend flavors. Sauce can be prepared ahead and stored in the refrigerator. Yield: 6 servings.

Mrs. Ken Rector
(Peggy Booth)

Sweet Slaw

1 medium cabbage
½ cup sweet pickles, chopped
1 small white onion, chopped
½ cup shredded carrots (optional)
Salt and pepper to taste

½ cup sugar
1 cup mayonnaise (do not
  substitute salad dressing)
¼ cup white vinegar

Shred cabbage. Add pickles, onions, carrots, if desired, salt and pepper. Toss these together. Sprinkle sugar over mixture. Mix mayonnaise and vinegar together until all lumps are gone. Pour over cabbage mixture and toss. Chill for 2 hours or longer before serving. Yield: 10 servings.

Mrs. Robert R. Bailess
(Natalie Waring)

Kraut Salad

Sauce

⅔ cup vinegar
1¼ cups sugar

¼ cup vegetable oil
¼ cup water

Place vinegar, sugar, vegetable oil, and water in saucepan. Bring to a boil over high heat. Boil 1 to 3 minutes until sugar dissolves. Let cool while preparing salad.

Salad

1 quart sauerkraut
1 cup diced celery
1 cup diced bell pepper
1 cup diced onion

1 (2-ounce) jar pimento, drained
  and diced
1 (8-ounce) can water chestnuts,
  drained and thinly sliced

Squeeze out all liquid from kraut. Place in colander and rinse with hot water. Do this several times. Place well-drained kraut in mixing bowl and add celery, bell pepper, onion, pimento, and water chestnuts. Mix well. Pour cooled sauce over this and mix again to coat all ingredients. Cover bowl or transfer to a jar and store in refrigerator overnight. Keeps for 1 to 2 weeks covered in refrigerator. It improves the longer it marinates. Yield: 6 to 8 servings.

Nick Cassino

Red Slaw Relish

¼ cup vinegar
⅓ cup sugar
1 Tablespoon mustard seed
1 teaspoon celery seed
½ cup red wine
½ cup water
2 teaspoons salt
Red pepper to taste

1 large head cabbage, cut into
*   chunks or shredded*
1 large green pepper, chopped
1 quart tomatoes, cubed and
*   drained*
1 (6-ounce) jar dill pickles, chopped
Cayenne pepper to taste

In a medium saucepan over medium heat, bring to a boil the first 8 ingredients. Reduce heat and simmer, uncovered for 5 minutes. Cool. In a large bowl, combine the above mixture and remaining ingredients. Cover and refrigerate; toss occasionally. Good with barbecue. Yield: 8 servings.

Herb Jones

English Pea Salad

1 (8-ounce) jar dill pickles, chopped
1 (9-ounce) jar chopped salad olives
3 (17-ounce) cans small English
*   peas*
1 large white onion, chopped
1 large bell pepper, chopped
½ cup mayonnaise
1 teaspoon mustard

Dash of TABASCO brand pepper
*   sauce*
Sprinkle of dill weed
Sprinkle of seasoned salt
Sprinkle of celery seed (optional)
Lettuce cups
Sprinkle of paprika

Put dill pickles and salad olives into colander and squeeze out all juice. Drain English peas well. Mix peas, onion, bell pepper, olives, and pickles in a large mixing bowl. Make dressing using mayonnaise, mustard, and TABASCO. Sprinkle salad with dill weed, seasoned salt, and celery seed if desired. Add dressing to salad. Serve in lettuce cups topped with a sprinkle of paprika. Yield: 10 to 12 servings.

Mrs. Bubba Rainer
(Tricia Frey)

 To peel tomatoes easily, pour boiling water over tomatoes and let stand for 60 seconds.

Gazpacho Salad

3 cups tomatoes, fresh in season or
  canned Italian plum tomatoes
1 teaspoon salt, divided
1 Tablespoon plus 1 teaspoon wine
  vinegar, divided
3 cucumbers
¼ teaspoon sugar
2 green bell peppers, diced
2 red bell peppers, diced

⅔ cup diced mild red onion
2 celery ribs, diced
3 firm avocados
2 cups French bread crumbs
3 green onions, minced
½ cup fresh parsley, minced
Capers, dark olives, and anchovies
  to garnish

Peel, seed, juice, and dice tomatoes. Place in bowl and add ½ teaspoon salt and 1 teaspoon wine vinegar. Let stand 5 minutes. Drain. Peel cucumbers, halve lengthwise, and scoop out seeds with a teaspoon. Dice and toss in a bowl with 1 Tablespoon wine vinegar, ½ teaspoon salt, and sugar. Let stand 5 minutes. Drain. Dice peppers and place in a bowl. Drop onions in boiling water for 15 seconds. Drain, rinse in cold water, drain again, and add to peppers. Add celery and toss together with salt and wine vinegar to taste. Halve, seed, peel, and dice avocados. Rinse in cold water to prevent discoloration. In a 2-quart glass bowl spread ¼ bread crumbs evenly on the bottom. Dry tomatoes, cucumbers, and pepper-onion mixture on paper towels. Cover crumbs with ⅓ pepper-onion mixture, ⅓ avocados, ⅓ tomatoes, ⅓ cucumbers, and ¼ dressing. Continue ending with remaining crumbs and dressing. Toss green onions and parsley. Place on top. Cover with plastic wrap and refrigerate 4 to 6 hours. Just before serving garnish with capers, olives, and anchovies. Serve with Herbal and Garlic Dressing. Yield: 15 to 20 servings.

Herbal and Garlic Dressing

2 to 3 large cloves garlic
1 teaspoon salt
Yellow peel of ½ lemon
Fresh basil
2 teaspoons Dijon mustard

3 Tablespoons fresh lemon juice
½ cup olive oil
Wine vinegar
Pepper and hot sauce to taste

Purée garlic in small bowl to a smooth paste with salt. Mince lemon peel and pound with garlic; pound in basil. Beat in mustard; then lemon juice and oil added by droplets. Season with salt, vinegar, pepper, and hot pepper sauce.

Mrs. Ernest Thomas
(Camille Sanders)

Chinese Salad

½ pound fresh bean sprouts
1 cucumber
1 teaspoon salt, divided
2 garlic cloves, minced
2 Tablespoons soy sauce

½ teaspoon sugar
2 Tablespoons white vinegar
1 (8-ounce) can water chestnuts,
    chopped (optional)

Rinse bean sprouts in cold water. Set aside in a medium-sized bowl. Peel and slice cucumber lengthwise in half. Remove seeds. Slice in very thin strips and then into 1-inch pieces. Place cucumbers in another bowl. Sprinkle ½ teaspoon salt on bean sprouts and ½ teaspoon on cucumber. Mix each well and let stand 30 minutes. Squeeze excess water and salt from each. Combine cucumber and bean sprouts and add remaining ingredients. Chill 45 minutes. Yield: 4 servings.

Mrs. Joseph P. Harris
(Susan Gunn)

Green Bean Salad

3 (16-ounce) cans French-style green
    beans
1 Vidalia onion or 1 medium onion,
    thinly sliced
¼ cup Italian salad dressing

2 Tablespoons vinegar
1 (8-ounce) can water chestnuts,
    chopped (optional)
12 small tomatoes, peeled and cored

Wash and drain beans. Add onion, Italian dressing, vinegar, and water chestnuts. Marinate overnight. Drain bean marinade and add enough sour cream dressing to coat beans. Serve bean mixture in tomato. Yield: 12 servings.

Sour Cream Dressing

1 cup sour cream
½ cup mayonnaise
1 teaspoon lemon juice
1 teaspoon dry mustard

1 teaspoon onion juice
Dash of garlic salt
2 teaspoons chopped chives

Combine all ingredients and refrigerate.

Mrs. John Hadad, III
(Susan Phillips)

Marinated Vegetables

¾ cup wine vinegar
1½ cups vegetable oil
2 teaspoons salt
1 teaspoon pepper
2 cloves garlic
1 head cauliflower, thinly cut
1 large onion, thinly sliced

1 (6-ounce) can mushrooms,
  drained
1 (14-ounce) can artichoke hearts,
  quartered
1 cup pitted ripe olives
1 (16-ounce) can cut green beans

Combine and boil vinegar, oil, salt, pepper, and garlic. Cool. Remove garlic. Put vegetables into large bowl. Pour marinade over vegetables and mix. Refrigerate 2 or 3 days, stirring occasionally. Serve drained on lettuce for a salad for 10 or use as a cocktail pickup. To vary, double marinade and add different kinds of vegetables such as cherry tomatoes (halved), squash slices, bell pepper, carrots, or broccoli florets. Yield: 10 servings.

Mrs. Murray Pinkston, Jr.
(Clara Parks Booth)

Mr. B's Sesame Spinach Salad

2 to 3 Tablespoons sesame seed
2 hard-cooked eggs, finely chopped

1 pound fresh spinach, torn

Spread sesame seed evenly on a cookie sheet. Toast by baking for 10 to 15 minutes at 275° to 300°. Toss together sesame seed, eggs, and spinach. Serve immediately with dressing. Yield: 6 servings.

Dressing

¼ cup salad oil
2 Tablespoons soy sauce
2 Tablespoons wine vinegar
1 clove garlic, crushed

¼ teaspoon salt
¼ teaspoon sugar
⅛ teaspoon ginger
¼ teaspoon white pepper

Place all ingredients in blender or covered jar and mix well.

Mrs. Bill Horne
Jackson, Mississippi

Storing mushrooms in a brown paper bag in the refrigerator will keep them fresher longer.

Fresh Spinach Salad and Dressing

1½ pounds fresh spinach
6 strips bacon, fried
3 hard-cooked eggs

4 green onions, sliced
½ pound fresh mushrooms, sliced

Wash spinach well and pat dry. Remove stems and break leaves into bite-size pieces. Break bacon into bits and chop eggs. Toss spinach, bacon, eggs, onions, and mushrooms lightly. Yield: 8 servings.

Dressing

⅓ cup red wine vinegar
⅔ cup vegetable oil
1 teaspoon salt
¼ teaspoon dry mustard

½ teaspoon sugar
2 cloves garlic, crushed
Coarsely ground pepper to taste

Prepare dressing by combining vinegar, oil, salt, mustard, sugar, garlic, and pepper. Mix well. Store in refrigerator.

The Editors

Tabooli

1 cup cracked wheat
4 cups water
1 bunch green onions
1 bunch parsley
6 to 8 sprigs mint or 3 Tablespoons
    dried mint

4 large tomatoes
Juice of 4 lemons or ½ cup lemon
    juice
½ cup olive oil
Salt and pepper to taste
½ teaspoon cinnamon

Soak wheat in water for about 25 minutes until soft. Drain in fine strainer until dry. Chop onions, parsley, mint, and tomatoes very finely. Add wheat, lemon juice, olive oil, salt, pepper, and cinnamon. Mix well. Serve on lettuce leaves. Yield: 6 to 8 servings.

Mrs. Albert Nosser
(Delores Koury)

Leftover vegetables make great additions to tossed green or chef's salads.

Taco Salad

3 cups torn lettuce
1 (15-ounce) can kidney beans,
   drained
2 medium tomatoes, chopped
2 Tablespoons green chili peppers
   or jalapeños, chopped
½ cup ripe or Greek black olives,
   sliced

½ cup crushed tortilla chips
½ large red onion, sliced
6 green onions, chopped
½ cup shredded Cheddar cheese
¾ (12-ounce) jar avocado dressing

Place lettuce in large salad bowl. Cover with other ingredients in order listed except dressing. Add dressing and toss, taking care not to use too much dressing. Yield: 8 servings.

Mrs. George E. Abraham
(Mabel Ellis)

Citrus-Avocado Salad

1 medium pink grapefruit, peeled
   and sectioned
1 large orange, peeled and sectioned
1 medium avocado, peeled and
   sliced crosswise
4 cups torn escarole or romaine
   lettuce
3 Tablespoons wine vinegar

3 Tablespoons lime or lemon juice
3 Tablespoons honey
1 teaspoon poppy seed
½ teaspoon dry mustard
½ teaspoon paprika
¼ teaspoon salt
⅛ teaspoon pepper

Mix grapefruit, orange, avocado, and lettuce. Beat together vinegar, lime or lemon juice, honey, poppy seed, dry mustard, paprika, salt, and pepper. Serve over salad ingredients. Yield: 4 servings.

Mrs. Bill Horne
Jackson, Mississippi

To peel an avocado, pull the skin off by hand, being careful not to break the inner green surface. This will prevent the flesh from discoloring.

Macaroni Salad

1 (12-ounce) package elbow
   macaroni
1 small bell pepper, chopped
1 medium onion, chopped
2 ribs celery, chopped
1 medium cucumber, chopped

2 tomatoes, chopped
1 cup mayonnaise or salad dressing
2 Tablespoons vinegar
Salt, pepper, and garlic powder to
   taste

Cook macaroni. Drain hot water; rinse, and drain well. Mix chopped vegetables, mayonnaise or dressing, vinegar, salt, pepper, and garlic powder with drained macaroni. Refrigerate soon after preparation. Will keep several days. Yield: 10 to 12 servings.

Mrs. Lewis Miller, Sr.
(Carrie Paul)

Fantastic Potato Salad

12 medium white potatoes
2 Tablespoons cider vinegar
2 Tablespoons melted margarine
2 Tablespoons sugar
2 Tablespoons salt
1 whole bunch celery, chopped

12 hard-cooked eggs, sliced
1 cup minced parsley
2 (4-ounce) jars chopped pimentos
½ cup minced onion
1 (10-ounce) jar sweet pickle relish

Boil potatoes in skins until tender. While hot, peel, cube and toss potatoes lightly with vinegar, margarine, sugar and salt. Refrigerate until thoroughly chilled. Then add celery, eggs, parsley, pimento, onion and pickle relish. Chill until flavors blend. Moisten with chilled Mayonnaise-Horseradish Sauce 1 hour before serving. Yield: 12 to 15 servings.

Mayonnaise-Horseradish Sauce

1 quart mayonnaise

1 (5-ounce) jar prepared horseradish

Mix well and refrigerate. This sauce is also very good on roast beef or corned beef.

Mrs. Mel Richardson
(Ginger Bailess)

Minty Potato Salad

8 to 10 potatoes
1 medium onion, finely chopped
¼ cup fresh minced mint, or ¼ cup
  dried mint
3 Tablespoons vegetable oil or more
  if needed

2 Tablespoons lemon juice or more if
  needed
1 Tablespoon salt or more if desired

Wash and boil unpeeled potatoes until done. Let cool until easy to handle. Peel and mash with remaining ingredients. Yield: 8 to 10 servings.

Mrs. Abe Abraham
(Gloria Farris)

Rice-A-Roni Salad

1 (8-ounce) package chicken-
  flavored Rice-A-Roni®, cooked
  as directed
1 (14-ounce) can artichoke hearts,
  drained and chopped, reserve
  liquid

4 green onions, chopped
20 green stuffed olives, chopped
½ medium bell pepper, chopped
½ cup mayonnaise
1 teaspoon curry powder
1 Tablespoon Worcestershire sauce

Combine rice, artichoke hearts, green onions, olives, and bell pepper. In another bowl, mix mayonnaise, curry powder, Worcestershire sauce, and ⅔ artichoke liquid. Toss all ingredients together and chill. Yield: 8 servings.

Marinated artichokes may be substituted for a different taste.

Miss Helen Abraham

Horseradish Mold

1 (3-ounce) package lemon gelatin
1 cup boiling water
1 (4-ounce) jar horseradish
½ pint sour cream

1 Tablespoon grated onion
Juice of ½ lemon
Salt and pepper to taste

Dissolve gelatin in boiling water and cool. Add horseradish, sour cream, onion, lemon juice, salt, and pepper. Pour into a 2-cup mold. Yield: 8 servings.

Delicious with prime rib or any red meat.

Mrs. Bill Horne
Jackson, Mississippi

Cucumber Salad

1 envelope unflavored gelatin
2 Tablespoons cold water
2 Tablespoons sugar
¾ teaspoon salt
⅔ cup hot water
3 to 4 Tablespoons lemon juice

6 medium cucumbers, peeled,
  seeded, and diced
1 (8-ounce) package cream cheese
1 cup mayonnaise
¼ cup minced onion

Soften gelatin in cold water. Blend in sugar and salt. Add hot water. Cool. Add remaining ingredients. Pour into a 9 x 9-inch dish. Refrigerate until firm. Yield: 8 servings.

Mrs. Dick Peterson
(Josephine Coker)

Vegetable Aspic Salad

1 envelope unflavored gelatin
1¼ cups cold water, divided
1 (10¾-ounce) can tomato soup
1 (3-ounce) package lemon gelatin
¼ teaspoon salt
⅛ teaspoon garlic salt

Dash of hot sauce
½ cup finely chopped celery
½ cup chopped Spanish olives
¼ cup chopped sweet pickles
1 carrot, grated
½ cup chopped pecans

In a small bowl, dissolve unflavored gelatin in ¼ cup cold water. Heat soup and 1 cup cold water to boiling point in saucepan. Remove from heat. Add lemon gelatin to unflavored gelatin after it has set. Add gelatin mixture to hot soup and allow to dissolve. Add salt, garlic salt, and hot sauce. After soup mixture begins to set, add celery, olives, pickles, carrots, and pecans. Pour into individual molds or 1½-quart glass container that has been lightly greased with cooking oil. Refrigerate until set. Yield: 10 to 12 servings.

Mrs. Harold Blue
(Jean Johnson)

 Quick chill gelatin mixtures for aspics or molds by pouring into metal pan and placing in freezer for about 15 minutes.

Tomato Aspic

4 envelopes unflavored gelatin
1 (46-ounce) can V-8 Juice
4 teaspoons finely chopped purple
 onion
4 Tablespoons lemon juice
3 Tablespoons Worcestershire sauce

1 teaspoon celery salt
½ teaspoon garlic powder
TABASCO brand pepper sauce to
 taste
Salt and pepper to taste

Soften gelatin in 2 cups V-8 for 5 minutes; then heat to dissolve. Add remaining V-8, onion, lemon juice, and seasonings. Pour into a large ring mold, individual molds, or loaf pan and refrigerate until set. Yield: 10 to 12 servings.

Shrimp, black olives, stuffed olives, artichoke hearts, cucumber slices, or cream cheese balls may be added.

Mrs. Tom Harris, Jr.
(Josephine Good)

Green Goddess Molds

1 (3-ounce) package lemon gelatin
2 chicken bouillon cubes
1 cup boiling water
½ cup cold water
½ cup Green Goddess dressing
1 Tablespoon mayonnaise

1 Tablespoon lemon juice
1 (14½-ounce) can cut asparagus,
 drained
½ cup diced celery
2 Tablespoons finely chopped green
 pepper

Dissolve gelatin and bouillon cubes in boiling water. Add cold water, Green Goddess dressing, mayonnaise, and lemon juice, beating with rotary beater until smooth. Chill until partially set or about 20 minutes. Fold in drained asparagus, celery, and green pepper. Turn into six ½-cup individual salad molds. Chill until firm, about 3 hours. Yield: 6 servings.

Mrs. Bill Duncan
(Floy Williams)

 Wilted lettuce can be freshened by letting it stand for 10 minutes in cold water with a few drops of lemon juice added.

Carrot Salad

*1 (8-ounce) can crushed pineapple,
  drained and juice reserved
1 (3-ounce) package orange gelatin*

*1 (8-ounce) package cream cheese,
  softened
1 cup finely grated carrots
1 envelope whipped topping mix*

Add enough boiling water to pineapple juice to make ⅔ cup. Mix with gelatin. Let cool. Cream cheese well. Add carrots, pineapple, and gelatin to cream cheese. Prepare whipped topping mix according to package directions and fold into gelatin mixture. Pour into 8 x 12-inch glass dish. Refrigerate overnight. Cut into squares. Remove from pan with spatula as this is a soft salad. Yield: 15 to 18 servings.

*Mrs. Fred Massengale
Hattiesburg, Mississippi*

Sunshine Salad

*1 (6-ounce) package orange gelatin
2 cups boiling water
2 cups 7 UP*

*1 (16-ounce) can crushed pineapple,
  juice reserved
1 cup miniature marshmallows
2 bananas, sliced*

Dissolve gelatin in boiling water. Stir in remaining ingredients. Set in a 9 x 13-inch glass dish. Yield: 15 servings.

Custard

*2 Tablespoons melted butter
2 Tablespoons flour
½ cup sugar
1 cup pineapple juice*

*1 egg, slightly beaten
Non-dairy whipped topping or
  whipped cream*

Combine butter and flour. Beat in remaining ingredients and cook over medium heat until thick. Cool. Spread over congealed salad. Top with non-dairy whipped topping or whipped cream.

*Mrs. Dick Peterson
(Josephine Coker)*

Orange Chiffon Salad

2 (3-ounce) packages orange gelatin
1 (3-ounce) package lemon gelatin
1 envelope unflavored gelatin
Juice from drained fruits plus water
    to make 4½ cups, divided

1 (11-ounce) can mandarin orange
    sections, drained
1 (16-ounce) can crushed pineapple,
    drained
1 (8-ounce) package cream cheese
1 cup mayonnaise

Mix all gelatins together. Heat 2¼ cups fruit juice and water mixture; add gelatin mixtures and stir thoroughly until dissolved. Add 2¼ cups of juice and water. Refrigerate until partially gelled. If it becomes too hard, it will require more whipping. Take out of refrigerator and whip well until light and foamy. Add softened cream cheese and mayonnaise. Whip. Add pineapple and whip. Grease springform mold with oil. Place mandarin orange sections in mold in a pattern. Pour in gelatin mixture carefully and return mold to refrigerator for several hours. Unmold on lettuce leaves when set. Serve with dab of mayonnaise. Yield: 16 servings.

Mrs. John T. Pegg
(Marie Gueymard)

Strawberry Congealed Salad

2 (3-ounce) packages strawberry
    gelatin
1 cup boiling water
2 (10-ounce) packages frozen
    strawberries

1 (16-ounce) can crushed pineapple,
    drained
3 medium bananas, mashed
1 cup chopped nuts
1 pint sour cream

Combine gelatin with boiling water in large mixing bowl and stir until dissolved. Fold in thawed strawberries with juice. Next, fold in drained pineapple, bananas, and nuts. Pour ½ mixture into 9 x 13-inch dish or large gelatin mold and refrigerate until firm. Spread sour cream over firm mixture and then gently spoon rest of mixture on top of cream and refrigerate for at least 3 hours. Yield: 12 servings.

Mrs. Jerry Dykes
(Tina Hazzlerigg)

Bing Cherry Salad

1 (16-ounce) can chunk pineapple
1 (15-ounce) can bing cherries
2 (6-ounce) COCA-COLAS
Juice of 2 lemons
¼ cup cold water

2 envelopes unflavored gelatin
1 (3-ounce) package cream cheese
½ Tablespoon mayonnaise
½ cup chopped celery
1 cup chopped nuts

Drain juice from pineapple and cherries. Combine with COCA-COLAS and lemon juice. Bring to a boil. Dissolve gelatin in ¼ cup cold water. Add hot mixture to gelatin. Place in refrigerator until it cools to the consistency of unbeaten egg whites, about 1 hour. Soften cream cheese with ½ Tablespoon mayonnaise. Add gelatin mixture gradually. Fold in celery and nuts. Place in an 11-cup mold and return to refrigerator to congeal, about 4 to 6 hours. Yield: 8 to 10 servings.

"The trademark COCA-COLA is used with permission of The Coca-Cola Company."

Mrs. C. E. Gill, III
New Orleans, Louisiana

Raspberry Salad

2 (10-ounce) packages frozen red
    raspberries and juice
1¾ cups boiling water
3 (3-ounce) packages red raspberry
    gelatin
2 cups cold water

1 (29-ounce) can crushed pineapple
    with juice
1 cup chopped walnuts or pecans
3 bananas, diced
Lemon juice

Take raspberries out of freezer to partially thaw. Pour boiling water over gelatin to dissolve. Add cold water and pineapple with juice and refrigerate until just starting to set around edges. Fold in nuts, bananas, and frozen raspberries with juice. Pour into individual molds or 1 large bundt pan. Yield: 16 servings.

Mrs. C. B. Patterson
(Sue Nelson)

Dip fresh fruits (bananas, avocados, apples, etc.) in lemon juice to keep them from turning brown.

Easy Cranberry Salad

1 envelope unflavored gelatin
2 Tablespoons cold water
1 (3-ounce) box raspberry gelatin
1 cup hot water
1 (8¼-ounce) can crushed
  pineapple, undrained

1 (16-ounce) can whole berry
  cranberry sauce
1 cup orange juice
¼ teaspoon salt
¼ cup pecans (optional)

Dissolve unflavored gelatin in cold water. Dissolve raspberry gelatin in hot water and add unflavored gelatin mixture. Add undrained pineapple, cranberries, orange juice, and salt. Add pecans if desired. Stir well and pour into greased mold. Refrigerate until set. Yield: 8 to 10 servings.

Mrs. J. Carter Stamm, Sr.
(Dorothy Williams)

Frozen Layered Cranberry Salad

1 (16-ounce) can whole berry
  cranberry sauce
3 Tablespoons fresh lemon juice
1 cup heavy cream, whipped

¼ cup mayonnaise
¼ cup powdered sugar
1 cup finely chopped nuts
Mayonnaise for topping (optional)

Mash cranberry sauce with fork. Mix in lemon juice. Spread a little of this mixture into individual molds, paper muffin cups, or 1 larger mold. Mix remaining ingredients. Spread this on top on cranberry layer. Freeze. Unmold red-side up onto lettuce leaves. May be served with a dash of mayonnaise on top. Yield: 8 to 10 servings.

Mrs. Erna Lee Jones
Southberry, North Carolina

Cranberry Cream Salad

1 (3-ounce) package cherry gelatin
1 cup hot water
1 (16-ounce) can whole cranberry
  sauce

½ cup chopped pecans
1 (8-ounce) carton sour cream

Dissolve gelatin in water. Break up cranberry sauce with fork, then add to gelatin. Add pecans. Fold in sour cream and put mixture into 1-quart mold. Chill. Yield: 6 to 8 servings.

Mrs. Steve Barlow
(Lynda Wilson)

Christmas Salad

2 (3-ounce) packages raspberry
   gelatin
1½ cups boiling water
1 (20-ounce) can crushed pineapple,
   drained
1 can whole berry cranberry sauce

¾ cup port wine
1¼ cups chopped pecans, divided
1 (8-ounce) package cream cheese
½ cup sugar
½ pint sour cream

Dissolve gelatin in boiling water. Add pineapple, cranberry sauce, port wine, and 1 cup nuts. Mix and pour into a 9 x 13-inch dish. Refrigerate until firm. Mix cream cheese, sugar, and sour cream until creamy and smooth. Spread on top and sprinkle with ¼ cup nuts.

Mrs. Joe Weaver
(Lenora Bradford)

Spiced Peach in Wine Jelly Salad

6 spiced peaches
1 (3-ounce) package cream cheese
¼ cup finely chopped pecans
2 envelopes unflavored gelatin
½ cup cold water

2 cups boiling water
1 cup sugar
3 Tablespoons lemon juice
1 cup dry sherry or white wine
Mayonnaise for topping

Drain peaches and remove pits; reserve juice. Soften cream cheese with a little cream or peach juice and mix with nuts. Stuff peaches with cream cheese mixture. Soften gelatin in cold water. Add boiling water and stir until dissolved. Add sugar, lemon juice, and sherry or wine. Place a thin layer of gelatin mixture in bottom of 7½ x 12-inch dish and refrigerate. When mixture is slightly set, add peaches and cover with remaining gelatin mixture. Chill. To serve, place on lettuce leaf and top with mayonnaise. This can also be done in individual molds or custard cups. Yield: 6 servings.

Mrs. James P. Guerriero
(Margaret Webb)

Place individual salad plates in the freezer about an hour before using.

Pineapple and Cheese Salad

2 envelopes unflavored gelatin
½ cup cold water
1 (16-ounce) can crushed pineapple,
   drained

½ cup sugar
Juice of 2 lemons
1 cup shredded cheese
½ pint heavy cream, whipped

Soften gelatin in cold water. Mix pineapple, sugar, and lemon juice. Heat and stir in gelatin while hot. When cool, stir in cheese and whipped cream. Pour into individual molds and refrigerate. Serve with dressing. Yield: 8 servings.

Dressing

½ cup mayonnaise
2 Tablespoons finely chopped celery

1½ teaspoons finely chopped bell
   pepper
½ teaspoon grated onion

Mix mayonnaise and other ingredients.

Mrs. Robert L. Dent
(Mary Frances Martin)

Individual Frozen Fruit Salads

2 cups sugar
1 cup water
2 (10-ounce) packages frozen
   strawberries

1 (13¼-ounce) can crushed
   pineapple, drained
1 cup peaches, drained and diced
4 bananas, diced

Boil sugar with water until clear. Add strawberries. Stir until dissolved. Add pineapple, peaches, and bananas. Freeze in muffin tins lined with paper baking cups. Yield: 24 servings.

This can also be frozen in parfait glasses, topped with whipped topping, and used as a dessert.

Mrs. Ray McLaurin
(Marlene Anderson)

When trying to select a ripe pineapple, pull out a leaf from the pineapple's crown. If the leaf comes out easily, the pineapple is ripe.

Corky's Frozen Fruit Salad

1 (8-ounce) package cream cheese
1 cup sour cream
¼ cup sugar
¼ teaspoon salt
1½ cups cut maraschino cherries
1 (16-ounce) can unpeeled apricot
   halves, drained and sliced

1 (9-ounce) can crushed pineapple,
   drained
2 cups miniature marshmallows
Red food coloring (drops to desired
   color)

Mix softened cream cheese and sour cream together. Add other ingredients to cream cheese mixture and sour cream. Pour into a loaf pan and freeze for 6 hours. Slice and serve on a piece of lettuce. Yield: 6 to 8 servings.

Mrs. Mark Prewitt
(Susie Harmon)

Ticky's Pineapple Salad

1 (3-ounce) package lemon gelatin
1 (3-ounce) package lime gelatin
2 cups hot water
1 cup mayonnaise
1 (14-ounce) can sweetened
   condensed milk

2 Tablespoons lemon juice
1 (16-ounce) can crushed pineapple,
   undrained
16 ounces cottage cheese

Dissolve gelatins in water. Mix mayonnaise and sweetened condensed milk in large bowl until smooth and add to gelatin. Add remaining ingredients. Pour into a 9 x 13-inch dish. Chill until firm. Yield: 10 to 12 servings.

Mrs. C. H. Wilson, Jr.
(Jo Peterson)

Millionaire Salad

2 eggs, beaten
5 Tablespoons lemon juice
5 Tablespoons sugar
2 Tablespoons butter
32 miniature marshmallows
1 cup whipped cream

1 (15-ounce) can pineapple tidbits,
  drained
1 (17-ounce) can fruit cocktail,
  drained
3 bananas, sliced

Combine eggs, juice, sugar, butter, and marshmallows in saucepan. Simmer until marshmallows are melted. Cool. Add remaining ingredients. Pour into 8 x 8-inch pan. Chill. Yield: 9 servings.

Mrs. Robert Moss
(Marilyn Quave)

Fruit Francine

1 quart strawberries, hulled and
  sliced
2 (11-ounce) cans mandarin orange
  sections

1 (5¼-ounce) can chunk pineapple
1 large or 2 small bananas, sliced
1 cup white wine or sherry
¼ cup sugar

Do not drain canned fruit. Combine all ingredients and chill at least 1 hour before serving to mingle flavors. Yield: 4 to 6 servings.

Mrs. Joseph P. Harris
(Susan Gunn)

Buttermilk Salad Dressing

2 cups mayonnaise
2 cups buttermilk
½ teaspoon garlic powder
1 teaspoon onion powder

2 Tablespoons monosodium
  glutamate
¾ teaspoon pepper
2 teaspoons salt

Mix all ingredients and let stand in refrigerator overnight before using.

Mrs. George Nasif
(Judy Bailess)

Bleu Cheese Dressing

¾ cup sour cream
½ teaspoon dry mustard
½ teaspoon black pepper
½ teaspoon salt
⅓ teaspoon garlic powder

1 teaspoon Worcestershire sauce
1 cup mayonnaise
4 ounces imported Danish bleu cheese, crumbled into small pieces

Place sour cream, dry mustard, black pepper, salt, garlic powder, and Worcestershire sauce in mixing bowl and blend for 2 minutes at low speed. Add mayonnaise and blend ½ minute at low speed. Then blend 2 minutes at medium speed. Add crumbled bleu cheese and blend for 3 minutes at medium speed. Must sit for 24 hours before using. Yield: 2½ cups.

Mrs. Jerry Yelverton
(Suzanne Smith)

Honey French Dressing

1 teaspoon salt
1 teaspoon paprika
½ teaspoon dry mustard

⅓ cup white vinegar
⅔ cup vegetable oil
6 Tablespoons honey

Put dry ingredients into measuring cup or cruet. Mix well. Fill to ⅓ cup mark with vinegar. Shake well. Add oil, filling to 1 cup mark. Add honey. Shake well; keep refrigerated. Good on fruit salads. Yield: 1 cup.

Mrs. Robert R. Bailess
(Natalie Waring)

Roquefort Dressing

2 cups mayonnaise
2 (5-ounce) packages Roquefort cheese, shredded
⅔ cup evaporated milk

2 Tablespoons sugar
1 teaspoon garlic powder
½ teaspoon celery salt

Mix all ingredients well. Yield: 3 cups.

Mrs. Louis L. Patterson
(Theodocia Perry)

Creamy Caesar Salad Dressing

1 egg yolk
Juice of 1½ lemons
¾ teaspoon salt
1 teaspoon Worcestershire sauce

Black pepper
3 anchovies
1 cup vegetable oil

Put all ingredients, except oil, in food processor and blend. While processor is running, add oil very slowly. Blend well and store in refrigerator. Yield: 1¾ cups.

Mrs. Gerald Olsen
Columbia, South Carolina

Fresh Spinach Salad Dressing

2 green onions
1 cup vegetable oil
½ cup white vinegar
½ cup sugar

½ cup brown sugar
½ cup chili sauce
1 Tablespoon Worcestershire sauce

On high speed in food processor, drop in onions. Stop processor. Add remaining ingredients. Run on high speed a few seconds until well blended. Pour into a quart jar and refrigerate. Excellent on fresh spinach salad. Yield: 1½ pints.

Mrs. Gordon L. Carr, Sr.
(Betty Ann Williams)

B.A.'s Spicy Dressing

1 cup mayonnaise
¼ cup chili sauce
¼ cup ketchup
1 teaspoon mustard
½ cup salad oil
1 teaspoon black pepper

Dash of TABASCO brand pepper
  sauce
Dash of paprika
Juice of 1 onion, grated
2 Tablespoons water
2 cloves garlic, minced (optional)
Juice of 1 lemon

Put ingredients into a quart jar and shake well. Keep in refrigerator. Yield: 1 pint.

Mrs. Gordon Carr, Jr.
(Rainy Loe)

Honey-Celery Seed Dressing

½ cup sugar
1 teaspoon dry mustard
1 teaspoon paprika
¼ teaspoon salt
1 teaspoon celery seed
⅓ cup honey

1 Tablespoon lemon juice
¼ cup vinegar
⅓ cup water
1 teaspoon grated onion
1 cup salad oil

In blender, mix dry ingredients. Add honey, lemon juice, vinegar, water, and onion. Mix well. While mixture is blending, slowly pour in oil and continue to blend. Refrigerate. Yield: 2½ cups.

Serve over an avocado and citrus salad or melon ball fruit salad. Poppy seed may be substituted for celery seed.

Mrs. Hays Latham
(Suzanne Massengale)

Homemade Mayonnaise

1½ Tablespoons vegetable oil
1 to 1½ heaping Tablespoons Dijon
*   mustard*
1 teaspoon salt
1 whole egg plus 1 egg yolk

4 shakes TABASCO brand pepper
*   sauce*
1¼ cups vegetable oil
¼ cup lemon concentrate or juice of
*   1 lemon*

Combine first 5 ingredients in food processor or blender. Blend 45 seconds to 1 minute. Gradually add oil with food processor on high until mixture thickens. When thick, turn off and add lemon concentrate. Mix well. Yield: 2 cups.

J. Stanford Terry

Store mayonnaise in the warmest section of refrigerator, preferably on the door shelf.

To store salad greens which have already been cut, toss with a small amount of oil and refrigerate in a large plastic bag.

Spur-Of-The-Moment Salad Ideas

Halve a banana and split halves lengthwise. Place on lettuce leaves and spread with peanut butter. Top with mayonnaise.

Top lettuce leaves with sliced beets and sliced hard-cooked eggs. Drizzle Durkee Famous Sauce® over all. "Durkee" and "Famous Sauce" are registered trademarks of the SCM Corporation.

Toss together chopped and cubed apples, raisins, chopped celery, chopped nuts, and mayonnaise. Season if desired with salt and pepper. Chopped carrots can also be added.

Top pineapple slices, peach halves, or pear halves with cottage cheese or shredded Cheddar cheese and mayonnaise. Serve on lettuce leaves. Garnish with maraschino cherry, if desired.

Serve asparagus tips and sliced hard-cooked eggs on lettuce leaves. Top with mayonnaise and paprika.

Squeeze juice of 1 fresh orange over a mixture of strawberries and other fruits in season, such as apples, bananas, melons, blueberries, and oranges.

Sprinkle avocado half heavily with lemon pepper seasoning salt. Fill cavity with plain yogurt. Top with additional lemon pepper.

Mix mayonnaise, lemon juice, and garlic salt and pour over avocado slices.

Toss broccoli florets, chopped green onions, and Hidden Valley Ranch® buttermilk salad dressing.

Soak sliced tomatoes, cucumber slices, and red onion rings in bottled Italian dressing. Serve on lettuce leaves.

Cover sliced cucumbers with vinegar; add ½ cup water. Season with salt and pepper. Onion rings may be added.

Mix softened cream cheese with honey to taste and chopped nuts. Place on top of canned or fresh pear halves.

Anchuca

Anchuca, the white-columned mansion, preserves a part of the Old South that is breath-taking. Built in 1830 by one of the city's earliest public officials, it reflects an elegance typical of that important period. It portrays a carefree, leisurely lifestyle, and in addition, history was written indelibly in the cycles of wealth, war, and the New South of today.

Anchuca is an experience, a touch and feel of the good taste and quality life of long-gone ancestors. Fine fabrics, colorful drapes, silverware and china suggest a culture that thrived on cotton and commerce.

The home sits on high terraces overlooking streets where wagons and buggies mingled with stately carriages. Once inside its massive gates, the visitor is transformed into a land of yesteryear. Brick drives are bordered by flowers in profusion, outlining the two-story slave quarters now converted into palatial bed and breakfast accommodations.

Its galleries commanded a view of Springfield, the picnic area made famous by the Bodley Incident of 1835. In retaliation for the death of a stalwart physician, gambling dens on the bayou below were destroyed in a crusade to protect the young city's morals.

From Anchuca, the gunboats on the Mississippi River were visible during the Civil War. The home itself was in the line of fire, within view of Devil's Backbone which bristled with Confederate defenders.

Years after the war, Confederate President Jefferson Davis returned home to Vicksburg after his imprisonment. He visited his brother, Joe Davis, at Anchuca, and he is said to have addressed the townspeople from its balcony. Their pre-war plantations had been nearby on the river.

So steeped in history, so elegant in its structure and furnishings, the home beckons with a dignity and charm that transform the visitor into an enchanting world that is gone with the wind.

Cheese and Egg Dishes pictured:
Ham and Spinach Quiche, Sausage 'n Cheese Brunch Tarts, Eggs Benedict

Eggs, Cheese, Rice and Pasta

Egg, Sausage, and Potato Casserole

2 pounds mild or hot sausage
1 (15-ounce) package frozen hash
  brown potatoes, thawed
10 to 12 eggs
1¼ cups light cream

½ teaspoon salt
¼ teaspoon pepper
4 to 5 drops TABASCO brand
  pepper sauce

In a skillet brown sausage, breaking it up while stirring. Drain well on paper towel. To a small amount of sausage grease, add potatoes and cook until soft. Mix drained sausage with potatoes. In a separate bowl beat eggs with cream. Add seasonings. Combine the 2 mixtures. Bake in 9 x 13-inch casserole dish at 350° for 25 to 30 minutes. Cut into squares and serve. Yield: 10 to 12 servings.

Mrs. Robert M. Abraham
(Billie Patterson)

Bachelor's Brunch Egg Casserole

1 pound hot sausage
6 slices bread, cubed
1 cup shredded sharp Cheddar
  cheese
2 cups milk

6 eggs, slightly beaten
1 teaspoon salt
Pepper to taste
1 teaspoon dry mustard

Brown sausage and drain well. In a 9 x 13-inch casserole dish layer bread, sausage, and cheese. Repeat until all is used. Pour milk into eggs. Add salt, pepper, and mustard. Mix and pour over layers. Cover and place in refrigerator for 12 hours. Cook, covered at 350° for 1 hour. Yield: 10 to 12 servings.

Mrs. Clift Odom
(Susan Clements)

Betsy's Brunch Casserole

3 cups cubed French bread
3 cups cooked and cubed ham
½ cup cubed Cheddar cheese
3 Tablespoons flour
1 Tablespoon dry mustard

3 Tablespoons melted butter,
  divided
4 eggs
3 cups milk
TABASCO brand pepper sauce

Cube French bread, ham and Cheddar cheese. Mix flour and dry mustard. Melt butter and set aside. Beat eggs until foamy; add milk and a few drops of TABASCO. Butter a 2-quart baking dish. Make first layer using all the French bread. Sprinkle ⅓ dry ingredients over this layer. Drizzle 1 Tablespoon melted butter over layer. Make second layer using all the ham and ⅓ dry ingredients and 1 Tablespoon of melted butter. Make third layer using all of the cheese, remaining dry ingredients and melted butter. Pour liquid ingredients over all 3 layers. Cover and refrigerate overnight or at least 4 hours. Bake uncovered for 1 hour at 350°. Yield: 8 to 10 servings.

This makes an excellent brunch or luncheon menu when served with a congealed spinach salad and glazed carrots.

Mrs. Jerry Nations
Brookhaven, Mississippi

Breakfast Pizza

1 can crescent rolls
1 cup frozen hash browns
1 cup chopped ham or cooked
  sausage
1 cup shredded cheese

5 eggs
¼ cup milk
½ teaspoon salt
⅛ teaspoon pepper

Press crescent roll dough onto ungreased 10-inch pizza pan. Place hash browns, ham, and cheese on top. Mix eggs, milk, salt, and pepper. Pour over pizza. Bake at 350° for 30 minutes. Yield: 8 servings.

May be baked in oblong pan, cut into squares, and served for morning meetings or bridge.

Mrs. David Sessums
(Beverly Tucker)

 Hard-cooked eggs should never be frozen because egg whites get tough.

Easy Egg Brunch

Sauce

4 slices bacon
1 or 2 (4-ounce) cans mushrooms,
    reserving a few for garnish
½ pound dried beef

¼ cup butter
½ cup flour
1 quart milk
Pepper to taste

Sauté bacon until almost done. Add mushrooms, dried beef and butter. Stir in flour and milk. Add pepper, but no salt. Stir until thick and smooth.

Egg Mixture

16 eggs
½ teaspoon salt

1 cup evaporated milk
¼ cup butter

Beat eggs with salt and evaporated milk; scramble in butter. Do not overcook. Butter a 9 x 13 x 2-inch glass baking dish. Place small amount of sauce in bottom and then eggs. Top with sauce. Garnish with mushrooms. Heat, covered, 1 hour at 275°. May be prepared day before, refrigerated and heated. Yield: 12 servings.

Mrs. George Rogers, Sr.
(Marian Todd)

Cajun's Eggs

4 green onions (tops and bottoms),
    finely chopped
¼ bell pepper, finely chopped
½ cup or more crawfish tails

8 eggs, well beaten
¼ cup milk or cream
Salt and pepper to taste

Sauté onions and bell pepper. Add crawfish tails; cook until light pink. Add beaten eggs mixed with milk or cream; stir slowly until done but still moist. Season to taste. Yield: 4 to 6 servings.

Shrimp may be substituted for crawfish.

Mrs. W. T. Ewell
(Betty Price)

Creole Eggs

1 large onion, chopped
1 green onion, chopped
2 bell peppers, chopped
½ cup chopped celery
6 Tablespoons butter, divided
1 (16-ounce) can tomatoes
½ Tablespoon chili powder

Salt and pepper to taste
2 Tablespoons flour
1 cup milk
12 hard-cooked eggs
½ cup buttered bread crumbs
Parmesan cheese (optional)

Sauté onions, peppers, and celery in skillet with 4 Tablespoons butter. Add tomatoes, chili powder, salt and pepper. Cook until thick. In a separate pan melt 2 Tablespoons butter. Add flour and blend thoroughly. Add milk and stir until thickened to make a white sauce. Combine with tomato mixture. Slice eggs in round slices. In a buttered 9 x 13 x 2-inch glass baking dish place a layer of white sauce and tomato mixture and a layer of eggs alternately until ingredients are used, ending with sauce. Top with buttered bread crumbs and Parmesan cheese if desired. Bake at 350° for 30 minutes. Yield: 12 servings.

Mrs. Reeves Carter
Rolling Fork, Mississippi

Mardi Gras Eggs

4 large hard-cooked eggs
¼ cup flour
1 pound bulk sausage

1 egg, beaten
1 cup seasoned bread crumbs
Vegetable oil for frying

Roll hard-cooked eggs in flour. Mold sausage around eggs. Roll eggs in beaten egg and dredge in bread crumbs. Fry in deep fat heated 350° to 375° until golden brown. Yield: 4 servings.

Great with beer on fishing trips, football games, or picnics.

George M. Canaga
Bay St. Louis, Mississippi

 Peel hard-cooked eggs under cold running water to keep the shell from tearing the egg.

Eggs Benedict

4 egg yolks
½ pound lightly salted butter at
  room temperature
1 Tablespoon lemon juice
1 Tablespoon water
Dash of TABASCO brand pepper
  sauce

3 Tablespoons white vinegar
Dash of salt
4 eggs
4 English muffins
4 slices of ham or Canadian bacon
Dash of paprika

Prepare sauce first by beating egg yolks with a wire whisk in a double boiler. Over low heat add pieces of butter a little at a time, beating until dissolved. After all butter has been combined, add lemon juice and water. Raise heat to almost boiling, stirring constantly with a wooden spoon until thickened. Add a dash of TABASCO. Next, prepare eggs. Experiment with egg first. Into a large boiler put 6 inches of water, vinegar and salt. Heat water until just boiling. Stir water and ease egg into water. Cook for 1¾ to 2½ minutes. Keep water swirling. Remove eggs with a slotted spoon. Toast muffins; top with ham or Canadian bacon; toast again. Add egg, sauce and paprika to toasted muffin. Yield: 4 servings.

R. Gray Wiggers
Jackson, Mississippi

Easy Eggs Benedict

1 (10½-ounce) can cream of
  mushroom or cream of shrimp
  soup, undiluted
½ cup milk
1 Tablespoon dry sherry
¼ teaspoon white pepper
6 eggs

Salt, if desired
1 cup shredded sharp Cheddar
  cheese
Paprika
6 English muffin halves, toasted
  and buttered

Mix soup, milk, sherry, and white pepper until smooth. Spread about ⅓ mixture in bottom of a buttered glass casserole. With spoon make 6 indentions, spaced evenly in sauce. Then break eggs carefully into indentions. Sprinkle eggs with salt if desired. Cover eggs with rest of sauce. Top with cheese and sprinkle with paprika. Bake, uncovered, at 325° until eggs are set about 15 to 20 minutes. Serve on toasted English muffins. Yield: 6 servings.

Mrs. Donald Day
(Martha Hickman)

Swiss Omelet Roll

1½ cups mayonnaise, divided
2 Tablespoons mustard
½ cup chopped green onions,
    divided
2 Tablespoons flour
1 cup milk
12 eggs, separated

½ teaspoon salt
⅛ teaspoon pepper
Cooking spray
1½ cups finely chopped ham
1 cup shredded Swiss cheese
Watercress to garnish (optional)

Combine 1 cup mayonnaise, mustard, and ¼ cup green onions; mix well and set aside. Combine ½ cup mayonnaise and flour. Gradually add milk and beaten egg yolks. Cook, stirring constantly over low heat, until thickened. Remove from heat and cool 15 minutes. Beat egg whites until stiff. Fold mayonnaise mixture, salt, and pepper into whites, combining thoroughly. Pour into a 15½ x 10½-inch jellyroll pan lined with waxed paper coated with ½ cup mayonnaise and cooking spray. Bake at 425° for 20 minutes. Invert on towel; carefully remove the waxed paper. Mix the ham, cheese, and ¼ cup green onions together and spread on the roll. Roll from narrow end lifting with towel while rolling. Place on serving dish seam down and top with the mustard sauce. Garnish with the greenery of your choice; watercress is especially nice. Yield: 6 to 8 servings.

Mrs. David Boolos
(Kay Garret)

Swiss Bacon Pleasers

6 slices bacon
1 (8-ounce) package crescent rolls
4 slices Swiss cheese
3 eggs, slightly beaten

¾ cup milk
1 Tablespoon instant minced onion
1 Tablespoon diced parsley

Cook, drain, and crumble bacon; set aside. Separate rolls into 4 rectangles and press into 2 well-greased and floured 8 x 8 x 2-inch pans. Place 2 cheese slices over dough in each pan. Combine eggs, milk, and onion; pour ½ milk mixture over cheese in each pan. Sprinkle ½ bacon and parsley over each pan. Bake at 425° for 15 to 18 minutes. Cut into 2-inch squares. Yield: 32 squares.

Mrs. Robert Moss
(Marilyn Quave)

Soak bacon in cold water for a few minutes before placing in skillet. This will lessen the tendency to shrink and curl.

Mexican Omelet

¾ cup chopped avocado
⅓ cup sour cream
2 Tablespoons chopped green chilies
1 Tablespoon chopped green onion
1 teaspoon lemon juice
¼ teaspoon salt

Dash of bottled hot pepper sauce
(optional)
2 Tablespoons butter or margarine
1 corn tortilla, torn into pieces
6 beaten eggs
1 cup shredded Monterey Jack
cheese

In a small bowl combine the first 7 ingredients. In a 10-inch, oven-proof skillet, melt the butter over medium heat and add the tortilla pieces. When tortilla is soft, pour eggs into the skillet and cook 3 to 5 minutes, lifting eggs to allow the uncooked portion to flow underneath. Remove from heat; sprinkle egg evenly with cheese and place skillet in a 325° oven for 3 to 4 minutes or until the cheese melts. Spread avocado mixture on top ½ omelet and return it to the oven for 5 to 7 minutes. Fold the omelet in half to serve. Yield: 4 to 6 servings.

Mrs. Anne Hurt
(Anne Pearson)

Swiss and Ham Buns

1 (8-ounce) package refrigerated
crescent dinner rolls
1 (4-ounce) package sliced cooked
ham

½ (8-ounce) package sliced Swiss
cheese
2 teaspoons prepared mustard
1 egg, slightly beaten

Preheat oven to 375°. On floured surface, separate dough from the crescent dinner rolls into 4 rectangles. Gently pinch diagonal perforations together on each rectangle. With lightly floured rolling pin, roll each rectangle into a 7 x 5-inch rectangle. Arrange ham and cheese slices on dough rectangles, cutting ham and cheese to fit and leaving a ½-inch rim of dough all around. Spread filling with mustard. Brush rim of dough with some egg. Fold dough and filling over so 5-inch sides meet. With a fork, firmly press edges together to seal. Place on cookie sheet; brush with remaining egg. Bake 12 to 15 minutes until browned. Yield: 4 servings.

Mrs. Kenneth Grogan, III
(Anne Blackledge)

Grits Soufflé

1½ cups grits
6 cups water
2 teaspoons salt

¼ cup butter
1½ cups shredded Cheddar cheese
5 eggs, beaten

Boil grits in salted water according to time on package directions. Stir in butter and cheese until cheese is melted. Allow to cool until lukewarm. Add eggs and pour into a greased baking dish, 2-quart casserole, or soufflé dish. Bake 45 minutes at 350°. Yield: 6 to 8 servings.

Miss Enez Bourdon

Garlic Cheese Grits

4¼ cups water, divided
1 teaspoon salt
1 cup quick cooking grits

½ cup margarine
1 roll garlic or bacon cheese
2 eggs, beaten

Boil 4 cups water. Add salt and grits. Cut up margarine and cheese roll; add to grits, stirring often. Beat 2 eggs and add ¼ cup water. Dip out hot mixture and add to eggs until well mixed. Pour into a 1½-quart casserole dish and cook uncovered approximately 1 hour at 350°. Brown under broiler if desired. Freezes well. Yield: 6 to 8 servings.

Mrs. William Beard
(Karyn Tanksley)

Cheese Pudding

12 slices white bread
¼ cup margarine
½ pound sharp cheese, shredded
2 cups milk

3 eggs, well beaten
1 teaspoon salt
1 teaspoon dry mustard

Remove crust from bread. Butter each slice on both sides. Cut into cubes. Place bread in a 9 x 13-inch glass baking dish; layer with cheese. Repeat the bread-cheese layering ending with cheese on top. Mix milk with eggs, salt, and mustard. Pour mixture over layers. Cover with foil and refrigerate at least 8 hours or overnight. Take out of refrigerator; set in a pan of hot water. Bake for 1 hour at 325°. Yield: 8 servings.

Mrs. John T. Pegg
(Marie Gueymard)

Blintz Soufflé

½ cup butter, softened
⅓ cup sugar
6 eggs
1½ cups sour cream
½ cup orange juice
1 cup flour

2 teaspoons baking powder
Blintz filling
Sour cream (for topping)
Blueberry syrup or assorted jams
  (for topping)

Preheat oven to 350°. Butter a 9 x 13-inch dish and set aside. In a large bowl mix butter, sugar, eggs, sour cream, orange juice, flour, and baking powder until well blended. Pour ½ batter into 9 x 13-inch dish. Place remaining ½ aside. Prepare blintz filling. Yield: 8 servings.

Blintz Filling

1 (8-ounce) package cream cheese,
  softened
1 pint small curd cottage cheese

2 egg yolks
1 Tablespoon sugar
1 teaspoon vanilla extract

In medium bowl or food processor fitted with metal blade, combine all ingredients. Mix until well blended. Drop filling by heaping spoonfuls over batter in dish. With a spatula or knife spread filling evenly over batter; it will mix slightly with batter. Pour remaining batter over filling. Bake uncovered at 350° for 50 to 60 minutes or until puffed and golden. Serve immediately with sour cream and blueberry syrup or assorted jams. May be made a day ahead. Cover and refrigerate until ready to use. Before baking, bring to room temperature.

This is a wonderful brunch or morning bridge dish.

Mrs. Stan Terry, Jr.
(Sallie Bingham)

127

Sausage 'n Cheese Brunch Tarts

½ pound bulk pork sausage
1¼ cups buttermilk baking mix
¼ cup margarine or butter, softened
2 Tablespoons boiling water
½ cup light cream

1 egg
2 Tablespoons thinly sliced green
  onions
¼ teaspoon salt
½ cup shredded Swiss cheese

Generously grease 12 muffin cups. Brown sausage and drain. Mix baking mix and margarine. Add boiling water; stir vigorously until soft dough forms. Press 1 level Tablespoon dough onto bottom and up side of each cup. Divide sausage evenly among cups. Beat cream and egg; stir in onions and salt. Spoon 1 Tablespoon into each cup; sprinkle cheese over tops. Bake at 375° about 25 minutes until edges are golden brown and centers are set. Yield: 1 dozen tarts.

Mrs. Guy Tucker
(Bernett Vance)

Ham and Spinach Quiche

2 (9-inch) pie shells
1 egg white, slightly beaten
1 envelope dry onion soup mix
3 Tablespoons flour
2 (9-ounce) packages frozen
  spinach, thawed and slightly
  drained
½ cup sour cream

½ cup mayonnaise
1 Tablespoon Cavender's All
  Purpose Greek Seasoning
½ pound ham, cut into ¼-inch
  cubes
½ pound Swiss cheese, shredded
1 whole egg plus 1 yolk
⅔ cup cream

Preheat oven to 375°. Lightly brush pie shells with egg white. Refrigerate. In a large bowl, blend onion soup mix with flour. Add spinach, sour cream, mayonnaise, and Cavender's Greek Seasoning. Mix well. Add ham and 1 cup Swiss cheese. Stir well. Spoon spinach mixture into pie shells, dividing evenly. In a small bowl, beat whole egg, yolk, and cream until well combined. Spoon egg mixture over quiches. Top each quiche with remaining Swiss cheese. Bake at 375° for 45 minutes. When done the quiches will be slightly puffed and nicely browned. Let cool slightly before serving. To freeze, bake at 375° for 25 to 30 minutes until partially set and not runny. Cool and freeze. Yield: 12 servings.

Mrs. Stan Terry, Jr.
(Sallie Bingham)

Beef Quiche

½ pound ground beef
½ cup mayonnaise
½ cup milk
2 eggs
1 Tablespoon cornstarch

1½ cups shredded sharp Cheddar
cheese
⅓ cup chopped green onions
Salt and pepper to taste
1 (9-inch) unbaked pie shell

Brown meat and drain fat from skillet. Add to meat in skillet, mayonnaise, milk, eggs and cornstarch. Stir over low heat until well mixed. Stir in cheese, onions, salt and pepper. Pour into pie shell and bake at 350° for 35 to 40 minutes. For a variation use 1 cup sharp Cheddar cheese and ½ cup mozzarella cheese. Yield: 6 to 8 servings.

This recipe can be tripled and placed in a 9 x 13 x 2-inch dish. Cut into 36 pieces and serve as an appetizer.

Miss Perry Patterson

Easy Spinach and Sausage Quiche

1 (12-ounce) frozen spinach soufflé,
thawed
2 eggs, beaten
3 Tablespoons milk
3 Tablespoons diced onion flakes
½ cup sliced fresh mushrooms or
canned mushrooms, drained

¾ cup shredded Swiss cheese
½ to 1 pound sausage, sautéed and
drained
TABASCO brand pepper sauce to
taste
1 (9-inch) unbaked pie shell or 1 box
refrigerator pie shells

Preheat oven to 425°. In a large bowl mix thoroughly soufflé, eggs, milk, onion flakes, mushrooms, cheese, sausage, and TABASCO. Pour into pie shell and bake at 425° for 15 minutes. Turn oven to 375° and continue cooking until center is firm and knife inserted into center comes out clean, about 25 minutes. Quiche may be frozen after baking. If frozen, thaw, heat, and serve. To use as an appetizer, choose hot sausage and decrease amount of TABASCO. For an appetizer use refrigerator pie shells. Follow directions on package and cut with 2-inch cookie cutter. Gently press into miniature muffin pans that have been coated with cooking spray. Fill with quiche. Bake at 350° for 15 to 20 minutes or until firm. Let cool slightly before removing from pans. Yield: 4 to 6 servings or approximately 36 small appetizers.

Mrs. Robert L. Pickett
(Jeneva Faulk)

Broccoli-Mushroom Quiche

1 (9⅝-inch) pie crust
1 (10-ounce) package frozen broccoli
   or ½ bunch fresh broccoli
½ pound fresh mushrooms
1 cup milk
3 eggs, beaten

2 Tablespoons margarine, melted
1 Tablespoon flour
1 teaspoon salt
½ to 1 teaspoon pepper
1 cup shredded Cheddar cheese,
   divided

Preheat oven to 375°. Bake pie crust about 10 minutes or until bottom is slightly brown. Let cool. Cook broccoli until tender. Drain well. Wash and dry mushrooms. Slice thinly. Combine milk, eggs, margarine, flour, salt, pepper and ¾ cup cheese. Beat with wire whisk. Sprinkle ¼ cup of cheese onto crust to seal flakiness. Layer broccoli and mushrooms on top of cheese. Pour milk mixture over this. Bake at 375° for 40 minutes or until custard is set and golden brown. Yield: 4 to 6 servings.

Mrs. Ben Hand
(Lana Toney)

Microwave Spinach Quiche

1 (10-ounce) package frozen
   chopped spinach
½ cup chopped onion
3 Tablespoons butter
1 teaspoon salt
½ Tablespoon pepper

Pinch of nutmeg
3 eggs
1 cup heavy cream
½ cup shredded Swiss cheese
1 (9-inch) pastry shell

In microwave cook spinach on high for 7 minutes according to directions on package. Sauté onions in butter for 3 minutes; add spinach and stir. Stir in salt, pepper, and nutmeg. Beat eggs in large glass measuring cup. Add cream and cheese and blend. Add spinach mixture. Pour into unbaked pie shell. Dot with butter. Cook 30 minutes on defrost setting of microwave. Yield: 8 servings.

Miss Mary Louise Cashman

Rubbing the grater with a little butter will keep soft cheese from sticking to the grater.

English Stuffed Eggs

*1 dozen eggs (preferably several
   days old)*
*3 Tablespoons mayonnaise
   (homemade is best)*
1 Tablespoon prepared mustard
*2 Tablespoons Durkee Famous
   Sauce®*
2 teaspoons curry powder

Dash of Worcestershire sauce
*2 or 3 dashes TABASCO brand
   pepper sauce*
½ teaspoon fresh lemon juice
6 to 8 drops fresh onion juice
Salt and pepper to taste
Paprika

Cover eggs with cold water. Bring to a rapid boil. Heat and cover for 20 minutes. Run cold water over eggs to cool. Peel and halve. Put egg yolks in bowl and mash. Add seasonings until desired consistency and taste. Stuff whites with mixture. Sprinkle with paprika before serving. "Durkee" and "Famous Sauce" are registered trademarks of SCM Corporation. Yield: 24 servings.

*Mrs. George Rogers, Jr.
Washington, D.C.*

Southern-Stuffed Eggs

12 hard-cooked eggs
½ teaspoon salt
1 teaspoon dry mustard
½ teaspoon pepper
*5 slices bacon, crisply fried and
   finely crumbled*

*½ cup mayonnaise or salad
   dressing*
½ to 1 teaspoon white vinegar
Paprika

Cut peeled eggs in half lengthwise. Take out yolks and mash with fork. Mix in salt, mustard, pepper, bacon, mayonnaise, and vinegar. Fill egg whites with yolk mixture. Sprinkle with paprika. Keep covered in refrigerator. ¼ cup finely chopped sweet pickles may be substituted for bacon for a different flavor. Yield: 24 stuffed eggs.

Miss Perry Patterson

Add a little vinegar to the water when an egg cracks during boiling. It will help seal the crack.

Newlywed Consommé Rice

1 cup raw rice
½ cup margarine or butter

2 cans beef consommé or bouillon

Spread rice over bottom of 9 x 13 x 2-inch casserole. Put butter in casserole. Pour in consommé. Cover and bake at 350° for 40 to 45 minutes or until all liquid is absorbed. Sautéed green onions and mushrooms may also be added. Yield: 6 to 8 servings.

Mrs. Howard Waring
(Belynda Lyons)

Confetti Rice

3 cups beef broth, boiling
½ cup butter or margarine
1½ cups long grain rice
½ teaspoon monosodium glutamate

¾ cup finely chopped carrots
¾ cup finely chopped celery
½ cup chopped green onions

Set oven to 350°. Place empty 1½-quart casserole in oven to heat. Bring broth to a boil in a saucepan. Put butter in skillet. When melted, add rice and heat 5 minutes. Remove casserole from oven; add rice and hot broth. Cook, covered, 35 to 40 minutes. 10 minutes before rice is done, remove and add monosodium glutamate and vegetables. Cover and continue cooking remaining 10 minutes. Can be reheated. Yield: 8 to 10 servings.

Mrs. Bill Pierce
(Pat Hand)

Dinner Party Rice

1 (17-ounce) can small early peas
½ cup sliced almonds
½ cup sliced green onions
½ cup sliced mushrooms

3 Tablespoons melted butter
2 cups cooked rice
Salt to taste
Pepper to taste

Sauté peas, almonds, onions, and mushrooms in butter for about 5 minutes until almonds are toasted. Add rice, salt and pepper. Cook until thoroughly heated. Doubles easily. Yield: 4 to 6 servings.

Mrs. Tom Harris, Jr.
(Josephine Good)

Curried Rice

½ cup butter
1 teaspoon curry powder
½ pound fresh mushrooms, sliced
2 Tablespoons minced green pepper
2 Tablespoons minced onion

1¼ cups long grain white rice
3 cups chicken broth
1 teaspoon salt
¼ teaspoon black pepper

Melt butter in a saucepan. Add curry powder and stir until blended. Add mushrooms, green pepper and onion; sauté until tender and onions are transparent. Add rice. Cook over low heat for 1 minute. Add chicken broth, salt, and pepper. Place in a 2-quart casserole; cover and refrigerate, if desired, at this point. Approximately 1 hour before serving, remove from refrigerator. Bake, covered, in a 325° oven for 1 hour or until the liquid is absorbed and rice is tender. Yield: 8 servings.

Mrs. Jeff King
(Anne Keene)

Greek-Style Skillet Rice

1 cup raw brown rice
2 Tablespoons olive oil
2 medium onions, chopped
1 clove garlic, minced
1 (10-ounce) package frozen
   chopped spinach, thawed and
   drained

Salt to taste
1 medium tomato, chopped
1 Tablespoon lemon juice
1 cup shredded Swiss cheese

Cook rice according to package directions. Meanwhile, heat oil in a 10-inch skillet. Add onions and garlic; cook until onions are tender. Add spinach and salt to taste; stir and cook until spinach is tender or about 5 minutes. Stir in hot cooked rice, tomato and lemon juice. Sprinkle with cheese. Cover and let stand 5 minutes until cheese melts. Yield: 6 servings.

Mrs. David Hosemann
(Connie Koury)

 To keep rice white when cooking in hard water, add 1 teaspoon vinegar or lemon juice to the water.

Wild Rice Casserole

1 (5-ounce) can mushrooms,
   drained or ½ pound fresh
   mushrooms, sliced
½ cup butter or margarine
2 Tablespoons flour

1 cup milk
1 (6-ounce) box long grain and wild
   rice, cooked according to package
   directions
Salt and pepper to taste

Sauté mushrooms in butter or margarine; add flour and blend well. Add milk and cook on medium heat, stirring until mixture has thickened. Add cooked rice and blend well. Add salt and pepper. Place in a greased 1-quart casserole and bake at 400° for 30 minutes. Yield: 4 to 6 servings.

Delicious with wild game or poultry.

Mrs. Joseph P. Harris
(Susan Gunn)

Sausage Jambalaya

1½ pounds hot sausage, sliced into
   rounds
1 large onion, minced
1 bell pepper, minced
4 ribs celery, chopped with leaves
2 cloves garlic, minced
2 cups raw rice
1 (16-ounce) can tomatoes, cut up
3¾ cups water

2 cups smoked ham, diced
Salt
Red pepper or TABASCO brand
   pepper sauce
Thyme
3 or 4 bay leaves
¼ cup chopped parsley
4 green onions and tops, minced

Sauté sausage until cooked. Remove sausage and in same oil sauté onion, bell pepper, celery, and garlic. Add rice and tomatoes. Stir well. Add liquid and ham. Add spices to taste and cooked sausage. Bring to a boil. Cook over low heat until rice is cooked, 30 to 40 minutes. Stir occasionally to prevent sticking. During last 10 minutes of cooking, add parsley and green onions. This may also be baked in a microwave or conventional oven. Yield: 8 to 10 servings.

Mrs. Jerry M. Hall
(Carolyn Buckner)

 One cup raw rice equals 3½ cups cooked rice.

Green Rice

½ cup corn oil
2 eggs
4 cups cooked rice (2 cups raw rice)
1 (5.33-ounce) can evaporated milk
1½ cups shredded sharp cheese
2 (10¾-ounce) cans cream of
   mushroom soup, undiluted

2 (4-ounce) cans mushroom stems
   and pieces
1 large onion, chopped
2 cups finely chopped parsley
1 teaspoon salt
1 teaspoon pepper

Add oil to beaten eggs. Add this and all other ingredients to cooked rice. Grease 2 medium casseroles. Add mixture and bake at 350° for 1 hour. Yield: 15 servings.

Mrs. James P. Guerriero
(Margaret Webb)

Hashwa
(Lebanese Rice and Meat Dressing for Fowl)

1 cup rice
1 teaspoon salt
2 pounds ground lean meat (beef or
   lamb)
1 onion, chopped
½ teaspoon salt
½ teaspoon cinnamon
½ teaspoon black pepper

¼ teaspoon nutmeg
¼ teaspoon cardamom seed
   (optional)
¼ teaspoon allspice (optional)
2 cups chicken broth
1 carrot, finely chopped
½ cup pine nuts
2 Tablespoons butter

Wash rice and cover with hot water; add salt and let stand 1 hour. Brown meat and onion in heavy saucepan. Add salt and spices and cook over low heat, about 3 minutes or until meat is tender and moisture gone. Drain water off rice and add to meat. Add chicken broth and carrots. Bring to a hard boil. Reduce heat and continue cooking until liquid has been absorbed and rice is done, about 15 to 20 minutes. In a small skillet, lightly brown pine nuts in butter. Pour dressing on platter and top with browned nuts. This dish can accompany roasted chicken, hen or turkey. Yield: 8 to 10 servings.

For a budget-stretcher serve as a main dish with a salad.

Mrs. George Jabour, Sr.
(Christine Varnado)

135

Rice Surprise

1 cup rice
2 cups chicken broth
1 cup sour cream
1½ Tablespoons jalapeño peppers,
minced and seeded
1½ Tablespoons jalapeño juice

⅓ cup creamy Italian dressing
1 (8-ounce) can sliced water
chestnuts
1 pound Monterey Jack cheese with
jalapeños, shredded

Cook rice according to package directions, substituting chicken broth for water. Combine all ingredients except cheese. Pour ½ mixture into a greased 2-quart casserole and top with ½ shredded cheese. Repeat layer. Bake uncovered at 350° for 30 minutes. Yield: 8 servings.

Mrs. David Sessums
(Beverly Tucker)

Sheareeya
(Lebanese Rice)

6 Tablespoons butter or margarine
1 cup vermicelli or thin spaghetti,
broken in ½-inch pieces
1 cup long grain rice
1 teaspoon salt

Dash of ground cinnamon
3 cups boiling water or chicken
broth
Laban or sour cream (optional)

Melt butter in medium saucepan over low heat, taking care not to burn. Add raw spaghetti and fry until golden brown, stirring occasionally to keep from burning. When brown, add rice, salt and cinnamon and fry for 2 minutes longer, stirring constantly. Add water and bring to a boil. Lower heat; cover and cook until all water is absorbed, approximately 20 minutes. May be topped with homemade yogurt (laban) or sour cream. Yield: 6 servings.

Serve as side dish with meats or vegetables.

Mrs. George Abraham
(Mabel Ellis)

 After rice is cooked, do not leave it in the pan for more than 10 minutes or it will become gummy.

 Pasta should be added to boiling water gradually so that the brisk boiling is not disturbed.

Homemade Noodles

1 egg
1 Tablespoon cooking oil
1 Tablespoon water

1 cup flour
¼ teaspoon baking powder

Combine egg, oil and water. Beat well. Add flour with baking powder sifted into it. A little more flour may be needed to make dough easy to roll. This depends on size of egg. Roll out the dough as thinly as possible. Leave on counter or table to dry. Turn over once. Cut into thin strips. Boil in salted broth in which chicken has cooked or use in homemade vegetable soup. Yield: 4 to 6 servings.

Mrs. Ober Anderson
Lake Mills, Iowa

Oysters and Pasta

2 (10 or 12-ounce) jars oysters or 2
  dozen fresh shucked oysters
⅜ to ½ cup lightly salted butter
⅜ to ½ cup olive oil
5 to 6 large garlic cloves, cut in
  chunks
4 to 5 quarts water

1 (12-ounce) package vermicelli
1 Tablespoon salt
1 teaspoon dried basil
1 teaspoon fresh ground or cracked
  pepper
½ to 1 teaspoon salt, if necessary
2 Tablespoons minced fresh parsley

Drain oysters in colander, but do not rinse. Remove shell remnants. Let oysters stand at room temperature. In a large heavy skillet (not iron) melt butter over low heat. Add olive oil; mix, and heat about 3 minutes. Add garlic chunks and cook, stirring often, for 4 minutes until golden brown. Remove garlic with slotted spoon. Remove from heat. Bring 4 to 5 quarts water in a large Dutch oven to a rolling boil. Add pasta slowly with salt. Stir to separate. Boil pasta for 7 to 8 minutes or until done, but not sticky. While pasta is boiling, return skillet to low heat. Add spices to garlic butter in skillet. Simmer on very low heat 3 minutes. Add oysters, stirring gently, 3 to 5 minutes until liquid in skillet becomes milky and edges on oysters slightly curl. Cover skillet and remove from heat. Drain vermicelli and return to Dutch oven. Add oyster mixture to vermicelli and toss gently to coat pasta evenly with butter and oysters. Serve on warm plates with French bread and salad. Yield: 4 to 6 servings.

W.C. Horne, Jr.
Jackson, Mississippi

Miriam's Scarpara Sauce with Pasta

1½ cups onions, finely chopped
3 Tablespoons olive oil
5 large cloves garlic, crushed
2 (1-pound) cans whole tomatoes or
    4 (10-ounce) cans tomato wedges
    (Use juice and cut up each tomato
    into 8 pieces)
2 Tablespoons capers, chopped
4 Tablespoons chopped ripe olives
    or 1 (4½-ounce) can chopped ripe
    olives

2 cups water
4 Tablespoons chopped pimento-
    stuffed olives
3 Tablespoons chopped parsley
½ teaspoon salt, black pepper
¾ teaspoon oregano
1 teaspoon sugar
1½ (12-ounce) packages linguine or
    spaghetti
6 quarts water with ¾ Tablespoon
    salt

Sauté onions in olive oil for 5 minutes stirring so it will not burn. Add
garlic; sauté 3 more minutes. Add all ingredients except linguine. Cook 45
minutes over medium heat. This will make 1½ quarts. Sauce is very thick.
Cook linguine in salted water. Cook pasta for 6 to 10 minutes or al dente,
slightly undercooked. Remove pasta from water and drain well. Add ½
linguine to sauce and let it absorb some sauce before adding remaining linguine. Yield: 5 servings.

Miriam Graeber Cohn
Port Gibson, Mississippi

Mock Fettuccine

2 quarts water
2 Tablespoons garlic purée or 3
    Tablespoons garlic juice or 12
    cloves garlic, minced
1 cup chopped green onions
1 (12-ounce) package broad flat
    noodles (fettuccine)

1½ cups mayonnaise
1 cup chopped fresh parsley
1 (14-ounce) can artichoke hearts,
    coarsely chopped
1 cup grated Parmesan cheese (not
    fresh)
Salt and white pepper to taste

Bring water, garlic, and onions to rolling boil in a Dutch oven. Add noodles and cook al dente according to package directions. Remove from heat
and carefully drain off all but approximately ½ cup water. Put noodles
back on low heat and add mayonnaise, parsley and artichokes, cooking
and tossing gently for 5 minutes. Add Parmesan cheese, salt and pepper,
then toss again. Cover and cook on low heat 1 or 2 more minutes. Let
stand a few minutes before serving. Excellent with beef. Taste noodles
before adding salt. Yield: 8 to 12 servings.

Mrs. Barry Holcomb
(Pat Horne)

Fettuccine with Shrimp

2 Tablespoons plus 1 teaspoon
  coarse kosher salt, divided
1 Tablespoon olive oil
1½ cups unsalted butter at room
  temperature, divided
½ pound medium white mushroom
  caps, thinly sliced
½ cup dry white wine
3 small cloves garlic, finely minced
1 medium bell pepper, chopped
1 (14-ounce) can artichoke hearts
  packed in water and citrus acid,
  drained and sliced

1 pound medium shrimp, 30 to 40
  count, peeled and deveined
1 pound fettuccine, preferably fresh
½ cup freshly grated Romano or
  Parmesan cheese
1 cup heavy cream at room
  temperature
2 ounces pimentos, diced
1 Tablespoon coarsely ground black
  pepper

Bring a large pot of water to a boil, adding 2 Tablespoons salt and olive oil to the water. In a large skillet, melt ½ cup butter over low heat. Add mushrooms and cook, stirring occasionally, until softened but not browned, about 3 minutes. Add 1 teaspoon salt and stir. Add wine; increase heat, and simmer until most of the wine has evaporated. Set aside on warm heat. In a large, heavy skillet, melt ¼ cup butter over low heat. Add garlic and cook over moderate heat, stirring occasionally, until barely softened, but not browned, about 3 minutes. Add bell pepper and artichoke hearts and toss for about 1 minute to soften, but do not cook through. Add additional ½ cup butter; allow to melt, then add shrimp and cook over moderate heat until opaque throughout and evenly cooked, about 3 minutes. Set aside on warm heat. Drop fettuccine into the boiling water and cook *al dente*, about 4 minutes for fresh, 10 minutes for dried. Drain well. Return cooked fettuccine to the pot. Off heat, drain butter from shrimp mixture into fettuccine and add remaining ¼ cup butter, stirring with fettuccine until butter is absorbed. Toss with cheese and gradually incorporate cream, stirring until mostly absorbed. More butter may be added here if needed. Drain mushrooms. Add shrimp mixture, mushrooms and pimentos to fettuccine and toss. Transfer to a warm platter and serve hot with a fresh grinding or sprinkling of black pepper and extra grated Parmesan cheese. Yield: 6 to 8 servings.

William L. Shappley, Jr.

When cooking pasta, do not add salt to water until it boils. Salt in cold water slows down the heating process.

Spinach Fettuccine with Italian Sausage

2 Tablespoons plus 1 teaspoon
coarse kosher salt, divided
3 Tablespoons virgin olive oil,
divided
1 cup unsalted butter at room
temperature, divided
½ pound medium white mushroom
caps, thinly sliced
½ cup dry white wine
1 pound sweet Italian sausage,
casing removed and cut into bite-
size pieces

1 pound spinach fettuccine,
preferably fresh
½ cup grated Parmesan or Romano
cheese
1 cup heavy cream at room
temperature
2 ounces pimentos
1 Tablespoon coarsely ground black
pepper

Bring a large pot of water to boil. Add 2 Tablespoons coarse salt and 1 Tablespoon olive oil. Return to boil. In a large skillet melt ½ cup butter over low heat. Add mushrooms and cook, stirring occasionally, until softened but not browned, about 3 minutes. Add 1 teaspoon kosher salt and stir. Add wine; increase heat, and simmer until most of wine has evaporated. Set aside on warm heat. In a large, heavy skillet add 2 Tablespoons olive oil and heat on moderately high heat until sizzling. Reduce heat and add sausage. Cook, turning frequently, until uniformly browned throughout, about 5 minutes. Drain and set aside on warm heat. Drop the fettuccine into boiling water and cook *al dente*, about 4 minutes for fresh or 10 minutes for dried. Drain well. Return cooked fettuccine to pot. Off heat, add ½ cup butter, stirring with fettuccini until butter is absorbed. Toss with cheese and gradually incorporate cream, stirring until mostly absorbed. Drain mushrooms. Add sausage, mushrooms and pimentos to fettuccine and toss. Transfer to a warm platter and serve hot with a fresh grinding or sprinkling of black pepper. Serve with additional grated cheese if desired. Yield: 6 to 8 servings.

May substitute hot Italian sausage for sweet sausage. If kosher salt is not used, reduce proportion by ½.

William L. Shappley, Jr.

To prevent olive oil from becoming rancid, add 1 lump sugar per pint of oil.

Add 1 or 2 Tablespoons of vegetable oil to the boiling water to keep pasta separated.

Fettuccine

2 quarts water
1 teaspoon salt
1 pound green or white fettuccine
noodles
¼ pound butter or margarine at
room temperature

⅓ pound grated Parmesan cheese
¼ cup milk or light cream at room
temperature
Freshly ground pepper
Chopped parsley to garnish
(optional)

Bring salted water to vigorous boil and drop in fettuccine, stirring until all noodles are separated. Boil for approximately 1 minute for white fettuccini and approximately 3 minutes for green fettuccine (overcooking will ruin noodles) and drain loosely, leaving a little water on noodles. Add butter and mix well with fork and spoon. Add cheese and mix well to avoid lumping. Add milk or cream and mix thoroughly until mixture is loose and creamy. Serve immediately, topped with fresh ground black pepper. Add parsley, if desired. The success of fettuccine depends on the correct consistency. It should not be watery or too dry. Add a little liquid at a time until the proper smooth, creamy consistency is reached. Yield: 8 to 10 servings.

Miss Mary Louise Cashman

Vermicelli Spinach Bake

2 cups cooked fresh spinach (10-
ounce bag equals 2 cups cooked)
¾ pound fresh mushrooms, sliced
4 or 5 green onions, sliced (use only
½ tops)
5 Tablespoons margarine, divided
2 Tablespoons flour

2 cups milk
½ teaspoon salt
⅛ teaspoon black pepper
¼ to ½ teaspoon basil
Dash of nutmeg
1 (8-ounce) package vermicelli
2 to 2¼ cups mozzarella, shredded

Cook spinach in salt water 12 to 15 minutes; drain well. Sauté mushrooms and green onions in 3 Tablespoons margarine. Melt remaining 2 Tablespoons margarine in pan; stir in flour and milk. Cook, stirring to make white sauce. Add salt, pepper, basil and nutmeg to sauce. Cook spaghetti according to package directions. Using an 8 x 12-inch baking dish, layer ½ spaghetti, then ½ mushroom and onion mixture, ½ of cheese and all of spinach. Make another layer of remaining spaghetti, mushrooms, onions and cheese. Cover with sauce. Bake at 350° until bubbly or about 20 to 30 minutes. Yield: 10 to 12 servings.

Mrs. Warner Byrum
(Sue Scanlon)

Shrimp Cabildo
(Spaghetti with Shrimp Sauce)

½ pound vermicelli or thin
  spaghetti
¼ cup margarine
1½ cups sliced fresh mushrooms
¼ cup sliced green onions (tops
  included)
1 pound frozen shrimp, peeled and
  deveined
3 Tablespoons flour

1½ teaspoons salt
½ teaspoon paprika
1 cup milk
1 cup light cream
½ cup shredded Swiss cheese
2 Tablespoons sherry
2 Tablespoons diced pimento
2 Tablespoons grated Parmesan
  cheese

Thaw shrimp. Cook vermicelli or spaghetti as directed on package. Drain well. Arrange in a shallow 2-quart baking dish sprayed with a vegetable cooking spray. Heat margarine. Add mushrooms and green onions; cook until mushrooms are tender. Add shrimp; cook until shrimp turn pink. Stir in flour, salt and paprika. Add milk and cream. Cook, stirring constantly, until sauce is thickened. Stir in Swiss cheese, sherry and pimento. Spoon shrimp mixture over vermicelli or spaghetti. Sprinkle with Parmesan cheese. Place under broiler 3 to 4 inches from heat. Broil about 5 minutes or until hot and bubbly and cheese browns slightly. 1 pound crabmeat may be used instead of shrimp. Yield: 6 servings.

Mrs. Robert McConnell
(Bobby Jo Moses)

Ravioli with Tomato Gravy

Tomato Gravy

1½ cups olive oil
5 pounds pork neck bones
3 pounds or 5 large onions
1 whole pod of garlic
1 small rib celery with leaves
2 (28-ounce) cans tomatoes
2 cans water
3 Tablespoons oregano leaves

4 Tablespoons basil leaves
5 Tablespoons parsley flakes
1 (4-ounce) bottle Kitchen
  Bouquet® browning and
  seasoning sauce and gravy aid
1 (12-ounce) can tomato paste
20 (15-ounce) cans tomato sauce
Salt and pepper

Put olive oil in large kettle to heat. Add neck bones to brown. Add onions, garlic, and celery to sauté. Mash tomatoes with hands. Add to kettle; then add seasonings, *Kitchen Bouquet®*, tomato paste, and tomato sauce. Rinse cans and add water, not to exceed 2 sauce cans full. Salt and pepper to taste and let simmer for 5 to 6 hours. Yield: 12 quarts.

Ravioli Filling

6 pounds pork butt, ground
2 Tablespoons salt
Pepper to taste
1 clove garlic
10 eggs, beaten
1½ cups olive oil

5 (6-ounce) packages Romano
  cheese
½ pound crackers, finely crushed
6 (10-ounce) packages chopped
  frozen spinach, cooked and
  squeezed
3 Tablespoons parsley flakes

Brown pork with salt and pepper. Add garlic, while cooking gently over low heat. Beat eggs in large container. Add olive oil, cheese and crackers, blending well. Add spinach and blend. Put meat mixture into egg mixture. Add parsley. Mix well with hands. Refrigerate overnight.

Ravioli Dough

4 cups flour, sifted
1 Tablespoon salt

1 egg
1 cup water

Sift together flour and salt. Make a little well and put egg in with a little water. With your hand, begin to mix adding a little water at a time. When thoroughly mixed, put on smooth surface and knead until dough is smooth, easy to handle, and quite elastic. With a rolling pin or dough stick roll out very very thin. This takes time and flour must be added as rolled to keep dough from sticking. When dough feels like a chamois, place balls of filling (about 1 Tablespoon) onto the dough about 1-inch apart. Roll dough over filling and seal by pressing dough with fingers. Press firmly between balls of filling with side of hand, making sure all air is out of ravioli pocket. Cut into squares with serrated wheel. Dust with flour. Seal individually in foil to freeze. To serve, drop ravioli in boiling salted water to which a few drops of oil have been added. Let cook at a slow boil 12 to 15 minutes and lift out gently with a slotted spoon. Pour small amount of sauce on plate. Place 2 to 4 ravioli on plate and top with additional sauce. Sprinkle generously with Romano cheese. Yield: 15 to 20 servings.

Tomato gravy may be used as a sauce for spaghetti either with or without ground beef.

Mrs. Harry Meyer
(Louise Angelo)

Spinach-Stuffed Manicotti

½ pound ground beef
Olive oil
2 cloves fresh garlic or ½ teaspoon
   garlic powder
1 package fresh spinach or 1 (10-
   ounce) box frozen spinach
1 cup ricotta or cottage cheese
1 cup grated Romano cheese

3 eggs, beaten
½ cup seasoned bread crumbs
Pinch of nutmeg
1 teaspoon oregano leaves
Salt and pepper to taste
12 to 14 manicotti noodles
4 cups spaghetti sauce
Grated Parmesan cheese

Brown meat in a little olive oil until meat loses its red color. Add garlic and sauté gently; do not brown. Set aside. If using fresh spinach, cook briefly in microwave or boil several minutes in just a little water. Drain, squeeze dry, and chop finely. If using frozen spinach, just squeeze out water. Combine meat and garlic mixture with spinach, cottage cheese, Romano, eggs, bread crumbs and seasonings. Blend well. Boil manicotti noodles according to package directions, adding a little olive oil to water to keep from sticking. When done, place in cold water to keep noodles from sticking together, but dry gently before stuffing. Stuff noodles with spinach mixture and place side by side in a greased casserole. Top manicotti with 2 to 3 cups of spaghetti sauce, covering well. Sprinkle with grated Parmesan. Bake at 350° for 30 minutes or until hot and bubbly. Serve with additional hot spaghetti sauce and grated cheese. Yield: 6 to 8 servings.

Mrs. Jack Stamm, Jr.
(Laurin Fields)

Elfo's Special For Two

4 ounces thin spaghetti
½ cup butter
1 or 2 cloves garlic, thinly sliced
½ teaspoon salt
½ teaspoon monosodium glutamate

Dash of pepper
6 to 8 jumbo shrimp
4 ounces mushrooms, sliced
3 Tablespoons grated Romano
   cheese

Cook spaghetti according to package directions. In skillet, melt butter over low heat. Add all other ingredients, except cheese, and sauté for 5 minutes, stirring occasionally. Combine shrimp mixture with spaghetti. Stir in cheese. Yield: 2 servings.

If using smaller shrimp, add more than amount specified.

Mrs. Sammy Ashley
(Carolyn Stricklin)

River Front

City Front once teemed with wagons and drays, cardsharps and sight-seers who met the famous packet boats. It must have been a sight to behold!

There's excitement now when the Mississippi Queen or the Delta Queen, sometimes both, reach port with their tourist passengers. Other excursion boats visit occasionally; also luxury yachts and motley rafts, the latter with adventuresome passengers replaying the Mark Twain saga.

Work boats pass too, some destined for the nearby port; others with heavy load, their diesels throbbing as they push heavy barges toward distant cities.

Excursion passengers re-live the romance of the river. They visit the National Military Park, the Old Court House Museum, antebellum homes—the places which set Vicksburg apart.

As the sun sinks in the west, they return from their sojourn into the past and walk the gangplank aboard the palatial boat. There is excitement as people board; deckhands cast off the massive lines and prepare to be under way.

The captain signals all aboard with a clanging of the bell; the whistle blows and the big paddlewheel at the stern begins to turn. The calliope plays familiar tunes of the river and passengers line the rails to wave good-bye as the boat moves away from the landing.

It's an experience one can feel only at City Front on the river.

Entrées pictured:
Stuffed Baked Ham, Stuffed Oysters, Fried Chicken, Shish Kabob, Eye of Round Roast

Entrées
Meats

Royal Stuffed Rib Eye Roast

¼ cup butter or margarine
1 medium onion, chopped
½ cup diced celery
1 (4-ounce) can sliced mushrooms
2 cups soft bread crumbs
1 teaspoon salt

1 teaspoon black pepper
½ teaspoon basil leaves
1 teaspoon parsley flakes
1 (3-pound) rib eye roast (trimmed)
4 slices bacon

Melt butter or margarine on low heat. Add onion, celery, and mushrooms; sauté until onions are transparent. Place bread crumbs in a 1-quart bowl and add salt, pepper, basil, parsley and melted butter and onion mixture. Lightly mix until well blended. Make a lengthwise cut ¾ way through rib eye. Place stuffing in pocket formed by cut. Close pocket by fastening meat with toothpicks. Place bacon diagonally across top, covering toothpicks. Place in 3-quart rectangular glass dish or pan. Bake, uncovered at 350° for 1 hour 15 minutes for medium-rare roast. Yield: 12 servings.

Mrs. Robert M. Abraham
(Billie Patterson)

Eye of Round Roast

1 (5-pound) eye of round roast
1 cup red wine
1 cup water
2 bunches green onions, chopped
4 fresh tomatoes, chopped

1 cup pitted ripe olives, sliced
2 bell peppers, chopped
3 teaspoons salt
2 Tablespoons wine vinegar
½ cup margarine, melted

Prepare meat for roasting. Mix wine and water; pour over meat. Roast meat uncovered at 325° until brown. Cover and continue roasting until meat is tender for total cooking time of about 3½ hours. Chop vegetables while meat is roasting. Add salt and wine vinegar to vegetables. When meat is done, remove from pan and slice ¾ to 1-inch thick. Put vegetables between slices; pour melted margarine over meat and vegetables. Wrap tightly in foil and let marinate 1 hour. Yield: 8 servings.

Mrs. Bill Pierce
(Pat Hand)

Marinated Chuck or Sirloin Tip Roast Beef

1 (4 to 6-pound) roast beef (chuck
   or sirloin tip)
½ cup vegetable oil
½ cup dry red wine
Juice of one lemon
¼ teaspoon each: oregano, thyme,
   rosemary
1 teaspoon monosodium glutamate

3 Tablespoons green onions or
   regular onion flakes
1 teaspoon salt
3 teaspoons cracked black pepper
1 garlic clove, crushed
2 bay leaves
2 Tablespoons meat tenderizer

Mix all ingredients and pour into a plastic or glass bowl deep enough to hold entire roast and marinade. Put roast in bowl and turn twice. Add more wine if roast is not completely submerged into marinade. Using meat fork, punch holes all over roast. Cover and marinate 48 hours at room temperature in a place without much light. Grill on red hot coals after draining marinade and sprinkling meat with more pepper. Cook 20 minutes each side. Allow roast to remain in grill with hood closed and while coals smolder for 10 to 15 minutes. Slice thickly and serve with horseradish sauce. Yield: 8 servings.

Excellent for cuts of meat that tend to be tough.

Carl Comer
Fulton, Mississippi

Smoker Roast

1 (4 to 5-pound) rump or sirloin tip
   roast
Salt to taste
Lemon pepper to taste

1 (5-pound) bag charcoal
3 to 4 hickory wood sticks
1 cup lighter fluid

Sprinkle roast thoroughly with salt and lemon pepper on all sides. Use ¾ to full pan charcoal, full pan water and hickory sticks. Pour lighter fluid on charcoal and let soak for 5 minutes. When coals turn gray, about 25 to 30 minutes, put water pan on smoker. After putting hickory sticks on fire, (sticks should be soaked in water for approximately 30 minutes before being placed on charcoal) place roast on grill; cover and cook. For rare roast allow 1 hour per pound. For medium, allow 1¼ hours per pound; for well done, allow 1½ hours per pound. Yield: 6 to 8 servings.

Removal of cover during cooking will extend cooking time and may require additional charcoal.

Leo Boolos, Jr.

Jane Bodron's Marinated Roast Beef

1 cup vegetable oil
¾ cup soy sauce
½ cup fresh lemon juice
¼ cup prepared mustard
¼ cup Worcestershire sauce

2 whole garlic bulbs, minced (not cloves)
1 Tablespoon cracked black pepper
1 (8 to 10-pound) rump roast or 1 or 2 (3 to 4-pound) eye of the round roasts

Mix first 7 ingredients. Punch deep holes in meat. Place roast in heavy-duty plastic bag. Pour marinade over roast. Refrigerate for 3 days, turning once daily. Drain marinade off meat and reserve marinade for another use. Place roast, fat-side up, in a large roasting pan without a rack. Cook to rare on a meat thermometer which is approximately 10 minutes per pound at 325° in a gas oven or 300° in an electric oven. Leftover marinade will keep refrigerated about 4 weeks. Good on steaks, burgers, chops, and chicken. Yield: 4 to 6 servings.

Mrs. Ellis Bodron
(Jane Workman)

Italian Beef

1 (5 to 6-pound) rump roast
1 teaspoon salt
¼ teaspoon black pepper
3 large onions, sliced
½ teaspoon onion salt
½ teaspoon oregano

½ teaspoon Italian seasoning
1 teaspoon monosodium glutamate
½ teaspoon garlic salt
¼ teaspoon basil
½ teaspoon seasoned salt

Cook roast the day before serving. Place rump roast in roaster or Dutch oven half filled with water; add salt, black pepper and onions. Cook, covered, in 325° oven for 3 hours. Place roast and liquid in container which can be placed in refrigerator. Store overnight. Next day, remove fat and slice beef in very thin slices. Strain liquid and add: onion salt, oregano, Italian seasoning, monosodium glutamate, garlic salt, basil, and seasoned salt. Bring all ingredients to boiling point and remove from stove. Place beef slices in layers and pour sauce over each layer. Pour remaining sauce to cover meat and place in 350° oven; bake for 30 minutes. Serve hot as a meat dish or serve on hard rolls. Yield: 12 to 15 servings.

Mrs. J. Lewis DeCell
(Coralee Smith)

Grilled Eye of the Round

1 (3 to 3½-pound) beef eye of the
  round
Whole black peppercorns
½ teaspoon garlic salt
½ teaspoon seasoned pepper

1½ cups Italian dressing
¾ cup Madeira wine
2 Tablespoons Worcestershire sauce
Parsley to garnish

Using a metal skewer, make holes 1-inch deep, spaced approximately ¾-inch apart around the entire roast. Insert 1 whole peppercorn into each hole. (Preparation of the roast should be done the night prior to cooking.) Rub the surface of the roast with your hand or skewer to close the holes after stuffing with peppercorns. Following this, rub garlic salt and seasoned pepper over the entire surface of the roast. Place roast in a large plastic bag with a seal. Combine Italian dressing with Madeira wine and Worcestershire sauce; pour into bag on top of meat. Marinate roast in the mixture for approximately 12 to 24 hours, turning the bag several times so as to cover the entire roast. Following this, remove roast from bag; pour marinade into a small saucepan. Loosely wrap roast in double thickness of heavy aluminum foil; place roast on a gas grill and cook over medium heat to desired degree of doneness, approximately 30 minutes per pound for medium rare. When ready to serve, heat reserved marinade to boiling point and pour over your roast. Slice meat approximately ¼-inch thick and garnish with parsley. Yield: 4 to 6 servings.

Dr. Briggs Hopson

Prime Rib

Garlic powder
Seasoning salt
MRS. DASH® Seasoning

Lemon pepper
Prime rib roast

Preheat oven to 500°. Rub seasonings into the prime rib. For medium rare, cook 5 minutes per pound. For medium, cook 7 minutes per pound. Turn oven off and do not open oven door for whatever time remains of 2 hours (total cooking time). MRS. DASH is a registered trademark of the Alberto-Culver Company.

Monsour's Restaurant
Vicksburg, Mississippi

When a roast is put into the oven, set a small foil pan partly filled with flour beside it; when the flour has browned, it's ready for making flavorful brown gravy.

Cold Beef Platter

1 (2½ to 3-pound) rolled beef rump
  roast
1 (14½-ounce) can asparagus
  spears, drained

1 (3-ounce) can sliced mushrooms,
  drained
Cherry tomatoes for garnish

Place roast on a rack in a shallow roasting pan at 325° until meat thermometer registers 140°. This is for a rare roast and takes approximately 1½ to 2 hours. Cool for 1 hour. Cut into 1¼-inch slices. Place in a shallow 10 x 13-inch dish. Drain the asparagus spears and mushrooms and arrange over roast.

Marinade

1⅓ cups salad oil
½ cup vinegar
2 cloves garlic, minced
2 teaspoons sugar

1½ teaspoons salt
1½ teaspoons dry mustard
Dash of pepper

Mix all ingredients together and pour over meat and vegetables. Cover with plastic wrap and refrigerate 2 to 24 hours. Before serving, drain the marinade and arrange meat, asparagus, and mushrooms on a platter. Garnish with cherry tomatoes. Yield: 15 to 20 servings.

Mrs. Jerry Mayfield
(Pam Jabour)

Very Special Brisket

½ teaspoon salt
¼ teaspoon garlic salt
1 (8 to 10-pound) brisket
¼ cup Worcestershire sauce
½ teaspoon sugar

¼ cup soy sauce
1 teaspoon liquid smoke
2 teaspoons bovril
1 teaspoon monosodium glutamate
1 Tablespoon chopped onion

Rub salt and garlic salt on brisket. Mix remaining ingredients and pour over meat. Wrap in foil. Marinate for at least 2 hours. Cook for 10 hours at 250°. Yield: 10 to 12 servings.

Mrs. Barry Holcomb
(Pat Horne)

A roast with the bone in will cook faster than a boneless roast because the bone carries the heat to the inside of the roast more quickly.

Barbecued Brisket

1 (4 to 5-pound) fresh beef brisket
1 (5-ounce) bottle liquid smoke
3 teaspoons garlic salt
2 teaspoons onion salt

2 teaspoons celery salt
1 (18-ounce) bottle barbecue sauce
Heavy-duty aluminum foil

Line a 9 x 12-inch or larger baking dish with heavy-duty aluminum foil, allowing enough foil to cover meat. Turn brisket fat-side down and pour entire bottle of liquid smoke over meat. Sprinkle the 3 salts over meat. Turn brisket over (fat-side on top) and seal with foil. Marinate overnight. Next morning pour off marinade; bake in a 225° oven for 5 hours. Let cool. Pour off gravy and refrigerate until cold. Slice meat with meat slicer on a thin setting or use an electric knife. Layer in casserole dish the brisket and barbecue sauce; repeat several times. Cook an additional 30 to 45 minutes in a 300° oven until warm. Yield: 8 to 10 servings.

Mrs. Richard Rula
Jackson, Mississippi

Corned Beef and Cabbage

3 to 4 pounds corned beef brisket
1 onion, halved
2 ribs celery with tops
1 carrot, peeled
2 bay leaves
1 teaspoon black pepper pods
2 cloves garlic

4 to 6 new potatoes, peeled and
  quartered
4 to 6 carrots, peeled and cut in
  bite-size pieces
1 medium head cabbage, cut in
  wedges

Cover meat with cold water and add onion, celery, 1 carrot, bay leaves, pepper, and garlic. Bring to a boil; reduce heat and simmer about 3 hours or until meat is tender. When fork pierces the meat easily, it is done. Leave in broth for an additional hour. Remove meat from broth. Boil potatoes, remaining carrots, and cabbage in corned beef broth until tender, about 10 minutes. When vegetables are done, serve on plate with several slices corned beef on top of vegetables. Yield: 4 to 6 servings.

Refrigerate leftover corned beef. It makes a delicious sandwich when served on rye bread spread with spicy mustard and topped with Swiss cheese. For a Reuben, add a dab of sauerkraut.

Father John Egan
(Saint Paul Catholic Church)

Swiss Bliss

1 Tablespoon margarine
2 pounds chuck roast, cut 1-inch
 thick
1 envelope onion soup mix
1 (4-ounce) can mushrooms,
 drained
½ medium green pepper, sliced

1 (20-ounce) can tomatoes, drained
 and chopped, reserving juice
Salt and pepper to taste
1 Tablespoon steak sauce
1 Tablespoon cornstarch
1 Tablespoon parsley flakes

Coat center of large sheet of heavy foil with margarine and place into a
9 x 13-inch dish. Place meat across foil, overlapping each piece slightly.
Sprinkle with soup mix, mushrooms, green pepper slices, and tomatoes.
Sprinkle lightly with salt and pepper. Mix tomato juice, steak sauce, and
cornstarch. Add enough water to make 2 cups liquid. Pour over meat
mixture and sprinkle with parsley flakes. Cover with foil and bake at 375°
for 2 hours. Yield: 4 servings.

Mrs. Chester Redditt
(Tricia Prewitt)

Carpetbagger Steak

1 cup fresh oysters, drained and
 chopped
½ cup chopped fresh mushrooms
2 teaspoons chopped fresh parsley
3 Tablespoons melted butter

4 slices bacon, cooked and crumbled
1 ounce crumbled bleu cheese
¼ cup sauterne or other dry white
 wine
4 thick-sliced rib eye or fillet steaks

Sauté oysters, mushrooms, and parsley in butter until mushrooms are
tender; drain. Stir in bacon, cheese, and sauterne; set aside. Make pocket
in side of steak. Stuff pocket with oyster mixture; secure with wooden
picks. Broil steaks about 6 inches from heat 8 to 10 minutes on each side
or until desired degree of doneness. Top steaks with any leftover stuffing.
Yield: 4 servings.

Mrs. Robert M. Abraham
(Billie Patterson)

A large roast can be carved more easily after it stands about 30 min-
utes.

For quick gravy, brown 2 cups flour in a dry skillet over medium
heat until it turns a rich beige color. Store in a tightly covered jar
and use as needed.

Tournedos in Wine Sauce

6 thin slices French bread
1½ pounds medium mushrooms
6 Tablespoons butter or margarine,
    divided
1¼ teaspoons seasoned salt,
    divided
½ teaspoon seasoned pepper,
    divided

6 beef loin tenderloin steaks, each
    cut 1¼ inches thick
¼ cup water
¼ cup port wine
Watercress sprigs or parsley for
    garnish

Toast French bread slices on both sides until golden brown. Cook mushrooms in skillet over medium-high heat in 4 Tablespoons butter or margarine, ¼ teaspoon seasoned salt and ¼ teaspoon seasoned pepper. When mushrooms are tender, remove from skillet and keep warm. Sprinkle steaks with 1 teaspoon seasoned salt and ¼ teaspoon seasoned pepper. In same skillet over medium-high heat, in 2 more Tablespoons hot butter or margarine, cook steaks until underside of steaks is browned, about 5 minutes; turn steaks and cook about 5 minutes longer for rare or until desired doneness. Arrange steaks on toast topped with mushrooms on a serving platter. Keep warm. Reduce heat to medium. To drippings in skillet, add water and port, stirring to loosen brown bits in skillet; heat to boiling. Pour sauce over steaks. Garnish with watercress or parsley. Yield: 6 servings.

Mrs. Robert M. Abraham
(Billie Patterson)

Pat's Perfect Steak Dinner

Have each filet mignon, rib eye, sirloin strip, or T-bone cut 1¼ to 1½ inches thick. Rub both sides of meat with olive oil. Sprinkle both sides with soy sauce. Coat both sides with lemon pepper seasoning and seasoned salt. Let meat sit out until it is room temperature. Tell your husband to start the grill 30 minutes before meal time. Make a salad, pour the water, and open the wine while the rolls and potatoes are warming and the grill is heating. Give your husband the steaks, tongs (not a fork), and another beer. Heat oven-proof plates or platter in a 250° to 300° oven or rinse in very hot water before placing steaks on them. Tell your husband to cook steaks on red hot coals 7 minutes per side for medium-rare steaks or 9 minutes for medium steaks. Turn only once. Serve immediately.

Dr. and Mrs. Barry W. Holcomb

Steak in a Bag

1 cup egg bread crumbs (3 to 4
  slices egg bread)
1 (2 to 3-pound) top sirloin steak,
  cut 2½ inches thick
4 Tablespoons butter or margarine,
  softened
4 Tablespoons vegetable oil
1 teaspoon garlic, crushed
2 teaspoons seasoned salt
2½ teaspoons seasoned pepper
1 cup shredded sharp Cheddar
  cheese

Prepare egg bread crumbs; set aside. Remove excess fat from steak. In a small bowl, mix butter or margarine, oil, garlic, seasoned salt and seasoned pepper until blended. Spread on all sides of steak. Mix bread crumbs and cheese. Press into butter mixture on steak, coating steak well. Place steak in brown grocery bag. Fold end over and secure with staples or paper clips. At this point steak may be refrigerated several hours. Before cooking, bring steak to room temperature. Preheat oven to 375°. Place bag on a rimmed baking sheet and bake 30 minutes. For medium rare steak, increase oven temperature to 425° and bake 15 minutes longer, a total of 45 minutes. For medium-well steak, reduce heat from 425° to 375° and bake 5 minutes longer before removing from oven, total of 50 minutes. Remove steak from bag. Let stand 5 minutes before carving into thin slices. Yield: 4 to 6 servings.

Mrs. Steve Rodman
Rockford, Illinois

Grilled Chuck Steak

1 (3 to 5-pound) chuck roast (about
  3 inches thick)
½ cup chopped onion
½ cup fresh lemon juice
¼ cup salad oil
½ teaspoon salt
½ teaspoon celery salt
½ teaspoon pepper
½ teaspoon dried thyme
½ teaspoon oregano flakes
½ teaspoon rosemary
1 to 2 cloves garlic, minced

Mix all ingredients except meat for marinade. In a non-metal pan marinate meat for at least 3 hours, turning several times and basting with mixture. Cook on grill over hot coals 10 minutes on each side for medium-rare meat. For medium to well-done meat, cook 2 to 3 minutes longer per side. If preferred, meat can be smoked for 1 to 2 hours instead of grilling. Yield: 6 to 8 servings.

Mrs. L. G. Horn
(Elizabeth Latimer)

Shish Kabob

½ cup Burgundy wine
½ teaspoon monosodium glutamate
½ cup vegetable oil
1 Tablespoon vinegar
1 clove garlic, minced
½ teaspoon salt
2 Tablespoons ketchup
½ teaspoon marjoram

½ teaspoon rosemary
1 teaspoon sugar
2 pounds sirloin steak, cut into 1½-inch cubes
Onion wedges
Tomato wedges
Green pepper pieces
Lemon pepper

Mix first 10 ingredients for marinade. Place marinade and sirloin cubes in container and marinate for 2 hours. Alternate meat with onions, tomatoes, and green peppers on skewers. Sprinkle generously with lemon pepper. Grill over charcoal fire, basting with remaining marinade. If any sauce remains, pour over meat when serving. May be served over rice. Yield: 4 servings.

Mrs. Robert R. Bailess
(Natalie Waring)

Hawaiian Beef Kabobs

½ cup ketchup
¼ cup vinegar
2 teaspoons brown sugar
3 Tablespoons lemon juice
3 teaspoons grated onion
½ teaspoon prepared mustard
1 Tablespoon Worcestershire sauce
3 Tablespoons dry sherry
¼ cup orange juice

½ teaspoon liquid smoke
Pinch of salt
Pinch of pepper
Pinch of paprika
2 pounds sirloin, cut into 1 to 1½-inch cubes
1 (20-ounce) can chunk pineapple
Bell pepper, cut in 1-inch pieces
Onions, cut in 1-inch pieces

Mix first 13 ingredients in a saucepan. Bring to a boil and let cool completely. Place raw meat in large, shallow plastic container with lid. Pour sauce over meat. Marinate for 24 hours, turning every 3 hours. Place meat on skewers alternating with pineapple chunks, bell pepper, and onion. Cook to desired doneness on barbecue grill or under oven broiler. Yield: 6 servings.

Mrs. Oscar Harvey
Yazoo City, Mississippi

Not Just Plain Stew

Salt and pepper to taste
2 pounds stew meat or small chuck
   roast, cut up
2 Tablespoons bacon drippings
2 onions; 1 chopped, 1 quartered
1 clove garlic, minced
1 (10½-ounce) can beef bouillon

1 (10½-ounce) can red wine or
   sherry
1 bay leaf
1 pound carrots, cut in 1-inch slices
4 to 6 potatoes, peeled and cut in 1-
   inch cubes

Salt and pepper meat; then slowly brown in bacon drippings on top of stove. Add chopped onions and minced garlic; let brown. Pour bouillon over meat, scraping sides and bottom to get browned bits. Transfer meat and gravy to a Dutch oven or casserole. Add wine, bay leaf, and quartered onion. Put in 350° oven and bake, covered, for 45 minutes. Add carrots and potatoes, sprinkle with salt and pepper and baste with gravy. Continue to cook for 1 to 1½ hours or until vegetables and meat are tender. If gravy is too thin, thicken with flour and water paste. Remove bay leaf. Yield: 4 to 6 servings.

Mrs. Jack Stamm, Jr.
(Laurin Fields)

Liver in Red Wine

4 slices calf or beef liver
Black pepper
2 Tablespoons bacon drippings
4 onions, thinly sliced

1 cup dry red wine
½ cup water
1 Tablespoon wheat germ (optional)

Sprinkle liver slices liberally with pepper. In a large skillet heat bacon drippings and brown liver quickly over high heat. Remove from skillet. Add onions to skillet and cook until browned. Add wine, water, and wheat germ; cover and let simmer for 10 to 15 minutes. Turn heat to medium high and add liver to wine mixture. Cook just until liver slices are thoroughly heated, about 5 to 10 minutes. Do not overcook or liver will be tough. Serve liver and wine sauce with onions over rice or grits.

Mrs. James B. Steen
(Dot Segrest)

Organ meats, such as liver, tend to toughen quickly so do not over-cook.

Beef Bourguignon

3 pounds lean beef chuck, cubed
½ cup shortening
3 Tablespoons flour
1½ teaspoons salt
½ teaspoon pepper
½ teaspoon thyme

1 cup beef consommé
2 to 3 cups dry red wine
1 (4-ounce) can or ½ pound fresh
  mushrooms, sautéed in 2
  Tablespoons butter
12 small white onions, parboiled

Brown meat in shortening; add flour and seasonings. Stir well. Pour into a 2-quart casserole. Add broth and wine. Bake 2 hours at 300°. Add mushrooms and onions. May add more broth and wine, if dry. Bake 1½ hours more, perhaps lowering oven temperature. Skim fat from gravy. Serve with mashed potatoes, noodles, or rice. Yield: 8 to 10 servings.

Mrs. J. Stanford Terry, Sr.
(Mary Frances Dent)

Vegetable-Beef Stir-Fry

4 Tablespoons soy sauce
2 Tablespoons wine
3 Tablespoons cooking oil, divided
1 teaspoon sugar
¼ teaspoon ginger
¾ to 1-pound beef round steak,
  partially frozen, thin-sliced
  diagonally

1 (16-ounce) can French-style green
  beans, drained, reserving liquid
2 beef bouillon cubes
4 carrots, thinly sliced diagonally
2 green onions with tops, sliced
  diagonally
3 ounces mushrooms, sliced
Hot cooked rice

In medium bowl, mix soy sauce, wine, 1 Tablespoon oil, sugar and ginger. Add beef; toss to mix and let stand about 20 minutes. Place reserved liquid from green beans in measuring cup and add water to make 1 cup. Boil this liquid, adding bouillon cubes, and set aside. Drain beef, reserving marinade. Heat remaining oil in large skillet or wok and stir-fry carrots and onions until crisp-tender, about 2 minutes. Push to one side of pan or remove from pan. Add drained beans; stir-fry 2 minutes, then push aside or remove. Add beef a few strips at a time; quickly stir-fry about 30 seconds, then mix with vegetables. Add mushrooms, reserved marinade and bouillon. Heat thoroughly and serve over rice. Cornstarch may be added to bouillon to thicken gravy if desired. Yield: 4 to 6 servings.

Mrs. Jerry Dykes
(Tina Hazzlerigg)

Chinese Pepper Steak

1 pound flank or round steak,
    partially frozen
¼ cup corn oil
½ cup coarsely chopped onion
½ cup coarsely diced green pepper
1 clove garlic, halved

1 teaspoon salt
¼ teaspoon pepper
¼ teaspoon ground ginger
1 Tablespoon cornstarch
1 cup beef broth
1 Tablespoon soy sauce

Cut steak, while partially frozen, diagonally across the grain into thin strips about 2 inches long. Thaw. Heat corn oil in heavy skillet or wok, if possible, over medium heat. Add meat and brown well on both sides. Add onion, green pepper, garlic, salt, pepper, and ginger; mix well. Cook over medium heat, stirring constantly, approximately 4 minutes or until tender and crisp. Remove garlic. Stir together cornstarch, broth, and soy sauce until smooth. Add to meat mixture and bring to boil, stirring constantly. Boil 2 minutes. Serve over hot fluffy rice. This recipe doubles beautifully. Yield: 4 servings.

Mrs. Russell Hawkins
(Brenda Davis)

Beef and Chou-Fleur

1 pound boneless round steak (⅓-
    inch thick)
2 Tablespoons butter
4 cups cauliflower, broken into
    florets
1 green pepper, cut in ¾-inch pieces
¼ cup soy sauce

1 clove garlic, minced
2 Tablespoons cornstarch
½ teaspoon sugar
2 cups beef broth
1 cup sliced green onions (optional)
2 cups hot, cooked rice

Cut half frozen meat into ½-inch squares. Brown meat in butter about 5 minutes. Add cauliflower, green pepper, soy sauce, and garlic. Stir lightly to coat vegetables with soy sauce. Cover pan and simmer about 10 minutes until vegetables are barely tender. Blend cornstarch, sugar, and broth. Add to meat mixture with green onions. Cook, stirring constantly, until thoroughly heated and sauce is thickened. Serve over rice. Yield: 4 to 6 servings.

Mrs. Bill Monsour
(Linda Shannon)

Beef and Bacon Roll-Ups

1 pound eye of the round roast,
  sliced ¼-inch thick
5 to 6 bacon slices, cut into thirds
½ cup flour
½ teaspoon salt
¼ teaspoon pepper

3 Tablespoons vegetable oil
2 cans hot water mixed with 1 can
  beef broth, divided
2 Tablespoons tomato paste
  (optional)

Trim excess fat from roast and pound on each side to tenderize. Place bacon piece in center of each roast slice. Roll up meat jellyroll fashion and secure with toothpicks. In a small bowl or plastic bag, mix flour, salt and pepper. Add meat rolls a few at a time and coat with seasoned flour. Heat oil in large skillet. Brown meat rolls over medium heat. Transfer meat to baking dish. Dissolve 3 Tablespoons of remaining seasoned flour in 1 cup hot water mixture. If necessary, add extra flour to make 3 Tablespoons. Add a little hot water to skillet, then stir in water with flour. Add remaining 2 cups of water mixture and tomato paste, if desired, and stir well. Bring to a boil, stirring constantly. Reduce heat and boil gravy for 1 minute. Pour gravy over meat and bake covered at 375° for 1 hour and 15 minutes or until tender. Yield: 4 servings.

Mrs. Jerry M. Hall
(Carolyn Buckner)

Hamburger Stroganoff

¾ cup chopped green onions and
  tops
1 clove garlic, minced
1 (8-ounce) can mushrooms,
  drained and chopped
½ cup margarine
1 pound ground chuck

½ to ¾ cup sherry or red wine
3 Tablespoons lemon juice
1 can beef consommé
1 teaspoon salt
1 teaspoon pepper
⅔ package medium egg noodles
1 (8-ounce) carton sour cream

Sauté onions, garlic, and mushrooms in melted margarine. Add meat and brown. Drain excess fat. Add liquids, salt and pepper. Simmer over medium heat for 15 minutes. Add uncooked noodles and cook with lid on until tender. The recipe may be made up to this point and stopped. Reheat later and add sour cream. It is also good when the sour cream is added and the casserole is refrigerated or frozen. Bake at 350° for 30 minutes. Yield: 4 to 6 servings.

Mrs. Joseph P. Harris
(Susan Gunn)

Grillades

1 round steak, full cut, ½-inch
  thick
½ teaspoon salt
¼ teaspoon pepper
2 Tablespoons flour
1 Tablespoon shortening
½ cup minced onions
2 green onions, chopped

1 clove garlic, minced
3 Tablespoons chopped parsley
1 Tablespoon chopped green pepper
½ (16-ounce) can tomatoes with
  juice
Beef bouillon
Water

Salt and pepper steak well; then flour and pound with a mallet. Cut meat into bite-sized pieces and brown in shortening. More shortening, flour, or both may need to be added at some point in browning. Remove to casserole. Brown onions, garlic, parsley, and green pepper. Put in casserole with meat and add tomatoes with juice. Add enough bouillon and water in equal parts to cover. Cover casserole dish and bake at 325° for 1½ to 2 hours or until fork tender. Stir occasionally and add bouillon and water, if needed, to keep gravy from getting too thick and dry. Remove from oven; skim off grease and serve with Cheese Grits (see Index). These can be done ahead of time and kept in refrigerator or freezer. More bouillon may be needed if dry when reheating. Yield: 4 to 6 servings.

Mrs. Elmer Platte
(Bob Logan)

Spicy Beef and Bean Casserole

1 pound ground beef
1 onion, chopped
1 bell pepper, chopped
1 cup ketchup

1 Tablespoon prepared mustard
1 Tablespoon Worcestershire sauce
1 to 2 Tablespoons chili powder
1 (16-ounce) can pork and beans

Brown meat and drain oil, reserving 1 Tablespoon. In same skillet, sauté onion and bell pepper in reserved oil. Mix all ingredients. Bake at 450° for 45 minutes. Yield: 6 servings.

Good with barbecued chicken or ribs or serve with a salad and bread for a low budget meal.

Mrs. Daniel Johnson
(Sue Buckner)

Stuffed Squash and Meatballs

6 to 8 crookneck squash
¾ cup raw rice
1½ pounds ground beef
Salt and pepper to taste
Pinch of cinnamon

3 large onions, sliced
3 to 4 Tablespoons olive oil
1 (6-ounce) can tomato paste
1 quart water

Wash and scrub squash; do not peel. Cut about a ¼-inch slice off the large end of the gourd and then core out most of the seeds making a pocket for stuffing. Rinse and set aside. Soak rice in cold water for 15 minutes. Drain. Mix with ground meat, salt, pepper, and cinnamon. Stuff squash lightly (do not pack) with mixture of meat and rice. Make small meatballs with leftover stuffing. Sauté sliced onions in oil until golden brown. Add tomato paste and stir well. Add water slowly to make a thin gravy, enough to almost cover the gourds. Season gravy with salt and pepper. Place squash in gravy; be sure to get the stuffed ends down into the liquid. Add meatballs to gravy. Let simmer about an hour or longer until squash is tender. Serve whole or, if the squash is large, slice the gourds; serve with plenty of gravy. Yield: 8 servings.

Mrs. John Dottley
(Nina Nosser)

Stuffed Bell Peppers

5 to 6 large bell peppers
1 pound ground beef
1 small onion, finely chopped
1 (20-ounce) can whole tomatoes
2 Tablespoons Worcestershire sauce

Salt and pepper to taste
1 to 1½ cups cooked rice
1 cup shredded Cheddar cheese
Grated Parmesan cheese

Cut tops off bell peppers and remove seeds. Parboil in salted, boiling water for 4 minutes. Drain and cool. Brown meat in skillet with onion. Drain oil. Add tomatoes that have been mashed. Add Worcestershire, salt, and pepper. Simmer 15 to 20 minutes. Add rice. Simmer, stirring occasionally, for 10 minutes. Remove from heat. Add Cheddar cheese, stirring until melted and well blended. Stuff mixture into peppers. Top with Parmesan cheese. Bake at 350° about 20 minutes or until hot. If freezing peppers, do not bake. Wrap individually and place in large freezer bag. Thaw well before baking. Yield: 5 to 6 servings.

Mrs. George Nasif
(Judy Bailess)

Moussaka

3 eggplants
Salt
2 onions, finely chopped
½ cup butter
1½ pounds ground beef
1½ teaspoons salt (more, if desired)
Pepper to taste
⅛ teaspoon cinnamon
½ teaspoon thyme
1 (8-ounce) can tomato sauce

1 (6-ounce) can tomato paste
½ cup olive oil (no substitute)
Italian bread crumbs
3 eggs, separated
1 cup milk
1 pound Swiss cheese, coarsely
  shredded
½ cup grated Romano cheese
3 Tablespoons dried parsley

Slice eggplants, rind and all, ¼-inch thick. Salt each slice thoroughly and set aside in large colander with plate on top for 20 minutes. This is to remove bitterness. Brown onions in butter; add beef, and sauté until brown. Season with salt, pepper, cinnamon, and thyme. Add tomato sauce and paste. If too thick, add a little water, bouillon, or red wine. Rinse and drain eggplant. Sauté slices in olive oil until golden. Butter and cover a 13 x 9 x 2-inch glass baking dish with bread crumbs. Beat egg whites until stiff and fold into meat mixture. Add 3 Tablespoons bread crumbs and mix well. Beat egg yolks with milk and Swiss cheese. Layer in casserole eggplant slices, then meat mixture, and then cheese mixture. Sprinkle with bread crumbs and top with Romano cheese and parsley. Bake at 350° for 30 minutes. Yield: 8 servings.

Mrs. Jack Stamm, Jr.
(Laurin Fields)

Anne's Meat Loaf

2 eggs
2 Tablespoons Worcestershire sauce
½ cup chopped celery
1 cup crushed corn flakes
⅓ cup chopped bell pepper
½ teaspoon pepper
½ cup evaporated milk

1 (20-ounce) can cooked tomatoes
½ cup grated carrots
1 cup chopped onions
1 cup cracker crumbs
1 teaspoon salt
2 pounds ground beef
½ cup ketchup

Beat eggs and put in a very large bowl. Add other ingredients except ketchup and mix thoroughly. Pack mixture into two 9 x 5 x 3-inch loaf pans and spread ketchup over top of meat. Bake at 350° for 1 hour or more. Yield: 8 to 10 servings.

Miss Anne Cashman

Chili Meat Loaf

Sauce

1 cup tomato sauce
2 Tablespoons brown sugar
1 Tablespoon vinegar
1 teaspoon Worcestershire sauce

½ teaspoon dried mustard
½ to 1 teaspoon chili powder
½ teaspoon salt

Combine above ingredients and simmer 5 minutes.

Meat Loaf

1 pound ground chuck or ground
  round
½ cup evaporated milk
⅓ cup bread crumbs

¼ cup chopped onions
⅛ teaspoon black pepper
½ to 1 teaspoon salt

Mix ½ sauce with meat loaf ingredients; form a loaf. Pour other half of sauce over meat loaf. Bake uncovered at 350° for 50 to 60 minutes. Yield: 4 to 6 servings.

Mrs. David Lee
(Janice Smart)

Tacos

1 pound ground round
1 cup chopped onion
2 garlic cloves, chopped
Salt and pepper
1½ teaspoons whole comino

1 large tomato, diced
Taco shells
Toppings
Taco sauce (optional)

Brown meat in skillet. Add onion and garlic and salt and pepper to taste. Cover and cook about 5 minutes, stirring occasionally. Using pestle and mortar, grind cominos until they crack open or place cominos in a clean cloth and pound. Add tomatoes and cracked cominos. Cover and cook over medium heat for 20 minutes. Prepare taco shells according to package. Fill with meat and toppings such as shredded lettuce, chopped tomato, shredded cheese or chopped onion. To make soft tacos, heat oil to 350°. Dip soft corn tortillas one at a time in oil for a few seconds. Drain. Fill with taco meat. Roll like a cigar. Top with shredded lettuce and chopped tomato. Serve with taco sauce if desired. Yield: 12 to 16 tacos.

Mrs. Daniel Johnson
(Sue Buckner)

Sour Cream Enchiladas

1 (10½-ounce) can cream of
   mushroom soup, undiluted
1 teaspoon salt
1 pint sour cream
2 small cans green chilies, diced

1 small can black olives, diced
1 cup chopped onions
1 pound ground beef
1 dozen flour tortillas
4 cups shredded longhorn cheese

In a large saucepan combine soup, salt, sour cream, chilies and olives and simmer. In skillet brown onions and ground beef. Spoon meat into tortilla centers; top with about 2 Tablespoons of soup mix and sprinkle with cheese. Roll and place in a 9 x 13-inch dish or 2 smaller dishes. After all are rolled and lined in dish pour in remaining soup mixture and sprinkle remaining cheese over this. Bake uncovered 30 minutes at 350°. Yield: 12 servings.

Mrs. Ron Wilson
(Linda Weaver)

Joanne's Spaghetti Gravy

5 large onions, chopped
½ cup olive oil
15 cloves garlic, chopped
2 (1-pound 12-ounce) cans whole
   tomatoes
6 (6-ounce) cans tomato paste
6 paste cans water
1 bell pepper, cut into strips
4 bay leaves

1 to 2 teaspoons basil
1 to 2 teaspoons oregano
½ teaspoon sugar
Salt and pepper to taste
3 (29-ounce) cans tomato sauce
3 to 4 pounds ground beef
1 pound mild pork sausage
   (optional)

In a large, heavy pot, sauté onions in olive oil, adding more olive oil if necessary. When onions are almost clear, add garlic and continue to sauté. Add tomatoes, tomato paste, water, bell pepper, and seasonings. Cook on low heat about 3 to 4 hours, stirring occasionally to check that gravy is not sticking to bottom of pot. Lower heat to simmer, if necessary. Add tomato sauce and more water, if gravy is too thick. Simmer 1 hour. Brown ground beef and sausage, if desired, in a skillet. Drain fat and add to gravy. Simmer at least 1 hour. This gravy cannot be overcooked; the longer it simmers the better the flavor. Use this gravy on spaghetti, lasagna or any recipe calling for Italian spaghetti sauce. Yield: 8 quarts.

For a variation, use Italian sausage instead of pork sausage. Remove from casing; brown; drain fat and add with ground beef.

Mrs. Dan Waring
(Janice Gerache)

Spaghetti Pie

6 ounces spaghetti
2 Tablespoons butter or margarine
⅓ cup grated Parmesan cheese
2 eggs, well beaten
1 pound ground beef
½ cup chopped onion
¼ cup chopped green pepper

1 (8-ounce) can tomatoes, cut up
1 (6-ounce) can tomato paste
1 teaspoon sugar
1 teaspoon dried oregano, crushed
½ teaspoon garlic salt
1 cup cottage cheese
½ cup shredded mozzarella cheese

Cook spaghetti according to package directions; drain. Stir butter or margarine into hot spaghetti. Stir in Parmesan cheese and eggs. Form spaghetti mixture into a "crust" in a buttered 10-inch pie plate. In skillet, cook ground beef, onion and green pepper until vegetables are tender and meat is browned. Drain excess fat. Stir in undrained tomatoes, tomato paste, sugar, oregano and garlic salt. Heat. Spread cottage cheese over spaghetti crust. Fill pie with tomato mixture. Bake, uncovered, at 350° for 20 minutes. Sprinkle mozzarella cheese on top. Bake 5 minutes longer or until cheese melts. Yield: 6 servings.

Mrs. Kenneth E. Hicks
(Margaret Bonney)

Gammie's Italian Casserole

1 (5-ounce) package medium egg
   noodles
Salt to season
1 pound ground chuck
1 large onion, chopped

2 (3-ounce) packages cream cheese,
   cubed
1 cup sour cream
1 (8-ounce) can tomato sauce
Cheddar cheese, shredded

Cook noodles in salted boiling water; drain. In a large skillet brown meat and onions; drain. Add cream cheese; stir until melted. Remove skillet from heat and add sour cream and tomato sauce. Combine sauce mixture and noodles. Pour into 2-quart greased casserole and cover with Cheddar cheese. Bake at 350° until bubbly. Yield: 6 servings.

Mrs. Bobby Robinson
(Jan Harris)

 Season stews and other meat dishes with slivered orange and lemon peel.

Spaghetti Sauce with Meatballs

5 pounds pork or beef neck bones
1½ cups olive oil
3 pounds or 5 large onions, chopped
1 whole bunch celery with leaves,
  chopped
1 whole garlic bulb, minced
2 (28-ounce) cans tomatoes
1 (12-ounce) can tomato paste
20 (15-ounce) cans tomato sauce

2 (15-ounce) cans water
3 Tablespoons oregano leaves
4 Tablespoons basil
5 Tablespoons parsley flakes
1 (4-ounce) bottle Kitchen Bouquet
  browning and seasoning sauce
  and gravy aid
Salt and pepper to taste

In a large pot brown neck bones in olive oil. Add onions, celery, and garlic. Mash tomatoes with hands and add to the bones. Add remaining ingredients and simmer 5 to 6 hours. Remove bones. Serve over spaghetti or use as a sauce in any Italian dish such as pizza or lasagna. Freezes well. Yield: 12 quarts.

Meatballs for Spaghetti Sauce

1 small onion, chopped
1 clove garlic, minced
2 Tablespoons olive oil
2 slices bread
¼ cup milk
1 pound ground beef
½ cup Romano cheese

¼ to ½ cup ketchup
1 Tablespoon parsley flakes
½ teaspoon basil
½ teaspoon oregano
Salt to taste
Pepper to taste

Sauté onions and garlic in oil until tender. Soak bread in milk. Mix vegetables with bread, ground beef, cheese, ketchup, and seasonings. Shape into meatballs 1½ to 2 inches in diameter. Brown slightly or add raw to 1 to 1½ quarts spaghetti sauce. Yield: Approximately 20 meatballs.

Mrs. Harry Meyer
(Louise Angelo)

 To freeze meatballs, place them on a cookie sheet until frozen. Store in plastic bags.

 To make slicing easier when cutting thin slices of raw meat, put meat in the freezer for half an hour.

Lasagna

3 Tablespoons olive oil
1 large onion, chopped
2 cloves garlic, crushed
1½ pounds ground lean beef
1 (6-ounce) can tomato paste
1 (29-ounce) can tomatoes
1 small can mushroom stems and
  pieces
1 teaspoon garlic salt
2 Tablespoons parsley flakes
½ teaspoon oregano

1 (8-ounce) package lasagna
  noodles
1½ cups creamed cottage cheese
2 eggs, beaten
2 teaspoons salt
½ teaspoon pepper
2 Tablespoons parsley flakes
¾ cup Parmesan cheese
1½ cups mozzarella cheese,
  shredded

In heavy Dutch oven heat oil and brown onions and garlic for 5 minutes. Add meat and cook for 10 minutes. Add paste, tomatoes, mushrooms and juice, garlic salt, parsley and oregano. Cover and simmer for 1 hour. Cook noodles according to package directions. Set aside and keep warm. Combine cottage cheese with eggs, salt, pepper, parsley flakes, and Parmesan cheese. Place ½ noodles side by side in 9 x 13-inch greased baking dish. Spread ½ cheese mixture. Add ½ meat mixture, then ½ shredded mozzarella cheese. Repeat layers. Bake at 350° 30 to 40 minutes. Let stand 10 minutes before cutting into squares. Yield: 8 servings.

Mrs. Bill Pierce
(Pat Hand)

Veal Lauren

1 pound veal tenderloin, thinly
  sliced
1 clove garlic, minced
½ Tablespoon butter
2 Tablespoons olive oil

Salt, black pepper and rosemary to
  taste
¼ cup white wine
1 onion, sliced
½ pound fresh mushrooms, sliced

Pound meat to ¼ to ⅜-inch thickness and cut into medallions. In a heavy skillet, sauté garlic in butter and olive oil. Add veal and sauté very lightly and quickly on both sides. Add salt, pepper and rosemary. Cook slowly for 10 minutes, covered, over low heat. Add wine; simmer for 5 more minutes. Add onions and mushrooms. Continue cooking, still covered, until meat and vegetables are tender. Yield: 4 servings

Mrs. John Wayne Jabour
(Becky Taylor)

My Veal Picotta for Four

2½ pounds veal round steak, thinly
  sliced
Salt and pepper to taste
¼ pound butter (approximately)

1 pound mushrooms, finely sliced
½ cup Chablis wine
1 Tablespoon Worcestershire sauce

Beat well the veal steak with wooden meat mallet. Salt and pepper each side. Place just enough butter in skillet to cover the bottom and add the thin strips of veal, browning lightly on each side. Add more butter as each strip of veal is sautéed until it is cooked lightly on both sides. Remove the strips of meat and set aside. Then add additional butter to the skillet; sauté finely slivered mushrooms in a similar manner, removing the mushrooms. Following this, add Chablis wine, Worcestershire, and remainder of butter. Place the veal strips and mushrooms back into skillet. Put a cover on skillet and let cook for approximately 5 minutes on medium high, tossing lightly twice while cooking. Remove; place in a covered dish in warm oven. Serve hot. Yield: 4 to 6 servings.

Dr. Briggs Hopson

Lamb Curry

¼ cup margarine
1 cup chopped onion
¼ cup chopped green pepper
¼ cup chopped celery
1 apple, diced
1 teaspoon curry powder
½ teaspoon salt

¼ cup flour
2 cups chicken broth (dissolve 2
  chicken bouillon cubes in 2 cups
  boiling water)
2 cups cubed lamb (from cooked
  roast)
3 cups hot cooked rice

Melt margarine in large saucepan. Add onion, green pepper, celery, and apple slices; cook gently until onion is tender. Stir in curry powder, salt and flour. Cook over low heat, stirring until mixture is hot. Remove from heat. Gradually stir in broth. Heat to boiling, stirring constantly. Boil and stir 1 minute. Stir in lamb; heat through, stirring occasionally, about 10 minutes. Serve over rice. May serve mashed hard-cooked eggs, bacon bits, or raisins to sprinkle on top. Yield: 4 to 6 servings.

This is a wonderful and delicious company recipe. Always a hit!

Mrs. J. E. Blackburn, Jr.
(Jeane McNeel)

Baked Filled Kibbee

2¼ cups cracked wheat (burghal)
3 cups lean finely ground lamb or
  beef
1 large onion, finely grated or
  ground

Salt and pepper to taste
1¼ cups butter or margarine,
  melted

Rinse wheat in pan of water several times. Cover with water and soak 15 minutes. Drain well through a fine strainer. Add meat, onion, salt and pepper to taste and mix well with fingers dipped in ice water. Grease an 11 x 3-inch pan with butter, leaving a small amount of butter in pan. Spread ½ kibbee (wheat mixture) smoothly over bottom of pan about ¼-inch thick. Spread meat filling over layer of kibbee. Cover with remaining kibbee and smooth surface well. Cut through entire 3 layers in squares. Score top layer diagonally to avoid puffing. Loosen edges from pan with spatula. Pour butter over top and bake at 375° until golden brown, approximately 45 minutes to 1 hour. Bakes better on oven rack higher than center. Yield: 3 dozen squares.

Meat Filling

1½ cups ground lamb or beef with
  little fat
¼ cup butter or margarine

1 large onion, finely chopped
Salt, pepper, and cinnamon to taste
1 cup pine nuts

Sauté meat in butter breaking with fork into fine pieces until meat loses color. Add onion, salt, pepper, and cinnamon and cook slowly until onion is transluscent. Add pine nuts and cook mixture until nuts are light golden.

Women of St. George Orthodox Church

Maudie's Leg o' Lamb Roast

1 leg of lamb roast
Lemon juice

Salt and pepper to taste
2 garlic cloves, thinly sliced

Cut all fat off roast. Rub with lemon juice, salt and pepper. Insert thinly sliced garlic in roast. Place in baking pan with a shallow amount of water in bottom.

Sauce

1 cup ketchup
½ cup vinegar
½ cup Worcestershire sauce

½ cup water
Dash of TABASCO brand pepper
sauce

Mix all ingredients in saucepan. Bring to a boil. Pour over lamb, turning to baste. Cook at 325° to 350° until done or 20 to 25 minutes per pound.

Mrs. Stan Terry, Jr.
(Sallie Bingham)

Pork and Chicken Kabobs

2 pounds bacon
1 (4½ to 5-pound) pork tenderloin,
   cubed
12 boneless chicken breasts, cut
   into pieces

Vegetables (Bell peppers, tomatoes,
   mushrooms, carrots, cherry
   tomatoes, onions, etc.)

Cut strips of bacon in thirds. Wrap each piece of pork and chicken with bacon. Skewer meats alternating with vegetables. Vegetables that do not tenderize quickly taste best when slightly parboiled or steamed before skewering. Marinate for several hours or overnight before grilling or smoking. Yield: Approximately 20 kabobs.

Marinade

28 to 32 ounces bottled Italian
   salad dressing
Juice of 3 lemons

½ cup Worcestershire sauce
1 teaspoon black pepper
Minced garlic or garlic salt to taste

Mix all ingredients and pour over kabobs to marinate.

Miss Helen Abraham

Country Ham

Whole country ham   *5 cups water*

Wash ham in hot water; scrub away mold and ashes with stiff brush. Place ham, skin-side up, in roaster. Add 5 cups water. Cover roaster. Preheat oven to 375°. Put roaster in oven. Turn oven to 500° for 10 minutes only. Turn oven off and leave for 3 hours. Do not open oven door. Turn oven to 500° for 15 minutes. Turn oven off and leave ham in oven 6 to 8 hours. Ham should not be exposed to 500° heat for more than 25 minutes total. It is extremely important not to open oven door after placing ham in oven.

Mrs. Jed Mihalyka
(Joy Hill)

Coca-Cola Ham

1 (6-pound) ham   *1 (12-ounce) can COCA-COLA*
Brown sugar

Preheat oven to 325°. Score top of ham. Place in oven just until hot. Remove from oven and cut skin off ham. Pack outside of ham well with brown sugar about ¼-inch thick. Pour Coke in bottom of pan. Do not pour over ham. Place ham in oven and let top of ham cook dry for about 10 minutes. Remove and baste. Continue cooking ham, uncovered for 1 hour, basting every 10 minutes. Take ham out of oven and baste occasionally as it cools.

"The trademark COCA-COLA is used with permission of The Coca-Cola Company."

Mrs. Stan Terry, Jr.
(Sallie Bingham)

A Vicksburg confectioner, searching for a way in the summer of 1894 to expand his sales of the popular soda-fountain drink Coca-Cola, launched an enterprise that was to become world-wide.

Joseph A. Biedenharn, the eldest of seven brothers who operated Biedenharn Candy Co., proposed the process when country people came to town and visited their fountain for a cold Coke. He tried carbonated Coca-Cola in the old 6-ounce Hutchinson pop bottles; and it became an instant success, not only to individuals, but to country picnics and church gatherings.

The Biedenharns expanded with bottling plants in Mississippi, Louisiana and Texas. Others adopted the process as it spread to remote parts of the world. It became the universal "pause that refreshes."

The old confectionary, now known as the Biedenharn Candy Co. Museum, is an authentic restoration of the place where Coca-Cola was first bottled.

172

Stuffed Baked Ham

1 (3 to 5-pound) piece of ham
(shank or butt picnic)
1 small loaf white bread
4 Tablespoons butter or margarine
3 ribs celery, chopped
2 medium-sized onions, chopped
1 bell pepper, chopped

1 (1⅜-ounce) can dry mustard
4 Tablespoons white vinegar
3 Tablespoons sugar
¼ teaspoon celery seed
Salt and red pepper to taste
3 eggs, beaten
Water or ham stock

Cook ham until done. Let cool slightly and carefully remove bone, trying not to tear ham out of shape. Trim excess fat from ham. In 250° oven, dry out bread. Roll bread to make crumbs or use food processor. In skillet sauté in margarine the celery, onions, and bell pepper until clear. Add this to bread crumbs along with mustard, vinegar, sugar, celery seed, salt and red pepper. Mix well. Add eggs and enough water or ham juice to stick together, similar to stuffing for turkey. Put stuffing in ham cavity where bone was removed. Tie ham with string in at least 3 places. Place on cookie sheet. Put rest of stuffing on top and sides of ham. Bake in preheated oven 350° for 15 to 20 minutes, just long enough to dry it out. Do not brown. Store in refrigerator overnight or several days. Cut in thin slices making sure dressing is on slices. Yield: 6 to 10 servings.

Mrs. Charles Faulk
(Elizabeth Young)

Oven-Smoked Canned Ham

1 (3-pound) canned ham

1 (4-ounce) bottle liquid smoke

Remove key from bottom side of can. With a beverage can opener, punch 4 to 6 openings in bottom side of ham can. Place can bottom-side up in 350° oven for 15 minutes or until jelly-like substance is melted. Remove can from oven and pour off juices. Pour liquid smoke through holes into can. Place can bottom-side up in oven. Cook 35 to 45 minutes. Remove from oven; cool and pour off liquid smoke. Open can with key. The ham is ready to slice and the cooking pan is ready to throw away. No clean-up!

Mrs. Sam Lusco
(Margaret Roy Gibson)

Ham and Broccoli Pie

1 small bunch fresh broccoli
2 Tablespoons margarine
2 ribs celery, sliced (1 cup)
1 onion, coarsely chopped (1 cup)
2 Tablespoons cornstarch
2 teaspoons dry mustard
1/4 teaspoon dried leaf marjoram, crushed

1/4 teaspoon grated lemon rind
1/8 teaspoon pepper
2 cups milk
2 Tablespoons freshly squeezed lemon juice
2 cups cooked, cubed ham
1 recipe single crust pastry

Wash broccoli and remove large leaves and tough part of stalks; separate into florets. Place in large saucepan with 1/2-inch boiling water. Cover. Simmer 5 minutes; drain and set aside. In small skillet melt margarine over medium heat. Add celery and onion; cook 3 minutes or until tender. In medium saucepan stir together cornstarch, mustard, marjoram, lemon rind, and pepper. Gradually stir in milk until smooth. Add celery and onion mixture. Stirring constantly, bring to boil over medium heat and boil 1 minute. Remove from heat. Stir in lemon juice, broccoli and ham. Pour mixture into 2-quart casserole. Roll out pastry for top crust. Cut slits to permit steam to escape during baking and place over filling. Seal and flute edges. Bake at 375° for 35 minutes or until crust is golden brown. Yield: 4 to 6 servings.

Mrs. Albert Dornbusch
(Gloria Abraham)

Sweet and Sour Pork Chops

1 teaspoon ginger
1 teaspoon salt
1/2 teaspoon pepper
1/2 teaspoon paprika
1/4 cup unbleached flour

6 pork chops
3 Tablespoons oil
1 cup pineapple juice
2 Tablespoons vinegar
3 Tablespoons brown sugar

Mix together ginger, salt, pepper, paprika, and unbleached flour. Use this to coat pork chops. Brown pork chops in oil. After browning chops, place in a baking dish and cover with combination of pineapple juice, vinegar, and brown sugar. Cover casserole dish with foil and bake 1 hour at 350°. Yield: 4 to 6 servings.

Mrs. George Jabour, Jr.
(Miriam Penton)

Hawaiian Ham Casserole

½ cup melted butter
2 (15¼-ounce) cans chunk
  pineapple and juice
1½ cups brown sugar
2 Tablespoons mustard
1 Tablespoon Worcestershire sauce
½ teaspoon salt
½ teaspoon pepper

½ teaspoon cinnamon
6 cups ham, cubed
1½ cups raisins
30 maraschino cherries, cut in half
1½ cups chopped walnuts
  (optional)
8 cups cooked rice

Over medium heat in a large pot combine melted butter, pineapple juice and brown sugar. After brown sugar has dissolved, add mustard, Worcestershire sauce, salt, pepper and cinnamon. Stir cubed ham into sauce and let simmer for 5 to 10 minutes. Add pineapple chunks, raisins, cherries and walnuts. Let mixture simmer for about 5 minutes. Spread cooked rice into a 9 x 13-inch baking dish. Stir some sauce (liquid only) into rice until it is all wet; then top rice with the rest of mixture. Be sure to arrange ingredients so that they are equally distributed over rice. Heat at 350° for 15 to 20 minutes. Yield: 8 servings.

Chicken can be substituted for ham.

Miss Helen Abraham

Smothered Pork Chops in Milk Gravy

4 pork chops
Salt
Pepper

Flour
4 Tablespoons oil
2 cups milk

Trim all fat from pork chops. Place salt, pepper, and flour in a sack. Put pork chops in sack and shake to coat. Brown pork chops on both sides in hot oil. Remove pork chops from skillet and add 2 Tablespoons or more flour. Brown flour lightly and slowly stir in milk to make a white gravy. Stir in salt and pepper to taste. Return pork chops to skillet and roll in gravy. Cover and simmer on low heat for 45 minutes, basting every 15 minutes. Serve gravy and pork chops over rice. Yield: 4 servings.

The Editors

To sear meat to a rich brown color, add 1 Tablespoon sugar to the heated oil; stir until it browns, then add meat.

Sweet and Sour Pork with Mixed Vegetables

1 (2 to 3-pound) pork loin

Marinade

1 Tablespoon wine
2 Tablespoons soy sauce
1 teaspoon ginger, minced

1 clove garlic, minced
½ teaspoon monosodium glutamate

Cut meat into 1-inch cubes. Marinate meat 2 to 3 hours or overnight.

Batter

2 egg yolks or 1 egg

4 Tablespoons cornstarch

Mix batter ingredients. Add additional cornstarch if necessary to achieve a stiff batter. Drain meat well and combine with batter. Deep-fry at 420° until crisp and golden brown. Turn out onto a warm platter.

Sauce

6 Tablespoons sugar
2 Tablespoons soy sauce
1 Tablespoon wine
3 Tablespoons vinegar

½ cup pineapple juice
3 Tablespoons ketchup
2 Tablespoons cornstarch
½ cup water

Combine sugar, soy sauce, wine, vinegar, pineapple juice, and ketchup. Bring to a boil. Mix cornstarch and water. Add to boiling ingredients and stir until thick.

Vegetable Mixture

½ cup green peppers cut in 1-inch
* squares*
½ cup carrots cut on diagonal
½ cup bamboo shoots cut on
* diagonal*

½ cup quartered pineapple slices
½ cup quartered onion
6 Tablespoons vegetable oil

Fry vegetable mixture in oil at 420° for a few minutes or just until vegetables are transparent. Add sauce and blend. Add meat and combine well. Serve immediately. Yield: 6 to 8 servings.

I learned this from a Taiwanese lady in Okinawa, Japan.

Mrs. James W. Cook
(Naomi Paquette)

Apple-Stuffed Pork Chops

1 Tablespoon butter
¼ cup finely chopped onion
1½ cups bread crumbs
¾ cup peeled and diced tart apples
1 teaspoon poultry seasoning
1½ teaspoons salt, divided
¼ teaspoon ground black pepper, divided

1 egg, slightly beaten
¼ cup water
6 rib pork chops, 1-inch thick with pocket
1 Tablespoon vegetable oil
2 cups orange juice

Melt butter in small skillet; add onion and sauté until transparent. In a medium size mixing bowl, blend onion with bread crumbs, apples, poultry seasoning, ½ teaspoon salt, ⅛ teaspoon pepper, egg, and water. Spoon about 2 Tablespoons of stuffing into the pocket of each pork chop. Fasten with toothpicks. Sprinkle remaining salt and pepper on chops. Heat oil in heavy skillet; add pork chops and brown on both sides. Remove to 9 x 13-inch baking dish. Pour orange juice over all. Cover and bake in 300° oven for 4 hours. Yield: 6 servings.

The ¾ cup apples may be substituted with ½ cup raisins and ¼ cup finely chopped walnuts.

Mrs. Vern Stairs
(Kim Brockman)

Sausage and Rice Casserole

1 pound hot pork sausage
1 pound regular pork sausage
1 large onion, finely chopped
1 large bell pepper, finely chopped
1 (8-ounce) can water chestnuts, finely chopped

1 bunch celery, finely chopped
2 packages dry chicken noodle soup
2 cups boiling water
1 cup raw rice
1 package slivered almonds

In a large pot, sauté sausage. Drain meat and reserve drippings. Sauté all chopped vegetables in reserved drippings. Meanwhile cook soup in boiling water. Remove boiling soup from the heat after 7 minutes. Add raw rice, vegetables, and sausage. If mixture seems dry, add ¼ cup water and place in a covered casserole. Bake, covered, at 300° for 1½ hours or until all liquid is absorbed and rice is fluffy. Serve on a large platter garnished with slivered almonds. Yield: 10 to 12 servings.

Also makes a good stuffing for bell peppers.

Mrs. Kurt Schrock
(Megan Thornton)

177

Medallions of Pork

3 pork tenderloins
2 teaspoons dry mustard
1 teaspoon salt
¼ teaspoon ground pepper
2 Tablespoons butter
2 cloves garlic, minced
½ cup dry vermouth
½ cup white wine

¾ to 1 cup orange juice
1 Tablespoon flour
2 Tablespoons water
Minced parsley
Zests of orange rind
Parsley sprigs
Orange slices

Trim fat and sinew from loins and cut in ½-inch thick slices. Combine dry mustard, salt and pepper and lightly rub into meat. In a large, heavy skillet, melt butter over medium-high heat and add pork slices and garlic. Brown meat for 3 to 5 minutes on each side. Add vermouth, wine, and orange juice; reduce heat. Simmer, covered, for 8 to 10 minutes until meat is tender. Remove medallions to a warm plate and cover. Make a paste of flour and water. With a flat whisk, stir paste into pan juices and simmer to thicken. When ready to serve, return medallions to hot pan gravy for a minute; then arrange on a warmed serving platter; cover with gravy. Sprinkle with minced parsley and zests of orange rind; place a sprig of parsley and slices of orange around the plate. Yield: 6 servings.

Mrs. Louis P. Cashman, Jr.
(Frances Reid)

Bobby's Barbecued Ribs

5 pounds spare ribs
1 cup butter
¾ cup chopped onions
¼ cup light brown sugar
2 teaspoons salt
2 teaspoons chili powder
1 teaspoon dry mustard

1 cup pineapple juice
½ cup lime juice
1 cup ketchup
½ cup chili sauce
1 Tablespoon soy sauce
Dash of TABASCO brand pepper
  sauce

Cut ribs into 2 or 3 rib portions. Place in shallow roasting pan, meaty-side up. Roast uncovered in preheated 350° oven for 1 hour. Meanwhile, in a quart saucepan, melt butter and sauté onions until tender. Blend in sugar, salt, chili powder, and mustard. Stir in pineapple juice, lime juice, ketchup, chili sauce, soy sauce and TABASCO. Heat to boiling. Reduce heat and simmer 30 minutes. Place ribs on grill and brush on sauce. Cook ribs for 20 to 30 minutes while brushing on sauce every 10 minutes. Yield: 4 to 6 servings.

Robert R. Bailess

Pork Chop and Rice Casserole

Salt
Pepper
6 thick loin pork chops
4 teaspoons prepared mustard
1 cup raw rice

6 thick slices onion
6 thick slices bell pepper
6 thick slices tomato
2 (10½-ounce) cans beef bouillon or
  consommé

Salt and pepper pork chops and spread with mustard. Place in 9 x 13-inch casserole and sprinkle rice over chops. Top each chop with a slice of onion, a slice of bell pepper, and a slice of tomato. Pour bouillon over all. Cover casserole with foil and bake 1 to 1½ hours in 350° oven or until rice is done. Yield: 6 servings.

Mrs. Daniel Johnson
(Sue Buckner)

Chinese Spareribs

6 pounds spareribs
1 Tablespoon ground ginger
½ cup soy sauce

Juice of 1 lemon
2 cloves garlic, crushed

Brown spareribs in hot oven 450° about 15 minutes. Pour off fat. Mix ginger, soy sauce, lemon, and garlic to make sauce. Pour over ribs. Reduce oven temperature to 325°. Cover and bake 1½ hours, basting often. Yield: 4 to 6 servings.

Serve with Hot Mustard Sauce.

Mrs. Ann Emmich
(Ann Grundfest)

Hot Mustard Sauce

1 cup sugar
1 cup wine vinegar
⅛ teaspoon salt

1 cup COLMAN'S English Mustard
  (no substitute)
2 large or 3 medium eggs

Mix all ingredients and cook in double boiler until thick. Do not use blender to mix. Can be stored in refrigerator for several months and can be reheated. It loses "hotness" the longer it is stored. Use as a dip or spread for crackers and sandwiches or to accompany ham or shrimp. Yield: 2½ cups.

Mrs. James William Jones
Meridian, Mississippi

Béarnaise Sauce

¼ cup tarragon wine vinegar
¼ cup dry white wine
1 Tablespoon minced green onion
1½ teaspoons dried tarragon
⅛ teaspoon pepper

⅛ teaspoon salt
3 egg yolks
3 Tablespoons boiling water
1 cup butter, sliced into thin piece

Boil vinegar, wine, green onion, tarragon, pepper, and salt over medium heat until liquid is reduced to 2 Tablespoons. Cool. Place egg yolks and water in top of double boiler. Have water in bottom of double boiler shallow enough so that it doesn't touch upper saucepan. Bring water in bottom of double boiler to barely boiling. Stir egg mixture constantly with wire whisk until it begins to thicken. Do not cook too long. Remove boiler from heat and add butter, one slice at a time, beating until dissolved. Remove top of double boiler from hot water. Blend in wine and vinegar mixture. Do not use an aluminum pan. Do not let sauce stand over heat. If prepared ahead, serve at room temperature. If sauce curdles, slowly add 1 Tablespoon boiling water while beating with a mixer. Serve with steak or prime rib. Yield: 1½ cups.

Mrs. Stan Terry, Jr.
(Sallie Bingham)

Jezebel Sauce

1 (1.12-ounce) can dry mustard
1 (5-ounce) jar horseradish
1 (18-ounce) jar apple jelly

1 (18-ounce) jar pineapple preserves
2 Tablespoons coarsely ground
  pepper

Mix mustard and horseradish well. Add remaining ingredients. Blend well and store in jars in refrigerator. Yield: 4 cups.

Serve with ham or with cheese and sausage chunks to dip as an appetizer.

The Editors

 One pound of boneless meat will serve 4 people.

 Meat that has been marinated will cook more quickly.

Meat Marinade

Meat tenderizer
Monosodium glutamate
½ cup soy sauce
½ cup strong coffee

1 Tablespoon Worcestershire sauce
1 Tablespoon vinegar
1 Tablespoon sesame seed, browned

Rub meat with tenderizer and monosodium glutamate. Mix remaining ingredients. Marinate meat overnight in refrigerator or for at least 1 hour or more. This is an excellent marinade for steaks and roasts of all kinds, including venison. Yield: 1½ cups marinade.

Mrs. Melvin R. Dykes
Jackson, Mississippi

Shish Kabob Marinade or Basting Sauce

¾ cup hot water
½ cup soy sauce
¼ cup honey

2 Tablespoons salad oil
2 Tablespoons fresh lemon juice
4 cloves garlic, minced

Combine all ingredients and marinate meat overnight.

Also delicious as a basting sauce for grilled pork chops.

Mrs. Joseph P. Harris
(Susan Gunn)

Dr. Edley's Rubbing Sauce

1 Tablespoon cooking oil
1½ teaspoons soy sauce
1 teaspoon garlic salt

1 teaspoon black pepper
1 teaspoon paprika
1 teaspoon monosodium glutamate

Rub sauce on meat. Let sit overnight. If not enough liquid to moisten well, add more oil.

Dr. Edley Jones

Raisin Sauce for Ham

¼ cup raisins
2 cups water
1 cup light brown sugar
2 Tablespoons cornstarch

1 pinch salt
¼ teaspoon ginger
2 Tablespoons vinegar
6 to 8 slices ham

Cook raisins in water for 5 minutes. Mix sugar, cornstarch, salt, ginger, and vinegar. Add to raisin mixture, stirring constantly. Cook until thickened and add sliced ham. Continue simmering until meat is thoroughly heated. Serve. Sauce may be prepared ahead of time and reheated when ready to add ham. Yield: 6 to 8 servings.

Mrs. John G. Collins
(Anita Sheffield)

Orange Cranberry Sauce

1 pound fresh cranberries
2 oranges, quartered
1 envelope unflavored gelatin

1 cup lukewarm water
¾ cup pecans, chopped
1 cup sugar

Put cranberries and oranges with peel into food processor. Chop finely. Pour into a bowl or serving dish. Dissolve gelatin in water. Add this to cranberry mixture. Add chopped pecans and sugar. Blend well. Refrigerate until set, 4 to 6 hours. Serve with turkey or pork. Yield: 8 servings.

Mrs. Jeff King
(Anne Keen)

Poultry

Old Plantation-Style Chicken

2 small fryers
Salt and pepper to taste
4 Tablespoons butter or margarine

Juice of 2 lemons
¼ cup dry sherry

Quarter fryers; wash and pat dry. Salt and pepper each quarter. Place skin-side up in large but shallow roasting pan. Put a pat of butter or margarine on each quarter and pour lemon juice over chicken. With oven on broil, place chicken on lower rack of oven and close oven door. Cook for 15 minutes. Turn chicken; baste and cook 15 minutes longer. Turn once again and baste; with skin-side up again, cook 15 minutes for a total of 45 minutes cooking time. Add sherry to chicken and baste with drippings. Put a cover of foil on chicken; turn oven to 325° and bake until tender, basting every 10 minutes. Serve with mushroom sauce. Yield: 8 servings.

Mushroom Sauce

½ pound fresh mushrooms
2 Tablespoons butter
1 (10½-ounce) can consommé or
   bouillon
Dash of Worcestershire sauce
Lemon juice

Dash of TABASCO brand pepper
   sauce
2 Tablespoons cornstarch
¼ cup water
Drippings from broiled chicken

Sauté mushrooms in butter. Add consommé and season with Worcestershire, lemon juice and TABASCO. Blend cornstarch and water into a paste and add to mixture. Add a little of the drippings from the chicken pan and cook, stirring constantly, until sauce is slightly thickened.

Warren Asher

 To turn a chicken while cooking, use 2 wooden spoons rather than a fork so that the flesh will not be pierced.

Smoked Chickens

½ bag hickory chips   6 whole chickens
10 pounds charcoal

Soak hickory chips in water overnight. Place charcoal in bottom of
smoker. Start fire and let burn 30 minutes. Coals will be glowing but not
flaming. Remove hickory chips; save water. Place soaked chips directly on
hot coals. Fill water pan with hickory water. Add more water until pan is
filled. Place 3 chickens on each rack. Outside temperature will determine
the length of time to cook. Very cold winter nights will require about 5
hours. Warmer weather will take less time, about 4 hours. Yield: 6
chickens.

Dr. Robert M. Abraham

Civil War Chicken

1 whole fryer or favorite chicken   6 slices salt meat
   pieces   3 Tablespoons flour
Pepper to taste

Split chicken down the back and place in iron skillet with 1-inch water.
Pepper to taste. Place thinly sliced salt meat evenly onto chicken pieces.
Cover tightly and bake 3 hours at 250°. Thicken gravy with flour paste.
Good with rice. Yield: 4 servings.

*Due to the shortage of salt during the war, Southerners were compelled to use salted
meat for their fowl.*

Mrs. Tom Harris, Jr.
(Josephine Good)

Barbecued Chicken

4 Tablespoons brown sugar   1 teaspoon salt
4 Tablespoons vinegar   1 Tablespoon mustard (optional)
2 Tablespoons Worcestershire sauce   ½ to 1 cup ketchup
2 Tablespoons cooking oil or melted 1 whole cut chicken or favorite
   margarine   pieces with skin removed

Mix all ingredients. Dip chicken in sauce. Pour remainder over chicken.
Bake in a 9 x 13 x 2-inch covered casserole at 350° for 1½ hours. Yield: 4 to
6 servings.

Mrs. Bobby Miller
(Beverly Beard)

Oven-Roasted Chicken

2 large broiler-fryers
Salt and pepper to taste

2 Tablespoons margarine
½ cup cooking oil

Bring chickens to room temperature. Remove fat and rinse out cavity. Season with salt and pepper and rub with margarine. Preheat oven to 475°. Lay chickens on side in a pan not much bigger than chickens themselves. Add oil to pan. Cook 10 minutes. Baste. Turn and baste again. Cook 10 minutes longer. Baste. Lower oven to 425°. Bake for 30 minutes, turning and basting every 10 minutes. Let rest 10 minutes before carving.

The Vicksburg Junior Auxiliary

Rosie's Chicken in Pastry

½ cup plus 3 Tablespoons butter,
  divided
4 ounces cream cheese
1 cup flour
3 Tablespoons white wine
2 chicken breasts, boned and cut in
  half
½ teaspoon salt

¼ teaspoon black pepper
¼ teaspoon tarragon
1 carrot, cut into 4 slices
8 to 10 fresh mushrooms, thinly
  sliced
4 thin slices baked ham
1 egg, beaten
½ cup sour cream

Soften ½ cup butter with cream cheese. Blend together and mix well. Add flour to this and mix until pastry leaves sides of bowl. Divide pastry into 4 equal parts and chill at least 1 hour. Melt 3 Tablespoons butter in a small skillet and add wine. Sauté the chicken in wine and butter mixture for approximately 3 to 4 minutes on each side. Sprinkle chicken with salt, pepper, and tarragon. Remove chicken from skillet and set aside. Sauté carrot slices and mushrooms with ham slices in butter and wine sauce in skillet. Remove from skillet and cool. Roll each portion of chilled pastry into a 7 x 5-inch rectangle. This may be adjusted according to size of chicken pieces. On each piece of pastry put 1 piece of chicken, 1 carrot slice, 1 ham slice, and ¼ mushroom slices. Fold pastry and seal edges by moistening ends. Place pastry-wrapped chicken seam-side down in baking dish and brush each piece with beaten egg. Prick pastry several times with fork tines. Bake at 375° for 10 to 15 minutes or until browned. While pastries are baking, heat butter and wine mixture and add sour cream. Stir continuously over heat until smooth and thoroughly heated. Pour sauce over each pastry. Yield: 4 servings.

Mrs. J. Lewis Decell
(Coralee Smith)

Italian Chicken

3 Tablespoons olive oil
1 large onion, coarsely chopped
3 to 4 ribs celery, coarsely chopped
1 large bell pepper, coarsely
  chopped
2 to 3 cloves garlic
4 to 6 chicken breasts, cut in half,
  boned and skinned
2 (16-ounce) jars Italian zucchini
1 (16-ounce) jar spaghetti sauce

12 to 15 pitted black olives
1 (4-ounce) can sliced mushrooms,
  drained
⅓ cup red wine
Salt, pepper and Italian seasoning
  to taste
Cooked rice
Freshly grated Romano cheese
Fresh parsley

Pour olive oil in skillet and sauté onion, celery, bell pepper and garlic. Remove garlic and discard. Remove vegetables and sauté chicken pieces until golden brown, but not too brown. Place chicken in oblong baking pan that has been oiled lightly or sprayed with cooking oil. Mix jars of zucchini, spaghetti sauce, olives and mushrooms. Add sautéed onion, bell pepper, celery and red wine. Pour over chicken. Cover with foil. Place in a preheated 350° oven for 35 to 45 minutes or until chicken is done. Check after 30 minutes and add water or wine if getting too dry. Serve over rice. Garnish with cheese and parsley. Yield: 8 to 10 servings.

Nick Cassino

Fiesta Microwave Chicken Kiev

7 Tablespoons butter, divided
3 Tablespoons Old English sharp
  cheese spread
2 teaspoons instant minced onion
1 teaspoon salt
1 teaspoon monosodium glutamate

2 Tablespoons chopped green chilies
4 whole chicken breasts, boned
1 cup crushed Cheddar cheese
  crackers
1½ Tablespoons taco seasoning mix

In small bowl beat together 3 Tablespoons butter and cheese; blend well. Mix in onion, salt, monosodium glutamate and chilies. Place a portion of mixture at 1 end of each chicken breast, dividing evenly. Roll up each piece, tucking in ends to completely enclose filling. Fasten with toothpicks. Dip each roll into 4 Tablespoons melted butter to coat; cover with mixture of crackers and taco seasoning mix. Arrange rolls in 12 x 8 x 2-inch dish. Cover with waxed paper. Microwave on high 10 to 12 minutes rotating ½ turn every 5 minutes until done. Yield: 4 servings.

Lee Kennedy Windham

Ham-Stuffed Chicken Breasts

4 to 6 chicken breasts, skinned and
  boned
4 to 6 cubes or thin strips cooked
  ham
4 to 6 cubes Cheddar cheese

1 (10¾-ounce) can cream of celery
  soup, undiluted
1 (5-ounce) can evaporated milk
6 drops Worcestershire sauce
Dash of pepper

Pound chicken breasts between sheets of waxed paper until thin. Place 1
piece ham and cheese on each chicken breast. Roll and secure with toothpick, making sure cheese is completely covered by chicken. Place in baking dish. Mix remaining ingredients and pour over chicken. Cover and
bake at 375° for 1 hour. Uncover and bake 15 minutes until sauce is thickened slightly. Remove toothpicks before serving. Good served over rice.
Yield: 4 to 6 servings.

Chicken can be stuffed with artichoke hearts, also.

Mrs. Bobby Robinson
(Jan Harris)

Supreme of Chicken with Mozzarella Cheese

6 Tablespoons butter, divided
1 Tablespoon vegetable oil
½ pound button mushrooms,
  minced
Salt
Freshly ground pepper
½ cup flour

4 boned chicken breasts
2 Tablespoons Madeira, port or
  sherry
⅓ cup dry white wine
½ pound mozzarella or Bel Paese
  cheese

Heat 2 Tablespoons butter with oil in heavy skillet. When hot, add mushrooms and cook 4 to 5 minutes, stirring occasionally. Do not allow to
brown. Season lightly with salt and pepper. Set aside. In paper bag combine flour, salt and pepper to taste. Add chicken breasts 1 at a time and
shake. Heat remaining butter in skillet over moderate heat. When butter
foams, add chicken. Sauté 3 minutes on 1 side and 2 minutes on second
side. Put in shallow pan. Spoon mushrooms over chicken breasts. Keep
warm. Add wines to skillet; turn heat to high and cook, scraping down
bits around pan. Reduce heat slightly and boil down about half of mixture
and pour over chicken. Slice cheese thin and place 1 slice on top of each
breast. Slide pan under preheated broiler 4 to 5 inches from heat and broil
long enough to melt cheese, about 2 to 3 minutes. Yield: 4 servings.

Mrs. Philip Jabour
(Linda Batschelet)

Chicken Wing Skillet

2 pounds broiler-fryer chicken
  wings (about 12)
¼ cup vegetable oil
¼ cup orange juice
¼ cup honey
¼ cup soy sauce
1 bunch green onions, cut in 2-inch
  lengths

4 to 6 carrots, sliced
2 cloves garlic, peeled and halved
½ teaspoon powdered ginger
¼ to ½ cup chicken bouillon
Cooked rice

Fold chicken wing tips under wing's thickest joint. Heat oil in fry pan over medium heat. Add chicken and brown on all sides. Drain off excess fat. Reduce heat. Add orange juice, honey, soy sauce, onions, carrots, garlic, and ginger. Stir wings and carrots to coat with sauce. Cover and simmer 15 to 20 minutes. Add bouillon to sauce and stir gently. Continue cooking until wings and carrots are tender. Remove garlic. Serve wings with sauce over rice. Yield: 4 servings.

Mrs. Bob Cunny
(Nell Pinkston)

Fried Chicken

1 (2 to 3-pound) fryer cut into
  pieces
Vegetable oil for frying

Salt
Pepper
¾ cup flour

Wash chicken and let it drain. Put enough cooking oil in a large skillet to a depth of 1-inch. Heat oil on medium high setting. Salt chicken liberally. Pepper to taste. Put flour in a bag and shake each piece of chicken individually to coat well. When oil is hot, place chicken in skillet; don't crowd pieces. Cook on 1 side until light brown, about 15 to 20 minutes. Lower heat to simmer and cover. Cook covered 5 to 7 minutes. Return heat to medium-high and finish. Yield: 4 to 6 servings.

Mrs. John Wayne Jabour
(Becky Taylor)

 When straining grease after frying chicken, put a napkin on top of a can and fasten with a rubber band. Pour grease through napkin to strain.

 When frying chicken in deep fat, cooked pieces will float to surface.

Chicken and Artichokes

Salt and pepper to taste
Paprika to taste
4 chicken breasts, skinned
½ cup butter, divided
1 (4-ounce) can mushrooms,
  drained or 6 to 8 large fresh
  mushrooms, sliced

2 Tablespoons flour
1 cup chicken broth
½ cup cooking sherry
1 (14-ounce) can artichoke hearts,
  drained

Sprinkle salt, pepper, and paprika over chicken breasts and brown in ¼ cup butter. Set aside. Sauté mushrooms in remaining butter. Add flour, chicken broth and sherry. Mix. Place artichoke hearts in bottom of 2-quart casserole or 10-inch oven skillet. Place chicken breasts over this. Pour mushroom, flour, chicken broth and sherry mixture over chicken breasts and artichokes. Bake, covered, at 300° for 60 minutes. Uncover and bake for an additional 60 minutes. Serve over rice. Yield: 4 servings.

Mrs. Donnie Harris
(Linda Aldrich)

Chicken Parisienne

6 chicken breast halves (skin on)
1 (10½-ounce) can condensed cream
  of mushroom soup, undiluted
1 (3-ounce) can mushrooms with
  liquid
1 cup dairy sour cream

½ cup cooking sherry or cocktail
  sherry
Paprika
Lemon pepper seasoning
Cooked rice

Place chicken breasts skin-side up in a large baking dish deep enough to accommodate chicken and liquid produced in cooking (at least 2 inches deep). Combine soup, mushrooms with liquid, sour cream and sherry. Pour over chicken, covering all pieces completely. Sprinkle generously with paprika and dust with lemon pepper. Bake at 350° uncovered 1¼ to 1½ hours until tender and gravy is golden on top of chicken. Serve over hot fluffy rice. Yield: 6 servings.

Mrs. Barry W. Holcomb
(Pat Horne)

Rub chicken with a good brandy before roasting along with other seasonings for extra flavor.

Poulet Marengo

1 (3-pound) chicken
1 small onion, quartered
½ cup parsley
3 ribs celery
2 Tablespoons butter
1 teaspoon salt
1 teaspoon pepper
⅛ teaspoon red pepper
⅛ teaspoon tarragon

1 pound fresh mushrooms
2 or 3 ripe tomatoes or 1 can whole
   tomatoes
3 green onions, chopped
Dry white wine
1 pound crawfish tails, boiled and
   peeled
Cooked rice

Boil chicken in water seasoned with onion, parsley, and celery; bone and shred. Melt butter to film bottom of a large, heavy pot. Sauté chicken in butter seasoned with salt, black and red pepper and tarragon until golden on all sides. Clean and trim mushrooms; peel fresh tomatoes. When chicken is well browned, add tomatoes and green onions. Cook a few minutes, adding enough dry wine to moisten the bottom of the pot. Cook, partially covered, until chicken is tender, adding more wine if necessary. Add crawfish tails and mushrooms to chicken when done. Continue to cook for 15 minutes. Boil gravy and let it reduce, if necessary. Serve over rice. Yield: 6 servings.

Mrs. James Penley
(Betty Prewitt)

Jo's Dilled Chicken with Vegetables

¼ cup butter or margarine
3½ to 4-pounds chicken, cut up
1 medium onion, sliced
1 medium green pepper, sliced
½ pound mushrooms, sliced
¼ teaspoon dill

1 teaspoon rosemary
½ cup dry white wine
1 teaspoon salt
¼ teaspoon pepper
1 medium zucchini or yellow
   squash, sliced

Melt butter in skillet over medium heat. Brown chicken on all sides. Remove to platter. Drain off all but 2 Tablespoons fat. Sauté onions, peppers, and mushrooms in remaining fat until tender, about 5 minutes. Add dill and rosemary. Return chicken to pan; add wine; sprinkle with salt and pepper. Reduce heat; cover; simmer ½ hour. Add sliced zucchini or yellow squash. Cover and simmer ½ hour or until tender. Yield: 4 servings.

Joanne G. Rake
Brandon, Florida

Nan's Chicken and Dumplings

1 (2 to 3-pound) chicken and 4
   breasts
½ medium onion, peeled
1 inside rib of celery with leaves
1 carrot peeled
Salt and pepper to taste

3 heaping Tablespoons solid
   vegetable shortening
2 cups flour
1 heaping teaspoon salt
9 Tablespoons ice water

Cover chicken with water. Add onion, celery, carrot, salt and pepper. Cook, covered, until meat comes off bone. Remove chicken; bone and break into bite-size pieces. Strain broth and return to large pot. In a large bowl cut shortening into flour with a pastry blender or fork until dough is pea-size. Add salt. Add ice water, 1 Tablespoon at a time, and mix lightly with a fork. On a lightly floured surface, roll dough very thinly. Keep roller floured. Cut into strips and layer on waxed paper. Lightly sprinkle flour over each layer. Chill 30 to 45 minutes. Drop into boiling broth with chicken pieces. Pinch each dumpling as thin as possible. Do not stir. Jiggle or shake the pot. Stirring will break dumplings. Cook on medium heat 30 minutes. To reheat, cover and warm slowly in oven or microwave. Yield: 6 to 8 servings.

Mrs. Joseph P. Harris
(Susan Gunn)

Chinese Chicken

1 chicken, cooked and cut in bite-
   size pieces
1 (6¼-ounce) package wild rice
   with seasoning, cooked as
   directed
1 (10¾-ounce) can cream of celery
   soup, undiluted
1 onion, chopped

1 cup mayonnaise
1 (14-ounce) can mixed Chinese
   vegetables
1 (2-ounce) jar pimentos
1 (16-ounce) can French-style beans,
   drained
Salt and pepper to taste

Mix above ingredients. Salt and pepper to taste. Bake to heat at 350° until bubbly. Freezes well. Yield: 8 servings.

Mrs. Gordon L. Carr, Jr.
(Rainy Loe)

Chicken à la King in Patty Shells

½ pound mushrooms, chopped
¼ cup green pepper, chopped
¼ cup onion, chopped
6 Tablespoons margarine
6 Tablespoons flour

3 cups evaporated milk
4 cups cubed, cooked chicken
1 (4-ounce) jar pimento
1 teaspoon salt
2 Tablespoons sherry

Sauté mushrooms, green pepper, and onion in margarine. Add flour and stir until smooth. Add milk slowly, stirring constantly. Add chicken, pimento, salt, and sherry. Simmer until heated thoroughly and slightly thickened. Serve in patty shells or over toast. Yield: 8 to 10 servings.

Mrs. George Guider
(Annie Lee Faulk)

Chinese Chicken-In-A-Garden

3 whole chicken breasts, skinned
  and boned
½ teaspoon garlic powder
3 Tablespoons vegetable oil, divided
2 Tablespoons soy sauce, divided
3 Tablespoons cornstarch, divided
½ teaspoon salt
¼ teaspoon pepper
3 green peppers, cut into 1-inch
  pieces
1 cup celery, cut into 1-inch pieces

8 green onions, cut into ½-inch
  slices
1 (6-ounce) package frozen Chinese
  pea pods, thawed and drained
¾ cup chicken bouillon
3 medium tomatoes, sliced into
  eighths
Fresh chopped mushrooms
  (optional)
Hot cooked rice

Cut chicken breasts into 1-inch pieces. Combine garlic powder, 1 Tablespoon oil, 1 Tablespoon soy sauce, 1 teaspoon cornstarch, salt, pepper and chicken. Mix well and let stand 20 minutes. Pour remaining oil in wok or large skillet. Allow to heat at medium high for 2 minutes. Add green pepper and stir-fry 4 minutes. Add celery, green onions and pea pods; stir-fry 2 minutes. Remove vegetables from skillet and set aside. Combine remaining soy sauce and cornstarch; stir in chicken bouillon. Set aside. Add chicken to skillet and stir-fry 3 minutes or until almost done. Add stir-fried vegetables, tomatoes and bouillon mixture. Mushrooms may be added at this time. Stir-fry over low heat for 3 minutes or until thickened and bubbly. Serve over hot cooked rice. Pour soy sauce on top, if desired. Yield: 6 servings.

Mrs. Ben Hand
(Lana Toney)

Parmesan Oven-Fried Chicken

½ cup fine, dry bread crumbs
⅓ cup grated Parmesan cheese
¼ teaspoon garlic salt
¼ teaspoon pepper

6 chicken breast halves, skinned
¼ cup Italian salad dressing
Vegetable cooking spray

In a small mixing bowl, combine bread crumbs, Parmesan cheese, garlic salt and pepper; set aside. Dip chicken in salad dressing; then dredge in bread crumb mixture. Place chicken, bone-side down, in a 9 x 13 x 2-inch baking pan coated with cooking spray. Bake at 350° for 45 minutes or until tender. Chicken may also be rolled in crushed corn or wheat flakes. Yield: 4 to 6 servings.

Mrs. Wayne Thornton
(Donna Nasif)

Favorite Chicken Tetrazzini

½ bell pepper, chopped
1 onion, chopped
2 Tablespoons butter
3 (10½-ounce) cans cream of
*   mushroom soup, undiluted*
5 Tablespoons light cream
1 cup shredded sharp cheese,
*   divided*
1 (5-ounce) can mushroom pieces
2 cups or more chicken, cooked and
*   chopped*

4 Tablespoons sherry
1 teaspoon salt
1 Tablespoon Worcestershire sauce
Black pepper to taste
Red pepper to taste
TABASCO brand pepper sauce
1 package noodles, cooked in
*   chicken broth*

Sauté green pepper and onions in butter. Add soup, thinned with light cream. Add ½ cup cheese to sauce. Add all other ingredients, including seasonings to taste and omitting noodles. Mix well and let thicken. Set aside. Cook noodles in chicken broth saved from cooking chicken. In greased 9 x 13-inch casserole, place layers of noodles, chicken, and sauce mixture. Repeat. Top with remaining cheese. Bake at 375° for 20 to 30 minutes. Freezes well. Yield: 8 to 10 servings.

Mrs. Louis P. Cashman, Jr.
(Frances Reid)

Chicken Tetrazzini

4 Tablespoons margarine
2 onions, chopped
1 medium bell pepper, chopped
1 (16-ounce) can tomatoes
4 Tablespoons chili powder
Salt to taste
Pepper to taste

¾ cup sharp cheese, shredded
1 pint light cream
Pinch of soda
1 (4 to 5-pound) chicken
1 (16-ounce) package thin spaghetti,
  cooked

Sauté margarine, onion and pepper. Add tomatoes and seasonings. Cook slowly until sauce thickens; add cheese and light cream with a pinch of soda cooking a little longer. Boil chicken, cool, and pull pieces from chicken. Butter large casserole and line with part of the cooked spaghetti. Layer chicken, tomato sauce, more spaghetti, and cheese. Continue until all is used ending with sauce and topped with cheese. Freezes well. Yield: 8 servings.

Mrs. Preston Herring
(Helen Greenoe)

Chicken-Asparagus Casserole

4 chicken breast halves, boned and
  skinned
½ cup vegetable oil
1 (14-ounce) can asparagus
1 (10¾-ounce) can cream of chicken
  soup, undiluted

½ cup mayonnaise
1 teaspoon lemon juice
½ teaspoon curry powder
1 cup Cheddar cheese, shredded

Sauté chicken in oil until no longer pink. Drain. Place asparagus on bottom of 9 x 9 x 2-inch baking dish. Place chicken on top of asparagus. Mix soup, mayonnaise, lemon juice, and curry powder. Pour mixture over chicken. Sprinkle cheese over top. Bake at 375° for 30 minutes. Yield: 4 servings.

Mrs. Sylvia Green
Shawnee, Kansas

To determine if oil is hot enough for frying chicken, fish, or potatoes, drop a kernel of popcorn into oil. When the corn pops, the oil is ready for frying.

Chicken Pie

1 (3 to 4-pound) chicken, cut into
  pieces
1 (10¾-ounce) can cream of chicken
  soup, undiluted
2½ cups flour

¾ cup shortening
½ cup cold water
3 hard-cooked eggs, sliced
¼ cup butter, melted
Pepper

Wash and cut chicken. Place in Dutch oven and cover with seasoned water. Boil until tender. Remove from broth and reserve broth. Remove skin and bones from chicken and shred. Add chicken soup to broth and mix well. Make a dough using flour, shortening and water. Roll ⅓ of dough thinly and cut into 1-inch strips. Break strips into dumplings and drop into boiling broth. Do not stir with spoon. Add sliced eggs and chicken pieces. Put in large casserole dish. Roll rest of dough very thinly and cover the dish. Brush with melted butter and sprinkle with pepper. Bake at 400° for 30 minutes or until brown. Yield: 6 to 8 servings.

Mrs. Leon Henry
(Modena Ray)

Easy Chicken Pot Pie

1 (3 to 4-pound) hen
1½ Tablespoons seasoned salt
4 hard-cooked eggs
1¼ cups chicken broth
1 (10½-ounce) can cream of celery
  soup, undiluted

1 (8½-ounce) can peas (optional)
1 (8½-ounce) can sliced carrots
  (optional)
1 cup self-rising flour
½ cup margarine, melted
1 cup milk

Boil hen in water with seasoned salt added. Remove from bone and cut into bite-size pieces. Layer in a 9 x 12-inch baking dish. Add eggs which have been grated. Top with chicken broth and soup. Layer peas and carrots, if desired. Mix flour, margarine, and milk well to form crust. Place on top of chicken mixture only when ready to bake. Cook at 350° for 45 minutes. Yield: 8 servings.

Mrs. Jack Palmer
(Sandy Holliday)

 For a brown crust on roasted chicken, rub mayonnaise generously over skin before cooking.

195

Old-Fashioned Chicken Loaf

1 (3 to 4-pound) chicken
3 eggs
1 cup cooked rice
1 cup bread crumbs
3 Tablespoons chicken fat or butter,
　melted

2 cups chicken broth or milk
1½ teaspoons salt
¼ teaspoon pepper

Boil chicken. Remove meat from bones and cut in small pieces. Beat eggs slightly; stir in rice, bread crumbs, fat or butter, broth or milk, seasonings and chicken. Spoon into greased 1½-quart casserole and bake at 350° for 50 minutes or until firm. Yield: 6 servings.

Sauce

3 Tablespoons chicken fat or butter
3 Tablespoons flour
1 cup chicken broth
3 Tablespoons cream
1 teaspoon minced parsley

½ teaspoon salt
½ teaspoon paprika
¼ cup sliced mushrooms or stuffed
　olives

Blend fat and flour. Stir in chicken broth and cream. Cook slowly until thickened, stirring constantly. Add parsley, salt and paprika. Add olives or mushrooms.

Mrs. R. R. Morrison, Jr.
(Twick Cooper)

Russian Chicken

¼ cup corn oil
1 (8-ounce) bottle Russian salad
　dressing
1 envelope dry onion soup mix

1 (10-ounce) jar apricot preserves
1 teaspoon salt
2 broiler-fryer chickens, cut in parts
　or 8 chicken breasts

Mix together all ingredients except chicken. Place chicken in single layer, skin-side up, in large shallow baking pan. Pour preserves mixture on chicken. Bake covered in 350° oven for 1½ hours or until tender, basting occasionally with pan drippings. Uncover last ½ hour. Serve hot with plain rice and sweet and sour sauce. Yield: 8 servings.

Miss Caroline Compton

Chicken-On-A-Skewer

10 to 12 chicken breast halves,
  boned and skinned
⅔ cup soy sauce
½ cup minced onion
2 cloves garlic, crushed or minced
4 Tablespoons salad oil

4 Tablespoons dry white wine
5 medium green peppers, seeded
  and cut into pieces
2 (15¼-ounce) cans pineapple
  chunks
Cooked rice

Cut chicken breasts into bite-size pieces. Combine soy sauce, onion, garlic, oil, and wine to make marinade. Cover chicken with marinade and refrigerate 30 minutes. Meanwhile, parboil pepper pieces for 2 minutes in boiling water; drain and cool. Place chicken, peppers, and pineapple chunks on metal or bamboo skewers. Alternate pieces of each. Grill over medium-hot coals for 15 minutes, basting once or twice with marinade. Serve over rice. Yield: 8 servings.

Mrs. Robert H. Weatherly
(Dannie Compton)

Savory Crescent Chicken Squares

1 (3-ounce) package cream cheese
6 Tablespoons melted butter,
  divided
2 Tablespoons chopped onions
2 cups cooked, cubed chicken
¼ teaspoon salt
⅛ teaspoon pepper

2 Tablespoons milk
½ cup slivered almonds
1 (8-ounce) package crescent rolls
Slivered almonds for garnish
  (optional)

Preheat oven to 350°. Blend cream cheese and 2 Tablespoons butter until smooth. Add chopped onions, chicken, salt, pepper, milk and almonds. Separate crescent rolls into 4 rectangles. Pat at the seams; spoon ½ cup chicken mixture onto crescent rolls. Seal the edges completely. Place sealed side on baking sheet. Brush with ¼ cup butter. Bake for 25 minutes. Garnish with slivered almonds, if desired. Yield: 4 servings.

This recipe freezes beautifully. Place on a cookie sheet and wrap in a baggie. Remove from baggie and cook for 40 minutes at 350°.

Mrs. Al Windham
(Cindy Shelton)

Spicy Mushroom Chicken

4 to 6 large chicken breasts
1 (4-ounce) jar sliced mushrooms
1 (20-ounce) can tomato sauce
1 cup coarsely chopped celery
½ cup finely chopped onion

1 clove garlic, finely minced
1 teaspoon salt
1 teaspoon Italian seasoning
¼ teaspoon black pepper

Remove skin from chicken breasts. Place chicken in baking dish and brown in 500° oven for 15 minutes, turning once. Reduce heat to 350°. In a small saucepan, combine remaining ingredients. Bring to a boil. Reduce heat and simmer 10 minutes. Pour sauce over chicken. Cover and bake for 45 minutes or until tender. Yield: 4 to 6 servings.

Mrs. Scooter Havard
Gloster, Mississippi

Sherried Chicken Livers

1 pound chicken livers
¼ teaspoon salt
¼ teaspoon black pepper
1 teaspoon lemon pepper seasoning
Juice of 1 lemon

4 Tablespoons butter or margarine,
*   melted*
2 Tablespoons sherry or white wine
4 pieces unbuttered toast

Wash livers and place in shallow pan. Cut livers in half if too large. Sprinkle with salt, pepper, and lemon pepper. Drizzle with lemon juice and butter. Preheat broiler. Place livers under broiler about 5 inches from heat. Cook until sizzling, about 4 or 5 minutes. Turn livers and baste adding a bit more lemon pepper and butter, if necessary. Continue to broil 3 or 4 minutes more until livers are brown but not dry. Livers should still be pink in center. Sprinkle wine over livers. Finish broiling 2 to 3 minutes. Serve over toast with pan juices. Yield: 4 to 6 servings.

Mrs. Herb Jones
(Mary Ruth Smith)

Always wait to stuff a turkey until just before roasting, and fill the cavity only ¾'s full, as dressing will expand.

Easy Chicken Divan

3 cups cooked, boned chicken, cut
 into bite-size pieces
1 cup sour cream
1 cup mayonnaise
1 cup shredded Cheddar cheese

1 Tablespoon fresh lemon juice (no
 substitution)
2 (10-ounce) packages frozen
 broccoli, cooked
¼ cup Parmesan cheese

Prepare chicken. Mix sour cream, mayonnaise, cheese, and lemon juice together in a bowl. Cook broccoli according to package directions; drain well. Layer ingredients with broccoli, chicken, and cheese mixture. Top with Parmesan cheese. Bake at 350° for 25 minutes in a 9 x 12 x 2-inch pan. Yield: 6 to 8 servings.

Mrs. Steve Harris
(Linda Walker)

Chicken Spaghetti

10 to 12 chicken breasts
4 to 6 chicken thighs
Salt and pepper to taste
3 quarts chicken broth
2 large green peppers, chopped
2 large onions, chopped
¼ cup butter
1 pound vermicelli

3 pounds processed cheese
1 (10-ounce) can ROTEL Tomatoes
 and Green Chilies
2 Tablespoons Worcestershire sauce
1 (6-ounce) can sliced mushrooms,
 drained
1 (17-ounce) can English peas,
 drained

In a large pot, boil chicken pieces until tender. Salt and pepper to taste. Cool meat in broth; reserve broth. Supplement reserved broth with canned broth to make 3 quarts. Remove skin and bones and cut chicken into bite-size pieces. In a medium skillet, sauté peppers and onions in butter or margarine until soft. In a very large pot, bring broth to a boil and cook vermicelli in broth until tender. Do not overcook. Leave vermicelli in broth. Add cheese cut in chunks. Stir until melted. Add ROTEL, Worcestershire, mushrooms, peas, onion mixture and chicken. Pour into 1 large or several small casserole dishes. Bake at 350° for 45 minutes or until bubbly. Yield: 16 servings.

Mrs. John Hadad, III
(Susan Phillips)

Hot Chicken Salad Soufflé

6 slices white bread, divided
2 cups diced cooked chicken
¼ cup chopped onion
½ cup chopped green pepper
½ cup chopped celery
½ cup mayonnaise
¾ teaspoon salt

Dash of pepper
2 eggs
1½ cups milk
1 (10½-ounce) can cream of
   mushroom soup, undiluted
½ cup shredded Cheddar cheese

Cube 2 slices bread and put in a greased 8 x 8 x 2-inch dish. Mix chicken, onion, pepper, celery, mayonnaise, salt and pepper and spoon over bread cubes. Beat eggs well. Add milk and beat to mix. Place 4 slices bread over salad; cover with egg and milk mixture. Cover and refrigerate overnight. When ready to serve, pour soup over soufflé. Cover and bake at 325° for 50 minutes. Remove soufflé from oven and sprinkle cheese over top. Yield: 6 servings.

Mrs. H. C. Fielder
(Mary Louise Mackey)

Chicken Soufflé

9 slices bread, crusts removed
4 cups cooked, cubed chicken
½ pound fresh mushrooms, sliced
¼ pound butter
1 (8-ounce) can water chestnuts,
   drained and sliced
½ cup mayonnaise
9 slices Old English cheese
4 eggs

2 cups milk
½ teaspoon salt
1 (10½-ounce) can cream of celery
   soup, undiluted
1 (10½-ounce) can cream of
   mushroom soup, undiluted
1 small can pimentos, sliced
Buttered bread crumbs

Butter a 9 x 13 x 2-inch pan; line with bread; top with chicken. Sauté mushrooms in butter; spread over chicken. Add water chestnuts; dot with mayonnaise. Place slices of cheese on top of layers. Beat eggs and milk with salt. Mix soups and pimento with egg and milk mixture; spoon over top of casserole. Cover with foil and refrigerate overnight or 24 hours. Bake at 350° for 1 hour and 45 minutes. The last 15 minutes, top with buttered bread crumbs. Crusts from bread slices may be used. Yield: 8 to 10 servings.

Mrs. Larry Lambiotte
(Carolyn Walker)

Hot Chicken Salad

4 cups cold, cut-up chicken chunks
2 Tablespoons lemon juice
¾ cup mayonnaise
1 teaspoon salt
½ teaspoon monosodium glutamate
2 cups chopped celery
4 hard-cooked eggs, sliced
¾ cup cream of chicken soup,
  undiluted

1 teaspoon finely chopped onion
1 (2-ounce) jar chopped pimento
  (optional)
1 cup shredded Cheddar cheese
1½ cups crushed potato chips
⅔ cup slivered, toasted almonds

Combine all but last 3 ingredients. Place in 9 x 13 x 2-inch baking dish. Top with cheese, potato chips, and almonds. Bake at 400° for 20 to 25 minutes or until bubbly. Flavor improves if refrigerated overnight before cooking. Yield: 8 servings.

Mrs. E. A. Buckner, Jr.
(Ruth Vicknair)

One-Dish Mexican Chicken

5 to 6 chicken breasts
1 large bag tortilla chips
1 (4-ounce) can green chilies
1 (10½-ounce) can chicken and rice
  soup, undiluted
1 (10½-ounce) can cream of chicken
  soup, undiluted

1 (8-ounce) carton sour cream
¾ pound shredded Cheddar cheese
1 head lettuce
2 tomatoes
Black olives
¼ pound Cheddar cheese
1 (8-ounce) jar picante sauce

Boil and bone chicken breasts. Chop into bite-size pieces. Crush ¾ bag of tortilla chips and place in bottom of 9 x 13-inch casserole dish. Mix green chilies, soups, sour cream, and ½ to ¾ pound of shredded cheese with chicken. Top with remaining crushed tortilla chips and bake at 350° for 30 minutes. Chop lettuce, tomatoes, and black olives and place on top of tortilla chips. Sprinkle remaining cheese and can of picante sauce over all. Yield: 6 to 8 servings.

Mrs. Hays Latham
(Suzanne Massengale)

Chicken Enchiladas

6 to 8 chicken breasts
2 cups chopped onion, divided
1 cup chopped green pepper
1/3 cup chopped fresh parsley
1 clove garlic, finely minced
1/2 cup butter
1 pound fresh mushrooms, sliced
3 cups chicken broth
2 Tablespoons flour
1 teaspoon chili powder
1 teaspoon cumin
1 teaspoon salt

1/2 teaspoon pepper
1 Tablespoon coriander
1/4 teaspoon TABASCO brand
   pepper sauce
2 teaspoons sugar
1/2 teaspoon celery salt
1/2 teaspoon thyme
8 fresh tomatoes, chopped
2 packages flour tortillas
2 cups shredded Colby cheese
2 cups shredded Monterey Jack
   cheese

Boil chicken and reserve 3 cups broth. Bone chicken and tear into bite-size pieces. Sauté 1 cup chopped onions, green pepper, parsley, and garlic in butter. Add fresh mushrooms and sauté lightly with other ingredients. Add chicken broth. Bring to boil and add flour to thicken sauce. Lower heat. Season sauce with chili powder, cumin, salt, pepper, coriander, TABASCO, sugar, celery salt, and thyme. Add chopped tomatoes. Simmer for 30 minutes, stirring frequently. Add chicken. Sauce may be kept warm or frozen for future use. Preheat flour tortillas to soften. Fill each tortilla with 2 to 3 Tablespoons sauce, 1 Tablespoon Colby cheese, 1 Tablespoon Monterey Jack cheese, and 1 Tablespoon onion. Roll up and place flap-side down in a buttered 9 x 13-inch glass dish. Heat covered with foil for 30 minutes at 350°. Cover with sauce, sprinkle with cheeses, and continue to cook uncovered for 15 to 20 minutes until cheese bubbles. Yield: 8 to 10 servings.

Enchiladas may be frozen after covered with sauce. Add cheese topping when ready to use. Thaw slightly, top with cheeses, and heat.

Mrs. Steve Harris
(Linda Walker)

Coq au Vin

1 (4-pound) chicken, cut into pieces
½ to ¾ cup flour
Salad oil
2 cloves garlic, minced
1 small onion, sliced
3 large potatoes, cut in quarters
3 large carrots, cut in half

3 Tablespoons butter, melted
3 cups dry red wine
1 (3-ounce) can sliced mushrooms,
  liquid reserved
1½ teaspoons salt
1½ cups rice, cooked

Coat chicken pieces with flour. Brown a few pieces at a time in salad oil in a large skillet. Place pieces in a 9 x 13 x 2-inch casserole. Arrange garlic, onion, potatoes, and carrots around the chicken. Drain oil from skillet. Add butter, wine, mushrooms with liquid, and salt. Scrape browned bits from bottom. Pour over chicken. Cover and bake at 325° for 2 hours. Cook rice and mound in center of platter. Arrange chicken and vegetables around rice. Pour sauce over rice. Yield: 4 to 6 servings.

Mrs. Joseph P. Harris
(Susan Gunn)

Breast of Turkey in Marsala

1 pound thinly sliced raw turkey
  breast meat
½ lemon
½ cup or more seasoned flour

4 to 6 Tablespoons butter
⅓ cup Marsala wine
⅓ cup grated Parmesan cheese
⅓ cup chicken stock

Cut turkey into convenient size pieces for serving and flatten with a knife. Rub each piece on both sides with cut lemon; coat with seasoned flour. Melt butter in large frying pan over gentle heat; fry breasts for 10 minutes, turning until golden on both sides. Pour in Marsala and allow to bubble for a minute or so. Sprinkle each breast thickly with Parmesan and moisten with chicken stock. Cover pan and cook gently for another 5 to 10 minutes until turkey is tender and cheese is melted. Serve with pan juices poured over turkey. Chicken breasts or veal may be substituted for turkey. Yield: 4 servings.

Mrs. Kenneth Kussmann
New Orleans, Louisiana

Roast Turkey

1 turkey	1 onion, quartered
Salt	1 rib celery
Pepper	½ cup margarine
1 carrot	

If turkey is frozen, thaw according to package directions. Remove neck and giblets from neck and body cavity and reserve. Rinse and pat dry. Sprinkle cavity of turkey with salt and pepper. Place carrot, onion, and celery in cavity of turkey. Place on rack breast-side up in an open roasting pan. Drizzle margarine over entire turkey. Sprinkle lightly with salt and pepper. Place meat thermometer in fatty part of thigh, being careful not to let thermometer touch bone. Roast at 325° until meat thermometer reaches 185° or until the fleshy parts of drumstick feel soft when pressed with fingers. If turkey begins to get too brown during cooking, cover breast lightly with foil tent. When done, remove from pan, reserving drippings for giblet gravy.

The Editors

Corn Bread Dressing

1 recipe corn bread	½ cup chopped parsley
1 (6-ounce) package herb-seasoned bread stuffing	Salt
	Pepper
2 large onions, chopped	½ teaspoon leaf sage
4 to 6 ribs celery, chopped	1 teaspoon poultry seasoning
2 to 3 cloves garlic (optional)	Red pepper to taste
4 green onions and tops, sliced	½ cup chopped cooked giblets
1 cup butter, melted	
Turkey stock and drippings to moisten	

Crumble corn bread and mix with bread stuffing in large bowl. Sauté onions, celery, garlic, and green onions in melted butter. Add to bread stuffing mixture. Gradually add stock, mixing well. Dressing should be moist enough not to be dry after baking. Stir in parsley, seasonings, and giblets. Pour into 9 x 13-inch casserole and bake at 350° for 30 to 40 minutes. Yield: 12 servings.

Canned chicken stock may be used if turkey stock is not available.

The Editors

Sausage Stuffing

1 (16-ounce) package mild or sage
   pork sausage (½ pound chopped
   beef and ½ pound pork sausage
   may be substituted)
½ medium onion, finely chopped

2 ribs celery, thinly sliced
½ cup chopped parsley
Salt and pepper to taste
1 (8-ounce) package of herb-
   seasoned stuffing mix

Over medium heat, fry together sausage, onion, and celery until pork is browned and celery is tender. Stir in parsley. Salt and pepper to taste. Prepare stuffing mix as directed. Blend together stuffing and sausage mixtures. Yield: 8 servings.

This may be used to stuff poultry or as an accompaniment to a poultry dish.

Mrs. Joseph Letter, Jr.
(Linda Arlotta)

Giblet Gravy

Giblets and neck from 1 turkey
1½ quarts water
2 chicken bouillon cubes
1 onion, quartered
1 carrot, quartered
2 ribs celery with leaves
1 bay leaf
1 teaspoon salt

1 teaspoon black pepper pods
6 Tablespoons flour
½ cup water
2 hard-cooked eggs, sliced or
   chopped
½ to 1 Tablespoon Kitchen Bouquet®
   browning and seasoning sauce
   and gravy aid

Cover neck and giblets except liver with water in a pot. Add bouillon cubes, onion, carrot, celery, bay leaf, salt, and pepper. Boil, covered, for 1 hour. Add liver and cook 15 minutes longer. Add 1 cup stock to drippings in turkey roaster. Bring to a boil, stirring well to loosen all brown bits from sides of pan. Degrease if necessary. Add about 2 more cups giblet broth, stirring to blend. Reduce heat. Make a paste from flour and water until very smooth. Add slowly to gravy mixture and continue to cook slowly, stirring constantly until slightly thickened. Remove giblets and chop. Add to gravy along with eggs. Pieces of meat pulled from neckbone may be added also. Adjust seasonings. If color of gravy is not dark enough, add up to 1 Tablespoon *Kitchen Bouquet®.* Yield: 5 cups.

The Editors

Uncle Barney's Basting Sauce

½ cup butter
¾ cup vegetable oil
4 lemons and peel
1 (5-ounce) bottle Worcestershire
sauce

1 (5-ounce) bottle soy sauce
1 Tablespoon mustard
1 Tablespoon lemon pepper
½ cup white vinegar

Mix all ingredients in small saucepan. Bring to a boil. Use on any grilled meat. Especially good on chicken. Yield: 2 cups.

Mrs. Bubba Rainer
(Tricia Frey)

Best Barbecue Sauce

¾ cup chopped onion
½ cup salad oil
¾ cup ketchup
¾ cup water
½ cup lemon juice

3 Tablespoons brown sugar
3 Tablespoons Worcestershire sauce
2 Tablespoons prepared mustard
2 teaspoons salt
½ teaspoon pepper

Cook chopped onion in salad oil until tender and clear but not brown. Add remaining ingredients; mix well. Simmer 15 to 20 minutes. Yield: 2 cups.

Mrs. James A. Dupuy
(Kathryn Roussel)

Red Wine Barbecue Sauce for Chicken

2 cups white vinegar
2 cups sweet red wine
2 cups lemon juice
½ teaspoon paprika
1 Tablespoon TABASCO brand
pepper sauce

2 Tablespoons Worcestershire sauce
3 bay leaves, crumbled
1 teaspoon salt
1 teaspoon black pepper
1 teaspoon red pepper
Melted margarine

Heat slowly all ingredients except margarine. Simmer 20 minutes. Brush sauce on chickens last 15 minutes of cooking time over charcoal or on gas grill. Remove chickens from heat and brush with melted margarine to seal in flavor. Yield: 6 cups.

Mrs. Oren Bailess
(Betty Dement)

Seafood

Shrimp Pontalba

½ pound mushrooms, thinly sliced
¾ cup butter, divided
1½ cups finely chopped green
   onions
5½ Tablespoons flour
3 cups milk

1 teaspoon salt
½ teaspoon red pepper
⅔ cup white wine
3 cups precooked shrimp
2 egg yolks, beaten
Paprika

Sauté mushrooms in 2 Tablespoons butter and set aside. In a large skillet, melt remaining butter and sauté onions until tender. Blend in flour and cook slowly for 5 minutes, stirring constantly. Remove from heat. Gradually stir in milk until smooth. Add salt, pepper, and wine. Bring to a boil. Reduce heat and simmer and stir 10 minutes to thicken sauce. Add shrimp and mushrooms, stirring lightly for 1 minute. Remove from heat and quickly beat in egg yolks. Spoon into 8 ramekins. Sprinkle with paprika and heat under broiler. Yield: 8 servings.

Mrs. James W. Cook
(Naomi Paquette)

East Indian Curried Shrimp

1 small onion, minced
1 celery heart, finely chopped
2 Tablespoons butter
2 Tablespoons flour
1 teaspoon curry powder
Pinch of thyme
1 bay leaf
3 pints chicken broth
1 small tart apple, peeled and cut
   up

Dash of TABASCO brand pepper
   sauce
Salt and pepper to taste
1 teaspoon monosodium glutamate
2 pounds shrimp, cooked
2 Tablespoons butter
Steamed rice, buttered and parslied

To make sauce, sauté onion and celery in butter. Add flour, curry powder, thyme and bay leaf. Blend well. Add chicken broth, apple (do not omit), TABASCO, salt and pepper. After apple begins to soften, strain. Add monosodium glutamate. Sauté shrimp in butter. Blend with sauce and serve over rice. Yield: 8 servings.

Mrs. Earl Hilderbrand
(Vivian Penley)

Curry of Shrimp

⅓ cup butter or margarine	3 cups cleaned, cooked shrimp
3 Tablespoons flour	1 Tablespoon freshly squeezed
1 to 3 Tablespoons curry powder	lemon juice
½ teaspoon salt	1 teaspoon sherry
¼ teaspoon paprika	1 teaspoon onion juice
Dash of ground nutmeg	Dash of Worcestershire sauce
2 cups light cream	Salt to taste

Melt butter; blend in flour, curry powder, salt, paprika, and nutmeg. Gradually stir in cream; cook until mixture thickens, stirring constantly. Add remaining ingredients; heat thoroughly. Serve with curry condiments and Orange Rice. Yield: 4 to 6 servings.

Orange Rice

1 cup uncooked long grain rice	1 Tablespoon grated orange peel
2 cups water	½ cup orange juice
1 teaspoon salt	

Cook rice in boiling salted water until done. Add orange peel and juice. Stir and serve.

Mrs. Glover Warner
(Peggy Holder)

Beer Batter Shrimp

1 pound large raw shrimp	1 egg
1 cup flour	¾ cup beer
½ teaspoon lemon pepper seasoning	Oil for frying

Shell and clean shrimp and split partially down back. Open and flatten slightly. Lightly mix flour, lemon pepper seasoning, egg, and beer to a medium batter. Don't overmix. Dip shrimp in batter and then deep fry at 375° until lightly browned. Drain and serve with favorite seafood sauce. Yield: 2 to 3 servings.

Let opened beer stand for a few minutes or it will foam up when added to mixture.

Mrs. William L. Murphy
(Rosemary Hosemann)

Boiled Shrimp with Remoulade Sauce

2 pounds shrimp, thawed, boiled,
  and peeled
½ lemon
1 small onion, cut up
2 bay leaves

1 rib celery, cut up
Peppercorns
¼ cup salt
Shrimp-crab boil can be
  substituted for above seasonings

To cook 2 pounds of shrimp, bring 2½ quarts water to a boil. Add lemon, onion, bay leaves, celery, and a few peppercorns. Add shrimp and boil for exactly 10 minutes. Add salt, take off heat, and let sit 15 minutes. Drain.

Remoulade Sauce

1 cup mayonnaise, preferably
  homemade
½ cup (5¼-ounce) jar Creole
  mustard
3 teaspoons grated onion

1 teaspoon horseradish
1 teaspoon lemon juice
1 teaspoon Worcestershire sauce
Shredded lettuce
Tomatoes, wedged or whole

Combine first 6 ingredients. Adjust seasonings to taste. Mix with peeled shrimp and serve over shredded lettuce and tomato wedges or stuff into whole tomatoes for main dish. Yield: 4 servings.

Mrs. C. B. Patterson
(Sue Nelson)

Shrimp Normon

2 to 3 pounds raw headless shrimp
  in shell
½ cup vegetable oil
1 Tablespoon salt

½ teaspoon red pepper
Black pepper
2 medium onions, thinly sliced
2 to 3 cups water

Rinse shrimp and drain well. Shrimp should be almost dry. Heat oil over medium heat in a large, heavy pot. Add shrimp and toss until all completely turn pink. Add salt, red pepper, and a generous amount of black pepper. Add onions; stir and cook about 5 minutes. Add water to half cover shrimp. Cover and simmer about 20 minutes until tender. Let cool until barely warm. Serve with sauce for dipping shrimp. Yield: 4 to 6 servings.

Mrs. Kermit Hymel
Metairie, Louisiana

Scampi I

4 pounds headless jumbo shrimp (10
* to 12 shrimp per pound)*
1 lemon, divided
2 cups butter

6 cloves garlic
1 Tablespoon finely chopped parsley
1 Tablespoon cayenne pepper

Thoroughly wash shrimp. Peel and place side by side in glass baking dish, making sure shrimp are not on top of each other. Squeeze juice of ½ lemon over shrimp. Slice remaining ½ lemon into 6 finely sliced pieces and place in baking dish. Melt butter. Finely chop garlic and place in butter. Add chopped parsley to butter and garlic mixture. Sprinkle pepper over shrimp, then pour butter and garlic mixture over this. Cover tightly and bake at 350° for 30 minutes. Yield: 6 to 8 servings.

Garlic-butter combination may be poured over French bread and served with shrimp as a side dish.

Dr. Briggs Hopson

Scampi II

2 pounds shrimp, fresh or frozen
1 small clove garlic, finely chopped
1 cup butter or margarine
¼ teaspoon rosemary
¼ teaspoon basil

3 Tablespoons lemon juice
3 Tablespoons dry white wine
½ teaspoon salt
¼ teaspoon pepper, freshly ground

If shrimp are frozen, thaw in shell just to separate. Rinse in cold water and place in boiling water. Bring to a boil and cook for 1 minute. Drain shrimp and cool enough to handle. Remove shells and devein shrimp. If shrimp are already shelled, use only 1 pound and separate. Put minced garlic into melted butter in a medium skillet. Let stand over heat for a few minutes to frizzle garlic. Add herbs, lemon juice, wine, salt and pepper. Arrange shrimp in skillet and heat until shrimp are cooked, approximately 8 to 10 minutes. Yield: 4 servings.

Mrs. Jerry Mayfield
(Pam Jabour)

 Lemons will yield nearly twice the amount of juice if they are dropped into hot water a few minutes before squeezing.

Shrimp-Stuffed Bell Peppers

6 large bell peppers
2 onions, minced
3 cloves garlic, minced
4 Tablespoons cooking oil
½ pound shrimp, shelled and
    cleaned
1 teaspoon minced celery
½ teaspoon black pepper

1 bay leaf
1 teaspoon Worcestershire sauce
1 teaspoon salt
1 large pinch of thyme
8 to 10 slices toast
1 egg
Bread crumbs
Butter

Split peppers; clean and trim. Boil 3 minutes. Take out and cool. Chop and set aside trimmings. Put onions and garlic in cooking oil and cook until brown. Add trimmings. Cut shrimp finely and add to onions and garlic. Add celery and seasonings. Cook for 10 minutes. Moisten the toast. Mix in well with onion and shrimp mixture; stir in egg. Cook an additional 5 minutes. Stuff pepper halves and lay flat on a pan; sprinkle with bread crumbs and dot with melted butter. Bake 20 minutes in 400° oven. Yield: 8 to 10 servings.

Louis Theobald

Spanish Supper

3 avocados
¼ cup lemon juice
3 Tablespoons olive oil or butter
2 Tablespoons chopped onion
1 clove garlic, minced
3 Tablespoons flour
1½ teaspoons chili powder
⅛ teaspoon TABASCO brand
    pepper sauce

½ teaspoon salt
1¼ cups tomato juice
2 cups diced cooked chicken or
    shrimp
¼ cup sliced ripe olives (optional)
½ cup shredded Cheddar cheese
Buttered bread crumbs or cracker
    crumbs

Cut avocados in half. Brush with lemon juice. Heat olive oil in skillet; add onion and garlic; cook until tender, but not brown. Add flour, chili powder, TABASCO, and salt; blend. Gradually add tomato juice, stirring constantly until mixture thickens and comes to a boil. Add diced chicken and olives. Heat. Remove from heat; add cheese and stir until melted. Spoon about ⅓ cup of hot mixture into cavity of avocado half. Top with buttered bread crumbs or cracker crumbs. Place in broiler. Broil until crumbs are lightly browned. Serve immediately. Yield: 6 servings.

Miss Mary Jane Jackson

Bill's Barbecued Shrimp

5 pounds shrimp with heads (26 to
  30-count per pound)
Salt and pepper to taste
3 bay leaves
¼ cup oregano

⅓ (2-ounce) bottle garlic juice
1 teaspoon TABASCO brand pepper
  sauce
2 pounds butter
6 large or 8 small lemons

Place shrimp evenly in large casserole or metal pan. Completely coat with salt and pepper until you think they are ruined. Crumble bay leaves and sprinkle evenly over shrimp. Sprinkle oregano, garlic juice, and TABASCO over shrimp. In separate pan melt butter. Squeeze lemon juice, pulp, and seeds into butter. Mix thoroughly and pour over shrimp. Preheat oven to 350° and cook covered for 30 to 40 minutes. Yield: 6 to 8 servings.

William W. (Bill) Ramsey

Chicken and Shrimp Casserole

8 whole cooked chicken breasts, cut
  into cubes
4 pounds boiled shrimp, peeled
3 (14-ounce) cans artichoke hearts,
  quartered
3 pounds fresh mushrooms, sautéed
  in butter

6 cups white sauce
2 Tablespoons Worcestershire sauce
1 cup sherry or white wine
½ cup freshly grated Parmesan
  cheese

Divide chicken, shrimp, artichokes, and mushrooms equally in 2 greased 3-quart or 9 x 13-inch casserole dishes. Make white sauce, adding Worcestershire and wine. Pour over chicken, shrimp, artichoke, and mushroom mixture. Top with cheese. Bake uncovered at 375° for 45 minutes. Yield: 18 to 20 servings.

White Sauce

2½ Tablespoons butter
2½ Tablespoons flour
½ teaspoon salt

Dash of white pepper and nutmeg
1 cup milk

Blend butter, flour, salt, pepper, and nutmeg over low heat until blended. Add milk and stir. Cook until thickened.

Mrs. William T. Harris
(Teresa Vaughn)

Shrimp Creole

⅔ cup vegetable oil
½ cup flour
1½ cups sliced green onions
1 cup chopped onion
¾ cup chopped green pepper
4 cloves garlic, minced
3 Tablespoons fresh parsley
1 (16-ounce) can tomatoes
1 (8-ounce) can tomato sauce
4 Tablespoons red wine
2 bay leaves

2 teaspoons salt
¾ teaspoon black pepper
½ teaspoon red pepper
¼ teaspoon dried basil
½ teaspoon dried thyme
2 slices fresh lemon
2 cups water or fish stock
  (approximately)
2 pounds raw shrimp, peeled
4 cups cooked rice

In a very heavy kettle heat oil and flour, stirring constantly. Cook and stir until a medium brown roux is formed. Add onions, peppers, garlic and parsley to cool the roux, then lower heat and continue cooking until vegetables brown slightly. Mix in tomatoes and tomato sauce. Add wine and seasonings and mix. Bring mixture to a low boil. Add water or stock to desired consistency. When mixture boils, reduce heat and simmer about 1 hour. Add shrimp; cover, and simmer for 20 minutes more; do not overcook shrimp. Adjust seasonings if necessary. Serve over boiled rice. Yield: 6 to 8 servings.

Mrs. Jack Stamm, Jr.
(Laurin Fields)

Susie's Shrimp Creole

1⅓ cups chopped green pepper
1⅓ cups chopped onion
2½ cups chopped celery
½ cup butter
2 (16-ounce) cans tomatoes
1 (10-ounce) can tomato soup,
  undiluted
1½ Tablespoons salt
½ teaspoon pepper
2 Tablespoons brown sugar

3 bay leaves
8 whole cloves
2 teaspoons Worcestershire sauce
½ teaspoon TABASCO brand
  pepper sauce
1 Tablespoon lemon juice
⅔ cup white wine
5 pounds cooked shrimp
Cooked rice

Sauté green peppers, onions, and celery in butter in a Dutch oven. Add other ingredients except wine and shrimp. Simmer for about 2 hours. Add wine and shrimp. Serve over rice. Yield: 6 to 8 servings.

Mrs. Mark Prewitt
(Susie Harmon)

Beth's Shrimp Casserole

3 cups raw shrimp, peeled
9 Tablespoons margarine, divided
2 Tablespoons liquid shrimp boil
1 cup chopped onion
1 cup chopped green pepper
1 cup chopped celery
2 cloves garlic, minced
1 (10¾-ounce) can cream of shrimp
   soup, undiluted

1 (10¾-ounce) can Cheddar cheese
   soup, undiluted
⅓ cup chopped parsley
1 cup chopped green onion tops
1 (2-ounce) jar pimento
2 cups cooked rice
1 teaspoon salt
1 teaspoon pepper
¼ cup bread crumbs

Sauté shrimp in 1 Tablespoon margarine and shrimp boil. Set aside. Sauté onion, green pepper, celery, and garlic in remaining margarine. Add soups, parsley, onion tops, and pimento. Drain shrimp and add. Stir in rice, salt, and pepper. Pour into a 3-quart casserole. Sprinkle with bread crumbs. Bake for 30 minutes at 350°. Yield: 8 to 10 servings.

1½ pounds shrimp equal approximately 3 cups peeled shrimp.

Mrs. Mark Mazzanti
(Beth Guin)

Oysters Rockefeller

1 (10-ounce) package frozen
   chopped spinach
½ cup butter, softened
¼ cup cracker crumbs
½ cup bread crumbs, divided
6 green onions, finely chopped
2 ribs celery, finely chopped
⅓ bunch parsley
⅓ head lettuce, shredded

Dash of TABASCO brand pepper
   sauce
1 Tablespoon Worcestershire sauce
½ teaspoon salt
1 teaspoon anchovy paste
¼ cup grated Parmesan cheese
Ice cream salt
2 dozen oyster shells or ramekins
2 to 3 dozen oysters

Purée spinach in a blender or processor. Mix softened butter and ¼ cup cracker crumbs in a separate bowl. Add spinach and all other ingredients except ice cream salt and oysters. Fill a pie pan with ice cream salt. Heat in a 450° oven for 20 minutes. Place shells in pan and fill each with 2 or 3 oysters. Cover with 2 Tablespoons sauce. Bake at 450° for 30 minutes. If not brown, broil slightly. Yield: 4 servings.

Mrs. George Martin
(Barbara Gilmore)

Deviled Oysters

2 cups finely chopped onions
1¼ cups finely chopped bell pepper
1½ cups finely chopped celery
5 large cloves garlic, finely chopped
1 cup margarine
1¼ teaspoons salt
1 teaspoon dry mustard
½ teaspoon red pepper
½ teaspoon black pepper
3 Tablespoons Worcestershire sauce

2 Tablespoons lemon juice
½ gallon oysters, drained and
   chopped
3 cups toasted French bread crumbs
2 eggs
¾ cup milk
1½ cups chopped fresh parsley
½ cup chopped green onion tops
Melba rounds

Sauté onions, bell pepper, celery, and garlic in margarine for 10 minutes; do not brown. Add all seasonings, lemon juice, and oysters. Bring to boil. Remove from heat. Add bread crumbs. Beat eggs in milk and add to oysters. Mix in parsley and green onion. Check salt and red pepper as more may be needed, but as it "sits," it gets hotter. Will make a heaping ½ gallon. Serve in chafing dish with melba rounds. Can be made in the morning and reheated later. May be served as a casserole. Yield: 60 servings.

Miriam Graeber Cohn
Port Gibson, Mississippi

Oysters Randall

2 (12-ounce) jars oysters
1 cup chopped celery
1 cup chopped green onions
1 clove garlic
1 Tablespoon chopped parsley
¼ cup chopped bell pepper
½ cup butter
2 (14-ounce) cans artichokes,
   drained

1 (6-ounce) can sliced mushrooms
1 (10½-ounce) can cream of
   mushroom soup, undiluted
½ teaspoon salt
½ cup white wine
1 cup coarse bread crumbs

Bring oysters to a boil in own juice. Drain and reserve liquid. Sauté celery, green onions, garlic, parsley, and bell pepper in butter. To vegetable mix add oysters, artichokes, mushrooms, and oyster liquid. Add mushroom soup, salt, and wine. Slowly stir in bread crumbs. Spoon into 12 ramekins or a 9 x 13-inch casserole. Heat 20 to 30 minutes in 350° preheated oven. Yield: 12 servings.

Mrs. E. A. Buckner, Jr.
(Ruth Vicknair)

Oysters Bienville

2 (8-ounce) cans shrimp, chopped
1 (6-ounce) can sliced mushrooms
3 ounces white wine, divided
1 bunch green onions, finely
  chopped
½ cup butter
3 Tablespoons flour
1 pint chicken broth
3 egg yolks
½ cup evaporated milk
3 pints oysters
¼ teaspoon paprika
1 teaspoon oregano
Salt and white pepper to taste
TABASCO brand pepper sauce to
  taste
¼ cup shredded Cheddar cheese

Mix shrimp, mushrooms, and 1½ ounces wine. Set aside. Sauté onions in butter; add flour, and stir over low heat. Add chicken broth, which has been heated, slowly stirring constantly. Add shrimp mixture and cook slowly until thick. Beat egg yolks well with 1½ ounces wine and evaporated milk. Slowly pour the warm sauce into this egg mixture; cook, stirring constantly until thick, about 2 to 3 minutes. Cook oysters in their own liquor until edges curl. Strain oysters from liquor reserving ½ cup liquor to pour in sauce. Pour liquor into sauce. Cook sauce an additional 8 to 10 minutes. Pour ½ sauce in casserole. Add seasonings, then layer oysters, and the last of the sauce. Sprinkle with cheese. Bake at 400° for 35 to 40 minutes. Yield: 8 to 10 servings.

Mrs. Gerald Rankin
(Judy McClure)

Fried Oysters

1½ pints fresh oysters
1 cup yellow corn meal
2 teaspoons salt
1 Tablespoon flour
¾ teaspoon black pepper
⅛ teaspoon cayenne
Vegetable oil for frying

Drain oysters thoroughly in colander. Combine corn meal, salt, flour, black pepper, and cayenne in a small bowl. Roll oysters in meal a few at a time, coating evenly. Fry a few at a time in deep oil heated to 375°. Fry about 2 minutes or just until light brown. Drain on paper towels. Keep warm in 200° oven until all oysters are fried. Yield: 4 servings.

Serve with Red Carpet Cocktail Sauce (see Index).

Mrs. Bill Beanland
(Martha Spencer)

Oysters Johnny Reb

2 quarts oysters, drained
½ cup finely chopped parsley
½ cup chopped green onions
2 Tablespoons lemon juice
½ cup butter or margarine, melted
2 cups fine cracker crumbs

1 Tablespoon Worcestershire sauce
Salt and pepper to taste
TABASCO brand pepper sauce
Paprika
6 Tablespoons milk
6 Tablespoons light cream

Place a layer of oysters in bottom of greased, shallow, 2-quart baking dish. Sprinkle ½ parsley, onions, lemon juice, butter, crumbs, Worcestershire, salt, pepper and TABASCO over oysters. Make another layer of same. Sprinkle with paprika. Just before baking, make evenly spaced holes in oyster mixture. Pour milk mixed with cream into holes, being careful not to moisten crumb topping all over. Bake at 375° for 30 minutes or until firm. Yield: 10 to 15 servings.

Warren Asher

Mother's Deviled Oysters

4 slices stale bread
2 pints oysters, drained, reserving
   juice
3 eggs
Grated rind of 1 lemon
6 green onions, finely chopped
1 cup finely chopped celery
1 cup finely chopped bell pepper

½ cup margarine or butter
1 Tablespoon Worcestershire sauce
TABASCO brand pepper sauce to
   taste
Black pepper to taste
Cracker crumbs
Butter or margarine

Crumble bread in mixing bowl. Add oysters, oyster juice and eggs. Mix well. Add grated lemon rind. Beat well. Sauté onions, celery and bell pepper in margarine until transparent. Be careful not to let burn. Add oyster mixture, Worcestershire, TABASCO and black pepper. Cook, stirring constantly, until oysters curl. Place mixture in casserole or individual ramekins or shells sprayed with non-stick cooking spray. Sprinkle cracker crumbs on top. Dot with butter or margarine. Bake in preheated 350° oven about 30 to 40 minutes until bubbly and slightly browned. Yield: 6 to 8 servings.

Mrs. Charles J. Faulk
(Elizabeth Young)

Stuffed Oysters in Shells

1 rib celery, finely chopped
1 medium onion, finely chopped
1 Tablespoon chopped parsley
½ cup butter or margarine, divided
6 or more slices of bread
1 pint oysters
1 large or 2 small eggs, beaten
Dash of red pepper, salt, and black
*   pepper*
1 Tablespoon Worcestershire sauce
*   or to taste*
Bread or cracker crumbs

Cook finely chopped celery, onion, and parsley in ¼ cup butter slowly until tender. Soak bread in water then squeeze out. Wash oysters; then cut up fine. Mix beaten eggs, bread, vegetables, and seasonings well. Add oysters and cook slowly until eggs and oysters are done. Spray oyster shells with non-stick cooking spray. Fill shells with this mixture; then sprinkle cracker or bread crumbs over top and pour ¼ cup melted butter on top of crumbs. Place filled shells on baking tin or shallow pan. Bake when ready to serve in 400° oven until light brown. Serve hot. Yield: 12 servings.

Mrs. J. T. Selby
(Ella Beth Rhodes)

Oyster Shells

Scrub oyster shells with stiff brush, using lots of water. Get all debris off. Put shells in hot water with a strong dry detergent. Let soak for 24 hours. Rinse thoroughly. Mix ¼ cup bleach with 2 gallons of water. Soak shells for another 24 hours. Rinse again. Now put shells in flat cardboard boxes or trays in single layers. Let sun dry for 24 hours. Rinse again. Put shells in a 300° oven for 1 hour. If any odor at all remains, wait for a rainy day and let sit out in the rain. In an emergency put shells in dishwasher in a large colander and run through regular cycle. This is enough solution to clean 6 dozen oyster shells. To reuse, just wash in the dishwasher as you would any serving shell.

Mrs. Barry W. Holcomb
(Pat Horne)

 Wash hands with toothpaste to remove the smell after cleaning or shelling fish or seafood.

Barbecued Oysters

3 cups oysters
¾ cup flour

Seasoned salt and pepper to taste
1½ cups barbecue sauce

Drain oysters. Mix flour, salt, and pepper in grocery sack. Shake oysters in flour mixture. Sauté oysters in hot oil just enough to form a crust, but not enough to completely cook. Place oysters in an oblong baking dish and cover oysters with barbecue sauce. Bake in 350° oven for 20 to 25 minutes. Yield: 6 to 8 servings.

Mrs. Robert M. Abraham
(Billie Patterson)

Wild Rice and Oyster Casserole

2 (6-ounce) packages long grain and
   wild rice with seasonings
5 cups beef stock
½ cup butter or margarine

3 pints oysters, drained and liquid
   reserved
3 cups mushroom sauce

Cook rice according to directions using beef stock in place of water. When rice is cooked, add butter. Heat oysters in pan just long enough for the edges to curl. Spoon ½ the rice mixture in buttered 2-quart casserole. Arrange ½ oysters on top. Cover with remaining rice mixture and oysters. Spoon mushroom sauce over all. Bake for 30 minutes in a 325° oven. Yield: 8 to 10 servings.

Mushroom Sauce

¼ cup chopped onion
3 Tablespoons butter or margarine
3 Tablespoons flour
1 cup oyster liquid

1 (8-ounce) can mushroom pieces
2 teaspoons curry powder
½ cup heavy cream

Sauté onions in butter. Add flour. Stir gently and when bubbly, add oyster liquid, stirring with wire whisk or wooden spoon until thickened. Add remaining ingredients.

Mrs. Richard G. Hastings
Port Gibson, Mississippi

Escalloped Oysters

1 cup margarine
1 cup flour
1½ teaspoons paprika
½ teaspoon salt
¼ teaspoon black pepper
Dash of cayenne pepper
2 medium onions, chopped

1 green pepper, chopped
½ clove garlic, minced
1 Tablespoon lemon juice
1 Tablespoon Worcestershire sauce
1 quart oysters, liquid reserved
¼ cup cracker crumbs

Heat margarine in pan until melted. Mix in flour, stirring with a whisk until smooth. Return to heat and slowly brown to light color. Add paprika, salt, pepper, and cayenne. Take off heat and add onions, green pepper, and garlic. Cook slowly for 5 minutes, stirring constantly. Take off heat again; add lemon juice, Worcestershire, oysters, and their liquid. Stir well. Pour into a 9 x 13-inch baking dish; sprinkle with crumbs and bake in 400° oven for 30 minutes. Yield: 4 to 6 servings.

Mrs. William Patterson
Union City, Tennessee

Sandy's Oyster and Eggplant Casserole

2 medium or 3 small eggplants
Salt
3 green onions, chopped
1 small yellow onion, chopped
2 ribs celery, chopped
¼ cup chopped fresh parsley

5 Tablespoons margarine, divided
1 (12-ounce) jar oysters
¼ to ½ cup dried bread crumbs
½ cup Parmesan cheese
Salt and pepper to taste

Peel and cube eggplants and boil in salted water until tender. Drain. Meanwhile, sauté onions, celery, and parsley in 3 Tablespoons margarine until clear and tender. Combine with eggplant. Cook oysters in their juice over medium heat just until edges curl. Drain, reserving juice, and chop into small pieces. Stir oysters into eggplant mixture. Add bread crumbs until consistency of dressing. If mixture gets too dry, add a little oyster juice. Stir in Parmesan cheese, reserving a little for top. Season with salt and pepper. Place mixture in buttered 2-quart casserole. Dot with remaining margarine and sprinkle with Parmesan. Bake at 350° until hot and bubbly, about 45 minutes. Yield: 6 to 8 servings.

Mrs. George Guider
(Annie Lee Faulk)

Crabmeat Casserole

5 Tablespoons butter
3 Tablespoons flour
2 cups milk, warmed
2 Tablespoons minced onion
½ teaspoon celery salt
1 Tablespoon grated orange rind
   (optional)
1 Tablespoon minced parsley
1 Tablespoon minced green pepper

1 pimento, minced
2 Tablespoons sherry
1 egg, beaten
Dash of hot sauce
1 teaspoon salt
Pepper to taste
1 pound fresh crabmeat
Bread crumbs
1 Tablespoon butter

Melt butter in a heavy-bottomed saucepan. Stir flour into the melted butter until mixture is smooth. Cook over low heat for several minutes, stirring to eliminate any raw flour taste. Remove pan from heat and add milk, beating constantly with wire whisk. Return sauce to medium heat and cook until thickened. Add next 6 ingredients and remove from heat. Add sherry. Add a little of the above hot sauce to egg; then add egg to rest of the sauce. To this mixture add hot sauce, salt, pepper, and crabmeat. Pour into 1½-quart casserole. Top with bread crumbs mixed with melted butter. Bake at 350° for 15 to 20 minutes. Yield: 6 to 8 servings.

Mrs. Bill Monsour
(Linda Shannon)

Deviled Crab

2 eggs, well beaten
1 (5½-ounce) can evaporated milk
2 Tablespoons butter
4 to 5 green onions with tops,
   chopped

1 Tablespoon Worcestershire sauce
Salt to taste
1 teaspoon dry mustard
1 pound crabmeat
Cracker crumbs

Mix eggs, milk, butter, onion, and seasonings. Mix well, but gently to leave lumps of crabmeat. Add just enough cracker crumbs to hold mixture together. Place in crab backs, crab foils, individual ramekins or a casserole. Sprinkle lightly with cracker crumbs. Bake at 400° for 20 minutes or until lightly browned. Yield: 4 to 6 servings.

This is an excellent stuffing for bell peppers.

Mrs. W. J. Gunn
(Blanche Simmons)

Nancy's Crab and Shrimp Casserole

¼ cup butter
1 pound fresh mushrooms, sliced
5 Tablespoons flour
2 cups light cream
¼ cup sherry
2 cups mayonnaise
½ cup minced parsley

½ cup green onions, chopped
3 cups bread crumbs
1 pound crab, well cleaned
1 pound shrimp, cooked and peeled
2 (14-ounce) cans artichokes,
    chopped
Parmesan cheese to taste

Melt butter; sauté mushrooms. Add flour. Carefully blend in cream, adding a little at a time until thick sauce forms. Add sherry and cool. Next add mayonnaise, parsley, green onions, and bread crumbs. Carefully stir in crab and shrimp. Grease a 9 x 13-inch casserole. Place chopped artichokes in casserole and spread crab and shrimp mixture over artichokes. Sprinkle top with Parmesan cheese. Bake at 350° for 30 to 40 minutes. Yield: 12 servings.

Mrs. Henry Dowling
Meridian, Mississippi

Crabmeat Elegant

1 cup soft bread pieces without
    crust (pieces should be nickel-
    size)
1 cup heavy cream
1 teaspoon hot Creole mustard
1 Tablespoon dry vermouth or
    sherry
Salt to taste

White pepper to taste
2 egg yolks
1 pound lump crabmeat
½ cup crushed Ritz crackers
¼ cup butter, softened
Celery salt
Paprika

In a pan, stir together bread and cream. Cook, stirring until thickened, but do not boil. Add mustard, vermouth, salt, white pepper, and eggs. Blend over heat, but do not boil. Fold in crabmeat. Place in buttered 2-quart casserole dish or ramekins. Mix cracker crumbs, butter, celery salt, and enough paprika to make topping red. Spread over casserole. Heat in 350° oven for 15 to 20 minutes. Yield: 6 to 8 servings.

Mrs. William L. Geary
New Orleans, Louisiana

When serving crab as an appetizer, allow ¼ to ⅓ cup flaked, fresh crab per person.

Crab St. Jacques

½ cup butter or margarine, divided
2 Tablespoons flour
½ teaspoon salt
1 cup light cream
½ pound mushrooms, sliced

1 medium onion, minced
2 Tablespoons parsley
8 ounces to 1 pound frozen or fresh
 lump crabmeat
3 Tablespoons sherry

In a small saucepan, blend ¼ cup melted butter with flour and salt. Stir in cream gradually. Cook, stirring constantly over a medium heat until thick and smooth. In another pan, sauté mushrooms, onion, and parsley in the remaining ¼ cup butter. Add crabmeat and sherry and toss to mix. Add cream sauce and mix well. Spoon into shells or ramekins. Broil until bubbly. Yield: 6 servings.

Mrs. Jerry Mayfield
(Pam Jabour)

Easy Crabmeat Casserole

1 pound fresh lump crabmeat
4 ounces cream cheese, cubed
4 ounces shredded Cheddar cheese

¼ cup milk
2 ounces sherry

Mix all ingredients and put into a 2-quart glass casserole dish. Bake at 350° for about 35 minutes. Yield: 4 to 6 servings.

Mrs. Landy Teller, Jr.
(Peggy Hossfeld)

Catfish with Christianne Sauce

8 catfish fillets
2 Tablespoons butter
Juice of 1 lemon
½ cup butter
2 Tablespoons flour
½ cup milk

Liquid from mushrooms
Juice of 1½ to 2 lemons
1 cup mushrooms, liquid reserved
¼ cup dry white wine
¼ cup chopped parsley

Bake fish at 375° approximately 20 minutes with butter and sprinkled lemon juice. Combine in saucepan all but last 3 ingredients. Simmer for 10 minutes. Add mushrooms, wine, and chopped parsley. Pour over fish. Bake 10 minutes more. Yield: 6 to 8 servings.

Mrs. Arthur Pigott
Indianola, Mississippi

Shrimp-Stuffed Catfish

2 cups shrimp, cooked and peeled
2 eggs
1 cup light cream
½ cup cooking sherry
1 cup chopped green onions
2 Tablespoons chopped fresh
   parsley

½ cup chopped mushrooms
Salt, pepper, and paprika to taste
12 large catfish fillets
Lemon wedges
Fresh parsley

Finely chop shrimp. Add eggs, cream, sherry, onions, 2 Tablespoons parsley, mushrooms, and seasonings. Divide mixture evenly on 6 fillets in a 9 x 13-inch baking dish. Spread out and top with remaining fillets. Bake at 350° for 45 minutes. Serve with lemon wedges and parsley. Yield: 6 servings.

Mrs. Buddy Baker
(Lynn Hilderbrand)

Fish Fillet Baked in Foil

1 medium red onion, sliced
2 Tablespoons chopped parsley
½ teaspoon thyme
3 Tablespoons white wine
6 Tablespoons olive oil
Salt and freshly ground pepper to
   taste, divided
¾ cup flour

3 pounds firm white fish fillets
   (flounder, trout, bass, catfish),
   cut into 6 fillets
Hot vegetable oil
2 large tomatoes, sliced
1 bay leaf, crushed
Juice of 1 lemon
6 lemon wedges

Combine onion, parsley, thyme, wine, oil, and salt and pepper. Line a pan with sufficient foil to cover and seal in the fillets tightly. Mix flour, salt, and pepper to taste in grocery sack. Shake fillets in flour mixture in sack. Sauté fillets in small amount of hot oil. Place fillets in foil and pour over wine and oil mixture. Cover fish with tomato slices and sprinkle with crushed bay leaf and lemon juice. Wrap and seal fish in foil and bake in 350° oven for 30 to 45 minutes. Check toward the end to prevent overcooking. Serve with lemon wedges. Yield: 6 servings.

Dr. Robert M. Abraham

 For 4 servings, allow 3 pounds of whole fish, 1½ pounds of fillets.

Maxwell's Trout Amandine

6 fillets of trout
1 cup milk
1 cup flour
1 teaspoon salt

¼ teaspoon pepper
¼ cup butter
3 Tablespoons light sherry
½ cup sliced almonds

Dip fillets into milk. Mix flour, salt, and pepper and sift. Roll fillets into flour so entire fillet is coated. Melt butter in skillet and sauté fillets, browning evenly on both sides. Just before removing fillets from skillet to warm platter, sprinkle fillets with sherry. After fillets have been removed, add almonds to skillet and sauté. Sprinkle almonds over fish. Yield: 6 servings.

Maxwell's Restaurant
Louise Maxwell

Red Fish Courtbouillon

1 cup vegetable oil, margarine, or
  butter
1 cup flour
1 bell pepper, chopped
1 bunch green onions, chopped
2 onions, chopped
4 cloves garlic, chopped
1 (6-ounce) can tomato paste
1 (8-ounce) can tomato sauce
8 cups warm water

1 Tablespoon Worcestershire sauce
½ lemon, sliced (no more)
Dash of TABASCO brand pepper
  sauce
6 to 8 pounds red fish or catfish,
  cut into pieces
Creole seasoning to taste
½ cup parsley flakes
Hot boiled rice

Heat oil in heavy skillet. When oil is hot, gradually sift in flour, stirring continuously until well mixed. Lower heat and continue stirring until chocolate brown. Remove roux from heat and pour into a Dutch oven. Place bell pepper, green onions, onions, and garlic into roux, stirring mixture until it stops sizzling. Add tomato paste and tomato sauce. Return to stove on low heat for a few minutes. Add warm water. Stir well. Bring to a boil. Add Worcestershire, lemon slices, and TABASCO. Lower heat, cover, and simmer at least 2 hours. Stir occasionally to prevent sticking on bottom. Season fish with seasoned salt and add to mixture. Bring to a boil; lower heat and simmer for 1 hour. Add more water if too thick. Add parsley before serving over boiled rice in a soup bowl. Yield: 8 servings.

Only use a spoonful of rice in each bowl. This is better when eaten like soup, not rice and gravy.

Mrs. Bubba Rainer
(Tricia Frey)

Market Red Fish

2 cloves garlic
½ cup margarine
Juice of 2 lemons
2 pounds fresh red fish

Fresh or dried basil
Creole seasoning salt
Pepper and paprika to taste
2 Tablespoons flour

Mince garlic finely. Melt the margarine and mix with garlic and lemon juice. Pour this over both sides of the cold fish and let sit until butter mixture firms, 3 to 4 minutes. Season fish with lots of basil and seasoning salt and pepper and paprika. Use any seasonings but do not leave out basil. Lightly coat with sifted flour. In a very hot non-stick skillet sear the fish fillets quickly, about 30 seconds on each side. This seals in the juices and lightly browns the fish. Remove from skillet and place fish in a jellyroll pan or shallow baking dish. Then run the red fish under a preheated oven broiler 2 to 3 minutes to a side, just until fish flakes easily with a fork. Do not overcook. Serve with pan juices. Yield: 4 to 6 servings.

Mrs. Jack Stamm, Jr.
(Laurin Fields)

Red Fish with Lump Crabmeat

6 pounds red fish fillets
Butter
2 lemons
⅓ cup finely chopped parsley
Cayenne pepper
2 pounds lump crabmeat
1½ pounds mushrooms, sliced

½ pound butter
1 Tablespoon lemon juice
⅓ cup finely chopped green onion
 tops
2 Tablespoons mayonnaise
½ cup Chablis wine

Wash red fish thoroughly and place individual strips into glass baking dish. Place 1 small slice butter on each piece red fish and squeeze small amount of lemon juice over each fillet. Sprinkle parsley on each piece of red fish; then sprinkle pepper lightly over each. Cover and bake at 350° for 20 minutes. While fish is baking, wash crabmeat thoroughly in cold water. Place in large mixing bowl. Sauté mushrooms in ½ pound butter with 1 Tablespoon lemon juice until lightly browned. Combine mushrooms with crabmeat. Add onions, mayonnaise, and wine, and mix well. Place crabmeat mixture on top of red fish and bake 20 more minutes. Yield: 12 servings.

Dr. Briggs Hopson

Red Fish Royale

1 pound red fish fillets (or flounder,
  snapper, or scamp)
1 Tablespoon lemon juice
⅛ teaspoon paprika
Salt and pepper
2 Tablespoons butter, melted and
  divided

1 Tablespoon flour
½ cup milk
¼ cup Italian bread crumbs
Parsley and lemon slices for garnish

Cut fillets into serving pieces. Place into greased shallow baking dish.
Sprinkle with lemon juice, paprika, and a dash of salt and pepper. In
saucepan, blend 1 Tablespoon butter with flour and a dash of salt and pepper; add milk all at once. Cook and stir until thick and bubbly; pour over
fish. Blend crumbs with rest of butter. Sprinkle over fish. Bake at 350° for
35 minutes. Garnish with parsley and lemon slices. Yield: 3 or 4 servings.

Mrs. R. R. Morrison, Jr.
(Twick Cooper)

Stuffed Flounder

6 (½-pound) flounder
2 medium onions, chopped
3 ribs celery, chopped
1 small bell pepper, chopped
2 eggs, beaten
3 teaspoons lemon juice
1½ cups seasoned bread crumbs

Salt and pepper to taste
Dash of TABASCO brand pepper
  sauce
Dash of cayenne pepper
1 pound lump crabmeat
1 (8-ounce) can shrimp
Butter to baste

Cut flounder down the middle. Take knife and cut around inside under
skin to make a pocket on each side of the slit. Sauté onions, celery, and bell
pepper until tender. Mix eggs, lemon juice, and bread crumbs. Add salt,
pepper, TABASCO, and cayenne. Check crabmeat for shells and add.
Drain shrimp and add. Stuff flounder with crab and shrimp mixture. Cook
1 hour at 350°, basting with butter. Watch carefully. Do not overcook.
Yield: 6 servings.

Mrs. Ben McLeod
Meridian, Mississippi

 *To thaw frozen fish, thaw slowly in the refrigerator instead of at
room temperature.*

Fried Bass Fillets

2 (8-ounce) packages frozen or fresh
    bass fillets
6 ounces beer
1 large egg

2 cups flour
2 cups yellow corn meal
1 teaspoon seasoned salt
1 (48-ounce) bottle cooking oil

If frozen, thaw fillets under cool, running water. Combine beer and egg and beat with fork until frothy. Combine flour, corn meal, and seasoned salt. Dip each fillet into egg mixture, then in meal mixture, breading evenly. Allow fish to stand 5 to 10 minutes. Meanwhile, heat oil in deep 9-inch iron skillet. Oil should be about 2 inches deep. When oil is sizzling hot, using tongs drop each fillet into oil. Allow to cook 2 to 3 minutes until lightly browned. Other fish may be substituted. Yield: 8 servings.

Mrs. Walter Heslep
Jackson, Mississippi

Bass and Artichoke Supreme

1 (14-ounce) can artichokes, drained
1 pound fillet of bass or other firm
    fish
¼ cup chopped onion
⅛ teaspoon tarragon leaves,
    crushed
2 Tablespoons butter

1 (10¾-ounce) can condensed cream
    of mushroom soup, undiluted
¼ cup milk
½ cup shredded sharp Cheddar
    cheese
4 cups cooked rice

Cut artichokes into fourths and arrange in a 10 x 6 x 2-inch or 1½-quart shallow baking dish. Top with fish cut into small fillets. In saucepan, cook onion with tarragon in butter until tender. Blend in soup and milk; pour over fish. Bake at 350° for 25 minutes or until done; top with cheese. Bake until cheese melts. Serve with rice. Yield: 4 servings.

Mrs. John F. Gussio, Jr.
(Shirley Nejam)

Microwave Roux

⅔ cup vegetable oil

⅔ cup flour

Mix oil and flour together in 1-quart measuring bowl. Microwave uncovered on high for 6 minutes. Stir. Cook for 30 seconds to 1 minute longer or until it reaches the desired brown color. Yield: 1⅓ cups.

The Editors

Crawfish or Shrimp Etouffée

1 cup butter
¼ teaspoon cayenne pepper
¼ teaspoon black pepper
1½ teaspoons salt
¼ teaspoon chili powder
2 Tablespoons paprika
2 pounds peeled crawfish or shrimp
   tails
2 medium onions, chopped
1 bunch green onions, chopped

1 bell pepper, chopped
4 cloves garlic, minced
4 cups water
2 Tablespoons flour
Scant ⅛ teaspoon liquid crab boil
2 Tablespoons finely chopped
   parsley
Cooked rice

Melt butter in Dutch oven. Measure all dry seasonings and add to butter. Sauté crawfish in seasoned butter for 6 minutes. Remove crawfish and set aside. Add chopped onion, green onions, bell pepper, and garlic to butter. Sauté well. Return crawfish to pan. Put water in a jar. Add flour and liquid crab boil to the water. Shake well. Pour into pan. Cook on low heat about 45 minutes. Stir occasionally. Sprinkle with parsley before serving over boiled rice. Yield: 8 servings.

Mrs. Bubba Rainer
(Tricia Frey)

Salmon Croquettes

4 slices bread
⅓ to ½ cup milk
1 (15½-ounce) can salmon
1 egg, slightly beaten
¼ teaspoon salt
⅛ teaspoon pepper

2 to 3 Tablespoons finely chopped
   onion
1 Tablespoon chopped parsley
   (optional)
¾ cup cracker crumbs
Vegetable oil for frying

Tear bread into pieces in a small bowl. Pour milk over bread and let soak. Drain oil from salmon. Remove bones, skin, and any dark brown parts of salmon. Lightly mash salmon in small bowl. Squeeze milk from bread. Mash well and add to salmon. Add egg, salt, pepper, onion, and parsley if desired and blend. Shape salmon mixture into patties, balls, or small logs. Roll in cracker crumbs. Fry in hot oil a few minutes on each side until golden brown. Yield: 4 servings.

May be served with a white sauce and a sprinkling of parsley.

Mrs. Walter Heslep
Jackson, Mississippi

Bay Scallops with Scallions

4 Tablespoons butter
1½ pounds bay scallops
Black pepper to taste
1 small bunch green onions, sliced

⅓ cup dry white wine
3 Tablespoons fresh parsley, finely
  chopped
Lemon wedges

In a large heavy skillet heat butter and sauté scallops seasoned with pepper very quickly until slightly browned, about 4 minutes. Remove scallops with a slotted spoon and put on a warmed serving dish. Sauté the onions in the same skillet over medium-high heat for 5 minutes. Do not brown. Add wine to deglaze the pan over high heat and cook until wine is reduced by half. Pour sauce over scallops; sprinkle with parsley and serve with lemon wedges to squeeze over scallops. Serve with additional hot butter if desired.

Mrs. Jack Stamm, Jr.
(Laurin Fields)

Seafood Quiche

1 (6-ounce) package frozen
  crabmeat, drained
1½ cups shrimp, deveined, cooked
  and chopped
8 ounces Swiss cheese, shredded
½ cup chopped celery

½ cup chopped green onions
2 (9⅝-inch) unbaked pie shells
1 cup mayonnaise
2 Tablespoons flour
½ cup dry white wine
4 eggs, slightly beaten

Combine crabmeat, shrimp, Swiss cheese, celery, and onions. Divide evenly, pouring into pie shells. Mix mayonnaise, flour, wine, and eggs. Divide evenly and pour over seafood mixture. Bake in a preheated 350° oven for 35 to 40 minutes.

Mrs. E. A. Buckner, Jr.
(Ruth Vicknair)

Sailing Stew

2 pounds shrimp, cooked and peeled
½ cup butter
1 Tablespoon garlic powder
1 (8-ounce) can crabmeat
1 (8-ounce) can minced clams with juice
1 (10½-ounce) can she-crab soup, undiluted
1 (19-ounce) can chunky clam chowder
1 cup parsley
4 Tablespoons flaked onions
¼ cup cooking vermouth
2 cartons light cream
Seasoned croutons
Dash of cayenne

Mix all but last 3 ingredients. Simmer for 20 minutes. Add cream just before serving. Float seasoned croutons on top with a dash of cayenne. Yield: 6 to 8 servings.

Mrs. Earl Hilderbrand
(Vivian Penley)

White Sauce

2 Tablespoons butter
2 Tablespoons flour
1 cup milk or cream
Salt
White pepper

Melt butter in a heavy pot or double boiler. Stir in flour to make a smooth paste. Very slowly, add milk to flour mixture. Stir over low heat until thickened. Add salt and white pepper to taste. Yield: 1 cup.

To prepare velouté sauce, substitute chicken broth for milk.

The Editors

Curry Sauce for Shrimp

1 (8-ounce) carton sour cream
⅓ cup mayonnaise
1 teaspoon grated onion
1 teaspoon curry powder
1 teaspoon lemon juice
¼ teaspoon Worcestershire sauce
⅛ teaspoon TABASCO brand pepper sauce

Mix all ingredients together in small glass or plastic bowl. Cover bowl and refrigerate for several hours before serving. It is important to make this several hours ahead of time or even a day or 2 in advance. Yield: 1 cup.

Mrs. Robert H. Weatherly
(Dannie Compton)

Spicy Remoulade Sauce

1 clove garlic, crushed
1 pint mayonnaise
2 Tablespoons horseradish Creole
  mustard
1 Tablespoon horseradish
4 Tablespoons lemon juice
2 Tablespoons Worcestershire sauce

Dash of TABASCO brand pepper
  sauce
Lemon pepper to taste
½ inch anchovy paste
3 Tablespoons chopped fresh
  parsley
2 Tablespoons grated onion

Mix all ingredients well. Adjust seasonings if necessary. Yield: 2 cups.

Mrs. Louis L. Patterson
(Theodocia Perry)

Vicksburg Dipping Sauce for Boiled Shrimp

½ cup chopped stuffed olives
½ cup finely chopped celery
2 medium onions, finely chopped
1 Tablespoon sweet pickle relish
1 pint mayonnaise
2 Tablespoons chili sauce

½ teaspoon horseradish
2 hard-cooked eggs, grated
1 Tablespoon Worcestershire sauce
Red pepper to taste
TABASCO brand pepper sauce to
  taste

Drain chopped vegetables between layers of paper towels. Stir vegetables into mayonnaise. Add chili sauce, horseradish, eggs, and Worcestershire. Add red pepper and TABASCO to taste and blend. Chill and serve with boiled shrimp. Yield: Approximately 5 cups.

Warren Asher

Red Carpet Cocktail Sauce

¾ cup ketchup
¼ cup chili sauce
2 Tablespoons fresh lemon juice
2 to 6 Tablespoons horseradish

1 Tablespoon Worcestershire sauce
2 to 4 dashes TABASCO brand
  pepper sauce

Mix all ingredients and chill. Yield: Approximately 1½ cups.

Serve with oysters, shrimp, or any seafood.

The Editors

Game

Venison Pepper Steak

2 pounds venison steak or round
  steak
½ teaspoon salt
¼ teaspoon pepper
¼ cup flour
¼ cup cooking oil
1 (16-ounce) can tomatoes

1¾ cups water
1 Tablespoon beef stock base or
  bouillon cube
½ cup chopped onion
1 clove garlic, minced
2 large green peppers, cut in strips
1½ teaspoons Worcestershire sauce

Cut steak into ½-inch strips and lightly salt. Mix salt and pepper with flour. Dredge meat and brown in hot oil. Set aside remaining seasoned flour. Drain tomatoes, reserving liquid. Add tomato liquid, water, beef stock base, onion, and garlic to the meat in skillet. Cover and simmer 1 hour and 15 minutes. Add green pepper strips and Worcestershire and simmer 5 minutes more. Blend in tomatoes and reserved flour and simmer about 5 minutes. Delicious with egg noodles or served over rice. Yield: 6 servings.

Butch Bailess

Venison Pie

1 pound ground venison
½ cup bread crumbs
¼ cup chopped onion
¼ cup chopped bell pepper
1½ teaspoons salt, divided
⅛ teaspoon oregano
⅛ teaspoon pepper

2 (8-ounce) cans tomato sauce,
  divided
1⅓ cups quick-cooking rice
1 cup water
1 cup shredded Cheddar cheese,
  divided

Combine venison, crumbs, onions, bell pepper, 1 teaspoon salt, oregano, pepper and ½ cup tomato sauce. Mix well and pat firmly in bottom and on sides of a 9-inch pie plate, fluting edges. Combine rice, water, ¼ cup cheese, remaining tomato sauce, and ½ teaspoon salt. Pour over meat. Cover with foil and bake at 350° for 25 minutes. Remove foil; add cheese and bake 15 minutes more. Cut into wedges. Yield: 6 servings.

Mrs. L. G. Horn
(Libby Latimer)

Venison Roast

1 venison roast
¼ cup vinegar
⅛ cup brown sugar
Salt
¼ cup flour
½ cup melted butter

½ cup ketchup
1 clove garlic, chopped
1 cup water
2 Tablespoons Worcestershire sauce
5 Tablespoons grated onion

Rub roast all over with vinegar mixed with sugar. Rub with salt. Sprinkle roast with flour. Place on rack in roasting pan. Pour a little water in bottom of pan. Bake uncovered in 500° oven until roast has browned. Make a sauce from remaining ingredients. Turn oven down to 350° and baste roast with sauce every 20 minutes, until all sauce has been used. If sauce gets too thick, add hot water. Cook until done, about 3 hours. Yield: 8 to 10 servings.

Mrs. George Rogers, Sr.
(Marion Todd)

Venison Ham

2 Tablespoons flour
2 Tablespoons vegetable oil
3 cups hot water
1 large venison ham roast
2 large onions, chopped coarsely
Salt and pepper to taste

1 (9-ounce) jar mustard pickle
3 Tablespoons vinegar
3 Tablespoons pancake syrup
4 Tablespoons Worcestershire sauce
1 (12-ounce) bottle chili sauce
Red pepper to taste

Combine flour and oil and cook over medium heat, stirring constantly, to make a brown roux. Add hot water gradually, stirring to blend. Place ham in roasting pan. Surround roast with onions, sprinkling some over top. Salt and pepper liberally. Pour roux over roast. Cover pan and bake 1 hour at 350°. Make a sauce with remaining ingredients. Pour sauce over roast and bake 3 more hours, uncovered for the last hour. Slice and serve with gravy over rice. Yield: 10 to 12 servings.

Mrs. Elmer Neill, Jr.
(Dorothy Stamm)

 Marinate venison in buttermilk overnight to lessen the wild flavor.

Venison Chili

3 Tablespoons bacon drippings
2 pounds ground venison
2 large onions, chopped
3 cloves garlic, minced
2 bell peppers, chopped
2 (1-pound) cans tomatoes
2 (8-ounce) cans tomato sauce
4 Tablespoons hot chili powder

1 teaspoon ground cumin
1 teaspoon paprika
2 to 3 teaspoons salt
Black pepper to taste
1 to 2 cups water
2 (16-ounce) cans chili hot beans or
kidney beans

Heat drippings in heavy pot. Add meat and cook until meat is slightly browned. Add onions, garlic, bell peppers and sauté until limp. Add tomatoes, tomato sauce, chili powder, cumin, paprika, salt, and pepper. Stir to blend. Add water and simmer about 30 minutes. Add beans and continue to cook about 30 to 45 minutes. Yield: 3 quarts.

Mrs. Debi Jones
Jackson, Mississippi

Bill's Baked Geese

2 geese
1 onion, quartered
1 rib celery, quartered
6 cloves garlic, smashed
1 Tablespoon salt
1 Tablespoon pepper
1 Tablespoon Tony Chachere's
Famous Creole Seasoning

8 strips thick-sliced bacon
1 cup vegetable oil
1 cup flour
TABASCO brand pepper sauce to
taste
Worcestershire sauce to taste
1 teaspoon leaf thyme

Place first 7 ingredients in large iron pot. Cover with water and cook covered 1 hour. Remove geese, reserving stock, and place in roaster. Sprinkle with additional Tony Chachere's seasoning. Layer 4 strips bacon over each goose. Bake in 400° oven for 15 minutes. Reduce heat to 300° and cook for 15 minutes. Meanwhile mix oil and flour in skillet. Cook over low heat to make a chestnut brown roux. Slowly add 3 or 4 cups goose stock to make a gravy. Season with TABASCO, Worcestershire, and thyme. Serve goose and gravy over white or wild rice. Yield: 4 servings.

William W. (Bill) Ramsey

Braised Goose with Wine Sauce

½ cup vegetable oil
2 medium onions, sliced
2 carrots, sliced
2 celery ribs, sliced
2 garlic cloves
½ teaspoon dried thyme, crumbled
1 bay leaf
1 (8 to 10-pound) goose

½ cup chopped fresh parsley leaves
Salt and freshly ground pepper to
taste
5 Tablespoons flour
4 cups chicken broth
2½ cups dry red wine
Watercress sprigs and brandied
fruit (optional garnish)

Preheat oven to 450°. Heat vegetable oil in heavy large skillet over medium heat. Add vegetables, garlic, thyme, and bay leaf and cook, stirring frequently, until browned, about 7 minutes. Add goose neck, heart, gizzard, and wing tips to skillet and cook, stirring, until browned, about 5 minutes. Remove from heat and stir in parsley. Pat goose dry with paper towels. Sprinkle cavity with salt and pepper. Spoon ½ vegetable mixture into goose. Truss goose. Transfer to deep roasting pan. Roast until browned on all sides, turning every 5 minutes, about 20 minutes total. Reduce oven to 325°. Add flour to vegetables remaining in skillet. Place over medium low heat and stir until browned, about 5 minutes. Whisk in chicken broth and wine; increase heat to medium high and bring to simmer, stirring. Add to goose. Cover goose and continue roasting until drumsticks move slightly in sockets and juices from fleshiest part of drumstick run yellow when flesh is pricked, about 1¾ to 3 hours, turning goose over halfway during cooking. Transfer goose to heated platter. Discard stuffing from cavity. Strain braising liquid into bowl and degrease. Pour into sauceboat. Garnish goose as desired. Serve sauce separately. Yield: 4 to 6 servings.

Mrs. Bob Coleman
(Cissy Wagner)

Gourmet Game Sauce

1 cup red currant jelly
2 Tablespoons prepared mustard
¼ teaspoon grated onion
⅛ teaspoon powdered ginger

Grated peel of 1 orange
Grated peel of 1 lemon
½ cup orange juice
2 Tablespoons lemon juice

Combine jelly and mustard in small saucepan; mix well. Add onion, ginger, and grated peels. Gradually stir in orange and lemon juice and cook over low heat, until sauce is blended. Use as a basting sauce when broiling or roasting game birds or serve hot or cold as a sauce for venison roast. Yield: 1½ cups.

Miss Enez Bourdon

Goose-In-A-Bag

1 large wild goose, cleaned and
  drawn
Garlic powder
Salt and pepper to taste
1 medium onion
1 rib celery

1 medium apple
1 stem fresh parsley
2 Tablespoons flour
1 (10½-ounce) can beef bouillon
½ can red wine

Sprinkle cavity of bird with garlic powder, salt, and pepper. Quarter onions, celery, and apple and stuff into cavity. Add parsley stem. Put flour in a commercial browning bag and shake well. Put goose into bag and carefully pour bouillon and ½ can red wine over goose. Twist end of bag lightly and secure according to directions on the package. Puncture top of browning bag with 6 slits. This is very important. Place in a preheated oven at 350° and roast 2 to 2½ hours. Remove goose from bag carefully. Pour gravy into pan and thicken with a little flour and water paste, if desired. Serve over rice. Ducks may be cooked the same way.

Mrs. Sally Wailes

Goose Kabobs

2 goose or duck breasts
1 (8-ounce) bottle Italian dressing

2 large onions
3 bell peppers
8 strips bacon

Skin goose breasts and remove from bone. Cut into 1-inch cubes. Marinate in Italian dressing for 48 hours, stirring twice daily. Light charcoal fire. While waiting for the fire to get to medium heat, quarter onions and separate into layers. Cut bell peppers into 1½-inch squares. Cut bacon into 1-inch pieces. On a skewer put bacon on each side of goose cube. Alternate onion and pepper with each piece of goose. Continue on skewers until all ingredients are used. Cook over medium heat 12 to 15 minutes, turning often and basting with remaining marinade. Yield: 4 servings.

German E. Jordan

Add 1 cup of orange marmalade to pan drippings for a quick and savory duck sauce.

Glenwood Duck

Water to cover ducks
4 wild ducks
2 onions, coarsely chopped
1 rib celery, coarsely chopped
1 Tablespoon black pepper

1 Tablespoon salt
4 Tablespoons vegetable oil
1 cup water
1 cup red wine
1 pound thick-cut bacon

Bring water to boil; add duck, onion, celery, pepper, and salt. Reduce heat. Cover pot and simmer for 1 hour. Remove duck; set aside to cool. Reserve stock. Rub ducks with oil inside and out. Salt and pepper ducks inside and out. Cut 3 slits on each side of each duck. Spoon stuffing lightly into duck cavity. Place on rack in roasting pan, breast side up. Put 1 cup water and red wine in pan. Cook at 450° for 15 minutes. Reduce heat to 325° for 1 hour. Last 15 minutes, cover breast of each duck with thick-cut bacon and baste with pan drippings. Yield: 6 to 8 servings.

Stuffing

Duck giblets or 2 chicken giblets
1 pound diced ham
3 Tablespoons cooking oil
1 large onion, chopped
1 bell pepper, chopped
1 rib celery, chopped
1 clove garlic, chopped

4 green onions, chopped
2 pints oysters, reserving juice
1 Tablespoon salt
1 Tablespoon black pepper
½ Tablespoon red pepper
4 cups cooked wild rice
1 cup chopped pecans

Brown giblets and ham in black iron pot in cooking oil until lightly browned. Add onions, bell pepper, celery, garlic, and green onions. Add oyster liquid. Cover and simmer 30 minutes. Add salt, pepper, and duck stock, if needed for moisture. Add red pepper and oysters. Cook slowly until oysters curl. Add wild rice. Mix gently and add pecans. Use extra dressing as a side dish.

William W. (Bill) Ramsey

Duck à l'Orange

3 to 4 ducks
Salt and pepper to taste
1 apple, quartered
1 onion, quartered
1 rib celery, cut in pieces
½ cup butter
1 (6-ounce) can frozen orange juice,
    not diluted

2 (6-ounce) cans mushrooms
1½ cups red wine
2 boxes long grain and wild rice
    with seasoning
½ cup chopped parsley

Season ducks with salt and pepper and stuff ducks with apple, onion, and celery. Place ducks in roaster and put pats of butter over duck. Pour orange juice, mushrooms, and wine over ducks. Bake covered for 4 hours at 400°. Baste once or twice during cooking. Sauce should thicken. Prepare rice according to package directions. Stir in parsley. Remove meat from ducks. Layer rice and ducks alternately. Pour sauce over and bake 1 hour at 375°. Freezes well. Yield: 10 to 12 servings.

Mrs. Babs Lopez
Opelousas, Louisiana

Enez's Wild Duck

2 wild ducks
2 Tablespoons butter
2 Tablespoons sherry
2 Tablespoons tomato paste
3 Tablespoons flour
1½ cups warm bouillon

1 teaspoon salt
¼ teaspoon pepper
½ cup dry red wine
½ pound sliced mushrooms
1 bay leaf

Cut ducks in half and completely cut out the backbones. Melt butter in a Dutch oven. Brown duck halves in butter, turning often, until they are dark brown. Pour sherry over ducks and allow to stand for 2 to 3 minutes. Remove ducks and stir well to deglaze the pan. Over low heat, stir in tomato paste. Stir in flour a little at a time until smooth. Gradually add bouillon, seasonings, and red wine. Bring mixture to a boil and add duck halves. Add mushrooms and bay leaf. Cover pot and cook over low heat for 1 hour. Remove duck pieces and strain; degrease sauce. Serve with rice. Yield: 4 servings.

Miss Enez Bourdon

Duck Gumbo

3 large or 6 small ducks
1 large onion, diced
½ Tablespoon black pepper

Tony Chachere's Famous Creole
Seasoning

Place ducks in large pot with enough water to cover. Add onion and pepper. Bring to a boil; reduce heat and simmer 2 to 6 hours. Remove ducks and let cool. Reserve stock. Bone ducks when cool and chop meat coarsely. Season generously with Chachere's seasoning.

1 cup vegetable oil mixed with 1
  cup flour
2 large onions, chopped
2 ribs celery, chopped
2 bell peppers, chopped
6 cloves garlic, chopped
1 pound fresh okra, chopped or 2
  (10-ounce) packages chopped okra
4 crumbled bay leaves

2 Tablespoons Worcestershire sauce
1 teaspoon red pepper
1 teaspoon thyme
2 teaspoons TABASCO brand
  pepper sauce
Salt and pepper to taste
Dash of filé powder
Rice, cooked

Make roux by cooking oil and flour mixture in a large pot until medium brown. Add onions, celery, bell peppers, garlic, and okra. Sauté for 15 to 20 minutes. Add duck meat and cook an additional 20 minutes. Skim grease from reserved stock and add to the mixture. (There should be enough stock to fill the pot ⅔ full; if not, add water.) Bring to a boil. Add bay leaves, Worcestershire sauce, red pepper, thyme, TABASCO, salt, and pepper. Reduce heat; cover and let simmer for 1 hour. Sprinkle with filé powder and serve over rice. Yield: 10 servings.

William W. (Bill) Ramsey

Baked Doves with Gravy

18 to 22 doves
Salt and pepper to taste
Flour
½ cup corn oil

½ cup chopped green onions
1½ cups water
½ cup sherry
½ cup chopped parsley

Salt, pepper, and flour doves. Brown in oil in Dutch oven at 400°. This takes about 1 hour. Add green onions, water, sherry, and parsley. Cover and reduce heat to 350°. Cook until tender, about 2 to 2½ hours. Makes a wonderful gravy. Serve with wild rice. Yield: 8 to 10 servings.

Mrs. German E. Jordan
(Judy Florian)

Julia's Ducks

2 wild ducks
1 onion, quartered
1 apple, quartered
1 orange, quartered

1½ cups butter (no substitute)
1 cup dry sherry
½ cup bourbon
Cooked wild or white rice

Rinse cleaned ducks. Stuff with the onion, apple, and orange pieces. Melt butter in a heavy Dutch oven. Add sherry and bourbon. Place ducks in Dutch oven and spoon liquid over ducks. Bring to a boil; reduce heat. Let simmer 2½ hours, basting several times during cooking. Serve over wild rice or wild and white rice mixed. Yield: 2 to 4 servings.

Mrs. Ted Houston
(Julia Donaldson)

Sis's Duck Recipe

4 ducks, cleaned thoroughly
1 apple
2 small onions
4 ribs celery
1 (3-ounce) box crab boil seasoning

Salt and pepper to taste
½ cup butter, melted
Lemon juice to taste
1 pound bacon

Stuff each whole duck with ¼ apple, ½ onion, and 1 rib celery. Simmer 3 to 5 hours in water, crab boil, salt, and pepper. Cook until tender or until meat separates from bone. Remove from water. Remove stuffing and score breast at ½-inch intervals diagonal to breastbone. Mix butter and lemon juice. Baste liberally with lemon butter. Completely cover duck breast with half pieces of bacon. Bake at 375° until bacon curls. Remove bacon before serving. Yield: 4 to 6 servings.

Mrs. Jerry Silver
(Sis Waring Hughes)

Easy Baked Doves

Black pepper to taste
4 wild doves

1 (10½-ounce) can French onion soup

Pepper doves and place in baking pan or dish. Pour soup over birds. Cover and bake at 350° for about 1 hour, basting every 15 minutes.

Vaughn Fields, Sr.

Dove Pie

6 doves
1 cup water
2 ribs celery
½ bell pepper
½ teaspoon crushed red pepper

1 teaspoon salt
1 recipe 2-crust pie pastry
¼ cup butter
Black pepper to taste

Place doves in pot with 1 cup water. Add celery, bell pepper, red pepper, and salt. Steam 45 to 60 minutes until birds are tender. Cool and bone doves. Reserve 1 cup broth. Line an 8-inch square baking dish with ½ pastry. Top with meat from doves. Dot with butter. Season with salt and pepper. Add reserved broth. Top with remaining pastry. Brush with melted butter. Bake at 350° until brown, about 1 hour. Yield: 4 to 6 servings.

Mrs. Buddy Bowen
Jackson, Mississippi

Smothered Duck, Dove or Quail

2 ducks or 6 to 8 dove or quail
2 Tablespoons white vinegar
½ cup butter
Seasoned salt and pepper to taste
1 (10½-ounce) can bouillon or
  consommé
½ envelope dry onion soup

2 Tablespoons Worcestershire sauce
Dash of TABASCO brand pepper
  sauce
Dash of Pickapeppa sauce
2 Tablespoons barbecue sauce
⅓ to ¾ cup wine, if desired

Pressure-cook game in water to which white vinegar has been added for 2 minutes. If a pressure cooker is unavailable, cook covered for 30 minutes. Transfer birds to a heavy skillet or Dutch oven. Salt and pepper birds. Brown quickly in butter. Lay breast-side down. Add bouillon or consommé and 1 can water. Add 3 Tablespoons vinegar water from pressure cooker. Add remaining ingredients. Cover skillet or Dutch oven and cook on low on range for 1 hour or until tender.

Mrs. George Martin
(Barbara Gilmore)

Freezing game and fish in water will keep it fresher longer.

Quail in Claret

2 quail, thoroughly cleaned and
  split lengthwise
1 ounce brandy
2 Tablespoons flour
4 Tablespoons butter or margarine
1 cup sliced fresh mushrooms

½ cup consommé or chicken stock
½ cup claret or any red Bordeaux
  wine
Pinch of celery salt
Fresh ground pepper
Juice of 1 orange, strained

Rub quail with a cloth soaked in brandy and dust with flour. Melt ½ butter in skillet and let it brown. Add quail and cover, allowing it to cook 5 minutes on each side. In a saucepan, melt remaining butter. When hot, add mushrooms and sauté until tender. To quail, add mushrooms, consommé, claret, celery salt, and pepper. Simmer gently about 10 minutes, until quail is tender. A minute or two before serving, add orange juice. Yield: 4 servings.

Mrs. Mickey Koestler
(Thelma Ragland)

Quail Bowen

Salt
Pepper
6 quail
½ cup water
2 bay leaves

¼ cup butter
2 cups pancake batter
½ teaspoon thyme
Vegetable oil for frying

Salt and pepper quail. In a large skillet put water, bay leaves, and butter. Add quail. Cover and steam on low for 1 hour or until quail are fork-tender. Make pancake batter and season with salt, pepper, and thyme. Dip each quail into batter, coating well. Fry in hot oil until lightly browned, just a few seconds. Yield: 3 to 6 servings.

Mrs. Buddy Bowen
Jackson, Mississippi

 When serving quail, allow 1 bird per serving.

Bill's Pheasant

1 pheasant
Salt to taste
White pepper to taste
1 cup flour
1 large white onion, chopped
1 bunch green onions, chopped

½ cup chopped parsley
4 cloves garlic, minced
1½ cups butter, divided
Dash of thyme
1½ cups dry white wine

Split in half or quarter pheasant. Salt and pepper pheasant; dredge in flour. Brown in pot or skillet and set aside. Sauté ½ chopped vegetables in same skillet. Line roasting pan with foil leaving enough foil to fold over. Preheat oven to 325°. Place sautéed vegetables in foil "boat" in roasting pan. Add ½ cup butter 2 Tablespoons at a time; add pheasant. Sprinkle thyme on pheasant and salt and pepper again. Pour 1 cup melted butter and wine over pheasant. Sprinkle remainder of vegetables over top. Seal foil and place in oven for 1½ hours. Yield: 2 to 4 servings.

William W. (Bill) Ramsey

Brunswick Stew

1 (5-pound) hen
1 squirrel or rabbit
¼ pound salt pork
3 cups water
1 pint butter beans
1 pint field peas
1 large onion, chopped
6 pods okra, sliced

½ cup celery, chopped
1 (16-ounce) can tomatoes
1 (16-ounce) can cream corn
4 medium potatoes, peeled and
    cubed
Salt and pepper to taste
TABASCO brand pepper sauce to
    taste

In a large pot, cook hen and squirrel or rabbit until meat falls off bone. Cut up with scissors and set aside. Cube salt pork and place in extra large container with water. Add butter beans, peas, onion, okra, and celery; cook over medium heat for 30 minutes. Add meat and remaining ingredients. Cook slowly for 1 hour, stirring occasionally to prevent sticking. This is best made a day before serving. Yield: 10 servings.

Mrs. Gordon L. Carr, Sr.
(Betty Ann Williams)

Sandwiches

Philadelphia Cheese Steak

1½ pounds beef (boneless rump or
  sirloin tip roast), sliced as thinly
  as possible
2 Tablespoons bacon drippings
1 medium onion, thinly sliced
1 medium bell pepper, cut in strips
  (optional)
Salt

Pepper
Butter or margarine, softened
4 to 6 po-boy or good sandwich
  buns
6 to 8 ounces white cheese
  (provolone, muenster, or
  mozzarella), shredded or thinly
  sliced

Cut beef slices into 1-inch strips. Heat bacon drippings in heavy skillet or grill. Add meat strips, onions, and green pepper all at once. Cook just until meat loses red color and vegetables are clear, tossing lightly as mixture cooks. *Do not overcook.* Move to heated platter. Salt and pepper to taste. Butter sandwich buns on both sides. Place butter-side down in hot skillet. Grill 2 to 3 minutes. Pile meat mixture onto buttered buns. Top with cheese and let heat from meat and bun melt cheese or run sandwich in microwave for 15 to 20 seconds on high. Yield: 4 to 6 servings.

Bruce Ebersole

Sausage Loaf

1 pound bulk sausage
1 loaf French bread
3 eggs
1 cup milk

6 ounces sharp Cheddar cheese,
  shredded
6 ounces Monterey Jack cheese,
  shredded

Cook sausage in heavy skillet until done; drain fat. Slice top off French bread lengthwise. Hollow out bottom of loaf; break into small pieces and toast to make about 3 cups bread crumbs. Beat eggs until foamy; add milk, ⅓ Cheddar cheese, ⅓ Monterey Jack cheese, drained sausage, and bread crumbs. Mix well. Fill bottom of bread loaf with mixture. Sprinkle remaining cheeses over mixture. Pack well. Cover with bread top. Wrap in foil. Bake at 300° for 30 minutes or until cheeses melt and seal the loaf together. To serve cut in 2-inch slices. Yield: 8 to 10 servings.

Mrs. Jerry Nations
Brookhaven, Mississippi

Reuben Sandwiches

8 slices rye bread
Creole mustard
4 slices corned beef

4 slices Swiss cheese
4 heaping Tablespoons sauerkraut
½ cup Thousand Island dressing

Spread each piece of bread with Creole mustard. Spread 1 slice corned beef, 1 slice Swiss cheese, and 1 heaping Tablespoon sauerkraut over 4 pieces of bread. Drizzle Thousand Island dressing over and cover with remaining bread. Heat, wrapped in foil for 10 to 15 minutes, at 350° in a conventional oven or microwave on medium 3 to 4½ minutes. Yield: 4 servings.

Mrs. Bill Beanland
(Martha Spencer)

Corned Beef Sandwich Spread

1 (12-ounce) can corned beef
1 rib celery, chopped
2 Tablespoons bell pepper, chopped
2 hard-cooked eggs, chopped
2 green onions, sliced
1 Tablespoon prepared mustard

2 Tablespoons Durkee Famous
   Sauce®
1 Tablespoon mayonnaise
TABASCO brand pepper sauce to
   taste
Black pepper to taste

Break up corned beef with fork. Mix with celery, bell pepper, eggs and onions. Toss lightly. Add mustard, Durkee Sauce® and mayonnaise to make spreading consistency. Season with TABASCO and pepper. "Durkee" and "Famous Sauce" are registered trademarks of SCM Corporation. Yield: 6 sandwiches.

Mrs. Jack Stamm, Jr.
(Laurin Fields)

 For a juicier hamburger, add cold water to ground beef before grilling (½ cup to 1 pound meat).

 Sprinkle salt in the bottom of the skillet when pan broiling chops, hamburgers, or steaks to prevent sticking and to help absorb the grease.

San Francisco Special

4 slices sour dough bread, buttered
    and toasted
4 slices cooked ham
4 slices Swiss cheese

4 large spinach leaves
2 hard-cooked eggs, sliced
Parmesan cheese
Mushroom sauce

On each slice of bread place a slice of ham and cheese. Top with spinach and egg slices. Pour mushroom sauce over top. Sprinkle with Parmesan cheese. Put under broiler until light and bubbly and cheese melts slightly. Yield: 4 sandwiches.

Mushroom Sauce

3 Tablespoons butter
3 Tablespoons flour
1 cup chicken stock
½ pound fresh mushrooms, sliced
2 green onions, sliced
1 clove garlic, crushed

½ cup white wine
1 egg yolk
½ cup milk or light cream
1 teaspoon lemon juice
Salt to taste
Pepper to taste

Mix together butter and flour over low heat to form a white roux. Add chicken stock and stir to blend. Meanwhile, simmer mushrooms, green onions, and garlic in wine. Add to roux. Beat egg yolk and stir in milk. Add a little of hot mixture to yolk mixture, beating well. Beat yolk mixture back into remaining sauce. Stir until slightly thickened. Season with lemon juice, salt, and pepper.

Miss Maggie Stamm

Corned Beef Burgers

1 (12-ounce) can corned beef
6 hot dog buns

1 (10-ounce) bottle Durkee Famous
    Sauce®

Crumble corned beef and warm in oven 10 to 15 minutes at 350°. Split buns and spread with Durkee Famous Sauce® Heap corned beef onto bun and drizzle with additional Durkee Sauce® Reheat slightly in warm oven. "Durkee" and "Famous Sauce" are registered trademarks of SCM Corporation. Yield: 6 sandwiches.

Mrs. Charles Faulk
(Elizabeth Young)

Muffaletto Sandwiches

1 loaf muffaletto bread
2 Tablespoons melted butter or
  margarine
Dash of oregano
½ cup olive oil
4 slices salami

4 slices bologna
Pepperoni (optional)
4 slices mozzarella cheese
4 slices Swiss cheese
4 slices American cheese
½ cup TIFFE'S Italian Salad Mix

Cut muffaletto bread in half horizontally. Brush butter, then olive oil on inside of bread. Sprinkle oregano on top of oil. Next layer meats and cheeses. Brush top of bread lightly with melted butter. Wrap in foil and bake at 350° for 20 minutes or until cheese melts. Remove from oven and spread Italian mix over the melted cheese. Cut into fourths. Serve hot or cold. Yield: 4 servings.

These can be made several hours ahead of time, adding Italian mix right before serving.

Mrs. Larry Rocconi
(Nina Dottley)

Barbecued Pork

1 (3½-pound) pork roast
2 ribs celery, chopped
1 medium purple onion, chopped
TABASCO brand pepper sauce to
  taste
Salt and pepper to taste
2 Tablespoons margarine
⅔ cup chopped purple onion

¼ cup vinegar
2 Tablespoons brown sugar
1 cup ketchup
¼ cup water
3 Tablespoons Worcestershire sauce
1 teaspoon prepared mustard
2 teaspoons salt

Place pork roast in large pot and cover with water that has celery, onion, TABASCO, salt, and pepper in it. Bring to a boil. Reduce to simmer and cook until tender and easy to shred, about 1 to 1½ hours. Remove from water and pull meat apart, discarding all fat. To prepare sauce, melt margarine; add onion and brown slightly. Add other ingredients and simmer until blended. Add shredded pork and simmer 15 to 20 minutes. Yield: 10 to 12 servings.

Dr. William Patterson
Union City, Tennessee

Barbara's Cheese Sandwich Spread

1 pound American cheese, shredded
1 large onion, chopped
1 large bell pepper, chopped

½ cup mayonnaise
1 loaf bread
Melted butter or margarine

Mix first 4 ingredients well. Trim crusts from bread. Roll each slice of bread thin. Spread with cheese mixture and roll up. Place seam-side down and brush with melted butter. Broil until bread is slightly toasted and cheese melts. This will keep in the refrigerator up to a week. It's also good as a cold sandwich spread or toasted open-face sandwich. Yield: 1½ cups.

Mrs. Charles Ramsay
(Barbara Parker)

Food Processor Three Cheese Pimento Spread

12 ounces sharp Cheddar cheese
1 (8-ounce) package cream cheese
1 (8-ounce) carton cottage cheese
1 teaspoon grated onion

¼ teaspoon salt
¼ teaspoon black pepper
½ teaspoon paprika (optional)
1 (2-ounce) jar chopped pimento

Shred Cheddar cheese in food processor. Remove. Cut cream cheese into pieces and place in food processor with cottage cheese. Add onion, salt, pepper, and paprika, if desired. Blend until smooth. With processor on, add grated cheese through feed tube. When well blended, add pimento with liquid. Process only until well blended. This will keep about 2 weeks in refrigerator. It will spread more easily if allowed to come to room temperature. Yield: 4 cups.

Mrs. Jerry M. Hall
(Carolyn Buckner)

Beer Cheese Spread for Sandwiches

1 pound American cheese, shredded
1 pound sharp New York State
  cheese, shredded
3 cloves garlic, chopped
1 (12-ounce) can beer at room
  temperature

3 Tablespoons dry COLMAN'S
  English Mustard
1 teaspoon salt
Dash of TABASCO brand pepper
  sauce to taste

Place all ingredients in food processor or blender and mix well. Yield: 4 cups.

Mrs. Charlie Faulk
(Elizabeth Young)

Ham on Croissant

4 large croissants
4 to 6 Tablespoons commercial
  Thousand Island salad dressing

½ pound thinly sliced ham
1 (4-ounce) carton alfalfa sprouts

Slice croissants in half lengthwise. Spread insides with dressing. Pile ham on bottom of each croissant. Top with desired amount of alfalfa sprouts. Place top half of croissant on top of alfalfa sprouts. Yield: 4 servings.

Delicious served with fresh fruit and kosher dill pickles.

Mrs. Walter Heslep
Jackson, Mississippi

Barbecue Frankburgers

1 pound wieners
1½ Tablespoons Worcestershire
  sauce
¼ cup vinegar
1 to 2 Tablespoons sugar

½ cup ketchup
½ cup water
½ cup chopped onions
½ cup chopped green pepper
Hot dog buns

In an oblong glass dish, place wieners. Combine remaining ingredients, except buns. Pour over wieners and bake at 350° for 1 hour. Serve in hot dog buns. Yield: 4 to 6 servings.

In place of wieners, use ground beef patties and serve on hamburger buns for a variation.

Mrs. Murray Pinkston
Clara Parks Booth

Mississippi Cotton Field

Strains of spirituals like "Swing Low, Sweet Chariot" no longer echo in the cotton fields. Instead, the mechanical pickers roll on rubber-tired wheels, gathering in the fluffy harvest that made cotton the king.

Legend described the Mississippi Delta as extending from the lobby of the Peabody Hotel in Memphis, Tennessee, to Catfish Row in Vicksburg. It was an agricultural kingdom where gentlemen were ranked by their plantings. Other crops vie now for the crown, but in the vast fields that stretch to the distant tree line, cotton is undisputed monarch of the realm.

There's no pretender for cotton's throne in the Delta.

Vegetables pictured:

Southern Black-Eyed Peas, Loaded Potatoes, Marinated Carrots, Pea-Stuffed Squash, Baked Tomatoes Rockefeller, Stir-Fried Vegetable Medley, Broccoli Elegant

Vegetables and Fruits

Nannie's Award-Winning Artichoke Casserole

1 clove garlic, minced
1/4 cup chopped green onions
2 Tablespoons parsley
1/4 cup olive oil
1 rounded Tablespoon flour
3/4 cup milk

1 (13¾-ounce) can artichoke hearts,
  cut up
1/2 cup shredded sharp Cheddar
  cheese
1/2 cup grated Parmesan cheese

Sauté garlic, onions, and parsley in oil. Add flour and gradually stir in milk. Fold in artichoke hearts. Place in a 2-quart casserole and cover with cheeses. Bake at 325° for 15 minutes. Yield: 4 servings.

Mrs. Robert L. Dent
(Mary Frances Martin)

Fresh Artichokes

4 fresh artichokes
Salt and pepper to taste
2 Tablespoons olive oil

3 dashes TABASCO brand pepper
  sauce
2 to 3 cups water

Cut stems off level with artichoke leaves so artichoke will sit on plate. Trim each leaf with scissors to remove the sticker. Place the artichoke in a heavy pot and add water so that it is several inches deep. Salt and pepper each artichoke well. Add olive oil and TABASCO to water in pan. Bring artichokes to a boil and then turn heat to low boil. Let cook 45 minutes to an hour, or until a leaf is easily pulled from artichoke base. When artichokes are tender, remove from pan and place on platter. To eat, pull off leaves 1 at a time and dip the bottom of the leaf into sauce, scraping meat of artichoke leaf with your teeth. Discard the rest of the leaf.

Sauce

1/4 cup margarine
1/4 cup lemon juice

Dash of salt

Blend above ingredients in a saucepan over low heat. Stir before serving.

Warren Asher

Cajun Red Beans and Rice

2 cups red or kidney beans, washed
  and drained
6 cups water
1 pound ground Italian or hot
  sausage, browned and drained
2 cloves garlic, minced
2 ribs celery, chopped
1 small bell pepper, chopped
2 teaspoons parsley

2 bay leaves
1 large onion, chopped
2 teaspoons sugar
1 pound link sausage, cut in 1-inch
  pieces
Ham bone with lots of ham
  (optional)
Cooked rice

Cover beans with water and bring to a boil. Remove from heat and let stand 1 hour or overnight, if possible. Add water and remaining ingredients except rice. Bring to boil. Lower to simmer and cook uncovered for 2½ to 3 hours, stirring occasionally. Can be frozen or refrigerated for several days. Serve over cooked rice. Yield: 6 servings.

Mrs. Ronnie Andrews
(Blue Paul)

Southern-Style Green Beans

2 (16-ounce) cans whole green beans
2 Tablespoons bacon drippings

Salt and pepper to taste

In a large pan cook canned green beans in own juice along with bacon drippings, salt, and pepper for approximately 45 minutes to 1 hour. After cooking, drain thoroughly and arrange lengthwise in a 9 x 13-inch serving dish.

Sauce

1 cup mayonnaise
⅓ cup mustard
2 to 4 Tablespoons horseradish

5 slices bacon, cooked and crumbled
½ cup sliced almonds, sautéed in
  butter

Prepare sauce by mixing together mayonnaise, mustard, and horseradish in a small bowl. These amounts may be changed to suit your own taste. This sauce is best prepared while beans are cooking so it can come to room temperature. Spoon sauce down the center of the row of beans. Garnish with crumbled bacon and sliced almonds. Yield: 6 to 8 servings.

Mrs. Robert Sadler
(Patricia Guider)

Tweety's Baked Beans

1 (31-ounce) can pork and beans
1 teaspoon dry mustard
½ Tablespoon thyme
¼ cup molasses
1 Tablespoon vinegar
1 cup ketchup

1 small onion, minced
1 clove garlic, minced
4 slices bacon, divided
4 Tablespoons barbecue sauce or
    liquid smoke to taste

Mix dry ingredients together. Stir into beans. Add molasses, vinegar, and ketchup. Mix in onion and garlic. Chop 1 slice bacon and stir into beans along with barbecue sauce or liquid smoke. Place other strips of bacon on top. Bake, uncovered, for 1 to 1½ hours in a 350° oven. Yield: 6 servings.

Mrs. J. E. Neill, Jr.
(Dorothy Stamm)

Green Bean Bundles with Cheese Sauce

2 (10-ounce) cans whole green
    beans, drained
1 pound bacon

1 (10-ounce) can new potatoes,
    drained
1 (10-ounce) jar onions, drained

Place 6 or more whole beans in a bundle and wrap with ½ strip bacon. Place bundles in casserole and place under broiler until bacon is cooked. Drain drippings. Add potatoes and onions and cover with Cheese Sauce. Bake at 350° for 10 to 15 minutes until onions and potatoes are heated. Yield: 10 to 12 servings.

Cheese Sauce

2 Tablespoons butter
½ teaspoon salt
Dash of white pepper
2 Tablespoons flour

1 cup milk
1 cup shredded medium sharp
    cheese

Melt butter in saucepan. Stir in flour, salt, and pepper until smooth. Add milk. Cook, stirring until thick. Add cheese and stir until melted. Pour over bean bundles.

Mrs. W. T. Ewell
(Betty Price)

 A fast method for preparing dried beans is to cover beans with water in a covered pan and bring to a boil; boil for 3 minutes then turn off and let set for 1 hour.

Marinated Green Beans and Artichokes

1½ cups sugar
2 cups vegetable oil
1 cup apple cider vinegar
2 cloves garlic, sliced
1 Tablespoon salt

3 (16-ounce) cans cut green beans,
 drained
1 (13¾-ounce) can artichoke
 hearts, drained

Combine sugar, oil, vinegar, garlic, and salt in mixing bowl. Mix with an electric mixer. Stir in beans and artichokes. Let sit 24 hours, then warm slowly. Yield: 10 to 12 servings.

Mrs. Robert R. Bailess
(Natalie Waring)

Green Bean Casserole

2 (10-ounce) packages French-style
 frozen green beans
1 small onion, chopped
6 Tablespoons margarine
2 Tablespoons flour
1⅓ cups light cream
1 (3-ounce) can sliced mushrooms
⅔ teaspoon salt
½ teaspoon soy sauce

⅔ teaspoon monosodium glutamate
½ teaspoon pepper
½ teaspoon TABASCO brand
 pepper sauce
1 (8-ounce) can sliced water
 chestnuts
16 ounces shredded cheese, divided
Cubed bread
¼ cup margarine, melted

Cook green beans according to package directions. Drain. Sauté onion in melted margarine. Add flour and mix well. Add cream, mushrooms, salt, soy sauce, monosodium glutamate, black pepper, TABASCO, and water chestnuts. Add green beans and ½ shredded cheese. Pour into a 2-quart casserole dish. Cover with remaining cheese and then bread cubes. Pour melted margarine over top. Bake 350° for 30 minutes. Freezes well. Yield: 8 servings.

Mrs. Randy Oswalt
(Lynda McAlpin)

 To prevent artichokes from turning gray, do not cook in iron or aluminum pots.

Broccoli Elegant

1½ cups water
¼ cup butter or margarine
1 (6-ounce) package corn bread
   stuffing mix
2 (10-ounce) packages frozen
   broccoli spears, thawed
2 Tablespoons butter or margarine
2 Tablespoons flour
1 teaspoon chicken-flavored
   bouillon granules

¾ cup milk
2 (3-ounce) packages cream cheese,
   softened
¼ teaspoon seasoned salt
4 green onions, sliced
1 cup shredded Cheddar cheese
Paprika

Combine water, butter, and packaged seasoning. Mix and bring to a boil. Remove from heat; stir in stuffing crumbs, and let stand 5 minutes. Spoon stuffing around inside edge of a lightly buttered 13 x 9 x 2-inch baking dish, leaving a well in the center. Place broccoli in well and set aside. Melt 2 Tablespoons butter in a heavy saucepan over low heat; add flour, stirring until smooth. Cook 1 minute, stirring constantly until thickened and bubbly. Stir in bouillon. Gradually add milk. Add cream cheese and salt, stirring until smooth. Stir in onion. Spoon mixture over center of broccoli; sprinkle with cheese and paprika. Cover with aluminum foil and bake at 350° for 35 minutes. Remove foil and bake an additional 10 minutes. Yield: 8 servings.

Mrs. Clyde Hughey, Jr.
Memphis, Tennessee

Baked Cream Cabbage

1 medium head cabbage, finely
   shredded
½ cup boiling salted water
3 Tablespoons butter or margarine
3 Tablespoons flour

½ teaspoon salt or more
1½ cups milk
¼ teaspoon white pepper
¼ cup seasoned bread crumbs

Cook cabbage 6 to 8 minutes in boiling water; drain well and put into buttered casserole. Melt butter in saucepan; stir in flour and salt until smooth. Add milk gradually, stirring mixture with wire whisk until smooth and thickened slightly. Add white pepper. Pour mixture over cabbage and sprinkle crumbs over top. Dot with butter and bake at 325° about 15 minutes or until bubbly. Yield: 6 servings.

Mrs. George A. Stevens
New Orleans, Louisiana

Broccoli with Almonds

2 pounds fresh broccoli	2 Tablespoons sherry
1 teaspoon salt	2 Tablespoons lemon juice
1 beef bouillon cube	1/8 teaspoon pepper
3/4 cup hot water	2 teaspoons monosodium
1 cup light cream	glutamate
1/4 cup butter or margarine	1/2 cup shredded Cheddar cheese
1/4 cup flour	1/4 cup slivered almonds

Trim off large leaves from broccoli. Remove tough ends of lower stalks and wash broccoli thoroughly; separate into spears. Cook broccoli, covered, in a small amount of boiling, salted water for 10 minutes or until tender-crisp. Drain well and place in a 12 x 8 x 2-inch baking dish. Dissolve bouillon cube in water, stir in cream, and set aside. Melt butter in a heavy saucepan over low heat; blend in flour, stirring until smooth. Cook 1 minute, stirring constantly. Gradually add bouillon mixture; cook over medium heat, stirring, until thick and bubbly. Stir in sherry, lemon juice, pepper, and monosodium glutamate. Pour sauce over broccoli and sprinkle with cheese and almonds. Bake at 375° for 25 to 30 minutes. Yield: 6 servings.

Mrs. Sammy Ashley
(Carolyn Stricklin)

Fresh Beets with Orange Sauce

2 pounds fresh beets	Salt

Cut tops off beets leaving 1 inch of stem and root end. Boil in salted water, covered, for 45 to 60 minutes or until tender. Drain and cut tops off. Slip off skins of beets and slice. Place in hot Orange Sauce and serve. Yield: 8 servings.

Orange Sauce

1/4 cup sugar	1 teaspoon grated orange rind
1/2 cup orange juice	2 Tablespoons margarine
2 Tablespoons lemon juice	1 Tablespoon cornstarch
1/2 teaspoon salt	

Mix all ingredients and cook in double boiler until cornstarch clears.

Miss Enez Bourdon

Broccoli and Carrots Amandine

1 pound fresh broccoli, trimmed
1 pound carrots, pared and
   diagonally sliced
½ cup slivered almonds
3 Tablespoons cooking oil
3 Tablespoons freshly squeezed
   lemon juice

3 Tablespoons butter or margarine
3 Tablespoons minced parsley
1½ teaspoons basil, crumbled
½ teaspoon thyme, crumbled
¼ teaspoon salt
¼ teaspoon pepper

Slice broccoli, keeping florets in serving-size pieces. Place broccoli stems and carrots in large skillet; top with florets. Add water to the depth of ½ inch and sprinkle with salt. Cover tightly and bring to a boil. Boil gently for 6 minutes or until tender-crisp. Drain any remaining water from skillet. Cover and keep warm. Roast almonds in oil in large saucepan, stirring over medium high heat. When almonds turn light gold, remove from pan with slotted spoon. Add lemon juice, butter, parsley, basil, thyme, salt, and pepper to oil left in pan. Stir until butter is melted. Pour over vegetables in skillet and toss well. Sprinkle with almonds. Yield: 4 to 6 servings.

Makes an attractive setting served with carrots centered on a tray of broccoli.

Mrs. Michael Engle
(Melanie Campbell)

Marinated Carrots

1 (10¾-ounce) can tomato soup,
   undiluted
½ cup salad oil
1 cup sugar
¾ cup vinegar
1 Tablespoon prepared mustard

1 Tablespoon Worcestershire sauce
Salt to taste
5 cups sliced carrots, cooked
1 bell pepper, sliced
1 onion, sliced

Mix first 7 ingredients. Bring to a boil. Pour over cooked carrots, bell pepper, and onion. Chill. Yield: 4 servings.

This may be served hot or cold and may be refrigerated for 2 weeks.

Mrs. Larry Lambiotte
(Carolyn Walker)

Always peel away the tough outer layer of skin on the stems of fresh broccoli before cooking.

Aunt Celie's Creole Stuffed Bell Peppers

6 large bell peppers
6 to 8 slices bacon
2 Tablespoons bacon drippings
1 large onion
1 (16-ounce) can tomatoes
1 (8-ounce) can tomato sauce
1 teaspoon sugar

Dash of hot sauce (optional)
Salt to taste
Pepper to taste
1 (16-ounce) can cream-style corn
2 eggs, well beaten
6 ounces sharp Cheddar cheese

Split bell peppers lengthwise; remove seeds and core. Cook in boiling salted water about 10 minutes or until peppers begin to change color and are tender. Remove peppers and drain on paper towels; set aside. Cook bacon and reserve 2 Tablespoons bacon drippings. Chop onion and cook in bacon drippings until clear. Add tomatoes, tomato sauce, sugar, hot sauce, salt, and pepper. Cook until almost dry. Be sure to cook long enough as this is very important to the success of the recipe. Add corn, mix in well and cook longer being careful not to burn. Remove from heat. Add eggs and cook a minute or 2 longer. Crumble bacon and add to mixture. Fill pepper shells; place a slice of cheese on top of each pepper and bake at 350° until cheese melts. Yield: 12 servings.

Mrs. Harry Klein
(Linda Mallory)

Corn Pudding

6 eggs
2 (16-ounce) cans cream-style corn
1 cup milk
½ cup flour

2 Tablespoons sugar
½ teaspoon salt
½ cup butter or margarine
Paprika

Beat eggs until well blended. Add corn, milk, flour, sugar, and salt. Mix well. Melt butter in a 12 x 7-inch baking dish. Pour in corn mixture, spooning butter over mixture. Bake at 350° for 50 minutes until brown on top and firm. Sprinkle with paprika. Yield: 10 servings.

Mrs. W. E. Bexley
(Betty Everett)

When boiling corn, add sugar to the water instead of salt. Salt will toughen the corn.

Cauliflower au Gratin

1 head cauliflower
1 Tablespoon vinegar
2 Tablespoons butter or margarine
2 Tablespoons flour
¾ cup milk

¼ teaspoon salt
Dash of white pepper
1¼ cups shredded Cheddar cheese,
    divided

Break cauliflower into florets. Boil in salted water with vinegar until tender but not mushy, about 15 to 20 minutes. Drain well. Melt butter in skillet. Add flour and stir until smooth. Add milk all at once and whisk until smooth. Cook quickly until thickened, stirring constantly. Stir in salt, pepper and ¼ cup cheese. Fold in cauliflower. Pour into a 1½-quart casserole. Cover with remaining cheese. Bake at 350° until bubbly and cheese has melted, about 20 minutes. Yield: 6 servings.

Casserole can be made a day ahead and refrigerated. Add cheese topping just before cooking.

Mrs. E. A. Buckner
(Ruth Vicknair)

Delta Eggplant

2 eggplants
Salt and pepper
3 Tablespoons butter
3 Tablespoons salad oil
1 cup onion, finely chopped
1 clove garlic, minced

2 cups peeled and chopped tomatoes
¼ teaspoon thyme
1 bay leaf
½ cup finely chopped parsley
½ cup bread crumbs
1 cup Gruyère cheese, shredded

Peel and cut five ½-inch thick circles from each eggplant. Sprinkle with salt and pepper. Place in a greased pan and broil 5 minutes. In a skillet, heat butter and oil and stir in onion and garlic. Sauté until onions are opaque. Add eggplant trimmings, tomatoes, thyme, and bay leaf. Cook until thick. Remove bay leaf and stir in bread crumbs and parsley. Season with salt and pepper. Pile tomato mixture on top each eggplant slice and sprinkle each slice with cheese. Bake at 350° until cheese is melted. Yield: 10 servings.

Mrs. Frank Maxwell
(Louise Middlebrook)

 To keep cauliflower white while cooking, add a little milk to the water.

Eggplant Soufflé

2 medium eggplants, peeled and
  cubed
½ teaspoon salt
½ cup chopped onion
3 green onions with tops, sliced
1 rib celery, chopped finely
2 Tablespoons finely chopped green
  pepper

2 Tablespoons margarine
3 eggs, beaten
1 cup shredded Cheddar cheese
Pinch of red pepper
Black pepper

Boil eggplant in salted water 20 minutes until tender. Drain. Sauté vegetables in margarine. Combine eggplant and vegetables. Mix eggs, cheese, red pepper, and black pepper to taste. Add to eggplant mixture. Pour into a buttered 2-quart casserole. Bake at 350° for 35 to 45 minutes until eggs are set. Soufflé should be puffy and lightly browned. Yield: 6 to 8 servings.

Mrs. D. P. Waring, Jr.
(Betty Jeanne Williams)

Fried Eggplant Sticks

1 (1-pound) eggplant, peeled
Salt and pepper
2 cups flour
⅔ cup evaporated milk

4 slices day-old bread
Vegetable oil for frying
Grated Romano cheese

Cut eggplant lengthwise into 3 x ½-inch sticks. Sprinkle with salt and let drain in a colander for 30 minutes. Pat the eggplant sticks dry. Place a little salt, pepper, and flour in a bag. Put eggplant in bag and shake, coating with seasoned flour. Place bread in food processor and process to make bread crumbs. Shake excess flour off eggplant sticks. Dip in milk, let excess milk drip off, then dredge in bread crumbs. Shake off excess bread crumbs. Heat deep oil to 350°. Fry in batches until golden brown. Drain on paper towels. Sprinkle with grated Romano cheese. Yield: 4 to 6 servings.

Mrs. Jack Stamm, Jr.
(Laurin Fields)

 Top cooked vegetables or casseroles with a mixture of 2 Tablespoons melted butter and ½ cup herb-seasoned stuffing mix, crushed. Sprinkle with shredded cheese.

Eggplant Stacks

1 eggplant, peeled if desired
1 large onion
2 tomatoes
Salt and pepper to taste
1 teaspoon basil leaves

2 teaspoons oregano leaves
¼ cup olive oil
½ cup grated Romano cheese
½ cup sour cream
6 Tablespoons chopped black olives

Slice eggplant into 8 rounds. Layer eggplant on bottom of 9 x 13-inch baking dish. Place a thin slice of onion on each slice of eggplant. Place a thick slice of tomato on top of each onion slice. Sprinkle lightly with salt and pepper. Sprinkle basil and oregano over all. Drizzle olive oil over and top with Romano cheese. Cover with foil. Bake at 350° for 40 to 45 minutes. Serve with sour cream and black olives. Yield: 8 servings.

Mrs. Harry Meyer
(Louise Angelo)

Mease's Mustard Greens

4 bunches mustard greens
2 cups water
1 teaspoon salt
⅛ teaspoon pepper

Pinch of sugar
1 ham hock or ¼ pound salt pork
1 hot green or red pepper

Soak and rinse greens well. Tear off thick parts of stems. Bring water to boil. Add remaining ingredients. Add greens and bring water back to a boil. Cover and simmer 30 to 45 minutes or until tender. Yield: 6 to 8 servings.

Mrs. B. J. Gunn
(Frances Kivett)

Sautéed Mushrooms

12 ounces fresh mushrooms
4 Tablespoons butter
½ teaspoon salt

½ teaspoon lemon pepper seasoning
⅛ teaspoon black pepper
1 Tablespoon fresh lemon juice

Wipe, but do not wash mushrooms. Slice mushrooms and sauté in butter for about 2 to 3 minutes until slightly browned. Do not overcook. Add seasonings and serve hot. Yield: 2 servings.

Delicious served with steak, broiled chicken, and roast.

The Editors

Mushroom Soufflé

¾ pound mushrooms
1 Tablespoon chopped onion
6 Tablespoons butter, divided
6 Tablespoons flour
2 cups scalded milk
½ cup shredded American cheese

Dash of TABASCO brand pepper
* sauce*
Salt and pepper to taste
6 egg yolks, well beaten
6 egg whites, stiffly beaten

Clean mushrooms. Chop caps and stems finely. Sauté mushrooms and onion in 3 Tablespoons butter. Set aside. To the liquid and fat in the pan, add remaining butter. Blend in flour and add hot milk gradually. Cook, stirring constantly until thick. Mix in cheese until melted. Add TABASCO, salt, and pepper. Cool. Stir egg yolks into mixture. Then fold in egg whites. Pour into a greased 2-quart soufflé dish and place in pan of warm water. Bake at 325° for about 1 hour or until firm. Serve at once. Serve with Shrimp and Almond Sauce. Yield: 8 servings.

Shrimp and Almond Sauce

1 (10½-ounce) can cream of shrimp
* soup, undiluted*
1 Tablespoon lemon juice

1 (3-ounce) package cream cheese
½ (3-ounce) package sliced almonds

Heat all ingredients in saucepan until melted. Serve over soufflé. This sauce is also good served over fresh broccoli or asparagus.

Mrs. R. R. Morrison, Jr.
(Twick Cooper)

Fried Okra

4 cups fresh okra, sliced
Salt
Pepper

½ to ¾ cup yellow corn meal
¼ cup flour
1 to 2 cups vegetable oil for frying

Rinse okra and slice. Lightly salt and pepper okra. Add corn meal and flour. Mix well. Heat vegetable oil in cast iron skillet until very hot. Add ½ okra mixture. Cook until light brown, about 5 or 6 minutes. Remove to platter with paper towels for draining. Add next batch of okra mixture. Cook the same as above. Yield: 6 servings.

Mrs. Richard H. Grau
(Sally Hines)

Imyl's Vidalia Apple Casserole

½ cup butter, divided
2 large Vidalia onions or 1 yellow
  onion, sliced ¼-inch thick
6 large tart apples, peeled and
  sliced ¼-inch thick

2 Tablespoons sugar
2 Tablespoons cinnamon
30 Ritz crackers, crushed
1 cup apple juice or cider

Butter a 1½-quart baking dish. Melt 2 Tablespoons butter in large skillet over medium-high heat. Add onions and sauté until golden, about 10 minutes. Remove onions with slotted spoon and set aside. Melt 3 Tablespoons butter in same skillet over medium-high heat. Add apples and cook until golden, about 12 minutes, stirring occasionally. Spread ½ apples evenly over bottom of baking dish. Top with ½ sautéed onions. Sprinkle with ½ sugar and cinnamon and ½ cracker crumbs. Repeat layering. Pour apple juice over top. Dot with remaining 3 Tablespoons butter. Cover and bake at 325° to 350° until bubbly, about 1 hour. Delicious with ham and roast pork. Yield: 10 to 12 servings.

Mrs. Lawrence Mullen
(Billie Ballard)

Happy New Year Peas

1 pound dried black-eyed peas
  (soaked overnight)
3 cups water or enough to cover
  peas
1 pound link sausage or your
  favorite

1 small onion, chopped
3 Tablespoons brown sugar
1 Tablespoon prepared mustard
1 teaspoon salt
8 ounces prepared barbecue sauce

Cook peas in water until just tender. Drain and retain ½ the liquid. Brown sausage and onions together. Drain. Place peas in a 3-quart casserole. Add sausage and onions. Stir in liquid, brown sugar, mustard, salt, and barbecue sauce. Bake for 1½ hours in 200° oven. Yield: 6 servings.

Delicious served over rice with garlic bread.

Mrs. T. P. Groome, Jr.
(Bettye Pierson)

 To keep cut and peeled carrots and celery fresh store in a covered bowl of water in refrigerator.

Bacon-Onion Pie

1½ cups seasoned bread crumbs
6 Tablespoons melted butter
2 medium onions, thinly sliced
¼ cup butter
½ pound bacon, cooked

¾ cup evaporated milk
3 eggs
Salt and pepper to taste
1 (6-ounce) roll jalapeño cheese

Line a 9-inch pie plate with combined crumbs and melted butter. Chill. Sauté onions in butter until golden in color, about 25 to 30 minutes. Arrange onions in crumb shell. Sprinkle well drained, crumbled bacon over onions. Mix milk, eggs, salt, and pepper well and pour over bacon and onion. Top with thinly sliced cheese. Bake at 350° for 30 minutes or until knife in center comes out clean. Yield: 8 servings.

Serve as a main dish or meat accompaniment or party style in small wedges.

Mrs. Mack Varner
(Penny Sanders)

Onion Pie

2 cups sliced onions
4 green onions diced, including tops
2 Tablespoons butter
Salt and pepper to taste
2 (9-inch) unbaked pie crusts
1 cup shredded sharp Cheddar
   cheese

1 egg, beaten
½ cup milk
¼ teaspoon paprika
2 teaspoons chopped parsley or 1
   teaspoon dried parsley

Sauté onions in butter with salt and pepper to taste. Into pie crust sprinkle alternate layers of cheese and sautéed onions, beginning and ending with cheese. Beat egg with milk, paprika and parsley. Pour over filling. Place second crust over top, sealing edges with fingers, then slash or puncture top crust in several places with fork or knife. Bake about 40 minutes at 375° until crust is firm and light golden brown. Let cool, then cut into pie-shaped wedges. Serve either hot or cold. Yield: 6 to 8 servings.

Gordon A. Cotton

Store chopped onions in a screw-top jar in the refrigerator. They will keep for several days.

Company Peas

¼ cup butter or margarine
3 ribs celery, sliced
2 Tablespoons chopped onion
¼ pound fresh mushrooms, sliced
   or 1 (4-ounce) can mushrooms

1 (2-ounce) jar pimentos, drained
2 (17-ounce) cans small English
   peas, drained
½ teaspoon garlic salt
Pepper to taste

Melt butter. Sauté celery, onion and mushrooms in butter until limp. Add pimento, peas, garlic salt and pepper. Bake at 350° for 20 to 30 minutes until hot. Yield: 6 to 8 servings.

Mrs. George Jabour, Jr.
(Miriam Penton)

Southern Black-Eyed Peas

1 pound dried black-eyed peas
1 smoked hog jowl or ham hock
1 large onion, chopped

Red pepper to taste
Salt

Put hog jowl or ham hock in large saucepan and cover with water. Boil for 10 to 15 minutes. Meanwhile wash and clean peas. Add to boiling water along with chopped onion. Water may be added in order to cover peas. Add red pepper, but be careful adding salt because meat will give peas some salty taste. Cook over medium heat until peas are soft, but not mushy, about 45 minutes to an hour. Yield: 6 servings.

Mrs. Woody Brumitt
(Debbie Dottley)

Baked Onions

4 medium to large onions
4 Tablespoons butter or margarine,
   divided
4 Tablespoons Worcestershire
   sauce, divided

4 Tablespoons soy sauce, divided
Tony Chachere's Famous Creole
   Seasoning to taste
Lemon pepper to taste

Peel onion and cut into sixths, being careful not to cut completely through to bottom. Inside each onion put 1 Tablespoon butter, 1 Tablespoon Worcestershire and 1 Tablespoon soy sauce. Sprinkle with Tony's seasoning and lemon pepper to taste. Wrap in foil and bake at 350° for 1 hour. Yield: 4 servings.

Joe Harris

Heavenly Hash Brown Casserole

1 (32-ounce) package frozen
  shredded potatoes, thawed
½ cup butter, melted
1 (10¾-ounce) can cream of chicken
  soup, undiluted
12 ounces American cheese,
  shredded

1 (8-ounce) carton sour cream
1 teaspoon salt
½ small onion, chopped
2 cups crushed corn flakes
½ cup melted butter

Place potatoes in a 9 x 13-inch casserole dish. Mix together the next 6 in-gredients and pour over potatoes. Top with corn flakes and melted butter. Bake, uncovered, at 350° for 45 minutes. Freezes well. Yield: 12 servings.

Mrs. William T. Harris
(Teresa Vaughn)

Loaded Potatoes

4 to 8 large baking potatoes

Salad oil

Wash potatoes. Rub with oil; wrap in foil. Bake at 400° for 1 hour or until tender. Serve with 1 or more of the following toppings. Yield: 4 to 8 servings.

Broccoli-Mushroom Topping

1 (10-ounce) package chopped
  broccoli
3 ribs celery, finely chopped
1 medium onion, finely chopped
2 Tablespoons vegetable oil
1 (10¾-ounce) can cream of
  mushroom soup, undiluted
1 (4-ounce) jar sliced mushrooms

1 (8-ounce) package processed
  cheese, cubed
½ teaspoon Worcestershire sauce
¼ teaspoon garlic salt
TABASCO brand pepper sauce to
  taste
¼ cup slivered almonds

Cook broccoli according to package directions and drain well. Sauté celery and onion in oil. Add broccoli to sautéed vegetables. Stir in soup and mushrooms. Add cheese and beat until cheese is thoroughly melted. Stir in Worcestershire, garlic salt, and TABASCO. Spoon over potatoes. Top with slivered almonds. Yield: 8 servings.

Spicy Sausage Topping

½ pound hot bulk sausage
1 small onion, chopped
1 (10-ounce) can ROTEL Tomatoes
  and Green Chilies

1 pound processed cheese
1½ cups shredded lettuce
1 to 2 tomatoes, chopped

Brown sausage and onion in skillet. Drain well. Mash tomatoes and green chilies and add to sausage. Simmer 5 to 10 minutes. Add cheese and stir over low heat until melted. Spoon over potatoes and top with lettuce and tomatoes. Yield: 6 servings.

Chili Topping

½ pound ground beef
1 small onion, finely chopped
1 clove garlic, minced
¼ cup bell pepper, finely chopped
2 Tablespoons vegetable oil
1 (8-ounce) can tomato sauce
½ cup water

1½ Tablespoons chili powder
½ teaspoon ground cumin
¼ teaspoon salt
¼ teaspoon black pepper
1½ cups shredded Cheddar cheese
¼ cup chopped green onions

Brown ground beef and drain. Sauté onion, garlic, and bell pepper in oil. Add to meat, Add tomato sauce, water, and spices to meat mixture. Simmer 30 minutes or until mixture thickens. Spoon over potatoes. Top with cheese and green onions. Yield: 4 servings.

Mrs. Kenneth Grogan, III
(Anne Blackledge)

Potatoes Romanoff

5 cups cooked, cold diced potatoes
2 teaspoons salt
Garlic powder to taste
½ cup chopped green onion,
  including tops
1 (8-ounce) carton sour cream

1 (16-ounce) carton large curd
  cottage cheese
½ cup shredded sharp Cheddar
  cheese
Paprika

Mix first 6 ingredients and place in a greased casserole dish. Top with cheese. Dust heavily with paprika. Bake at 350° for 30 minutes. Yield: 6 to 8 servings.

Mrs. Jim Chaney
(Karen Heern)

Auntie's au Gratin Potatoes

2 pounds unpeeled red potatoes
3 Tablespoons butter
3 Tablespoons flour
2 cups milk

½ pound sharp Cheddar cheese,
  shredded
Salt and white pepper to taste
Paprika

Boil potatoes in lightly salted water until fork-tender. Do not overcook. Cool, peel, and cut into bite-size cubes. Meanwhile melt butter in saucepan and stir in flour until mixture is smooth. Gradually add milk, stirring with whisk until sauce is slightly thickened. Salt to taste. In a deep buttered casserole put a layer of potatoes, a layer of sauce, and a layer of cheese; potatoes, sauce, cheese, etc. Season with salt and white pepper. Be sure to end with cheese on top. Season with paprika. Bake at 350° for 45 minutes or until bubbly. Brown under broiler if desired. Yield: 6 to 8 servings.

Mrs. Bruce Ebersole
(Story Stamm)

Parmesan Potato Casserole

5 pounds medium Irish potatoes
2 pounds small yellow onions
½ cup margarine, melted
½ cup flour
3 cups milk
1 cup chicken broth

1 pound sharp cheese, shredded
1 (4-ounce) can Parmesan cheese
½ teaspoon pepper
1¾ teaspoons salt
1 teaspoon seasoned salt

Peel, dice, and boil potatoes and onions in a large pot until tender. Drain and set aside. In a medium boiler, melt butter and whisk in flour. Add milk and broth. Stir with whisk making a cream sauce. As sauce thickens, add cheeses and seasonings. Place potatoes and onions in a 3-quart casserole and pour sauce over potatoes. Bake at 350° for 45 minutes. Can be divided into 3 small casseroles and frozen. Yield: 10 to 12 servings.

Mrs. Gordon L. Carr, Sr.
(Betty Ann Williams)

 When preparing mashed potatoes, boil potatoes with a small onion, a clove garlic, bay leaf, or celery rib with leaves for extra flavor.

Hawaiian Yams

2 cups cooked, mashed sweet
  potatoes
2 eggs
½ teaspoon salt

1 teaspoon vanilla extract
1 cup sugar
½ (3½-ounce) can coconut
1 (5-ounce) can evaporated milk

Mix together potatoes, eggs, salt, vanilla, and sugar with electric mixer. Mix in coconut and milk. Pour into large pie pan or small casserole dish. Bake 45 minutes at 350°. Yield: 6 to 8 servings.

Topping

1 (8-ounce) jar maraschino cherries
  with juice
1 (8-ounce) can crushed pineapple
  with juice

1½ Tablespoons cornstarch
¾ cup sugar

Mix together topping ingredients in saucepan. Boil for 2 minutes, stirring constantly. Pour and spread over potatoes after they are removed from oven. Cool about 10 minutes before serving.

Mrs. Douglas Huskey
(Becki Fields)

Terrific 'Taters

5 medium potatoes
1 (8-ounce) carton sour cream
1 (1-ounce) package buttermilk
  salad dressing mix

Salt and pepper to taste
1 cup shredded Cheddar cheese
2 pieces crisply fried bacon,
  crumbled

Peel and slice potatoes. Boil until tender. Drain, saving 1 Tablespoon liquid. Place potatoes in casserole dish. Add sour cream and potato liquid. Sprinkle with buttermilk salad dressing mix, salt, and pepper. Toss until potatoes are covered. Sprinkle Cheddar cheese on top. Bake at 350° for 15 minutes until cheese is melted and potatoes are bubbly. Remove and sprinkle with crumbled bacon pieces. Serve hot. Yield: 5 servings.

Mrs. W. E. Johnson
(Betty Miller)

Potatoes and onions should be kept in a cool, dark place with good air circulation to prevent sprouting.

Bacon-Wrapped Potatoes

4 large baking potatoes, peeled if
    desired
Salt and pepper to taste
4 thin slices onion

4 round slices bell pepper
4 slices bacon
Margarine

Cut potatoes in half lengthwise. Salt and pepper each ½ keeping the 2 halves of each potato together. Between halves of each potato, put 1 slice onion and 1 ring bell pepper. Wrap 1 slice of bacon around each potato and secure with toothpick. Butter 1 side of 4 pieces of tin foil. Wrap each potato with foil. Margarine will prevent potato from sticking to foil. Place potatoes on baking sheet and bake at 450° for 45 to 60 minutes or until done. During baking, turn potatoes once. Yield: 4 servings.

This may be cooked on the grill.

Mrs. Daniel Johnson
(Sue Buckner)

Georgie's Sweet Potatoes in Orange Cups

2 cups cooked sweet potatoes
3 large naval oranges
¼ cup butter
¼ cup sugar
½ cup milk

¼ cup bourbon or 1 teaspoon
    vanilla extract
½ teaspoon salt
½ cup chopped pecans
Miniature marshmallows

Cover sweet potatoes with cold water. Boil until tender. Peel and cube. Halve oranges and remove pulp with spoon; flute edges with sharp knife. Cream butter and sugar together. Add cooked sweet potatoes, milk, bourbon or vanilla, and salt. Beat until fluffy. Add chopped pecans. Fill orange cups right before serving and place marshmallows on top. Place on baking sheet and brown under broiler. Serve while hot. Yield: 6 servings.

May also be served as a casserole.

Mrs. Eddy Sorey
(Boo McAdams)

 To keep French fries from turning brown put cut potatoes in water until ready to use. Pat dry before frying.

272

Rockwood Scalloped Potatoes

6 large Irish potatoes
½ teaspoon salt
¼ teaspoon white pepper
4 white onions, thinly sliced

½ cup flour
2 cups milk
½ cup butter

Peel potatoes and slice very thinly. Butter bottom and sides of baking pan. Layer potatoes in pan and add salt and pepper. Layer onions. Sprinkle flour over potatoes and onion layer. Repeat each layer. Heat milk to simmer. Pour over potatoes and onions. Top with butter, cut into pats. Bake at 375° for 1 hour. Yield: 6 to 8 servings.

Mike Martinson
Jackson, Mississippi

Spanakopitta
(Greek Spinach Pies)

3 (10-ounce) packages frozen
  spinach leaves, thawed and
  chopped, or 4 bags fresh spinach
3 bunches green onions
½ bunch parsley
1 yellow onion, grated

1¼ cups vegetable oil, divided
¼ cup uncooked rice
½ pound feta cheese
4 eggs
Salt and pepper to taste
1 pound phyllo dough

Wash and chop spinach if fresh is used. Drain. Chop green onions and parsley; add yellow onion. Mix together in frying pan with ¼ cup vegetable oil. Sauté all the above ingredients. Add rice. Stir frequently until rice is softened. Set aside to cool. Crumble feta cheese. Beat eggs and add to cheese. Mix well. Add this to spinach mixture. Grease 10½ x 15½-inch pan with oil. Place 1 sheet of phyllo in bottom of pan. Layer the phyllo brushing each layer with oil. Allow phyllo to overhang about 2 inches on each side to fold over the spinach mixture. 10 layers of phyllo are on the bottom, then the spinach mixture, then 10 more layers on top. With a knife, gently divide into strips. Do not cut through. Cook at 350° until golden brown, about 45 minutes. Cook; then slice according to knife markings. Yield: 4 dozen.

Mrs. George Tzotzolas
(Irene Alissandrakis)

 To keep parsley fresh, rinse, drain well, and place in a tightly sealed plastic bag in refrigerator.

273

Sweet Potato and Apple Casserole

6 medium sweet potatoes or yams
1 cup maple syrup
¼ cup butter or margarine
¼ teaspoon salt

4 medium apples, peeled, cored, and
 sliced
Plain bread crumbs
Cinnamon

Boil sweet potatoes until tender. Let potatoes cool. In a medium saucepan over medium high heat put syrup, butter or margarine, and salt. Add prepared apples to syrup mixture and simmer gently until apples are just tender. Peel and chop cooled sweet potatoes into quarters or sixths. Layer sweet potatoes and apples in a 13 x 9 x 2-inch baking dish and top each layer with a sprinkling of plain bread crumbs and cinnamon. Bake at 400° for 20 to 30 minutes or until top is lightly browned. Yield: 8 to 10 servings.

Mrs. Joseph Letter, Jr.
(Linda Arlotta)

Spinach Gratin

4 Tablespoons butter, divided
1 Tablespoon finely chopped onion
½ cup white rice
1¼ cups hot water
Salt and pepper
½ cup milk
2 Tablespoons dry bread crumbs

1 pound spinach, parboiled,
 drained, and coarsely chopped
4 Tablespoons freshly grated
 Parmesan cheese
½ teaspoon freshly grated nutmeg
1½ Tablespoons lemon juice
1 egg, beaten

Melt 2 Tablespoons butter in a pan. Add onion; cover and simmer for 1 minute. Add rice; increase heat and stir for 1 minute, or until rice grains turn opaque. Add water, salt, and pepper to mixture; cover, reduce heat and cook 20 minutes. In a small bowl, stir milk into bread crumbs and put aside. Add spinach, ½ cheese, nutmeg, lemon juice, and more salt and pepper. Mix together cooked rice, spinach mixture, egg, and melted butter. Butter a 9-inch pie dish and scoop spinach-rice mixture into it. Smooth top and sprinkle with remaining cheese. Bake in a preheated oven at 375° for 15 minutes. Serve hot from dish. Yield: 4 to 6 servings.

Mrs. Bob Coleman
(Cissy Wagner)

 Sweet potatoes will not turn brown if put in salted water (5 teaspoons to 1 quart water) immediately after peeling.

Spinach-Artichoke Casserole

2 (3-ounce) packages cream cheese
2 ounces bleu cheese
Juice of 1 lemon
½ cup butter
2 (10-ounce) packages frozen
    chopped spinach

1 (13¾-ounce) can artichoke hearts,
    drained
¼ cup buttered bread crumbs
Paprika to taste

In a small saucepan, cook cream cheese, bleu cheese, lemon juice, and butter over low heat until smooth. Cook spinach only until thawed; drain well. Combine spinach with cream cheese mixture. In the bottom of a greased 1½-quart casserole, arrange artichoke hearts and pour spinach mixture over them. Top with bread crumbs and paprika. Cook at 350° for 15 to 20 minutes. Yield: 3 to 4 servings.

Mrs. Jeff King
(Anne Keen)

Spinach Madeleine

2 (10-ounce) packages frozen
    chopped spinach
4 Tablespoons butter
2 Tablespoons flour
2 Tablespoons chopped onion
½ cup evaporated milk
½ cup vegetable liquor

½ teaspoon black pepper
¾ teaspoon celery salt
¾ teaspoon garlic salt
½ teaspoon salt
1 teaspoon Worcestershire sauce
1 (6-ounce) roll jalapeño cheese
Red pepper to taste

Cook spinach according to directions on package. Drain and reserve liquor. Melt butter in saucepan over low heat. Add flour, stirring until blended and smooth, but not brown. Add onion and cook until soft, but not brown. Add liquids slowly, stirring constantly to avoid lumps. Cook until smooth and thick; continue stirring. Add seasonings and cheese, which has been cut into small pieces. Stir until melted and combine with cooked spinach. This may be served immediately or put into a casserole and topped with buttered crumbs. The flavor is improved if the latter is done and kept in refrigerator overnight. Also freezes well. Yield: 5 to 6 servings.

Mrs. Virginia Ray

Spinach Parmesan

2 (10-ounce) packages frozen
  chopped spinach
1 (8-ounce) carton sour cream
⅓ cup Parmesan cheese

½ teaspoon garlic salt
3 slices white bread, cubed
3 Tablespoons margarine, melted

Cook spinach according to package directions. Drain and press water out of spinach. Mix spinach, sour cream, cheese, and garlic salt. Pour into buttered baking dish and top with bread cubes. Pour margarine over bread cubes. Bake at 350° until bread cubes are lightly browned, about 20 minutes. Can be prepared ahead and refrigerated before baking. Yield: 4 to 6 servings.

Spinach can also be stuffed into tomatoes, drizzled with melted margarine, and baked.

Mrs. John Newton
(Cathie Bailess)

Stuffed Zucchini Squash

2 large zucchini squash (3-inch
  diameter, 12 inches long)
2 pounds lean ground beef
1 pound roll hot pork sausage
2 large onions, grated
2 (6-ounce) cans tomato sauce
1½ teaspoons garlic powder
1 teaspoon onion powder

1 teaspoon seasoned salt
Dash of TABASCO brand pepper
  sauce
Black pepper to taste
½ cup grated Parmesan cheese,
  divided
2 Tablespoons Worcestershire sauce

Boil squash in hot salted water until tender. Remove from water; drain. Cut a slice from the top and using a spoon, scoop out pulp, forming a boat-shaped shell. Reserve pulp. Place the 2 shells in a large baking dish. Brown ground beef and sausage in a large skillet. Drain well and put in large mixing bowl. Add grated onion, tomato sauce, and all seasonings, except 2 Tablespoons Parmesan cheese. Add zucchini pulp. If pulp is watery, drain well before adding to meat mixture. Fill zucchini squash shells with meat mixture. Sprinkle top with remaining Parmesan cheese. Bake at 350°, uncovered, for 1 hour. Yield: 6 to 8 servings.

Mrs. George Jabour, Jr.
(Miriam Penton)

Squash Casserole

2 pounds squash
2 eggs
½ to ¾ medium onion, chopped
6 Tablespoons margarine
½ cup milk

3 Tablespoons brown sugar
1 teaspoon salt
1½ cups shredded Cheddar cheese
Round butter crackers, crushed
Butter or margarine

Cook squash in small amount of water until tender. Drain well and mash. In a separate bowl beat eggs. Sauté onion in margarine. Add squash, eggs, milk, brown sugar, and salt to onions. Mix well. In a buttered 2-quart casserole put 1 layer of 10 crushed crackers, 1 layer of squash mixture, and 1 layer of cheese. Repeat the 3 layers; top with cracker crumbs and dots of butter. Bake, uncovered, at 350° for 45 minutes. Can be frozen. Yield: 8 to 10 servings.

Mrs. Don Miller, Jr.
(Deanna Blanchard)

Summer Vegetable Casserole

2 Tablespoons raw rice
3 zucchini squash, sliced in rounds
3 yellow squash, sliced in rounds
1 large onion, sliced in wedges
2 large tomatoes, sliced in wedges

½ teaspoon salt
¼ teaspoon pepper
1 Tablespoon brown sugar
2 Tablespoons butter or margarine

Butter a 2-quart casserole dish. Put raw rice in the bottom. Layer sliced vegetables in order listed above. Sprinkle salt, pepper, and brown sugar between each layer and on top. Cut butter into small pieces and dot on top of casserole. Cover and bake at 325° for 1 hour. These are all juicy vegetables so cut into thick slices. Do not add any liquid. Yield: 8 servings.

The vegetables make a wonderful broth while cooking that can be used for soup bases.

Mrs. Steve Harris
(Linda Walker)

 A lettuce leaf added to canned vegetables when heating will add fresh vegetable taste.

Pea-Stuffed Squash

4 medium yellow squash
1 (17-ounce) can small early peas
4 Tablespoons melted butter
¼ cup light cream, warmed
Salt to taste

Pepper to taste
Bread crumbs
Butter
Parmesan cheese, grated

Cut squash lengthwise and boil in salted water, about 7 to 10 minutes. The squash must be slightly firm. Remove inside of squash. Drain peas and put in blender with butter, cream, salt, and pepper. Purée thoroughly. Fill squash cavity with purée of peas. Cover with bread crumbs; dot with butter and sprinkle with Parmesan cheese. Bake at 350° until hot, about 15 minutes and then run under broiler to brown. Yield: 8 servings.

Mrs. Clyde Hughey, Jr.
Memphis, Tennessee

Southern-Style Stuffed Squash

6 to 8 medium yellow squash
1 slice country ham
1 medium onion, chopped
4 ribs celery, thinly sliced
3 cloves garlic, finely chopped

2 slices bread, toasted
Salt and pepper to taste
1 egg, beaten
Bread crumbs
Butter

Peel yellow squash. Slice and boil until tender. Drain and set aside. Trim fat from country ham and render grease. Remove remaining fat and chop ham. Using grease from ham, sauté onion, celery, and garlic until slightly wilted. Add squash and ham. Cook over medium heat about 15 minutes, stirring frequently. Soak toasted bread in water and wring thoroughly. Mix into squash mixture and cook several minutes, stirring often. Salt and pepper to taste. Add beaten egg, stir, and place into serving dish. Top with bread crumbs and pats of butter. Bake at 350° for 15 minutes. Yield: 6 to 8 servings.

Mrs. Mike Cappaert
(Patty Graham)

 A clove of garlic is a piece of garlic; the bulb or pod means the whole garlic.

Zucchini Casserole

1 cup buttermilk baking mix
2 Tablespoons parsley flakes
½ cup finely chopped onion
½ teaspoon salt
½ cup Parmesan cheese
¼ teaspoon seasoned pepper
¼ teaspoon oregano

Dash of pepper
½ teaspoon garlic powder
½ cup vegetable oil
4 eggs, slightly beaten
3 cups sliced zucchini, unpeeled and
    uncooked

Mix all ingredients; add zucchini last. Bake in a greased 9 x 13-inch casserole at 350° for 25 minutes or until brown. Yield: 8 servings.

Serve as a casserole or cut into 1-inch squares as an appetizer.

Mrs. Jerry Beard
(Mallory Wilkerson)

Mixed Vegetable Casserole

2 (10-ounce) packages frozen mixed
    vegetables
1 medium onion, chopped
1 cup chopped celery
1 cup shredded processed cheese

1 cup mayonnaise
1 tube Ritz crackers, crushed
½ cup butter, melted

Cook vegetables according to package directions. Drain and place in a greased 1½-quart casserole. Mix onion, celery, cheese, and mayonnaise. Spread on top of vegetables. Mix cracker crumbs and melted butter. Top casserole with crumb mixture and bake 30 minutes at 350°. Yield: 8 servings.

Mrs. David Sessums
(Beverly Tucker)

Fried Green Tomatoes

2 medium firm green tomatoes
1 cup corn meal
½ teaspoon salt

½ teaspoon black pepper
Vegetable oil for frying

Slice tomatoes ¼-inch thick. Season corn meal with salt and pepper. Dredge tomatoes in corn meal. Fry immediately in hot oil on both sides until golden brown. Drain on paper towels. Yield: 4 servings.

Miriam Graeber Cohn
Port Gibson, Mississippi

Baked Tomatoes

5 to 6 medium-sized firm, ripe
 tomatoes
Salt
Freshly ground black pepper
Red pepper
¼ to ½ cup Grey Poupon Dijon
 Mustard

6 Tablespoons margarine, melted
½ cup Italian seasoned bread
 crumbs
½ cup grated Parmesan cheese

Wash tomatoes, remove stems, and halve crosswise. Place cut-side up in a lightly greased baking dish. Sprinkle lightly with salt, pepper, and red pepper. Spread each with mustard. Mix together margarine, bread crumbs, and cheese. Spread mixture over tomatoes. Bake in 350° oven for 20 to 30 minutes. Yield: 10 to 12 servings.

Mrs. Joseph R. Compton
(Emily Raworth)

Baked Tomatoes Rockefeller

2 (10-ounce) packages chopped
 spinach
2 cups seasoned bread crumbs
6 green onions, chopped
6 eggs, slightly beaten
¾ cup butter, melted
½ cup Parmesan cheese
¼ teaspoon Worcestershire sauce

½ teaspoon minced garlic
1 teaspoon salt
½ teaspoon black pepper
1 teaspoon thyme
1 teaspoon monosodium glutamate
¼ teaspoon TABASCO brand
 pepper sauce
12 thick tomato slices

Cook spinach according to directions. Add remaining ingredients except tomato. Arrange tomato slices in a single layer in buttered 9 x 13-inch baking dish. Mound spinach mixture on tomato slices. Sprinkle lightly with more Parmesan cheese. Bake at 350° for 15 minutes. The spinach mixture may be made well in advance and it freezes well. Yield: 12 servings.

Mrs. Mack Varner
(Penny Sanders)

 To ripen tomatoes, put them in a brown paper bag in a dark pantry and they will ripen overnight.

Okra and Tomatoes

3 Tablespoons bacon grease
2 large onions, chopped
1 (20-ounce) can sliced okra

1 (1-pound 13-ounce) can whole
  tomatoes
Salt and pepper to taste

In a large iron skillet heat grease and sauté onions over low heat until clear, about 10 minutes. Add okra with liquid and tomatoes with liquid. Simmer over low heat, stirring often to avoid sticking. Cook until most of juice evaporates, about 1½ hours. Add salt and pepper to taste.

Fresh okra and tomatoes may be substituted. Fresh or canned corn may also be added.

Mrs. Ernest Lipscomb
(Betty McCabe)

Oriental Vegetables with Horseradish Sauce

1 (10-ounce) package frozen broccoli
1 (10-ounce) package oriental-style
  vegetables
1 (3-ounce) package cream cheese,
  softened

⅓ cup light cream
¼ teaspoon mustard
½ teaspoon sugar
2 teaspoons horseradish
2 teaspoons lemon juice

Cook vegetables according to directions. Blend cream cheese to a paste with cream. Gradually add remaining ingredients and blend well. Heat to serve over vegetables. Yield: 6 to 8 servings.

Mrs. James McAdams
Greenwood, Mississippi

Tempura Batter for Vegetables

1 cup flour
¼ cup cornstarch
1 teaspoon baking powder
1 teaspoon salt

1 egg, slightly beaten
¾ cup cold water
¼ cup vegetable oil
Cayenne pepper to taste (optional)

Mix together dry ingredients. Add egg, water and oil and cayenne pepper if desired. Stir to blend. Use to dip slices of yellow squash, zucchini, eggplant, green tomatoes, onion rings, mushrooms or fish fillets for frying. Fry in small bit of oil in skillet or wok on very high heat. Batter will keep, covered, in refrigerator for a few days. Yield: 2 cups.

Mrs. Bill Fenwick
(Dot Chew)

Stir-Fried Vegetable Medley

2 medium carrots
2 celery ribs
1 medium red onion
1 medium bunch broccoli
½ pound large mushrooms

¼ cup salad oil
¼ cup water
1¼ teaspoons salt
½ teaspoon sugar

Cut each carrot crosswise in half, then lengthwise into matchstick-thin strips. Cut each celery rib crosswise in 3 pieces, then lengthwise into matchstick-thin strips. Thinly slice onion. Cut broccoli in 2 x ½-inch pieces. Cut mushrooms in quarters or cut in half if small. In a 12-inch skillet over high heat, cook carrots, celery, onion, and broccoli in hot salad oil, stirring quickly and frequently, about 3 to 4 minutes. Add mushrooms, water, salt, and sugar; cover and cook 5 to 6 minutes longer until vegetables are tender-crisp, stirring occasionally. Yield: 8 servings.

Jeannie Abraham

Foolproof Hollandaise Sauce

¾ cup water
Salt, red pepper, and paprika to
taste
2 Tablespoons fresh lemon juice

1 Tablespoon cornstarch
2 egg yolks, beaten
3 Tablespoons butter, divided

Pour water in top of double boiler. Heat water and add salt, red pepper, paprika, and lemon juice. Dissolve cornstarch in small amount of cold water. Add to seasoned water, stirring constantly. Remove from heat when slightly thickened. Add beaten egg yolks and 1 Tablespoon butter. Stir eggs and butter in mixture and place over hot water until thickened. Before serving add 2 Tablespoons butter. Can be reheated over hot, not boiling water, for 5 minutes. Yield: 1 cup.

Mrs. Bruce Ebersole
(Story Stamm)

 To freeze fresh mushrooms, clean and pat dry quickly; store in plastic bag. Do not defrost before using. It's impossible to tell they've been frozen.

Cheese Fruit

1 (17-ounce) can mixed fruits
1 (17-ounce) can apricot halves
1 (20-ounce) can pineapple chunks

2 (5-ounce) jars Old English cheese
  spread
¾ cup sugar
¼ cup flour

Drain fruits, reserving 2 cups fluid. Heat juice in saucepan, adding slowly sugar and flour. When mixture is smooth, add cheese spread. Stir sauce until it bubbles; sauce should be very smooth. Put drained fruit in 9 x 12-inch pan. Pour sauce over fruit and bake at 350° for 30 minutes. Yield: 8 to 12 servings.

If doubling this recipe, make only 1½ amount cheese sauce

Mrs. Harry H. Gilliland, Jr.
(Meta Klaus)

Pineapple Cheese Casserole

2 (20-ounce) cans pineapple chunks
Scant ½ cup sugar
½ cup flour

½ teaspoon salt
1 cup shredded medium Cheddar
  cheese

Drain pineapple, reserving juice. In a saucepan, combine pineapple juice, sugar, flour, and salt. Cook until clear. In a buttered 1¾-quart casserole dish, layer pineapple and cheese. Pour in a little sauce. Continue layering until all ingredients are used ending with sauce. Bake at 375° for 30 minutes or until bubbly. Yield: 8 servings.

Mrs. Marion Blalock Haraway
Brookhaven, Mississippi

Hot Fruit Compote

1 (20-ounce) can pineapple chunks
1 (17-ounce) can blackberries
1 (14.5-ounce) can peeled apricots
1 (20-ounce) jar applesauce

1 cup brown sugar
¾ cup sherry wine
3 Tablespoons butter or margarine
Sour cream

Drain first 3 fruits. Mix these and applesauce in a 9 x 13-inch baking dish. Add brown sugar and mix well. Pour sherry over fruit. Dot with pats of butter. Cook at 350° for 30 minutes or until it bubbles. Remove from oven and top each serving with a dollop of sour cream. Yield: 8 servings.

Mrs. Bobby Robinson
(Jan Harris)

Lemon Cream Sauce

2 cups mayonnaise
2 cups sour cream
¼ cup fresh lemon juice
2½ teaspoons grated lemon peel

2 teaspoons white horseradish
2 teaspoons Dijon mustard
1 teaspoon salt

Combine all ingredients in large bowl and blend. Cover and refrigerate. Adjust seasoning before serving. Delicious for use as a dip with steamed artichokes. For lime sauce substitute ⅓ cup lime juice for lemon juice and 1 teaspoon grated lime peel for lemon peel. Good served with broccoli florets that have been cooked, cooled and lightly sprinkled with Italian salad dressing. Yield: 4 cups.

Mrs. Jerry Nations
Brookhaven, Mississippi

Hot Fruit Dish

1 (29-ounce) can peach halves
1 (16-ounce) can pear halves
1 (15-ounce) can pineapple slices
1 (15-ounce) jar spiced apple rings,
  reserving juice

½ cup butter or margarine
3 Tablespoons flour
1 cup sugar
1 cup cooking sherry

Drain fruits and arrange them in a 9 x 13-inch baking dish. Reserve juice from apple rings. Melt butter or margarine and stir in flour and sugar. Add sherry and juice from apple rings. Cook this mixture until thickened and pour over fruits. Cook at 350° for 30 to 45 minutes. Yield: Approximately 12 servings.

Mrs. William Bost, Jr.
(Carolyn Walden)

Microwave Apples in Wine

2 large baking apples
¼ cup white wine
¼ teaspoon cinnamon

1 Tablespoon butter or margarine
2 Tablespoons brown sugar,
  softened

Core apples; pare strip from top of each. Pour wine in 1-quart casserole. Stir together cinnamon, butter and brown sugar. Spoon into apple centers. Bake, uncovered, on high for 3½ to 4 minutes or until tender. Turn pan and baste several times during cooking. Yield: 2 servings.

The Editors

Christ Episcopal Church

Standing on old streets in Vicksburg, one can imagine the loaded wagons and buggies of another era passing by. Weathered brick pavement suggests a bygone day, adding quaintness and authentic antiquity particularly on steep slopes, where the bricks were beveled to give horses a foothold.

Nearby ran old Jackson Road, a winding route travelers would take through the plantation country to the capital at Jackson. Watering troughs were spaced at intervals along the streets.

At the gabled door of historic Christ Episcopal Church, oldest place of assembly in Vicksburg, the pattern is especially pleasing. Christ Church was built in 1839 and has survived through war and disease without relenting in its Divine mission.

As solid as the surrounding hills, it prevails.

Breads pictured:
Bubble Wreath, Yeast Rolls, Easy French Bread, Lebanese Church Bread, Viola's Biscuits, Coconut Muffins, Strawberry Butter, Cheesy Jalapeño Corn Bread, Holiday Cranberry Bread, Cinnamon Rolls, Cream Cheese Stollen, Braided Parsley Bread, Sour Dough Refrigerator Rolls, Carol Robbie's Bread, French Bread

Breads

Cheesy Jalapeño Corn Bread

5 slices bacon
2 eggs
1¼ cups milk
2 cups self-rising corn meal
1 Tablespoon sugar
¼ teaspoon garlic powder
1 (8½-ounce) can creamed corn

1 cup chopped onion
1 cup shredded medium Cheddar
cheese
2 Tablespoons canned chopped
jalapeños
2 Tablespoons chopped pimento
(optional)

Cook bacon in 9-inch skillet until crisp. Crumble. Reserve 5 Tablespoons bacon drippings. Use 1 Tablespoon bacon drippings to grease skillet. Preheat skillet in 400° oven while mixing other ingredients. Beat eggs; stir in milk and 4 Tablespoons bacon drippings. Add bacon and other ingredients. Mix well. Pour into heated skillet. Bake at 400° for 35 minutes. Yield: 6 servings.

Mrs. David Sessums
(Beverly Tucker)

Geneva's Sour Cream Corn Bread

¼ cup plus 3 Tablespoons bacon
  drippings, divided
1 cup white corn meal
½ cup flour
1 teaspoon salt

2 teaspoons baking powder
1 cup sour cream
¾ cup buttermilk
1 egg

Heat 1 Tablespoon bacon drippings in a 10-inch iron skillet. Mix together well all other ingredients. Mix well. To Tablespoon of bacon drippings in skillet, sprinkle corn meal to cover very lightly the bottom of skillet. Pour batter into skillet. Bake at 475° for 18 minutes or until browned. Yield: 4 to 6 servings.

Mrs. Karl Hatten
(Ruth Land)

Before cooking corn bread, grease skillet or pan and place in oven until grease sizzles. Remove pan from oven, sprinkle a little corn meal in bottom, then pour in batter.

287

Corn Bread

1 cup white corn meal
1 Tablespoon flour
1 teaspoon baking powder
½ teaspoon soda
½ teaspoon salt

1 cup buttermilk
1 egg
3 Tablespoons vegetable oil or
   bacon grease

Stir all dry ingredients together. Pour in buttermilk and stir. Put egg in the middle of batter and stir until well mixed. Pour oil into batter and stir. Pour corn bread into a 10-inch iron skillet or 12 muffin tins which have been heated in the oven with oil to coat bottom for a crispy crust. Bake at 425° for 20 minutes. Yield: 4 to 8 servings.

Mrs. Bobby Robinson
(Jan Harris)

Spoon Bread

3 cups milk
1 cup white corn meal
1 teaspoon butter
1 teaspoon sugar

1 teaspoon salt
3 egg yolks, beaten
3 egg whites, beaten

Heat milk in heavy pan; add meal slowly and stir until thickened. When slightly cooled, add butter, sugar, and salt. Add beaten egg yolks. Fold in beaten egg whites. Bake in buttered 9 x 13-inch casserole at 350° for 45 minutes. Serve immediately with lemon butter. Yield: 4 to 6 servings.

Mrs. Jerry Silver
("Sis" Waring Hughes)

Cheesy Hush Puppies

½ cup shredded processed cheese
2 small onions, grated
½ cup flour
1½ cups self-rising corn meal

1 cup buttermilk
½ teaspoon sugar
1 egg, slightly beaten
½ teaspoon salt

Mix all ingredients together in a medium-size mixing bowl. Spoon into 300° grease, ½ teaspoon at a time. As the hush puppies rise to the top, turn them over and brown. Yield: 10 servings.

Mrs. Jerry Mayfield
(Pam Jabour)

Hush Puppies

1½ cups self-rising corn meal
½ cup flour
2 eggs
1 large onion, chopped
3 Tablespoons green onion tops,
    chopped

⅛ teaspoon red pepper
¼ teaspoon garlic powder
1½ teaspoons salt
Scant ¾ cup beer
Cooking oil

Mix corn meal, flour, eggs, chopped vegetables, red pepper, garlic powder, and salt. Add beer. Store in refrigerator. When ready to cook, drop by teaspoon into deep oil and fry to desired color. Yield: 4 to 6 servings.

Mrs. Bubba Rainer
(Tricia Frey)

Viola's Biscuits

2 Tablespoons sugar
2 Tablespoons baking powder
6 cups self-rising flour

1 cup solid vegetable shortening
2 cups buttermilk

Combine first 3 ingredients and sift. Cut in shortening. Add buttermilk. Roll out on a floured surface ¼-inch thick. Cut into 1½-inch circles. Bake in a preheated 400° oven for 10 minutes. Cool and freeze if desired or bake 8 minutes longer to serve immediately. If frozen, remove as many as desired and bake in a preheated 450° oven for 15 minutes. Yield: 5 dozen small biscuits.

Mrs. D. P. Waring, Jr.
(Betty Jeanne Williams)

Old-Fashioned Sally Lund Bread

½ cup butter
½ cup sugar
2 eggs

2 cups flour
2 teaspoons baking powder
½ cup milk

Cream butter and sugar. Add eggs 1 at a time. Beat well. Combine flour and baking powder. Add to batter alternately with milk. Beat well. Bake in small loaf pan, approximately 8½ x 4½-inches, which has been greased and floured, at 350° for 1 hour. Yield: 1 loaf.

Mrs. R. C. Odom
(Idamae Ellzey)

Sour Dough Refrigerator Rolls

2 packages dry yeast
⅓ cup warm water (110°)
1 cup sour dough starter
½ cup vegetable oil
3 eggs, well beaten

1 cup warm water (110°)
½ cup sugar
2 teaspoons salt
4½ to 5½ cups flour, divided
Melted butter (not margarine)

Soften yeast in ⅓ cup warm water; set aside. In a large bowl combine sour dough starter, vegetable oil, eggs, 1 cup warm water, sugar, salt, and 2 cups flour. Stir vigorously by hand for 1 minute. Stir in softened yeast and enough flour to make a dough that pulls away from sides of the bowl. Cover with a cloth. Set in a warm place free from drafts and let rise until doubled in size. Punch down; cover with plastic wrap or seal in plastic bowl, and refrigerate overnight. 3 hours before baking, roll dough onto a floured surface ¼ to ½-inch thick. Cut with biscuit cutter and dip into melted butter; fold in half, pocket-book style, and place in greased baking pans. Cover and let rise, about 2½ to 3 hours. Bake at 425° for 12 to 15 minutes or until golden brown. These can be frozen after baking only 10 minutes. After they are thawed, reheat in a 375° oven for 5 minutes. Yield: 2 to 3 dozen.

Basic Sour Dough Starter

2 cups flour
1 teaspoon salt
3 Tablespoons sugar

1 Tablespoon dry yeast
2 cups lukewarm water

With a wooden or plastic spoon stir dry ingredients into a large mixing bowl and gradually add liquid. Stir until it resembles a smooth paste. Cover and set in warm place (85°) to sour. In 2 to 3 days it will be ready to use. Stir several times a day. Store in refrigerator. Never use any type of metal utensil or bowl in contact with sour dough as this ruins the flavor; instead, use wooden, plastic, or ceramic containers and utensils. Always return at least 1 cup starter to the refrigerator. Feed it once a month by adding equal parts of water and flour, allowing it to bubble and expand. At this time return 1 cup to refrigerator stock and use the rest in recipes or share with a friend.

Mrs. Steve Parris

To proof yeast add 1 teaspoon sugar to yeast-warm water mixture in recipes. If mixture bubbles up fairly quickly, yeast is good.

Yeast Rolls

1 cup milk
½ cup margarine
½ cup sugar
2 packages yeast

1 teaspoon salt
3 eggs
4 cups flour
Butter

Scald milk and remove from heat. Add margarine. Combine sugar and yeast. Mix well. Using a yeast thermometer, the milk should test between 105° and 115°, not exceeding in order to dissolve the yeast. Add yeast and sugar mixture to milk and margarine. Add salt and slightly beaten eggs. Add flour. Mix well. Let rise until doubled in bulk, 2 to 3 hours. Roll out; add flour as needed. Cut with biscuit cutter. Butter each roll; fold over. Let rise again until doubled in size. Bake in preheated 400° oven until browned. May be half baked and then frozen. When removing from freezer, allow about 15 minutes to thaw. Finish baking in 400° oven. Yield: 6 dozen.

Mrs. James P. Guerriero
(Margaret Webb)

Light-As-A-Feather Rolls

2 packages yeast
½ cup warm water
⅔ cup sugar
1 teaspoon salt
2 Tablespoons soft butter or
   margarine

1½ cups warm milk
1 egg, slightly beaten
6 to 7 cups flour (bleached or
   unbleached)

Sprinkle yeast on warm water. Add sugar, salt, butter, milk, and egg. Add flour 1 cup at a time and mix well with spoon. When a sticky consistency has been reached, turn out on floured board and knead slightly. Place in buttered bowl and cover; let rise in warm place until doubled. Knead on floured board; roll out and cut into desired shape and place in buttered pans. Let rise until doubled and place in 400° oven to bake 20 to 25 minutes or until browned. Butter tops when removed from oven. Yield: Approximately 72 medium rolls.

Mrs. Robert Evans, III
(Sheila Lawler)

 To glaze the tops of rolls or pastry, brush before baking with egg white beaten slightly with 1 Tablespoon water.

French Onion Bread

1 package dry yeast
¼ cup lukewarm water
1 envelope dry onion soup mix
2 cups water
2 Tablespoons sugar
1 teaspoon salt
2 Tablespoons grated Parmesan
  cheese

2 Tablespoons shortening
6 to 6½ cups sifted enriched flour
2 Tablespoons corn meal
1 egg white, beaten with fork with
  1 Tablespoon water

Dissolve yeast in lukewarm water. Simmer dry onion soup mix with 2 cups water, covered, for 10 minutes. Remove from stove. Add sugar, salt, cheese and shortening. Cool to lukewarm. Remove to large mixing bowl. Add yeast mixture; stir well until all yeast particles are dissolved. Stir flour in gradually, mixing well after each addition. Knead mixture on floured board until smooth and elastic, about 5 minutes. Return to mixing bowl; cover with plastic wrap, cloth or plate. Let rise until doubled, about 1½ hours. Punch down with fingers. Divide in half; cover and let mixture rest for 10 minutes. By hand, shape into 2 long loaves. Place on a greased baking sheet that has been sprinkled with corn meal. Cover with towel and let rise 1 hour. Bake in preheated oven at 375° for 20 minutes. With pastry brush, brush loaves with beaten egg white and water. Bake additional 10 to 15 minutes or until browned and done. Yield: 2 loaves.

Mrs. R. Crofton Sloan
(Mary Bayer)

Refrigerator Spoon Rolls

1 package dry yeast
2 cups warm water
¼ cup sugar
½ cup vegetable oil

4 cups self-rising flour
1 egg, slightly beaten
1 teaspoon salt
3 Tablespoons bran

Dissolve yeast in warm water with sugar in large mixing bowl. Add all other ingredients and beat until well mixed. Place in airtight covered container and store in refrigerator. As needed, spoon into greased muffin tins and bake at 400° for about 20 minutes. The dough can be kept a week to 10 days with no rising time required. Yield: 24 to 30 rolls.

Mrs. Jerry Dykes
(Tina Hazzlerigg)

Carol Robbie's Bread

1 cup boiling water
¾ cup margarine, sliced into pats
¾ cup sugar
1 teaspoon salt
1 cup warm water

2 packages dry yeast
Pinch of sugar
2 eggs, beaten
6 cups bread flour
Butter

Grease 2 large or 5 small loaf pans well and set aside. In a large bowl combine water, margarine, sugar, and salt. Stir until cool. In a small bowl combine warm water (105° to 115°), yeast, and sugar. Stir gently to dissolve yeast. Next, check temperature of margarine mixture. When it is cool enough so as not to kill the yeast (below 105°), combine the 2 mixtures into the large bowl. Stir in beaten eggs. Gradually add flour. At this point dough should taste sweet. The mixture will be very gummy in consistency. Pour or spoon mixture into loaf pans filling almost ½ full. Cover the loaf pans with a dish towel and let dough rise for about 45 minutes or until dough is not quite to the top of pan. Bake risen dough for 45 minutes at 350°. Rub butter over the tops immediately. Serve hot or cool or wrap for gift giving. Freezes well. Yield: 2 regular or 5 miniature loaves.

Carol Bonelli-Rosser

Easy French Bread

1 package yeast
1½ cups very warm water, not
   boiling
1 Tablespoon shortening

1 Tablespoon sugar
1½ teaspoons salt
4 cups flour
Butter

Put yeast in very warm water in large mixing bowl and stir with wooden spoon. Add shortening, sugar, and salt. Add flour, 1 cup at a time, and work dough with wooden spoon until it "cleans the bowl." Cover and let rise 10 minutes; then stir down; let rise 10 minutes and stir down again. Do this 5 times at 10 minute intervals. Turn dough out on lightly floured board. Divide into 2 balls. Let stand 5 to 10 minutes. Roll each ball into a rectangle approximately 12 x 9 inches. Roll long-side up firmly as for jelly-roll. Seal edges. Place on greased cookie sheet with sealed edges down. Score top 5 or 6 times diagonally. Cover with towel and place in warm spot. Let rise 1½ hours. Bake at 400° for 30 minutes. Brush top with butter and cool. Freezes well and there is no kneading in this bread. Yield: 12 to 15 servings.

Mrs. Duane Anderson
Enid, Oklahoma

Easy Wheat Bread

1 package dry yeast
1¼ cups warm water (110° to 115°)
1½ cups whole wheat flour, sifted
1½ cups flour, sifted

2 Tablespoons soft shortening
2 teaspoons salt
2 Tablespoons sugar
Melted butter

In a medium-size mixing bowl, dissolve yeast in warm water. Add ½ the flours. Add shortening, salt, and sugar. Beat 2 minutes at medium speed with electric mixer or 300 vigorous strokes by hand. Scrape sides and bottom of bowl frequently. Add remaining flours and blend in with spoon until smooth. Scrape batter from sides of bowl. Cover with cloth and let rise in warm place (85°) until doubled in size, 30 to 60 minutes. Stir down batter about 25 strokes. Spread batter evenly in greased 8½ x 4½ x 2¾-inch or 9 x 5 x 3-inch pan. Batter will be sticky. Smooth out top of loaf by flouring hand and patting. Let rise in warm place (85°) until batter is ½ inch from top of 8½-inch pan or 1 inch from top of 9-inch pan, 40 to 60 minutes. Bake at 375° for 45 to 50 minutes or until browned. To test loaf, tap the top crust; it should sound hollow. Immediately remove from pan. Place on cooling rack or across bread pans. Brush top with melted butter or shortening. Do not place in direct draft. Cool before cutting; use a serrated knife. Doubles and freezes well. Yield: 1 loaf.

Mrs. H. Donald Barnes
(Betty Haraway)

Pull-Apart Bread

1 cup milk
1 cup butter, divided
4 Tablespoons sugar
1 teaspoon salt

1 package yeast
¼ cup warm water
Pinch of sugar
3½ cups flour

Combine milk, ½ cup butter, sugar, and salt in saucepan. Heat until butter is melted. Cool until lukewarm. Stir yeast into warm water and sugar. Stir until yeast dissolves. Stir yeast into cooled milk mixture. Stir in flour and blend with mixer. Cover and let rise in warm place until doubled in size, about 1½ hours. Turn dough out onto floured surface. Roll ¼-inch thick. Cut into 3-inch squares. Dip each square into remaining butter that has been melted. Layer squares in bread pan. Let rise until doubled in size, about 40 minutes. Bake at 375° for 30 to 40 minutes. Yield: 1 loaf.

Mrs. Donald Seago
(Rosemary Moore)

Braided Parsley Bread

1 package dry yeast
¼ cup warm water
4 cups flour, divided
¼ cup sugar
1½ teaspoons salt

½ cup hot water
½ cup milk
¼ cup butter, softened
1 egg

Dissolve yeast in warm water in large bowl. Add 2 cups flour, sugar, salt, hot water, milk, butter, and egg. Beat with mixer for 2 minutes at medium speed. Add remaining 2 cups flour. Mix well with spoon. Cover bowl and set in warm place. Let dough rise 45 to 60 minutes or until doubled in size. Stir down dough. On a floured surface toss dough until no longer sticky. Roll out to an 18 x 12-inch rectangle. Cut dough lengthwise into three 4-inch strips. Spread filling down center of each strip. Roll up each strip starting on long side. Moisten edges to seal. On a greased cookie sheet braid the 3 strips. Brush on glaze with pastry brush and sprinkle with poppy seed or sesame seed. Cover and put in a warm place. Let rise 45 to 60 minutes or until doubled in size. Bake at 350° for 30 to 35 minutes or until golden brown. Yield: 10 to 12 servings.

Filling

½ cup melted butter
1 cup chopped parsley
2 Tablespoons Parmesan cheese
1 Tablespoon poppy seed

1 teaspoon garlic salt
2 Tablespoons chopped onion
1 teaspoon paprika

Mix all ingredients well.

Glaze

1 egg white
1 Tablespoon water

Poppy seed or sesame seed

Mix all ingredients.

Mrs. Jerry M. Hall
(Carolyn Buckner)

 Let dough rise in an unheated oven with a large pan of hot water beneath it.

Lebanese Church Bread

1 package yeast	*1 Tablespoon salt*
2½ cups warm water	*1½ teaspoons sugar*
2½ pounds flour	*1 Tablespoon vegetable oil*

Dissolve yeast in warm water. In large pan mix flour, salt, and sugar. Make a well in center of flour mixture. Add dissolved yeast and oil. Work mixture into flour until thoroughly blended. Dough will be stiff and sticky. Remove excess dough from hands. Dip hands into warm water to moisten dough. Knead dough for 5 minutes or until smooth on top. Turn over dough. Dip hands in warm water again and knead dough for 5 more minutes. Continue this kneading process until dough is smooth and elastic. Cover pan with cloth and then plastic wrap. Let rise in warm draft-free place for 2 hours or until dough has doubled in size. Cut dough into pieces the size of an orange. Smooth each piece into a ball. On a piece of white cloth, such as a sheet, roll out or pat each ball into a circle ½ inch in thickness and about 6 to 8 inches in diameter. Cover dough with cloth and then plastic wrap. Let set ½ hour. Bake at 450° on ungreased baking sheet on lower shelf about 5 minutes or until light brown. If necessary, brown a few minutes under broiler (watch carefully to prevent burning). Cool. Cover with white cloth to keep soft. Yield: 9 to 10 loaves.

Hifa Nicola

Asphodel Bread

5 cups biscuit mix	*2 cups warm milk*
4 Tablespoons sugar	*4 eggs*
½ teaspoon salt	*¼ teaspoon cream of tartar*
2 envelopes dry yeast	*Vegetable oil*

Into a very large bowl sift biscuit mix, sugar, and salt. Soften yeast in milk. Make sure the milk is only warm. Too much heat kills the yeast. Beat the eggs with a pinch of cream of tartar until thoroughly broken up. Combine milk and eggs and pour into dry ingredients. Stir until well mixed. This is a heavy, sticky mixture so be sure that it is well mixed. Set aside in a warm place covered with a damp dish towel or, even better, seal with plastic wrap. When doubled in bulk, stir down and fill oiled loaf pans about halfway. Again let rise and double the size before baking at 350° approximately 20 minutes. Serve very hot. The bread freezes quite well. Remember to allow to completely thaw before reheating. This also makes the most delicious toast the next day. Yield: 2 loaves.

Mrs. David Boolos
(Kay Garrett)

Aunt Margaret's Oatmeal Bread

2 cups boiling water
1 cup oats
2 Tablespoons margarine
2 teaspoons salt
¼ teaspoon sugar

⅓ cup warm water
2 packages dry yeast
½ cup honey
6 cups flour
Butter

Pour boiling water over oats, margarine, and salt and let stand about 20 to 30 minutes in a large mixing bowl. About 10 minutes before oats are ready, mix sugar and warm water and sprinkle yeast over top. When oats are ready, mix and add to oats mixture. Add honey and stir well. Add 2 cups flour and stir until flour disappears. Then add 2 more cups flour and stir until flour disappears. Last 2 cups of flour are added ½ cup at a time and kneaded each time until flour disappears. Form into ball and leave in same bowl. Cover and let rise in warm place until doubled in size. Then stick several times with a knife and let fall. Divide into 2 equal amounts and put in 2 well greased loaf pans. Cover and let rise until doubled in size. Bake 1 hour in preheated oven at 350°. Turn out of pans onto racks. Rub tops with butter and cool. Yield: 2 loaves.

This can also be made with 2 cups whole wheat flour and 4 cups white flour.

Mrs. Kenneth E. Hicks
(Margaret Bonney)

Italian Cheese Bread

½ cup margarine, softened
½ cup mayonnaise
6 green onions and tops, finely
  chopped
1 (4-ounce) can chopped ripe olives

½ teaspoon garlic powder
2 cups shredded mozzarella cheese
1 loaf New Orleans-style French
  bread, sliced lengthwise

In a medium-size mixing bowl, blend softened margarine with mayonnaise. Add onions, olives, garlic powder, and cheese. Mix well. Spread ½ mixture on each slice of bread. Bake at 350° for 15 to 20 minutes on a cookie sheet or until cheese melts. Cool slightly; slice and serve. Yield: 8 to 16 servings.

Mrs. F. S. McMillan, Jr.
(Lynn Foy)

For a crisp crust, do not grease loaves after baking. For a soft, tender crust, brush bread with soft butter or margarine while still hot.

Parmesan Twists

¼ cup margarine, softened
1 cup grated Parmesan cheese
½ cup commercial sour cream
1 cup flour

½ teaspoon Italian seasoning
1 egg yolk, beaten
1 Tablespoon tap water
Poppy seed

Cream margarine. Add cheese and sour cream, mixing well. Combine flour and seasoning. Gradually add to creamed mixture and blend until smooth. Turn dough out onto a lightly floured board; divide in half. Roll out ½ dough into a 12 x 7-rectangle and cut into 6 x ½-inch strips. Twist each strip 2 to 3 times and place on a greased cookie sheet. Repeat procedure with remaining dough. Combine egg yolk and water. Brush strips with egg and water mixture; sprinkle lightly with poppy seed. Bake at 350° about 10 minutes, just until lightly browned. Yield: Approximately 4½ dozen.

Mrs. Robert L. Fleming, Jr.
(Laura Sorrels)

Herb Bread

1 teaspoon basil
1 teaspoon rosemary
½ teaspoon thyme

¾ cup margarine
Day-old hot dog buns

Mix first 4 ingredients together and allow to stand for several hours at room temperature. Spread on buns and cut into strips. Bake at 325° for 15 minutes or until crisp. Yield: 8 to 10 servings.

Mrs. Jerry Mayfield
(Pam Jabour)

Company Carrot Bread

2 cups flour
2 teaspoons baking soda
2 teaspoons cinnamon
1½ cups sugar
1½ cups butter-flavored oil

3 eggs, beaten
2 teaspoons vanilla extract
2½ cups grated carrots
1 cup chopped pecans or raisins

Mix and beat together all ingredients except carrots and pecans. Fold in carrots and pecans and pour into a well greased 9 x 3-inch loaf pan. Bake at 300° for 1 hour. Yield: 1 loaf.

Mrs. Robert R. Bailess
(Natalie Waring)

Herb and Spice Butters

½ cup unsalted butter, softened

To softened butter add 1 of these ingredients:

¼ teaspoon dill weed or ¾
teaspoon fresh dill
1 Tablespoon finely chopped chives
1 Tablespoon finely chopped parsley
½ teaspoon basil leaves or 1½
teaspoons fresh basil

¼ teaspoon cinnamon
¼ teaspoon nutmeg
½ teaspoon garlic powder or 2
cloves garlic, boiled, drained,
and mashed

Mix well and refrigerate. Serve on appropriate breads, vegetables, meats, poultry, or seafood. Yield: ½ cup.

The Editors

Strawberry Bread

3 cups flour
2 cups sugar
1 teaspoon soda
1 teaspoon salt
1 Tablespoon cinnamon

3 eggs, beaten
2 (10-ounce) packages sliced frozen
strawberries, thawed
1¼ cups vegetable oil
1¼ cups pecans

Sift together flour, sugar, soda, salt, and cinnamon. Beat eggs and add strawberries, oil, and pecans. Pour into dry mixture. Mix well. Pour into 2 well greased and floured loaf pans. Bake at 350° for approximately 1 hour. Yield: 2 loaves.

Mrs. Robert O. Bailess
(Ruby Wilshire)

Banana Nut Bread

1 cup sugar
½ cup vegetable oil
2 eggs
3 large, very ripe bananas

2 cups flour
1 teaspoon soda
1 cup chopped nuts
1 teaspoon vanilla extract

Combine all ingredients. Mix well. Pour into a greased and floured loaf pan. Bake at 375° for approximately 45 minutes. Muffins may also be used with this recipe, but vary the cooking time accordingly. Yield: 1 large loaf.

Mrs. David Blackledge
(Jan Anderson)

Bubble Wreath

1 package dry yeast
3½ to 3¾ cups sifted flour
1¼ cups milk
¼ cup shortening
¼ cup sugar
1 teaspoon salt

1 egg, beaten
1 recipe Sugar Fruit Topping
½ cup melted butter
½ cup sugar, mixed with 1
   teaspoon cinnamon

Sugar Fruit Topping

2 Tablespoons butter
2 Tablespoons light corn syrup
½ cup packed light brown sugar

16 halved candied cherries
Pecan halves or whole blanched
   almonds

Mix all ingredients.

In a large mixing bowl, combine yeast and 2 cups flour. In a saucepan, heat together milk, shortening, sugar, and salt until warm (115° to 120°), stirring constantly to melt shortening. Add this to flour mixture in bowl, stirring well. Add the beaten egg and beat on low speed of electric mixer for ½ minute, scraping sides of bowl constantly. Beat 3 minutes on high speed. By hand, stir in enough of the remaining flour to make a soft dough. Turn out on a lightly floured surface; knead until smooth. Place dough in a greased bowl, turning once to grease surface of dough. Cover and let rise until doubled in volume, about 2 hours. Grease a 10-inch tube pan. Spread bottom with the sugar fruit topping. Arrange cherries and nuts in an attractive pattern. They will be on the top of the finished coffee cake. Shape dough into 48 small balls. Dip these dough balls in the melted butter and roll in cinnamon sugar mixture. Carefully place on top of sugar fruit topping in tube pan. Let rise again until doubled. Bake 35 minutes in a 400° oven. Loosen and turn out of pan while still hot or it will stick. Yield: 6 to 8 servings.

Mrs. George Jabour, Jr.
(Miriam Penton)

Cheddar Butter Spread

½ cup butter, softened
1 cup shredded Cheddar cheese

½ teaspoon Worcestershire sauce
¼ teaspoon garlic salt

Combine first 4 ingredients. Serve with warm bread. Yield: 1½ cups.

Mrs. Jim Davidson
(Tupper Jones)

Beignets

½ cup butter or margarine
1 teaspoon sugar
¼ teaspoon salt
1 cup cold water
1 cup plus 2 Tablespoons sifted
  flour

1 teaspoon vanilla extract
4 eggs
Salad oil for deep frying
Powdered sugar for dusting

In medium saucepan heat butter, sugar, salt, and cold water to boiling. Remove pan from heat and add flour all at once; stir vigorously until ingredients are combined thoroughly and dough leaves sides of pan and forms a ball. Add vanilla, then eggs, 1 at a time, stirring vigorously. Dough should be smooth and glossy. Meanwhile, in deep fat fryer or large saucepan, heat salad oil to 375° on deep fat thermometer. Drop heaping teaspoon of dough into hot oil and fry beignets a few at a time until golden. Each beignet will puff up to about 2 inches in diameter when done. Drain on paper towels. Dust beignets with powdered sugar and serve warm.

This recipe can also be rolled out and cut like small dumplings and dropped into deep fat.

Mrs. Glover Warner
(Peggy Holder)

Holiday Cranberry Bread

2 cups flour
1 cup plus 2 Tablespoons sugar
1½ teaspoons baking powder
1 teaspoon salt
½ teaspoon baking soda
¼ cup butter or margarine
1 large egg

1 teaspoon grated orange peel
¾ cup orange juice (freshly
  squeezed, if possible)
1 cup currants or raisins
½ cup pecan pieces
1½ cups fresh or frozen cranberries

In large bowl, sift together flour, sugar, baking powder, salt, and baking soda. Cut in butter until crumbly. Add egg, orange peel, and orange juice. Mix well. Add currants and pecans and mix. Fold in cranberries. Bake in greased 9 x 5 x 3-inch loaf pan at 350° for 1 hour and 10 minutes. Cool before removing from pan. Yield: 12 to 14 servings.

Great for a holiday brunch.

Miss Louise Hall
Cascilla, Mississippi

Pancakes

1 cup plus 2 Tablespoons milk,
   divided
2 Tablespoons cooking oil
1 egg, beaten

1 cup flour
½ teaspoon salt
2 Tablespoons baking powder

Mix 1 cup milk, oil and egg. Add sifted dry ingredients. Add 2 more Tablespoons milk. Cook on hot griddle. Yield: 3 to 4 servings.

Mrs. Ober Anderson
Lake Mills, Iowa

Pancake Surprise

2 Tablespoons butter
2 eggs
¼ cup flour
¼ cup milk

Dash of nutmeg
¼ cup powdered sugar
Juice of ½ lemon

Preheat oven to 425°. Melt butter in 12-inch skillet. In mixing bowl beat eggs slightly. Add flour, milk, and nutmeg. Beat together slightly, leaving the batter a little lumpy. When butter is very hot, pour batter in butter. Bake in oven 15 to 20 minutes or until golden brown. Sprinkle powdered sugar on top and run into oven briefly. Then sprinkle with lemon juice and serve with jelly, jam, or marmalade. Yield: 4 servings.

Miss Martha Wise
Greenville, Mississippi

Maid Service Pancakes

6 eggs
4 cups buttermilk
¼ cup vegetable oil
1 cup cream or canned milk
1 package dry yeast
4 cups flour

2 Tablespoons baking powder
2 Tablespoons baking soda
2 Tablespoons sugar, honey, or
   fructose
1 teaspoon salt

Beat eggs. Add buttermilk, oil, and cream. Combine remaining dry ingredients and add to liquids. Be sure and stir this mixture thoroughly. Set in refrigerator overnight before using. Bake on hot griddle, as needed. Batter will keep in refrigerator for 7 to 10 days. It makes a very light moist pancake with just a little hint of yeast flavor. Yield: ¾ gallon batter.

Mrs. Vaughn Varnado
Marietta, Georgia

Syrup for Pancakes

4 cups sugar, divided
2 cups water
¾ cup light corn syrup

Pinch of salt
1 teaspoon vanilla extract

In a heavy iron skillet caramelize 2 cups sugar until all sugar is dissolved. Add 2 cups sugar, water, and corn syrup. Bring to boil slowly and then simmer until all sugar is dissolved. Add salt and vanilla; cool. Yield: 4 to 5 cups.

Mrs. John Newton
(Cathie Bailess)

Fruit Fritters

1½ cups flour
2 teaspoons baking powder
¼ teaspoon salt
2 Tablespoons sugar
1 egg, beaten

⅔ cup milk
1 Tablespoon melted butter or
   margarine
2 cups sliced apples or bananas
Vegetable oil for frying

Sift flour, baking powder, salt, and sugar. Combine egg, milk, and butter. Pour into flour mixture and stir until smooth. Add 2 cups apples or banana slices. Drop by Tablespoons into hot oil. Fry 3 to 5 minutes until golden brown. Drain on paper towels. Yield: 6 servings.

Miriam Graeber Cohn
Port Gibson, Mississippi

Overnight French Toast

1 (10-ounce) loaf French bread
8 large eggs
3 cups milk
1 cup sugar

¾ teaspoon salt
2 Tablespoons vanilla extract
¼ cup butter
Syrup

Butter a 9 x 13-inch pan. Cut bread into 1-inch slices and arrange in single layer in pan. In a large bowl, beat eggs with milk, sugar, salt and vanilla. Pour over bread. Cover with foil and refrigerate. Next day, uncover and dot with butter. Bake at 350° until puffy and light brown. Serve with syrup. Yield: 6 to 8 servings.

Mrs. Buddy Baker
(Lynn Hilderbrand)

French Toast Special

½ teaspoon cinnamon
⅛ teaspoon nutmeg (optional)
1 cup pancake batter (may be made
  from a mix)
20 slices extra thin-sliced, firm
  bread

Hot vegetable oil
Maple syrup (optional)
Powdered sugar

Add cinnamon and nutmeg to pancake batter. Stir well. Trim bread (optional) and cut into triangles. Dip bread into batter and deep fry until golden brown. This can be a main dish by cutting bread into 2 large triangles and serving with syrup. This may also be served as a pick-up brunch item by cutting bread into 4 smaller triangles and serving only with powdered sugar. May be made a little ahead of time and kept in a low oven. Allow approximately 1½ slices per person. Yield: 12 servings.

Mrs. Stan Terry, Jr.
(Sallie Bingham)

Cinnamon Rolls

4½ cups unsifted flour, divided
1⅓ cups sugar, divided
1 teaspoon salt
2 packages yeast
¾ cup milk

½ cup water
½ cup margarine
2 eggs
3 Tablespoons melted margarine
1 Tablespoon cinnamon

Combine 1 cup flour, ⅓ cup sugar, salt, and yeast. Set aside. Heat milk, water, and margarine over low heat from 120° to 130°. Add to dry ingredients and beat 2 minutes at medium speed. Add ½ cup more flour and eggs. Beat at high speed 2 minutes. Add remaining flour. Batter will be stiff. Cover tightly and refrigerate 2 hours. Turn onto floured board. Roll into three 9 x 12-inch rectangles. Brush with melted margarine. Combine 1 cup sugar and cinnamon and sprinkle over the dough. Roll up from short ends and seal seams. Cut into 1-inch slices. Place 9 slices on each greased 8-inch round pan. Cover; let rise until doubled in size, 45 minutes to 1½ hours. Bake at 350° for 20 minutes. Remove from pan and cool. Yield: 27 rolls.

Mrs. Vernon Smith
(Alice Walker)

Cream Cheese Stollen

1 (8-ounce) carton sour cream,
   scalded
½ cup sugar
½ cup margarine, melted
1 teaspoon salt

2 packages dry yeast
½ cup warm water, 105° to 115°
2 eggs, beaten
4 cups flour

Combine scalded sour cream, sugar, margarine, and salt; mix well and let cool to lukewarm. Dissolve yeast in warm water in a large mixing bowl; stir in sour cream mixture and eggs. Gradually stir in flour (dough will be soft). Cover tightly and chill overnight. Divide dough into 4 equal portions. Turn each portion out onto heavily floured surface and knead 4 to 5 times. Roll each into 12 x 8-inch rectangle. Spread ¼ filling over each rectangle, leaving a ½-inch margin around the edges. Carefully roll up jellyroll fashion, beginning at long side. Firmly pinch edge and ends to seal. Carefully place rolls, seam-side down, onto greased baking sheets. Make 6 equally spaced x-shaped cuts across top of each loaf. Cover and let rise in a warm place (85°) free from drafts for 1 hour or until doubled in bulk. Bake at 375° for 15 to 20 minutes. Spread loaves with glaze while warm. Yield: 4 stollens.

Filling

2 (8-ounce) packages cream cheese,
   at room temperature
¾ cup sugar

1 egg, beaten
2 teaspoons vanilla extract

Combine all ingredients. Place in food processor or electric mixer until well blended. Yield: About 2 cups.

Glaze

2 cups powdered sugar, sifted
¼ cup milk

2 teaspoons vanilla extract

Combine all ingredients, mixing well.

Mrs. Jerry Mayfield
(Pam Jabour)

 Test water for dissolving yeast by dropping a little on the inside of your wrist. It should feel comfortably warm, not hot.

Danish Puff

Pastry

½ cup margarine
1 cup flour

¼ teaspoon salt
2 Tablespoons cold water

In a small mixing bowl cut margarine into flour and salt. Add cold water and stir until mixed. Spread on ungreased 13-inch pizza pan. Yield: 8 servings.

Filling

1 cup water
½ cup margarine
1 teaspoon almond flavoring

¾ cup flour
3 eggs

In saucepan, bring water to boil. Add margarine. When melted, add almond flavoring and remove from heat. Immediately stir in flour. Beat until smooth. Add eggs, 1 at a time, beating well after each addition. Spread mixture over pastry. Bake at 350° for 1 hour.

Icing

2 cups powdered sugar
¼ cup margarine
2 Tablespoons boiling water

¼ teaspoon almond extract
½ cup chopped pecans or almonds

Mix all ingredients, except nuts, in small bowl. Beat well. Add more hot water if necessary to make soft spreading consistency. Spread over warm, not hot, pastry. Garnish with nuts.

For a festive holiday pastry, garnish with red and green maraschino cherries.

Ober J. Anderson
Ankeny, Iowa

Sweet Potato Muffins

¾ cup canned or cooked fresh sweet
   potatoes, mashed
¼ cup margarine
½ cup sugar
1 egg
¾ cup flour
2 teaspoons baking powder

½ teaspoon salt
¾ teaspoon cinnamon
¼ teaspoon nutmeg
½ cup milk
¼ cup pecans, chopped finely
1 to 2 Tablespoons cinnamon sugar

Purée sweet potatoes in blender or food processor. Cream margarine and sugar. Beat in egg. Add sweet potatoes and mix well. Sift together flour, baking powder, salt, and spices. Add alternately with milk and pecans only until just blended. Do not overmix. Fill small greased muffin tins completely. Sprinkle tops with cinnamon sugar. Bake at 400° for 25 to 30 minutes. Yield: 2 to 2½ dozen.

Mrs. Billy Buckner
(Sandy Antoine)

Grandma's Coconut Muffins

½ cup shortening
1 cup sugar
2 eggs
1½ cups flour
2 teaspoons baking powder

Dash of salt
¾ cup milk
1 teaspoon vanilla extract
1 (3½-ounce) can flaked coconut

Cream together shortening and sugar. Add eggs and mix. Mix together flour, baking powder, and salt; add to shortening mixture alternating with milk. Add vanilla and coconut; mix well. Pour into miniature muffin pans. Bake at 400° for 6 to 10 minutes until lightly browned. Yield: 48 muffins.

Mrs. A. J. (Buddy) Dees, Jr.
(Carolyn Dillard)

Pecan Muffins

⅓ cup melted butter
½ cup flour
½ cup sugar
1 teaspoon vanilla extract

½ cup brown sugar
2 eggs, beaten
1 cup chopped pecans

Mix ingredients and bake at 350° for 25 minutes in greased muffin pans. Yield: 12 muffins or 24 miniature muffins.

Miss Mary Louise Cashman

Fresh Blueberry Muffins

2 cups flour
1 Tablespoon baking powder
¾ cup sugar
Pinch of salt
1 cup milk

⅓ cup vegetable oil
1 egg, beaten
1 cup fresh blueberries or frozen,
    not packed in sugar

Combine dry ingredients in large mixing bowl. Make well in center of flour mixture and add milk, oil, and egg. Stir only until combined. Stir berries gently into this. Spoon dough into greased muffin pans or pans lined with muffin papers. Bake in a preheated 400° oven 20 to 25 minutes. Let stand 5 minutes before removing from pan. Serve warm. For a coffee use miniature muffin pans and sprinkle top of dough with sugar before baking. Again, let set 5 minutes before removing. Yield: 1½ dozen.

Mrs. Robert L. Pickett
(Jeneva Faulk)

Raisin Bran Pecan Muffins

1 (15-ounce) box raisin bran
3 scant cups sugar
5 teaspoons soda
5 cups flour
2 teaspoons salt

4 eggs, beaten
¾ cup vegetable oil
1 cup pecans, chopped
1 quart buttermilk

Mix raisin bran, sugar, soda, flour, and salt in very large bowl. Add beaten eggs, oil, nuts and buttermilk. Mix well. Store in covered container in refrigerator and use as needed. Grease muffin pans. Fill muffin pans ⅔ full. Preheat oven to 400°. Bake 15 to 20 minutes. Batter will keep for 6 weeks in refrigerator or cook muffins and store in freezer.

Louise Davis
Jackson, Mississippi

Strawberry Butter

¾ cup frozen strawberries, thawed
    and drained

1 cup butter, softened
3 Tablespoons powdered sugar

Mix ingredients in blender until smooth. Refrigerate. Yield: Approximately 2 cups.

Mrs. Kenneth Hicks
(Margaret Bonney)

Apple Pecan Coffee Cake

2 cups sugar
1 cup vegetable oil
2 eggs
2½ cups flour
1 teaspoon salt
2 Tablespoons baking powder

1 teaspoon soda
1 teaspoon vanilla extract
2 cups chopped pecans
2 cups chopped Granny Smith
  apples

Grease and flour a 9 x 13-inch pan. Combine sugar and oil. Add well beaten eggs. Sift dry ingredients and add all at one time. Stir in vanilla, pecans, and apples. Bake in 9 x 13-inch pan in 350° oven for 25 to 30 minutes. Yield: 16 servings.

Mrs. B. J. Gunn
(Frances Kivett)

K.K.'s Colorado Coffee Cake

¼ cup butter
1 (8-ounce) package cream cheese
1½ cups sugar
2 eggs
2 cups flour

2 teaspoons baking powder
½ teaspoon salt
1 teaspoon baking soda
½ cup milk
1 teaspoon vanilla extract

In a large mixing bowl cream together butter, cream cheese, sugar, and eggs. In a medium bowl sift together flour, baking powder, salt, and baking soda. In a third smaller bowl combine the milk and vanilla. Add milk mixture to creamed butter mixture, stirring constantly until well blended. Add flour mixture to creamed ingredients, blending for 3 minutes or until well mixed. Spoon mixture into 3 greased and floured round 8-inch cake pans. Yield: 3 coffee cakes.

Topping

¼ cup butter
¼ cup flour
1 cup brown sugar

3 teaspoons cinnamon
Chopped nuts (optional)

Mix all ingredients together and sprinkle over dough mixture in each of 3 loaf pans. Bake cakes at 350° for 20 minutes. Delicious hot or cold. Yield: 3 coffee cakes.

K.K. Guider Jacobs
Denver, Colorado

Cinnamon Nut Coffee Cake

1 (18½-ounce) box yellow cake mix
1 (3-ounce) box instant vanilla
   pudding mix
½ cup vegetable oil
4 eggs, beaten
1 teaspoon butter flavoring

1 teaspoon vanilla extract
¾ cup water
¼ cup sugar
2 teaspoons ground cinnamon
¼ cup chopped pecans

Preheat oven to 350°. Into large mixing bowl put cake mix, pudding mix, oil, eggs, flavorings, and water. Mix well with electric hand mixer. Mix separately in small bowl sugar, cinnamon, and pecans. Sprinkle a little pecan mixture in bottom of bundt cake pan. Add a layer of cake mixture and then another layer of pecan mixture. Continue layering until both mixtures are all used. Bake in 350° oven 50 to 60 minutes. Yield: 12 servings.

Mrs. Thomas Dykes
(Rose Josey)

Oatmeal Coffee Cake

1 cup oatmeal
1¼ cups hot water
1¼ cups flour
1 cup sugar
1 cup brown sugar, packed

1 teaspoon baking powder
1 teaspoon cinnamon
½ cup margarine, melted
2 whole eggs
1 teaspoon vanilla extract

Cover oatmeal with hot water and let set for 20 minutes. While this mixture sets, mix together dry ingredients. Add margarine, eggs, vanilla and mix well. Add oatmeal and mix. Pour into a 9 x 13-inch pan and bake at 350° for 30 minutes. Spread topping on while hot. Yield: 12 to 15 servings.

Topping

⅔ cup brown sugar, packed
2 cups flaked coconut
1 cup pecans, chopped

¼ cup margarine, melted
2 teaspoons vanilla extract
⅓ cup evaporated milk

While cake is baking, mix together the above ingredients. When cake is done, but still hot, spread topping on and put back in oven for 15 minutes.

Mrs. Orlando L. Duncan
(Carol Conway)

Cedar Grove

Added to charm and elegance of old mansions are real-life stories of death and destruction in war. Cedar Grove bears the scars of conflict with a Civil War cannonball embedded in a wall near the piano in the living room. A shell hole in the floor, located exactly where Union gunboats fired it, is preserved for visitors to see.

Cedar Grove, built in the early 1840's, then faced open slopes that extended to the Mississippi River. It provided a prime target for the attacking boats during the Vicksburg Siege of 1863.

Its gardens are breath-taking with magnolias, flowering shrubs and trees, and a gazebo trimmed with lacy wrought iron. Above-ground cisterns make elevated observation decks.

Cedar Grove, a favorite of tourists and an elegant remnant of the past, offers bed and breakfast to overnight guests.

Desserts pictured:

Black Forest Torte, Old Time Lemon Pie, Bing Cherry Parfait, Raspberry Sorbet, Peppermint Ice Cream with Chocolate Sauce, Grasshopper Pie, Butter Creme Brownies, Divinity, Sis's Pralines, Thumbprint Cookies, Orange Balls

Desserts

Crêpes Fitzgerald

Crêpe Batter

1 cup flour
Pinch of salt
1 teaspoon powdered sugar

2 eggs
1 to 1¼ cups milk
¼ cup butter

Mix flour, salt, powdered sugar, eggs, and milk together until batter is consistency of heavy cream. Heat pan. Add small amount of butter to grease pan and melt. Using a small amount of batter, cook crêpes. Grease pan before making each crêpe.

Filling

2 ounces cream cheese
2 Tablespoons sour cream

1 Tablespoon powdered sugar

Mix cream cheese, sour cream, and powdered sugar to make a thick paste. Fill each crêpe with 1 Tablespoon of mixture; fold into quarters.

Flambée

2 ounces sugar
2 ounces butter
5 ounces strawberries or
   raspberries

5 Tablespoons Grand Marnier

Place sugar and butter in pan; heat and mix in fruit. Heat well. Add filled crêpes and coat with sauce. Pour in Grand Marnier and ignite. Magnificent! Yield: 4 to 6 crêpes.

Mrs. James W. Cook
(Naomi Paquette)

 When making crêpes, discard the first crêpe. It should be used only to absorb excess oil from pan.

Heavenly Delicious Cake

1 (20-ounce) can crushed pineapple,
  reserving juice
1½ cups sugar, divided
Juice of 2 lemons
6 eggs, separated
2 envelopes unflavored gelatin
1 packaged angel food cake, torn
  into small pieces

½ cup maraschino cherries,
  chopped
1 cup pecans, chopped
½ pint heavy cream, whipped
Additional cherries and nuts to
  garnish

Drain pineapple, saving 1 cup juice. In a double boiler combine pineapple, ¾ cup reserved pineapple juice, ¾ cup sugar, lemon juice, and egg yolks. Place over simmering water and cook about 10 minutes until mixture coats metal spoon. Soften gelatin in ¼ cup saved pineapple juice. Add to hot mixture and dissolve. Beat egg whites, adding ¾ cup sugar and fold into cooked mixture. Pour over combined cake, cherries, and nuts. Stir lightly. Pour into greased tube pan; refrigerate several hours before serving. May make ahead and keep 1 to 2 days. Serve garnished with whipped cream and additional cherries and nuts. Yield: 10 to 12 servings.

Mrs. William Dale
Huntsville, Alabama

Helen's Super Dessert

1 (18½-ounce) box yellow or white
  cake mix
1 cup milk
2 Tablespoons almond extract
1 (5¼-ounce) package instant
  vanilla pudding, prepared
  according to directions

1(5¼-ounce) package instant
  chocolate pudding, prepared
  according to directions
½ pint heavy cream, whipped
½ cup toasted almonds

Bake cake in 9 x 13-inch pan according to package directions. Let cool. Remove cake from pan and slice in ½ horizontally. Place 1 layer back in pan; put the other on a large platter or pan. Pour ½ cup milk mixed with 1 Tablespoon of almond extract over each layer. Prepare puddings. Over cake layer in pan, pour vanilla pudding; let set. Top with second cake layer. Then spread chocolate pudding over cake and top with whipped cream. Sprinkle toasted almonds to garnish. Yield: 12 to 14 servings.

Mrs. Jimmy Gouras
(Peggy Mayfield)

Blueberry Angel Dessert

½ cup sugar
½ cup powdered sugar
1 (8-ounce) package cream cheese
1 teaspoon vanilla extract
1 (12-ounce) carton non-dairy
    whipped topping

1 angel food cake
1 (21-ounce) can blueberry pie
    filling

In a medium size mixing bowl, combine sugar, powdered sugar, cream cheese, and vanilla. Fold in whipped topping. Slice cake into three layers. Spread whipped topping mixture onto each layer and top with pie filling. Repeat for all layers. Frost cake with remaining whipped topping mixture and pie filling. Refrigerate. Yield: 8 to 10 servings.

Mrs. Kenneth E. Hicks
(Margaret Bonney)

Chocolate Eclair Dessert

3 cups cold milk
1 (5¼-ounce) box vanilla instant
    pudding and pie filling

1 (8-ounce) carton non-dairy
    whipped topping
½ (16-ounce) box graham crackers

In a large mixing bowl, pour milk; add pudding mix, beating slowly with a wire whisk, rotary beater, or at the lowest speed of electric mixer until well blended, 1 to 2 minutes. Let set for 5 minutes. Fold in whipped topping. In 11 x 7 x 1½-inch dish, place a layer of graham crackers. Pour ½ of the above mixture over crackers, following with another layer of graham crackers, the remaining ½ of the mixture, ending with a final layer of crackers. Set aside.

Icing

¼ cup butter or margarine, melted
6 Tablespoons milk
3½ Tablespoons cocoa

1 teaspoon vanilla extract
1 (16-ounce) box powdered sugar
½ cup chopped pecans

In a 3½-quart saucepan, mix the melted butter, milk, and cocoa. Bring to a boil. Remove from heat. Blend in vanilla. With an electric mixer on high speed, beat the powdered sugar into the cocoa mixture until creamy. Add chopped pecans and beat at low speed until blended. Spread icing evenly over the final layer of crackers and refrigerate. Yield: 12 to 15 servings.

Mrs. John O. Curtis
(Leigh Wilson)

Chocolate Eclairs

Shells

1 cup water
½ cup butter or margarine

1 cup flour
4 eggs

Bring water to a boil and add butter. Boil until butter is melted. Add flour and stir well. Stir until mixture is smooth. Cool 5 to 10 minutes. Add eggs, 1 at a time; mix well after adding each egg. With a spoon or pastry tube, drop on a very lightly greased cookie sheet. Use about 1 to 1½ Tablespoons dough for each shell. Bake at 375° for 35 minutes and then 200° for 10 minutes. When cool, slice open and fill with custard.

Custard

1 quart milk
4 egg yolks
1½ cups sugar
4 Tablespoons flour

4 Tablespoons cornstarch
Pinch of salt
2 Tablespoons butter
1 teaspoon vanilla extract

Scald milk in top of double boiler. Add egg yolks, sugar, flour, cornstarch, and salt. Stir well to blend completely. Add butter and continue cooking until custard begins to thicken; stir constantly. Add vanilla. Custard should be thick enough to hold onto the spoon. Fill shells with cooled custard.

Chocolate Icing

½ cup margarine
1 cup sugar
⅓ cup evaporated milk

½ cup semisweet chocolate chips
1 teaspoon vanilla extract

Melt margarine in saucepan. Add sugar and evaporated milk. Bring to a boil. Boil for 2 minutes, stirring constantly. Add chocolate chips and vanilla. Remove from heat. Beat until thickened. Using a spoon, drizzle chocolate over éclairs. Yield: 12 servings.

Mrs. Dan Waring
(Janice Gerache)

Before whipping cream, chill the bowl and beaters in the freezer.

Chocolate Ice Box Cake

1 cup margarine
1 (1-pound) box powdered sugar
4 egg yolks
4 squares unsweetened chocolate
4 egg whites
1 teaspoon almond extract

4 Tablespoons sherry
1 cup chopped almonds
1 dozen almond macaroons (no substitute)
1 dozen lady fingers
½ pint heavy cream, whipped

Cream margarine thoroughly and beat in sugar, adding small amount at a time. Beat until light. Beat in egg yolks 1 at a time. Fold in chocolate which has been melted over hot water. Beat egg whites until stiff and fold into mixture. Add almond extract and sherry. Fold in chopped almonds. Line bottom of a 9-inch springform pan with crumbled macaroons. Split lady fingers and stand around sides of pan. Pour chocolate mixture into pan on top of macaroons and refrigerate overnight. To serve, remove sides of pan and spread ½ pint whipped cream over chocolate. Can be frozen without whipped cream added. Yield: 10 to 12 servings.

Mrs. Gorman Schaffer
(Margaret Patterson)

Effie's Delicious Dessert

4 eggs
1½ cups sugar, divided
1 teaspoon vanilla extract
½ cup flour
½ cup cream of wheat (farina)
1 cup water

1 (5¼-ounce) box instant chocolate or vanilla pudding
2 cups milk
1 cup heavy cream
3 Tablespoons sugar
Grated chocolate

Whip eggs, ½ cup sugar, and vanilla together for 15 minutes until light and fluffy. Add flour and cream of wheat. Beat together until well mixed. Pour into a 9 x 13-inch pan. Bake 15 minutes at 375°. While baking, boil 1 cup sugar and 1 cup water. When cake is done and hot, pour sugar syrup over cake. Let set until cool. Prepare pudding according to package directions. Top cake layer with pudding. Refrigerate until firm. Beat whipping cream until soft peaks form. Add sugar and beat until stiff. Top with whipped cream and garnish with grated chocolate. Refrigerate until time to serve. Yield: 12 to 14 servings.

Mrs. Jimmy Gouras
(Peggy Mayfield)

Strawberry Dessert

1 (5½-ounce) box strawberry
    gelatin
½ pint strawberries, frozen or fresh
2 cups crushed pretzels
¾ cup margarine

3 Tablespoons sugar
1 (8-ounce) package cream cheese
1 (16-ounce) carton whipped
    topping
¾ cup sugar

Prepare gelatin according to directions leaving out ½ cup water called for in gelatin recipe. Mix strawberries into gelatin and refrigerate until partially gelled. Mix pretzels, margarine, and sugar together and pat into bottom of 9 x 13-inch pan. Bake at 350° for 10 minutes. Cream together cream cheese, whipped topping and sugar and spread over pretzel mixture. Pour gelatin mixture over ingredients in pan. Refrigerate at least 4 hours. Yield: 8 servings.

Mrs. Joseph T. Wood
Laurel, Mississippi

Pavlova
(Meringue Shells)

4 egg whites
¼ teaspoon cream of tartar or 1
    teaspoon vinegar
Pinch of salt
1 teaspoon vanilla extract

1 cup sugar
Whipped cream
Fresh fruit (peaches, pineapple,
    kiwi, etc.)

Combine egg whites, cream of tartar, salt and vanilla in a large mixing bowl. Beat at low speed until eggs begin to froth, then at medium speed until egg whites hold soft peaks. Gradually add ¾ cup sugar, 1 teaspoon at a time, while beating on high speed. Beat until meringue is very stiff, dull, and no longer grainy. Gently fold in rest of sugar. Meringues should be dried rather than baked to obtain the proper texture. Shape meringue according to following directions: Pile the meringue high on a plate at least 12 inches in diameter. Bake the meringue in a slow oven for 1 hour. It will sink somewhat in the middle, and you should have a big crater-shaped disc when the meringue mixture is done. Turn heat off and let meringue remain in oven for at least 4 hours. When completely dry, meringue is ready. When cool, fill the meringue with slightly sweetened whipped cream and dot with fresh fruits. Yield: 4 to 6 servings.

Rosemary Deeb
Cairns, Australia

Southern-Style Baked Alaska

1 quart vanilla ice cream	½ teaspoon baking powder
½ cup margarine, softened	2 Tablespoons cocoa
2 cups sugar, divided	¼ teaspoon salt
2 eggs	1 teaspoon vanilla extract
1 cup flour	4 egg whites

Line a 1-quart mixing bowl (7 inches in diameter) with waxed paper, leaving overhang around the edges. Pack ice cream into bowl and freeze until firm. In a medium mixing bowl combine margarine and 1 cup sugar; cream until light and fluffy. Add eggs, 1 at a time, beating after each addition. In a separate bowl combine flour, baking powder, cocoa, and salt. Add to creamed mixture, mixing well. Stir in vanilla. Spoon this batter into a greased and floured 8-inch round cake pan. Bake at 350° for 25 to 30 minutes. Let cool in pan 10 minutes and then place on a wire rack until completely cooled. Place the cake on an ovenproof serving dish. Invert the bowl of ice cream onto the cake, leaving waxed paper intact. Remove bowl and place the ice cream-topped cake in freezer. Beat egg whites until frothy and gradually beat in remaining 1 cup sugar. Continue beating until stiff peaks form. Remove ice cream-topped cake from freezer and peel off waxed paper. Quickly spread meringue over entire surface. Place in a 500° oven just long enough to brown the meringue. Yield: 10 servings.

The ice cream-topped cake may be frozen the day before serving. The day of serving, the meringue may be prepared and refrigerated until ready to serve.

Mrs. Michael Harden
(Sharon Emery)

Hostess Twinkie Dessert

1 box (10 count) Hostess Twinkies	1 (20-ounce) can crushed pineapple,
3 or 4 medium bananas, sliced	drained
1 (5¼-ounce) package vanilla	1 (8-ounce) carton non-dairy
instant pudding (prepare as	whipped topping
directed)	Maraschino cherries

Slice Twinkies in half and place cream-side up in a 9 x 13-inch pan. Only 9 of the 10 Twinkies will be needed. Layer the sliced bananas, vanilla pudding, and crushed pineapple. Top with non-dairy topping and decorate with cherries. Chill 2 hours before serving. Yield: 24 servings.

Mrs. David Hosemann
(Connie Koury)

Caramel Custard

Custard

½ cup sugar
3 large eggs plus 2 large egg yolks
⅛ teaspoon salt

¼ teaspoon vanilla extract
2 Tablespoons light rum
2 cups milk

In a mixing bowl, combine sugar, eggs, and egg yolks beaten together, salt, vanilla, and rum. In a small saucepan scald the milk, then stir it gradually into egg mixture. Strain and pour into custard cups which have caramelized sugar in them. To cook custard, place custard cups in baking pan with about 1 to 1½ inches water in it. Bake in preheated 325° oven for 45 minutes or until knife inserted into center comes out clean. Place cups on cooling rack and cover.

Caramelized Sugar

½ cup sugar

¼ cup water

Microwave method: Combine sugar and water in 2-cup measuring cup. Heat on high for 7 minutes. Check to see if golden brown in color. If not, cook 30 seconds more. Continue at 15 second intervals until golden brown, watching carefully. Quickly pour caramelized sugar into six (4 to 5-ounce) custard cups which have been lightly greased. Fill cups with strained custard mixture. Range-top method: Combine sugar and water in small skillet. Cook over high heat stirring from time to time with a wooden spoon until golden brown in color. Proceed as directed in microwave method. Yield: 6 servings.

Mrs. Don S. Miller, Jr.
(Deanna Blanchard)

Peach Melba

1½ teaspoons cornstarch
1 Tablespoon water
1 (10-ounce) package frozen
   raspberries

½ cup currant jelly
Peach halves
Vanilla ice cream

In a small saucepan, mix cornstarch and water; add frozen raspberries and currant jelly. Cook on low heat until clear. Place peach half in bowl. Top with vanilla ice cream. Pour sauce over top.

Mrs. David May
(Martha Ann Johnston)

Cake Top Lemon Pudding

2 Tablespoons margarine
1 cup sugar
4 eggs, separated
3 Tablespoons flour

½ cup lemon juice
2 teaspoons grated lemon rind
¼ teaspoon salt
1 cup milk

Cream margarine and sugar. Add egg yolks, flour, lemon juice, lemon rind, and salt. Blend well. Stir in milk. Beat egg whites well. Fold into lemon mixture. Pour into 8 custard cups. Place custard cups in pan of hot water in oven. Bake at 325° for about 40 minutes. Turn up temperature in oven to brown top of pudding. Yield: 8 servings.

Mrs. George Rogers, Sr.
(Marion Todd)

Rice Pudding

1 egg, slightly beaten
2 cups cooked rice
Dash of cinnamon
1 Tablespoon margarine

¾ cup sugar
1 cup milk
½ teaspoon vanilla extract

Combine all ingredients in baking dish. Bake at 350° until pudding thickens. Yield: 2 to 4 servings.

Mrs. Marshall Whatley
(Wilma Pierce)

Banana Pudding

6 eggs, separated
1½ cups sugar, divided
½ cup flour
2 cups milk

¼ cup melted margarine
2 teaspoons vanilla extract
1 (9-ounce) bag vanilla wafers
4 bananas, sliced

Mix together 6 egg yolks and 2 egg whites. Add 1 cup sugar and flour. Mix well. Add gradually milk and melted margarine. Cook in double boiler until thickened. Add vanilla. Layer vanilla wafers, bananas, and pudding alternately. Beat 4 remaining egg whites until stiff. Add ½ cup sugar. Spread over banana pudding and bake at 350° for approximately 20 minutes or until meringue is brown. Chill and serve. Yield: 8 servings.

Mrs. Chester Redditt
(Tricia Prewitt)

Nanie's Plum Pudding

1½ cups sugar
4 eggs
3 cups raisins
2 cups flour, sifted
1½ cups margarine or butter
1½ cups bread crumbs
⅓ cup milk

½ cup citro (optional)
1 rounded teaspoon baking powder
1 teaspoon nutmeg
1 teaspoon ground cloves
1 teaspoon cinnamon
½ Tablespoon orange marmalade

Cream sugar and eggs, 1 at a time. Add raisins that have been coated with flour. Slice cold butter and add to mixture, then other ingredients. Put aside about 1 cup of the plum pudding mix for the sauce. Cook in plum pudding steamer for 3 hours. Check water level every hour.

Sauce

1 cup plum pudding mix
5 cups water
1 cup sugar

Rind of 1 or 2 oranges, cut in small pieces

Cook until thickened. Spoon over pudding. Yield: 12 to 14 servings.

Mrs. Brad Bradway
(Mary Dalrymple)

Ozark Pudding

1 egg
¾ cup sugar
3 rounded Tablespoons flour
1¼ teaspoons baking powder
⅛ teaspoon salt

½ cup chopped apples
½ cup chopped pecans
1 teaspoon vanilla extract
Ice cream or whipped cream

Beat egg well and add sugar, beating until light and creamy. Sift flour, baking powder and salt together and add to egg mixture; blend well. Fold in apples and nuts; add vanilla. Pour into greased, waxed paper-lined dish; bake at 325° for 30 minutes. Cut into squares and serve with whipped cream or vanilla ice cream.

This recipe was a favorite of Mrs. Harry Truman.

Mrs. George Stevens
(Sidney McLaurin)

 Place clear plastic wrap directly on top of pudding, smoothing wrap to sides of bowl, to keep top of pudding satiny.

Old-Fashioned Chocolate Pudding

1½ cups sugar
¾ cup cocoa
¾ cup flour
½ teaspoon salt

4 eggs
4 cups milk
2 Tablespoons butter
2 teaspoons vanilla extract

Mix together sugar, cocoa, flour and salt. Beat eggs until no white of egg shows. Add egg mixture along with milk to dry mixture. Cook over medium heat until thick, stirring constantly. When the pudding is thickened, stir in butter and vanilla. Pour in serving dish or dishes and refrigerate. This is also good warm served over vanilla ice cream or as a pie filling. Lemon pudding can be made by omitting cocoa, increasing flour to 1 cup, and adding ½ cup lemon juice. Omit vanilla. Coconut pudding can be made by omitting cocoa, increasing flour to 1 cup and adding 1 cup coconut and 2 teaspoons vanilla. Yield: 8 to 10 servings.

Mrs. Russell Hawkins
(Brenda Davis)

Bread Pudding with Hard Sauce

4 cups fine bread crumbs (made
  from stale French bread)
1 cup sugar
3 cups milk
2 cups seedless raisins

1 cup coarsely chopped pecans
Grated peel of 1 lemon or 3
  Tablespoons lemon extract
3 Tablespoons vanilla extract
½ teaspoon cinnamon

Combine all ingredients and pour into a 2-quart baking dish. Bake uncovered at 350° for 1 hour and 15 minutes. Cut into squares. Serve hot or cold.

Hard Sauce for Bread Pudding

4 Tablespoons butter
1 cup powdered sugar

1½ ounces bourbon or rum
Cherries to garnish (optional)

Cream butter and sugar together. Add liquor. Pour over bread pudding and garnish with a cherry, if desired. Yield: 10 to 12 servings.

Mrs. Frank Campbell
(Carole Blackledge)

 Before beating egg whites, be sure that bowl and beaters are completely free of any grease.

Caramel Bread Pudding

1 quart milk
½ plus ⅔ cup sugar, divided
2 cups broken bread slices (2 or 3
    pieces, lightly packed)

3 eggs
2 teaspoons vanilla extract
¼ teaspoon salt
Whipped cream

Heat milk to boiling point. At the same time, melt ½ cup sugar in iron skillet. When sugar is caramelized, pour it into heated milk and stir until sugar is completely dissolved in the milk. Remove from heat. Add broken bread slices to milk and sugar mixture. Let stand for ½ hour. In another bowl, beat eggs slightly. Add ⅔ cup sugar, vanilla, and salt to egg mixture. Mix ingredients thoroughly and add to milk, bread, and sugar mixture. Pour into greased pudding pan and bake at 350° for 1 hour. Let cool and serve with heavy or whipped cream. Yield: 8 servings.

It gets better after refrigerating for several days.

Mrs. Ben Dudding
Clinton, Mississippi

Tipsy Pudding

2 cups hot milk
½ cup sugar
⅛ teaspoon salt
2 large eggs, beaten
2 Tablespoons flour

2 or 3 Tablespoons bourbon or
    sherry
1 (8-ounce) carton heavy cream,
    whipped
1 pound cake

Heat milk in top of double boiler. Do not boil. Add sugar with salt to beaten eggs. Stir well. Stir flour with small amount of hot milk until smooth. Add egg mixture to hot milk. Place over gently boiling water. Stir in flour mixture. Stir often until mixture begins to thicken. It is done when the custard coats a silver spoon. Cool. Add bourbon and stir well. Whip cream until it holds peaks. Gently stir cream into custard. Alternate with layers of pound cake in bite-size pieces, beginning with cake and ending with custard. Chill at least 1 hour before serving. Stale pound cake or a purchased cake may be used. Lady fingers may be used instead of pound cake. Line a glass bowl with split lady fingers. Drizzle with sherry. Pour in custard and top with whipped cream. Garnish with maraschino cherries. Yield: 4 to 6 servings.

Mrs. T. P. Groome, Jr.
(Bettye Pierson)

Easy Bread Pudding with Vanilla Sauce

1 (14-ounce) can sweetened
  condensed milk
3 cups very hot water
3 cups finely diced day-old bread

3 eggs, slightly beaten
1 Tablespoon melted butter
½ teaspoon salt
1 teaspoon vanilla extract

Combine condensed milk and hot water. Pour over bread and let stand until lukewarm. Stir in eggs, butter, salt and vanilla. Pour into buttered 1½-quart casserole or baking dish. Set in shallow pan of hot water. Bake at 350° until a knife blade inserted near the center comes out clean, about 1 hour. Serve with vanilla sauce, chocolate sauce or your favorite plum jelly. Yield: 6 to 8 servings.

Vanilla Sauce

½ cup sugar
2 Tablespoons cornstarch
¼ teaspoon salt

2 cups boiling water
¼ cup real butter
2 teaspoons vanilla extract

In a saucepan combine sugar, cornstarch and salt. Gradually stir in water. Boil, stirring constantly, 5 minutes or until sauce is thickened. Add remaining ingredients.

3 Tablespoons bourbon may be substituted for vanilla.

Mrs. Vaughn Fields
(Lucy McLaurin)

Charlotte Russe

2 Tablespoons cornstarch
1 cup sugar
4 eggs, separated
2 envelopes unflavored gelatin
1 quart milk or 1 pint milk and 1
  pint light cream, divided

1 pint heavy cream
2 teaspoons vanilla extract
Pinch of salt

Add cornstarch to sugar; mix with egg yolks and cream well. Soften gelatin with ½ cup milk; set aside. Heat rest of milk and add slowly to egg and sugar mixture. Cook until thickened. Add gelatin mixture to hot custard mix. Whip egg whites until stiff and fold into custard. Add heavy cream, vanilla and salt. Refrigerate until congealed slightly. Serve in sherbet or custard dishes. Yield: 10 to 12 servings.

Mrs. Ethel C. Long

Normandy Chocolate Mousse

12 lady fingers, split
¾ cup butter
1¾ cups powdered sugar
6 eggs, separated
¼ cup milk
1½ teaspoons vanilla extract
1 teaspoon rum extract

4 ounces unsweetened chocolate,
   melted
1½ cups chopped pecans
⅓ pint heavy cream, whipped
Chocolate shavings to garnish
   (optional)

Line a 9 x 5 x 3-inch pan with waxed paper. Arrange lady fingers around the sides and bottom of pan. Cream butter; gradually add sugar, creaming until light and fluffy. Add egg yolks 1 at a time; beat until smooth after each addition. Blend in milk, vanilla, rum extract, and chocolate well. Beat egg whites until stiff but not dry (not as much as a meringue); fold into chocolate mixture. Add pecans. Pour into prepared pan. Refrigerate overnight. To serve, invert onto serving plate. Remove waxed paper. Decorate top with whipped cream and chocolate shavings. Cut into slices. Yield: 12 to 15 servings.

Mrs. David Sessums
(Beverly Tucker)

Pot de Crème Chocolat

½ pound semisweet chocolate bits
5 Tablespoons cold water
1 Tablespoon instant coffee
5 eggs, separated
2 Tablespoons light rum

½ cup heavy cream
2 teaspoons sugar
2 teaspoons ground almonds
2 teaspoons coffee liqueur

In top of double boiler heat semisweet chocolate bits, cold water, and instant coffee. Separate eggs. Beat yolks into the melted chocolate mixture. Beat in light rum and allow mixture to cool slightly. In separate bowl beat egg whites to soft peaks. Fold gently into chocolate mixture. Pour into 8 pot de crème cups with lids (or any small cups that can be covered). Refrigerate for 24 hours. To serve, whip cream until thick. Add sugar, ground almonds, and coffee liqueur and continue beating until cream holds its shape. Yield: 8 servings.

Mrs. Tommy Akers
(Jeanie Gerrard)

Butter the pot or cup before melting chocolate or measuring molasses or syrup. It will pour faster.

French Chocolate Mousse

6 squares semisweet chocolate,
  melted
¼ teaspoon salt
2 Tablespoons water

4 large eggs, separated
2 teaspoons vanilla extract
¾ cup heavy cream, divided
1½ teaspoons sugar

Melt chocolate with salt and water in top of double boiler. Beat egg yolks until light and lemon colored. Gradually beat in melted chocolate. Add vanilla. Beat egg whites until they stand in soft stiff peaks and fold into the chocolate mixture. Whip ½ cup cream and fold in. Spoon into sherbet dishes; chill. Use remaining cream, whipped with sugar to taste, to decorate top of each dish just before serving. Yield: 8 servings.

Mrs. Frank Maxwell
(Louise Middlebrook)

Ladyfingers

½ cup sifted unbleached flour
3 Tablespoons sifted cornstarch
3 large eggs, separated

½ cup sugar, divided
1 teaspoon vanilla extract
Powdered sugar

Grease and flour 2 large cookie sheets. On waxed paper sift together flour and cornstarch; reserve. In bowl of electric mixer at high speed beat egg whites until soft peaks form. Gradually beat in ¼ cup sugar until stiff peaks form. Without washing beater, in another bowl with mixer at high speed, beat egg yolks, remaining ¼ cup sugar and vanilla until thickened and lemon colored. With mixer at low speed, gradually beat in reserved flour mixture until blended. Gently fold in egg whites, about ⅓ at a time, until blended. Spoon batter, a portion at a time, into a pastry bag fitted with a plain round tube (½-inch wide). Holding the bag diagonally at a 45° angle, press batter onto prepared cookie sheets into "fingers" about 3½ inches long and 1 inch wide, well apart from one another. Sprinkle with powdered sugar. Let stand 5 minutes. Sprinkle again with powdered sugar. Bake 1 cookie sheet at a time in a preheated 350° oven until set and tinged with gold, 8 to 10 minutes. With a metal spatula remove from cookie sheet to wire rack. Cool completely. Store in airtight container. Yield: 2 dozen single ladyfingers.

Mrs. Dan Waring
(Janice Gerache)

Chocolate Charlotte Russe Dessert

4 squares unsweetened chocolate
¾ cup sugar
⅓ cup milk
6 eggs, separated
1½ cups unsalted butter or
  margarine

1 cup powdered sugar
Pinch of salt
½ teaspoon vanilla extract
4 packets lady fingers, split
1 (8-ounce) container non-dairy
  whipped topping

Melt chocolate squares in top part of double boiler over hot water. Mix sugar, milk, and egg yolks. Add to chocolate and cook until smooth and thickened, stirring constantly. Cool. Cream butter or margarine well. Fold ¾ cup powdered sugar and cream thoroughly. Add chocolate mixture and beat well. Beat egg whites with little salt until stiff. Gradually beat in vanilla and remaining powdered sugar. Fold into chocolate mixture. Line bottom and sides of a 9-inch springform pan with lady fingers. Put in alternate layers of ⅓ mixture and remaining lady fingers. Refrigerate for 12 hours before serving. Top with whipped topping. Yield: 16 servings.

Mrs. George Tzotzolas
(Irene Alissandrakis)

Peppermint Ice Cream Dessert

Crust

1 (6-ounce) package chocolate chips
2 Tablespoons margarine

2 cups rice cereal

Place chocolate chips and margarine in large glass bowl and microwave for 2 minutes or until melted. Stir in rice cereal. Line 10-inch pie plate with mixture. Refrigerate until set, about 15 minutes.

Filling

½ gallon peppermint stick ice
  cream

1 milk chocolate candy bar or
  crushed peppermint candy

Soften ice cream and fill crust. Sprinkle with shavings from chocolate bar or crushed peppermint candy. Freeze 3 to 4 hours. Cut and serve. Yield: 8 servings.

Iolene Anderson
Ankeny, Iowa

Angel Food Ice Cream Cake

1 large angel food cake
1 (18-ounce) jar chocolate fudge
   sauce

1 gallon vanilla ice cream, softened
½ pint heavy cream, whipped
Slivered chocolate (optional)

Tear cake into large pieces. Stir in chocolate sauce and coat pieces of cake. Mix in softened ice cream. Put into angel food cake pan and freeze 3 to 4 hours; turn out onto large cake plate and frost with whipped cream. Decorate with slivered chocolate or as desired; refreeze. Yield: 20 servings.

Mrs. Ed Buelow, Jr.
(Carol Cox)

Ambrosia

1 to 1¼ cups shredded fresh
   coconut
16 to 18 medium-size navel oranges

⅔ cup fresh coconut juice
10 to 12 ounces crushed pineapple
⅓ cup maraschino cherries, drained

Remove shell from coconut, reserving juice. Peel brown skin off coconut meat and wipe clean. Do not rinse. Shred coconut. A food processor does this quickly. Peel oranges over a large bowl. With knife, slit each section of orange, scraping outward to remove pulp. Try to keep pieces as large as possible. As each orange is finished, squeeze juice from membranes into bowl; discard membrane. Add remaining ingredients and mix gently. Refrigerate overnight. Serve with whipped topping and your favorite holiday cake or cookies.

Mrs. W. J. Gunn
(Blanche Simmons)

Baked Bananas

4 firm ripe bananas
¼ cup margarine
2 Tablespoons sugar
1 Tablespoon (or more) cinnamon

Whipped cream, whipped topping,
   ice cream, or coconut milk for
   topping

Peel bananas and slice into quarters. Place in shallow baking dish. Melt margarine and pour over bananas. Mix together sugar and cinnamon; sprinkle over bananas. Place bananas in preheated 350° oven and bake for 12 to 15 minutes. Spoon sauce and bananas into serving dish. Top with desired topping or serve plain. Yield: 4 to 6 servings.

Mrs. Allison Andrews
(Allison Walt)

Rum Trifle

½ cup light rum
¾ cup golden raisins
¾ cup slivered almonds
1 (3-ounce) package vanilla pudding
   (not instant)
2½ cups milk

1 cup chilled heavy cream
8 cups angel food cake cut into ½-
   inch cubes
8 maraschino cherries
Sliced almonds, toasted

Pour rum over raisins and slivered almonds in a small bowl. Let soak 1 hour. In a medium saucepan, mix pudding with 2½ cups milk. Cook over medium heat until it boils. When pudding has cooled, whip the chilled cream and fold ½ whipped cream into pudding. In trifle bowl or other pretty, clear crystal bowl, layer ⅓ cake cubes. Sprinkle with ⅓ rum mixture, then ⅓ pudding. Repeat each layer twice, ending with pudding. Cover and refrigerate a minimum of 3 hours and a maximum of 24 hours before serving. Garnish with remaining whipped cream, maraschino cherries, and toasted sliced almonds. Yield: 10 servings.

Mrs. Anne Hurt
(Anne Pearson)

Frozen Amaretto Torte

⅓ cup margarine, melted
2 cups chocolate wafer cookie
   crumbs (about 40 wafers)
½ cup slivered almonds, toasted
   and chopped
1 (6-ounce) package chocolate chips

1 (14-ounce) can sweetened
   condensed milk
1 (16-ounce) carton sour cream
⅓ cup amaretto
1 cup heavy cream, whipped

Combine margarine, crumbs, and almonds. Reserving 1½ cups crumbs, press firmly on bottom of 9-inch springform pan. In small saucepan over medium heat, melt chips with sweetened condensed milk. In large mixing bowl, combine sour cream and amaretto; mix well. Stir in chocolate mixture. Fold in whipped cream. Pour ½ amaretto mixture over prepared crust; top with 1 cup reserved crumbs and then rest of amaretto mixture. Top with remaining ½ cup crumbs; cover. Freeze 6 hours or until firm. Return leftovers to freezer. Yield: 12 to 15 servings.

Butterscotch chips may be substituted for chocolate chips.

Mrs. Tom Harris, Jr.
(Josephine Good)

Pineapple Blitz Torte

½ cup butter
½ cup sugar
4 egg yolks, well beaten
⅔ cup cake flour

¼ teaspoon salt
1 teaspoon baking powder
¼ cup milk

Thoroughly cream butter and sugar; add egg yolks and beat thoroughly. Add sifted dry ingredients, alternating with milk. Pour into 2 waxed paper-lined 8-inch pans. Bake at 325° for 15 minutes. Top with meringue.

Meringue Topping

4 egg whites
¾ cup sugar

1 teaspoon vanilla extract
1 cup chopped nuts

Beat egg whites to a stiff foam; add sugar 1 Tablespoon at a time. Add vanilla and spread meringue over partially baked layer. Sprinkle with nuts; return to oven and bake at 325° for 15 minutes. Cool; remove from pans and fill with pineapple filling.

Pineapple Filling

1½ Tablespoons powdered sugar
1 (8-ounce) can crushed pineapple

¼ teaspoon vanilla extract
½ pint heavy cream, whipped

Fold sugar, pineapple, and vanilla into stiffly whipped cream. Place 1 layer cake, meringue-side down onto plate; spread with filling. Place the other layer, meringue-side down on this; spread with filling. Yield: 8 servings.

Mrs. Ernest Thomas
(Camille Sanders)

Cakes

Praline Cheese Cake

1¼ cups crushed graham crackers
¼ cup sugar
¼ cup chopped pecans, toasted
¼ cup margarine, melted
3 (8-ounce) packages cream cheese, softened
1 cup brown sugar

1 (5½-ounce) can evaporated milk
2 Tablespoons flour
1½ teaspoons vanilla extract
3 eggs
1 cup pecan halves, toasted for garnish

In a small bowl combine first 3 ingredients. Stir in margarine. Press over bottom and ½ inch up sides of a 9-inch springform pan. Bake at 350° for 10 minutes. Beat together cream cheese, brown sugar, milk, flour and vanilla. Add eggs and beat until blended. Pour into baked crust. Bake at 350° for 50 to 55 minutes or until set. Cool in pan 30 minutes. Loosen sides and remove rim. Cool. Arrange nut halves on top. Yield: 12 to 15 servings.

Praline Sauce

⅔ cup light corn syrup
1½ cups light brown sugar

4 Tablespoons butter
1 (5½-ounce) can evaporated milk

Mix first 3 ingredients in medium saucepan and heat to boiling point. Remove from heat and cool to lukewarm. Add milk and blend well. Serve warm over praline cheese cake. This sauce can be stored in jars in the refrigerator and kept for a long time. Yield: 3½ cups.

This sauce is also delicious over ice cream and other cakes. It can easily be doubled and put into jars to make a nice gift during the holidays.

Mrs. Butch Bailess
(Ginner Kennedy)

 Dusting pecans with a little flour before mixing into cake batter prevents pecans from sinking to bottom.

Cheese Cake

1 (6-ounce) box zwieback crackers,
  crushed
1¼ cups sugar, divided
½ teaspoon cinnamon
¼ cup butter, melted
4 eggs, separated

1 cup sour cream
1 teaspoon vanilla extract
2 Tablespoons flour
¼ teaspoon salt
1 pound cream cheese, softened

Combine crackers, ¼ cup sugar, cinnamon, and butter; press into bottom of a 9-inch springform pan. Bake at 350° for 10 minutes and let cool. Beat egg whites until stiff with ¼ cup sugar. Set aside. Without washing the beater, beat egg yolks until thick. Add sour cream and vanilla. Beat in ¾ cup sugar, flour, salt, and cream cheese. Mix well and then fold in egg whites. Pour into springform pan. Bake at 350° for 50 to 55 minutes. Cool and chill. Top with Strawberry-Raspberry glaze if desired; or for an easy topping, use 1 can cherry or blueberry pie filling. Yield: 12 to 15 servings.

For a different flavor, add 1 teaspoon each of fresh lemon juice and lemon rind or fresh orange juice and orange rind.

Mrs. Mark Prewitt
(Susie Harmon)

Strawberry-Raspberry Glaze

2 pints strawberries
1 (12-ounce) jar red raspberry jelly
1 Tablespoon cornstarch

¼ cup Cointreau
¼ cup water

Wash and hull berries and let dry completely. Combine a little jelly with cornstarch in saucepan and mix well. Add remaining jelly, Cointreau and water and cook over medium heat, stirring frequently, until thickened and clear, about 5 to 10 minutes. Cool to lukewarm, stirring occasionally. Arrange berries pointed-end up all over top of cake. Spoon glaze over berries, allowing some to drip down sides of cake. Return to refrigerator until glaze is set.

Mrs. John Hennessey
(Joy Ann Howard)

 For ease in flouring pans, keep some flour in a large shaker and shake out the amount needed to cover the pan.

Mocha Chocolate Chip Cheese Cake

1½ cups chocolate wafer crumbs
   (about 24 wafers)
6 Tablespoons butter at room
   temperature
1⅓ cups sugar, divided
1½ pounds cream cheese at room
   temperature

4 eggs at room temperature
⅓ cup heavy cream
1 Tablespoon instant coffee powder
1½ teaspoons vanilla extract
1 cup miniature chocolate chips

Position rack in center of oven and preheat to 200°. Butter bottom and sides of 9-inch springform pan. Combine crumbs, butter and ⅓ cup sugar in food processor and mix well. Pat evenly onto bottom and sides of prepared pan. Set aside. Beat cream cheese in large bowl of electric mixer until fluffy. Blend in 1 cup sugar. Add eggs, 1 at a time, beating well after each addition. Add cream, coffee, and vanilla and beat 2 minutes. Turn mixture into prepared crust. Top with chocolate chips and swirl through with spatula. Set pan on baking sheet. Bake about 2 hours or longer or until it seems set. Yield: 10 to 12 servings.

Mrs. Steve Rodman
Rockford, Illinois

Cream Cheese Pound Cake

½ cup butter, softened
1 cup margarine, softened
3 cups sugar
1 (8-ounce) package cream cheese
6 eggs

3 cups cake flour
2 teaspoons vanilla extract
2 teaspoons fresh lemon juice
Powdered sugar

Cream butter and margarine until smooth. Add sugar and cream well. Add cream cheese and cream well. Alternate eggs and flour until thoroughly mixed. Add vanilla and lemon juice. Pour into greased and floured tube pan. Bake for 1½ hours at 300°. Sift powdered sugar over cake. Yield: 10 to 12 servings.

Almond extract can be substituted for lemon juice.

Mrs. Richard Johnson
(Saralie Prewitt)

 Save margarine wrappers to grease baking pans.

Amaretto Cheese Cake

⅓ cup plus 1 Tablespoon butter
1½ cups graham cracker crumbs
1 teaspoon ground cinnamon
3 (8-ounce) packages cream cheese

1 cup sugar
4 medium eggs
⅓ cup amaretto liqueur

Melt butter; add to graham cracker crumbs and cinnamon. Mix well. Pat into bottom and ½ inch on sides of a 9-inch springform pan. With electric mixer beat softened cream cheese until light and fluffy. Gradually add sugar. Add eggs 1 at a time, beating well after each addition. Stir in amaretto. Pour into pan. Bake at 375° for 45 to 55 minutes until set. Yield: 10 servings.

Glaze

2 Tablespoons plus 1 teaspoon
  sugar
1 (8-ounce) carton sour cream

1 Tablespoon amaretto
Grated chocolate (optional)

Add sugar to sour cream. Mix well; add amaretto. Spoon over cake when cooled. Put back into oven; set temperature at 400°. Leave in oven 5 minutes. Cool to room temperature. Refrigerate 24 to 48 hours for flavor to penetrate fully. Cover with grated chocolate if desired.

Mrs. W. F. McGehee
(Brownie Burton)

Whipping Cream Pound Cake

3 cups sugar
1 cup butter (no substitute)
6 eggs
3 cups cake flour

½ pint heavy cream
1 teaspoon vanilla extract
1 teaspoon butter extract

Grease and flour a bundt cake pan. In large bowl cream sugar and butter. Add eggs and flour alternately, mixing well. Add cream and flavorings. Beat at low speed of electric mixer until smooth. Pour in pan. Put in cold oven. Bake 1 hour and 25 minutes at 325°. Yield: 12 servings.

Mrs. Lindsey Blackledge
Laurel, Mississippi

Hershey Bar Pound Cake

2 cups sugar
1 cup butter
4 eggs
2 (5.5-ounce) cans chocolate syrup
7 (1.45-ounce) HERSHEY bars,
   melted

¼ teaspoon salt
2½ cups flour
½ teaspoon soda
1 cup buttermilk
1 teaspoon vanilla extract
Powdered sugar

Cream sugar and butter; add eggs 1 at a time, beating well. Add syrup and melted candy bars. Add salt to flour; stir soda into buttermilk and add to other ingredients alternately with flour, beginning and ending with flour. Add vanilla and pour into greased tube pan. Bake at 300° for 1½ hours. Cool in pan 10 minutes before removing. Sift powdered sugar over cooled cake. Yield: 10 to 12 servings. "HERSHEY'S" is a registered trademark of Hershey Foods Corporation and used with permission.

Mrs. Brad Bradway
(Mary Dalrymple)

Apricot Brandy Pound Cake

1 cup butter
3 cups sugar
6 eggs
3 cups flour
¼ teaspoon soda
½ teaspoon salt
1 cup sour cream

½ teaspoon rum flavoring
1 teaspoon orange flavoring
¼ teaspoon almond flavoring
½ teaspoon lemon flavoring
1 teaspoon vanilla extract
½ cup apricot brandy

Grease and flour one 10-inch tube pan. Preheat oven to 325°. Cream together butter and sugar until very light and fluffy. Add eggs 1 at a time, beating thoroughly after each. Sift together dry ingredients. Combine sour cream, flavorings, and brandy. Add dry ingredients alternately with sour cream mixture. Pour into prepared pan. Bake for 70 minutes or until done. Remove from oven and cool. This freezes well. Yield: 1 (10-inch) tube cake.

Mrs. George Jabour, Jr.
(Miriam Penton)

Flavoring extracts will be distributed better if they are added to the liquids.

Apple Cider Pound Cake

3 cups flour
½ teaspoon salt
½ teaspoon baking powder
¾ teaspoon cinnamon
½ teaspoon allspice
½ teaspoon nutmeg
¼ teaspoon cloves

1 cup butter
½ cup shortening
3 cups sugar
6 eggs
1 teaspoon vanilla extract
1 cup apple cider

Sift together flour, salt, baking powder, and spices; set aside. Cream butter, shortening, and sugar. Add eggs, 1 at a time, beating well after each. Add vanilla. Add dry ingredients alternately with cider to creamed mixture, beginning and ending with flour. Pour batter into greased and floured 10-inch tube pan. Bake at 325° for 1½ hours. Cool 15 minutes; remove from pan and finish cooling on wire rack.

Caramel Glaze

½ cup sugar
¼ teaspoon soda
¼ cup buttermilk

½ teaspoon light corn syrup
¼ teaspoon vanilla extract
¼ cup butter

Bring ingredients to rolling boil. Boil 10 minutes, stirring occasionally. Pour over slightly warm cake, allowing glaze to drip down sides of cake.

This is a large cake which can be divided into 3 loaf pans for gift giving.

Mrs. Elmer Bonney
Jackson, Mississippi

Delicate White Cake

½ cup plus 2 Tablespoons butter
2 cups sugar, divided
3 cups flour
2 teaspoons baking powder

1 teaspoon salt
1 cup milk
1 teaspoon vanilla extract
6 egg whites

Cream butter and 1 cup sugar. Mix dry ingredients; add alternately with milk. Add vanilla. Beat egg whites. Add 1 cup sugar. Fold into cake batter. Bake in two 8-inch pans at 350° for 30 minutes or until done. Yield: 10 to 12 servings.

Mrs. Elmer Neill, Sr.
Tallulah, Louisiana

Prize Angel Food Cake

1½ cups egg whites (11 to 13
  whites)
1⅛ cups sifted cake flour
1¾ cups sugar, divided
½ teaspoon salt

1½ teaspoons cream of tartar
1 teaspoon vanilla extract
1 scant teaspoon almond extract

Let egg whites stand until room temperature. Sift flour once before measuring. Sift flour and ¾ cup sugar together 5 times. Put egg whites and salt into large bowl of mixer. Beat until foamy. Add cream of tartar and continue beating until whites are stiff and stand in points, about 2½ to 3 minutes. Do not overbeat until dry. Sprinkle in gradually 1 cup sugar, while beating on medium speed. Beat only until sugar is blended, about 1½ minutes. Turn to low speed and add vanilla and almond extracts. Sprinkle in sifted flour mixture evenly and quickly. Beat only enough to blend, about 1½ minutes, scraping bowl to blend in quickly. Pour into 10-inch tube pan. Cut through batter with knife or spatula, going around in circular motion 3 times to release large air bubbles. Bake in preheated 375° oven for 30 to 35 minutes until golden brown. Turn oven off after 30 minutes. Leave cake in oven for 5 more minutes before removing. Can freeze. Yield: 12 to 15 servings.

Mary Ann Bingham Shaw
Greenwood, Mississippi

Sherry Cake

1 (18½-ounce) box yellow cake mix
1 (3-ounce) box vanilla instant
  pudding

¾ cup salad oil
¾ cup sherry
4 large eggs

Mix together cake mix and pudding. Add oil and sherry and blend. Beat in eggs 1 at a time. Bake in bundt pan at 325° for 50 minutes.

Glaze

1 cup powdered sugar

¼ cup sherry

Mix sugar and sherry until smooth. While cake is still hot in the pan, drizzle ⅓ glaze over bottom of cake. Let cake cool and turn out onto plate. Pour the rest of glaze over cake. Yield: 15 to 20 servings.

Mrs. J. Carter Stamm, Sr.
(Dorothy Williams)

Plain Layer Cake

1 cup butter
2 cups sugar
5 large eggs
1 teaspoon soda
1 teaspoon baking powder

Dash of salt
2¾ cups cake flour, sifted before
    measuring
1 cup buttermilk
1½ teaspoons vanilla extract

Preheat oven to 350°. Cream butter and sugar 15 minutes with electric mixer. Add eggs, 1 at a time, beating well after each addition. Sift dry ingredients together and add alternately with buttermilk. Add vanilla extract. Bake in greased and floured cake pans for 25 minutes. This batter will fill three 9-inch cake pans plus a few cupcakes, or it will fill two 9-inch and two 8-inch pans. (Use 2 layers and freeze 2 layers.) Cool in pans for 10 minutes; then cool on wire cake racks. Frost with desired frosting.

Never Fail Chocolate Frosting

2 cups sugar
2 (1-ounce) squares unsweetened
    chocolate

½ cup margarine
½ cup milk
½ teaspoon vanilla extract

Combine all ingredients except vanilla extract. Stir over medium heat until sugar and chocolate dissolve. Turn heat to high and boil rapidly 1 minute. Remove from heat and add vanilla. Beat until right consistency to spread. If it gets too hard to spread, add 1 or 2 Tablespoons water and mix. Yield: 15 to 20 servings.

Mrs. C. B. Patterson
(Sue Nelson)

Louise's Lemon Jelly Cake

1 (18½-ounce) box Duncan Hines
    Butter Recipe Cake Mix
8 egg yolks, slightly beaten

1½ cups sugar
8 Tablespoons lemon juice
½ cup butter (no substitute)

Prepare cake mix as directed in two 8-inch pans. Let cool and set aside. Mix egg yolks, sugar, lemon juice, and butter together in a saucepan. Cook mixture over low heat stirring constantly until it comes to a boil and thickens. If mixture becomes lumpy, strain. Put mixture in bowl and set in refrigerator until cold. Slice cake to make 4 layers and put lemon mixture between layers and on top of cake. Yield: 10 to 12 servings.

Mrs. Harry Meyer
(Louise Angelo)

My Favorite Sponge Cake

1 large or 2 medium lemons *2 cups sugar, divided*
8 large eggs, separated *2 cups flour*

Grate rind of lemons and set aside. Squeeze juice from lemons and add to rind. Beat egg yolks at high speed until almost doubled in size. Add lemon juice and rind to yolks. Gradually add 1 cup sugar to yolks, beating until sugar dissolves. This will double in amount. Set aside. Beat egg whites until stiff. Add remaining 1 cup sugar and beat well. Stir in flour gradually. Do not beat as this will toughen texture. Pour into greased tube pan or two 12 x 9 x 2-inch pans. Bake at 350° for about 1 hour. Cake is done when inserted broom straw or toothpick comes out clean. Cool for 20 minutes. Turn right-side up on cake plate. Frost with favorite icing or glaze. Be sure to use a serrated knife with sawing motions to cut clean slices. Yield: 15 to 20 servings.

Sister Mary Benigna Bové, R.S.M.

Prune Cake

3 eggs *1 teaspoon allspice*
1 cup vegetable oil *1 teaspoon nutmeg*
1½ cups sugar *1 teaspoon salt*
2 cups flour *1 cup buttermilk*
1 teaspoon soda *1 cup cooked pitted prunes, cut up*
1 teaspoon cinnamon *1 cup chopped nuts (optional)*

Mix all cake ingredients in order given. It is best to sift all dry ingredients together before adding to mixture. Grease and flour a large baking pan, 10 x 14-inch or larger. Pour in cake batter and bake at 350° about 40 minutes. Remove from oven and immediately prick all over top with a knife or fork before pouring icing over cake. Yield: 12 servings.

Icing

1 cup sugar *1 Tablespoon dark corn syrup*
½ cup buttermilk *¼ cup butter or margarine*
1 teaspoon soda *Whipped cream (optional)*

Mix first 5 ingredients in a boiler and bring to a rolling boil. Remove from heat and beat slightly. While still very warm, pour over hot cake which has been pricked. Serve with whipped cream if desired.

Mrs. George Jabour, Sr.
(Christine Varnado)

Fluffy Gold Coconut Cake

2½ cups sifted cake flour
1⅔ cups sugar
4 teaspoons baking powder
1 teaspoon salt
½ cup soft shortening

1¼ cups milk
1 teaspoon lemon extract
½ teaspoon vanilla extract
5 egg yolks (reserve 2 egg whites for
    frosting)

Grease generously and flour two 9-inch cake pans. Sift together cake flour, sugar, baking powder, and salt. Add shortening. Add a little over ½ milk with extracts and beat for 2 minutes. Add remaining milk and egg yolks. Beat 2 minutes and pour into prepared pans. Bake at 350° for 25 to 35 minutes. Cool. Ice with 7-Minute Coconut Frosting. Yield: 12 servings.

7-Minute Coconut Frosting

2 egg whites
¼ teaspoon cream of tartar
1½ cups sugar
⅓ cup water

1½ teaspoons vanilla extract
1 fresh coconut, grated or 1 package
    grated coconut

Combine in top of double boiler egg whites, cream of tartar, sugar, and water. Place over boiling water and beat with rotary beater about 5 minutes until mixture holds its shape. Fold in vanilla. Beat until cool. Then spread frosting between layers and pat coconut on top of frosting. Then frost remaining cake and pat coconut on top of frosting.

Mrs. James Robertson
(Elise Ethridge)

Lemon Sauce

½ cup sugar
1 Tablespoon cornstarch
Pinch of salt

1 cup boiling water
2 Tablespoons butter
3 Tablespoons lemon juice

In a saucepan combine sugar, cornstarch, and salt. Gradually stir in water. Boil, stirring constantly, 5 minutes. Remove from heat and stir in butter and lemon juice. Pour hot sauce over warm gingerbread. Yield: 2 cups.

This is good over other sweet breads, cakes and ice cream.

The Editors

Fresh Apple Cake with Icing

1 cup cooking oil	1 teaspoon soda
2 cups sugar	½ teaspoon cinnamon
3 eggs, well beaten	½ teaspoon nutmeg
2½ cups flour	1 teaspoon vanilla extract
2 teaspoons baking powder	3 cups peeled, chopped apples
½ teaspoon salt	1 cup chopped pecans

Combine oil and sugar. Beat in eggs. Sift together flour, baking powder, salt, soda, cinnamon and nutmeg. Add to creamed mixture. Fold in vanilla, apples and pecans. Pour into well-greased bundt pan and bake at 350° for 50 to 60 minutes. Remove cake from pan and cool. Drizzle brown icing over cooled cake. Yield: 16 servings.

Brown Icing

1½ cups light brown sugar	¼ cup evaporated milk
¼ cup butter	1 teaspoon vanilla extract

Bring sugar, butter and milk to a boil, stirring constantly. Remove from heat immediately and stir in vanilla. Beat by hand until icing has cooled. Drizzle over apple cake.

Mrs. Robert R. Bailess
(Natalie Waring)

Applesauce Cake

½ cup margarine	½ teaspoon soda
1½ cups sugar	1 teaspoon cinnamon
2 eggs, beaten	½ teaspoon cloves
1 cup applesauce	1 cup pecans, chopped
2 cups flour	1 cup raisins
¼ teaspoon salt	Powdered sugar (optional)
1 teaspoon baking powder	

In large mixing bowl cream margarine and sugar; add eggs and beat well. Add applesauce, then all sifted dry ingredients, and beat until smooth. Add chopped nuts and raisins. Bake in a tube or bundt pan. Bake at 350° for 45 to 60 minutes. Sift powdered sugar on top if desired. Yield: 10 to 12 servings.

Children love this made in small muffin tins.

Mrs. Tom Harris, Jr.
(Josephine Good)

Blackberry Jam Cake with Caramel Icing

1 cup butter, softened
2 cups sugar
6 eggs
2 teaspoons soda
1 cup buttermilk

3 cups sifted flour
1 teaspoon cinnamon
1 teaspoon allspice
1 teaspoon cloves
1½ cups blackberry jam

In a large mixing bowl, cream butter and sugar. Beat in eggs 1 at a time. In a separate bowl dissolve soda in buttermilk and stir into sugar mixture. Stir in flour and spices. Add jam, mixing well. Bake in 3 greased and lightly floured 8 or 9-inch cake pans at 350° for 45 minutes. Cool and remove from pans. Frost each layer and entire cake with caramel icing. Yield: 16 to 20 servings.

Caramel Icing

4 Tablespoons plus 3 cups sugar,
    divided
1 (15-ounce) can condensed milk

¾ cup butter
1 Tablespoon vanilla extract

In heavy skillet, slowly brown 4 Tablespoons sugar. In a large saucepan, combine 3 cups sugar, milk, and butter and bring to a boil. Reduce heat. Add browned sugar to this mixture; cook on medium heat until mixture forms a firm ball in cold water. Remove from heat and allow to cool. Add vanilla and beat until thick enough to spread easily. Add a bit of cream if icing becomes too hard while spreading.

Mrs. Harold Blue
(Jean Johnson)

Crème de Cacao Cake

1 (18½-ounce) box yellow cake mix
2 cups heavy cream

¼ cup or more to taste dry
    chocolate flavored drink mix
¼ cup crème de cacao

Bake cake according to package directions in two 9-inch pans. Cool and slice each layer horizontally, making 4 layers. Whip cream and fold in dry chocolate mix and crème de cacao. Ice each layer; stack layers and ice top and sides with whipped cream mixture. Put in refrigerator for at least 6 to 8 hours. Yield: 15 to 20 servings.

Mrs. Ann Emmich
(Ann Grundfest)

Carrot Cake

2 cups flour
2 cups sugar
2 teaspoons cinnamon
2 teaspoons soda

1 teaspoon salt
4 eggs
1½ cups vegetable oil
3 cups grated carrots

Sift dry ingredients. Add eggs, oil, and carrots. Mix well. Bake in three 9-inch cake pans at 375° for 25 to 30 minutes.

Icing

½ cup margarine
1 (8-ounce) package cream cheese,
    softened
1 (1-pound) box powdered sugar

2 teaspoons vanilla extract
1 teaspoon lemon juice
1 cup chopped pecans

Cream margarine and cream cheese. Add sugar and mix well. Add vanilla, lemon juice, and pecans; mix well. Spread icing between cooled cake layers and on top and sides. Yield: 15 to 20 servings.

Mrs. John Newton
(Cathie Bailess)

White Fruit Cake

1 pound butter
3 cups sugar
12 eggs
2½ pounds candied red and green
    cherries, chopped
2½ pounds candied red and green
    pineapple, chopped

2½ pounds pecans
6 cups flour, divided
½ teaspoon soda
2 teaspoons vanilla extract
2 teaspoons almond flavoring
2 teaspoons lemon flavoring

Cream butter and sugar. Add eggs, 1 at a time, and blend well. Chop cherries and pineapple. Break nuts or chop coarsely. Use 1½ cups flour to coat fruit and nuts. Sift soda with remaining flour. Add dry ingredients alternately with fruit and nuts, stirring and folding in carefully. Add flavorings. Grease pans, line with brown paper or waxed paper, and grease the paper. Fill pans no more than ¾ full with batter. Bake in a 300° oven. For a tube pan and 2 loaf pans, bake 2½ hours. For 4 loaf pans bake 1½ hours. Cake tester will come out moist but not doughy when cake is done. Yield: 24 to 30 servings.

Mrs. Dewey Blackledge, Sr.
Laurel, Mississippi

Miriam's Fruit Cake

¾ cup flour
¼ teaspoon baking powder
¼ teaspoon baking soda
½ teaspoon salt
¾ cup brown sugar
1 (8-ounce) box whole pitted dates

1 (6-ounce) package apricot halves
3 cups pecan halves
3 eggs
1 teaspoon vanilla extract
Cream cheese slices for topping

Sift flour; measure. Add baking powder, soda, and salt and sift into a 2-quart bowl. Stir in brown sugar. Add dates, apricots, and pecans. Stir to coat fruit. Beat eggs well in separate bowl; add vanilla. Mix with fruit until well blended. This takes time. Grease a 9 x 5 x 3-inch loaf pan and line with waxed paper. Grease paper. Pour in mixture and bake 1½ hours at 300° or until toothpick inserted comes out clean. Remove from pan immediately and pull away waxed paper. Serve with a small sliver of cream cheese on top of each slice. Yield: 12 to 15 servings.

May be frozen a year or stored 1 month in refrigerator.

Miriam Graeber Cohn
Port Gibson, Mississippi

Cranberry-Orange Cake

2¼ cups flour, sifted and divided
1 cup sugar, sifted
1 Tablespoon baking soda
1 teaspoon salt
1 cup buttermilk
2 eggs, beaten

¾ cup vegetable oil
Grated rind of 2 oranges
1 cup chopped dates
1 cup chopped pecans
1 cup whole raw cranberries

Mix together 1¼ cups flour, sugar, soda, and salt. Add buttermilk, eggs, oil, and orange rind. Mix well. In another bowl mix 1 cup flour, dates, nuts, and cranberries. Add to cake batter and mix well. Bake in bundt pan, which has been greased and floured, at 350° for 1 hour.

Glaze

1 cup orange juice

1 cup sugar

Mix orange juice and sugar. Heat slightly to dissolve sugar. Pour over cake in pan while cake is hot. Let cool completely, at least 3 hours, before removing from pan. Yield: 15 to 20 servings.

Mrs. James Hobson, Jr.
(Kay Varner)

White Chocolate Cake

¼ pound white chocolate
1 cup butter or margarine
2 cups sugar
4 eggs, separated

1 cup buttermilk
2½ cups cake flour
1 teaspoon baking powder
1 cup flaked coconut

Melt chocolate in double boiler and cool. Cream butter until light; add sugar gradually and continue to beat until very light and fluffy. Add 4 beaten egg yolks; beat 2 or 3 minutes; add cooled chocolate and mix well. Add alternately buttermilk, cake flour, and baking powder. Fold in beaten egg whites. Gently stir in coconut. Pour into 3 greased and floured 9-inch cake pans. Bake at 350° for 25 to 30 minutes. Yield: 12 servings.

Frosting

½ cup butter
2 (3-ounce) packages cream cheese
1 (16-ounce) box powdered sugar

1 teaspoon vanilla extract
½ cup chopped nuts

Cream butter and cream cheese. Add sugar and vanilla. Beat until spreading consistency and add nuts. If too stiff to spread, add small amount of milk or cream. Frost cake.

Mrs. Touphie Habeeb
(Mable Fulton)

Pumpkin Roll

3 eggs
1 cup sugar
⅔ cup pumpkin
1 teaspoon lemon juice
¾ cup flour
1 teaspoon baking powder

2 teaspoons cinnamon
1 teaspoon ginger
½ teaspoon nutmeg
½ teaspoon salt
1 cup chopped pecans
Powdered sugar

In a large mixing bowl, beat eggs on high speed with electric mixer for 5 minutes. Beat in sugar, then add pumpkin and lemon juice. In a separate bowl combine flour and spices; fold this into pumpkin mixture. Spread evenly on a greased and floured jellyroll pan. Sprinkle with 1 cup finely chopped pecans. Bake at 350° for 15 minutes. Remove from oven, loosen edges immediately, and turn out onto dish towel or cheesecloth sprinkled with powdered sugar. Roll up, starting with long side, and let cool. When cool, unroll; spread evenly with filling, and roll back up. Sprinkle with powdered sugar. Yield: 8 to 10 servings.

Filling

1 cup powdered sugar
2 (3-ounce) packages cream cheese, softened

4 Tablespoons butter
½ teaspoon vanilla extract

Mix all ingredients until smooth.

If the pumpkin bread cools at all before it is removed from the pan, it sticks terribly. It should be kept in the refrigerator and served cold.

Mrs. Anne Hurt
(Anne Pearson)

Black Raspberry Sheet Cake

3 cups flour
3 teaspoons baking powder
1 teaspoon salt
½ cup sugar
1 cup margarine

3 egg yolks, well beaten
½ cup milk
1 teaspoon vanilla extract
1 (21-ounce) can black raspberry pie filling or cherry pie filling

In a large bowl, add ingredients as listed in order, except pie filling. Mix very lightly and do not handle dough more than necessary. Take ¾ dough and roll out on pastry cloth or floured board. Roll out to fit a 9 x 12-inch cake pan and at least 1 inch up the sides of the pan and place in pan. Spread black raspberry pie filling on pastry; roll out rest of dough to a 6 x 12-inch rectangle and with pastry cutter, dipped in flour, cut strips of dough for lattice on top of filling. Bake 30 minutes at 350°. After cake is thoroughly cooled, make topping. Yield: 15 servings.

Topping

½ cup butter or margarine
½ cup shortening
1 (8-ounce) package cream cheese
1 pound powdered sugar

Dash of salt
1 pint marshmallow cream
1 cup shredded coconut

In large bowl, allow to soften to room temperature margarine, shortening, and cream cheese. Cream well. Add powdered sugar and salt. Cream well. Add marshmallow cream and spread on cake. Sprinkle with coconut. Refrigerate at least 2 hours.

Mrs. John Moro
(Betty DiMichele)

Wilma McCall's Chocolate Pudding Cake

1 cup sifted flour
¾ cup sugar
2 teaspoons baking powder
½ teaspoon salt
2½ Tablespoons cocoa

½ cup milk
1 teaspoon vanilla extract
3 Tablespoons margarine, melted
½ cup chopped pecans

Sift together flour, sugar, baking powder, salt, and cocoa. Add, stirring in with spoon, milk, vanilla, melted margarine, and chopped pecans. Pour into well-greased 8 x 8 x 2-inch pan.

Pudding

½ cup sugar
½ cup light brown sugar
2 Tablespoons cocoa

1 cup boiling water
Whipped topping (optional)
Cherries (optional)

Combine granulated sugar, light brown sugar, cocoa, and boiling water. Pour gently over batter. Bake at 350° for 30 to 40 minutes. When completely cooled, turn upside down on serving dish. May have to ease out with a knife. Garnish with whipped topping and cherries. Yield: 12 servings.

Mrs. Kenneth F. Grogan, III
(Anne Blackledge)

Black Forest Cake

⅔ cup whipped margarine
4 squares semisweet chocolate, melted
1¾ cups sugar
1½ cups flour
1¼ teaspoons baking soda

1 teaspoon salt
1¼ teaspoons baking powder
1¼ cups water
1 teaspoon vanilla extract
2 eggs, slightly beaten
Chocolate curls (optional)

Mix margarine, chocolate and sugar. Mix dry ingredients and then add to chocolate mixture. Add water, vanilla and eggs. Mix well. Divide batter evenly into 4 greased and floured 9-inch round cake pans. Bake at 350° for 15 to 18 minutes. Layer chocolate filling and cream filling between cake layers, ending with cream filling. Garnish with chocolate curls, if desired. Yield: 14 to 16 servings.

Chocolate Filling

1½ bars German sweet chocolate *½ cup chopped nuts*
¾ cup whipped margarine

Melt chocolate in double boiler. Blend in margarine. Add nuts.

Cream Filling

2 cups heavy cream *1 teaspoon vanilla extract*
1 Tablespoon sugar

Whip cream; add sugar and vanilla.

Mrs. Charles Gastrell
(Kathryn Caldwell)

Aunt Sue's "No Egg" Chocolate Cake

3 cups flour *12 Tablespoons melted butter or*
2 cups sugar *margarine*
6 Tablespoons cocoa *2 teaspoons vanilla extract*
1 teaspoon salt *2 Tablespoons vinegar*
2 teaspoons soda *2 cups cold water*

Put all dry ingredients into ungreased 13 x 9 x 2-inch pan. Mix together.
Add melted butter, vanilla, and vinegar. Pour water over all. Mix well until
batter is blended. Preheat oven to 350°. Bake 30 to 35 minutes. Frost in pan
while cake is still warm with chocolate icing. Yield: 12 servings.

Frosting

4 Tablespoons butter or margarine, *1 (16-ounce) box powdered sugar,*
melted *sifted*
6 Tablespoons cocoa *Small amount cream or milk*

Mix all ingredients until blended and consistency is right for spreading.
Frost warm cake.

Mrs. Jack Beard
(Carolyn Maly)

*Place a pan of water in the bottom of the oven when baking a fruit
cake to prevent it from drying out.*

Caramel Fudge Cake

1 (18½-ounce) package chocolate
   pudding recipe cake mix
28 light caramels

1 (15-ounce) can sweetened
   condensed milk
1 Tablespoon butter or margarine

Preheat oven to 350°. Grease and flour a 9 x 13-inch pan. Prepare cake according to directions. Combine caramels, milk, and butter in top of double boiler. Stir constantly until caramels are melted and let cool slightly. Spread ½ cake mix in pan. Bake for 10 minutes. Pour caramel mixture in thin stream over batter. Cover with remaining cake mix batter. Bake at 350° for 20 to 30 minutes. Cool. Prepare frosting. Yield: 12 to 16 servings.

Frosting

½ cup butter or margarine
2 squares unsweetened chocolate,
   melted

3 Tablespoons cream or milk
1 teaspoon vanilla extract
2 cups sifted powdered sugar

Beat first 4 ingredients until creamy, gradually adding powdered sugar. Frost cake.

Mrs. Jerry Hayes
(Cris Page)

Chocolate Mousse Cake

7 (1-ounce) squares semisweet
   chocolate
¼ pound butter
7 eggs, separated
1 cup sugar, divided

1 teaspoon vanilla extract
⅛ teaspoon cream of tartar
Chocolate leaves to garnish
   (optional)

In a small saucepan, melt chocolate and butter over low heat. In a large bowl, beat egg yolks and ¾ cup sugar 5 minutes or until light and fluffy. Gradually beat in warm chocolate mixture and vanilla. In another large bowl beat egg whites with cream of tartar until soft peaks form. Add remaining sugar, 1 Tablespoon at a time. Continue beating until stiff. Fold egg white mixture carefully into chocolate mixture. Pour ¾ of the batter into an ungreased 8 x 3-inch springform pan. Cover remaining batter and refrigerate. Bake cake in preheated oven 325° for 35 to 40 minutes. Remove cake from oven and cool. Cake will drop as it cools. Remove outside ring of springform pan leaving cake on the bottom for easier serving. Stir the refrigerated batter to soften slightly. Spread on top of cake, filling in hole where cake has fallen. Refrigerate until firm. 2 hours before serving, make whipped cream frosting; fill in hole on top of cake; garnish with chocolate leaves. Yield: 12 servings.

Whipped Cream Frosting

½ pint heavy cream　　　　　*1 teaspoon vanilla extract*
⅓ cup powdered sugar

In a small bowl, beat cream until soft peaks form. Add powdered sugar and vanilla. Beat until stiff.

Chocolate Leaves

7 camellia leaves (non-poisonous)
1 (1-ounce) square semisweet
*　chocolate*

Wash and dry leaves. Melt chocolate in small pan over hot water. With table knife, spread melted chocolate on underside of leaves. Place leaves, chocolate-side up, on waxed paper-lined baking sheet. Refrigerate until chocolate is firm. Remove leaf by grasping stem and gently pulling away from the chocolate. Discard leaves; use chocolate leaves to garnish. Yield: 12 servings.

This may be frozen by placing unwrapped in freezer until solid. Wrap well and return to freezer. Work quickly with chocolate leaves as warm fingers may melt chocolate.

Mrs. John C. Williams
(Jane Johnson)

Caramel Icing

3 cups sugar, divided　　　　*2 Tablespoons butter*
1 cup fresh or canned milk　　*1 teaspoon vanilla extract*

Caramelize 1 cup sugar. Bring 2 cups sugar and milk to a boil. Slowly add caramelized sugar and cook together, stirring until it forms soft ball in water. Remove and add butter and vanilla. Cool and beat until ready to spread.

Mrs. Elmer Neill, Sr.
Tallulah, Louisiana

 Shortening creams best between 70° and 80°.

 If using a glass pan when baking, lower oven temperature 25°.

Chocolate Buttermilk Sheet Cake

2 cups flour
2 cups sugar
½ teaspoon salt
½ cup margarine
1 cup water
½ cup vegetable shortening

3 heaping Tablespoons cocoa
2 eggs, beaten
1 teaspoon soda
½ cup buttermilk
1 teaspoon vanilla extract

Place in large mixing bowl, flour, sugar, and salt. Place in saucepan margarine, water, vegetable shortening, and cocoa. Bring to boil and pour over flour mixture. Mix well. Place in another bowl eggs, soda, buttermilk, and vanilla. Stir well and add to above mixture. Bake in greased and floured 9 x 13-inch pan at 350° for 20 minutes.

Icing

½ cup margarine
3 heaping Tablespoons cocoa
1 (16-ounce) box powdered sugar

1 teaspoon vanilla extract
½ cup chopped nuts
6 Tablespoons milk

Melt margarine and cocoa in a 2-quart pan, but do not boil. Take off heat and add powdered sugar, vanilla, chopped nuts, and milk. Stir well. Ice cake while hot. Yield: 12 servings.

Mrs. Jed Mihalyka
(Joy Hill)

Chocolate Nut Cupcakes

4 ounces semisweet chocolate
1 cup margarine
1½ cups pecans
1¾ cups sugar

1¼ cups sifted flour
¼ teaspoon salt
4 beaten eggs
1 teaspoon vanilla extract

Melt chocolate and margarine. Cool; add pecans. Mix sugar, flour and salt; add eggs and vanilla. Mix with spoon until moistened. Do not beat. Add chocolate mixture. Put in greased muffin tins. Bake at 325° about 30 minutes. Yield: 24 cupcakes.

Mrs. Fred Froehlig
(Rhoma Loflin)

Pies

Louise's Chocolate Cream Pie

1½ cups sugar
½ teaspoon salt
1 Tablespoon cornstarch
1 Tablespoon flour
3 squares unsweetened chocolate
3 cups milk

3 eggs, separated
1 Tablespoon butter
2 teaspoons vanilla extract, divided
¼ teaspoon cream of tartar
6 Tablespoons sugar
1 (9-inch) baked pie shell

In a saucepan mix 1½ cups sugar, salt, cornstarch, flour and chocolate, cut into small pieces. Gradually stir in milk. Cook over medium heat, stirring constantly, until mixture thickens and boils. Boil 3 minutes and remove from heat. Beat egg yolks slightly and add a little of hot mixture. Boil 1 to 2 minutes more, stirring constantly. Remove from heat and add butter and 1½ teaspoons vanilla. Let mixture cool, stirring occasionally. While mixture is cooling, beat egg whites with cream of tartar until soft peaks form. Add 6 Tablespoons sugar gradually and ½ teaspoon vanilla. Beat until stiff peaks form. Pour pie filling into pie shell. Spread meringue over top sealing to edge of pastry. Bake at 350° until meringue is very lightly browned on top about 12 to 15 minutes. Let cool and refrigerate several hours until set. Yield: 6 to 8 servings.

Miss Louise Hall
Cascilla, Mississippi

No-Crust Fudge Pie

⅓ cup butter
3 squares unsweetened chocolate
2 cups sugar
4 eggs, well beaten

¼ teaspoon salt
1 teaspoon vanilla extract
⅔ cup chopped nuts, finely chopped
Vanilla ice cream or whipped cream

Melt butter and chocolate together over low heat. Stir in sugar; blend beaten eggs with chocolate mixture. Add salt, vanilla, and nuts. Pour into a well greased 9-inch glass pie plate. Bake at 350° for 45 minutes. Serve with vanilla ice cream or whipped cream. Yield: 8 servings.

Mrs. Louis P. Cashman, Jr.
(Frances Reid)

Cal's Chocolate Pie

½ cup butter or margarine
2 eggs
1 cup sugar
1 (5-ounce) can evaporated milk
1 teaspoon vanilla extract

2 to 3 Tablespoons brandy
3½ Tablespoons cocoa
9-inch graham cracker crust
Whipped cream (optional)
Shaved chocolate curls (optional)

Mix first 7 ingredients 2 to 3 minutes in blender. Pour into graham cracker crust. Bake at 325° for 40 to 50 minutes. May be served with whipped cream topping and shaved chocolate curls. Yield: 6 servings.

John A. Lever
Clinton, Mississippi

Chocolate Pecan Pie

½ cup chopped pecans, soaked in 3
  Tablespoons bourbon
¼ cup margarine, melted
1 cup sugar
3 eggs, slightly beaten
¾ cup MRS. BUTTERWORTH'S
  Syrup®

1 teaspoon vanilla extract
Pinch of salt
½ cup chocolate chips
1 (9-inch) pie shell

Soak pecans in bourbon and set aside. In bowl beat margarine, sugar and eggs until fluffy. Blend in syrup, vanilla, and salt. Add chocolate chips. Pour filling into pie shell and put pecans on top. Bake 45 to 55 minutes in 375° oven. Can be doubled. Yield: 6 to 8 servings.

Miss Anne Cashman

Best-Ever Pie Crust

1 cup margarine, melted
2 cups flour

½ cup powdered sugar

Mix all ingredients well. Press into two 8 to 9-inch pie pans. Bake at 350° for 15 to 20 minutes. Fill with any cooked filling. Yield: 2 crusts.

Especially good for lemon or chocolate meringue pies.

Mrs. Robert C. Odom
(Idamae Ellzey)

Strawberry Pie

2 pints fresh strawberries, washed
  and hulled, divided
1 cup sugar
3 Tablespoons cornstarch

Dash of salt
1 (9-inch) pie shell, baked
Whipped cream

Crush 1 pint strawberries; add sugar and cornstarch. Cook until thick and clear. Add salt; cool. Place 1 pint halved strawberries in baked pie shell. Cover with cooked mixture. Serve with whipped cream. Yield: 6 to 8 servings.

Mrs. George Rogers, Jr.
Washington, D.C.

Fresh Strawberry Pie

1½ cups sugar
1½ cups water
¼ cup cornstarch
Pinch of salt
4 drops red food coloring
1 (3-ounce) package strawberry
  gelatin

1 quart fresh unsweetened
  strawberries
1 (9-inch) baked pie shell
Whipped cream for topping

Combine sugar, water, cornstarch and salt; cook until clear. Remove from heat; add red food coloring. Add gelatin and stir well. Let cool. Put strawberries into baked pie shell. Pour sauce over them and chill. Top with whipped cream before serving. Yield: 8 servings.

Mrs. Ed Buelow, Jr.
(Carol Cox)

Southern Pecan Pie

3 eggs, slightly beaten
1 cup sugar
½ cup light or dark corn syrup
2 Tablespoons melted butter

⅛ teaspoon salt
1 teaspoon vanilla extract
1 cup pecans, coarsely broken
1 (9-inch) unbaked pie shell

Mix together eggs, sugar, corn syrup, butter, salt, and vanilla. Stir to blend. Fold in pecans. Pour into unbaked pie shell. Cook in preheated oven at 375° for 45 minutes or until set.

Mrs. Bernard Booth
Drew, Mississippi

Lemon-Crusted Fresh Blueberry Pie

Lemon Pastry

2 cups sifted flour	⅔ cup shortening
1 teaspoon salt	4 to 6 Tablespoons cold water
½ teaspoon grated lemon peel	1 Tablespoon lemon juice

Sift together flour and salt; stir in lemon peel. Cut in shortening with pastry blender until pieces are the size of small peas. Mix together water and lemon juice. Sprinkle 1 Tablespoon liquid over part of flour mixture. Gently toss with fork; push to side of bowl. Sprinkle next Tablespoon liquid over dry portion; mix lightly; push to moistened part at side of bowl. Repeat with remaining liquid until all flour mixture is moistened. Divide dough into 2 portions and form each portion into a ball. Flatten pastry balls 1 at a time, on lightly floured surface. Roll from center to edge until dough is ⅛-inch thick.

Pie

1 recipe lemon pastry	½ teaspoon grated lemon peel
4 cups fresh blueberries	Dash of salt
¾ to 1 cup sugar	1 to 2 teaspoons lemon juice
3 Tablespoons flour	1 Tablespoon butter or margarine

In mixing bowl, combine blueberries, sugar, flour, lemon peel, and salt. Line a 9-inch pie plate with pastry; pour in filling. Drizzle with lemon juice and dot with butter or margarine. Adjust top crust, cutting slits or decorations for escape of steam. Seal and flute edges. If desired sprinkle top crust with additional sugar. Bake at 400° for 35 to 40 minutes. Yield: 8 servings.

Mrs. Glover Warner
(Peggy Holder)

No-Roll Pie Crust For Double Pie Crust

2 cups flour	⅔ cup vegetable oil
¼ cup cold water	1 teaspoon salt

Combine ingredients in mixing bowl until a ball is formed. Halve and press with fingers in pans for 2 pies; otherwise, press in oblong pan for 1 crust.

Miss Anne Cashman

Peach Custard Pie

1 cup sugar
2 Tablespoons flour
2 eggs, beaten
½ cup margarine, cut into pieces

1 teaspoon vanilla extract
1 (29-ounce) can sliced peaches,
    drained
1 (8-inch) pie shell

In a saucepan combine sugar, flour, and eggs. Add margarine and cook on low until margarine melts, stirring constantly. Add vanilla. Line un-baked pie shell with sliced peaches. Pour custard over peaches. Preheat oven to 400°. Bake at 400° for 8 minutes; reduce temperature to 350° and bake for 45 minutes or until set. Yield: 6 to 8 servings.

Mrs. Randy Oswalt
(Lynda McAlpin)

Luscious Peach Pie

Graham Cracker Crust

1¼ cups graham cracker crumbs
3 Tablespoons sugar

⅓ cup margarine, melted

Mix crumbs and sugar together in a small bowl. Pour melted margarine into crumbs and mix well. Press into bottom of a 9-inch pie plate. Bake at 350° for 8 minutes. Chill and fill with pie filling.

Filling

2 (3-ounce) packages cream cheese,
    softened
¾ cup sifted powdered sugar
½ teaspoon almond extract

¾ cup heavy cream, whipped
1 (16-ounce) can sliced peaches,
    drained

Combine softened cream cheese, powdered sugar, and almond extract in medium mixing bowl. Beat with hand mixer until smooth. Fold in whipped cream. Gently stir in peaches by hand. Pour into crust and chill well. Yield: One 9-inch pie.

Mrs. Wayne Thornton
(Donna Nasif)

Substitute gingersnap crumbs for graham cracker crumbs when making pie crust. This is especially good with pumpkin chiffon or lemon filling.

Apple Dumplings

2 cups sugar
2 cups water
¼ teaspoon cinnamon
¼ teaspoon nutmeg
¼ cup butter
6 small Granny Smith apples

2 cups enriched flour
1 teaspoon salt
2 teaspoons baking powder
¾ cup shortening
½ cup milk

To make sauce combine sugar, water, cinnamon, and nutmeg. Cook 5 minutes; add butter and set aside. Pare and core apples. In mixing bowl sift flour, salt, and baking powder; cut in shortening. Add milk all at once. Stir until flour is just moistened. Roll ¼-inch thick. Cut six 5-inch squares. Place 1 apple on each square of pastry. Sprinkle generously with additional sugar and spices; dot with butter, fold corners, and pinch edges together. Seal with water on finger tip. Place 1 inch apart in greased baking pan. Pour sauce over dumplings. Bake in moderately hot oven at 375° for 35 minutes. Serve hot with cream. Yield: 6 servings.

Can make slightly ahead of time and refrigerate if sauce is not added.

Mrs. Glover Warner
(Peggy Holder)

Meridian Dutch Apple Pie

Pastry

½ cup shortening
1½ cups flour

¼ teaspoon salt
3 Tablespoons ice water

Cut shortening into flour and salt until flaky. Add ice water 1 spoon at a time and mix. Roll thinly. Place ⅔ pastry mixture in bottom of pie plate, reserving ⅓ for lattice strips on top.

Filling

3 large apples, peeled and sliced
3 teaspoons cinnamon, divided
½ cup butter

1 cup brown sugar, packed
1 egg

Place apples in unbaked crust. Sprinkle with 1½ teaspoons cinnamon. Cream butter, brown sugar, egg, and remaining cinnamon. Pour over apples. Form lattice on top. Bake at 350° for 45 minutes. Yield: 6 to 8 servings.

Mrs. Louis L. Patterson
(Theodocia Perry)

Blue Ribbon Cherry Pie

Cherry Pie Filling

1¼ cups sugar
3 Tablespoons cornstarch
¼ teaspoon salt
1 Tablespoon soft butter
½ cup cherry juice

¼ teaspoon red food coloring
¼ teaspoon almond extract
2 teaspoons lemon juice
3 cups drained canned cherries
(reserve liquid)

Combine sugar, cornstarch, and salt. Stir in butter. Combine cherry juice, food coloring, almond extract, and lemon juice. Add this mixture to dry ingredients. Add cherries and let stand while preparing pastry. Line a 9-inch pie plate with pastry; fill with cherry mixture. Make lattice top; flute edges. Cut a 3-inch strip of aluminum foil and fold loosely around the edge of the pie. Bake at 400° for 50 to 55 minutes.

Rich Pastry

2¼ cups sifted flour
1 teaspoon salt
1 Tablespoon sugar
⅔ cup shortening

1 egg yolk
1 Tablespoon lemon juice
⅓ cup milk
1 egg white

Sift flour with salt and sugar. Cut in ½ shortening until mixture resembles corn meal. Cut in other ½ until mixture resembles large peas. Beat egg yolk and lemon juice together. Blend in juice and milk. Add to dry ingredients, tossing with a fork into a soft dough. Form into a ball. Divide ball into halves. Roll first half to ⅛-inch thickness. After putting dough into pie pan, brush bottom with egg white. Roll second half out and cut into strips to make lattice top. Yield: 8 servings.

This is an original recipe of Mrs. Randy Sherard. It won the Mississippi Cherry Pie Contest in 1962.

Mrs. James Sherard
(Florence Froehlig)

Caramel Pie

Syrup

3 cups sugar   1 cup hot water

Starting with ½ cup sugar, slowly begin browning in heavy skillet. Gradually add remaining sugar until all is caramel brown, about 30 minutes. Slowly add hot water, stirring constantly until syrup is formed. If not used right away, cool and store in jars in refrigerator.

Pie

6 egg yolks   2 Tablespoons butter
½ cup cornstarch   1 cup caramel syrup
1 cup sugar   2 (9-inch) baked pie shells
3 cups milk, heated to boiling

Beat together egg yolks, cornstarch, and sugar. Slowly add hot milk, butter, and caramel syrup. Cook over medium heat until thick, stirring constantly. Pour into 2 baked pie shells. Cool and top with meringue.

Meringue

6 egg whites   ½ teaspoon cream of tartar

Beat egg whites until stiff. Add cream of tartar and pour onto pies. Bake at 350° until lightly browned. Yield: 2 pies.

Mrs. Claude Taylor
Port Gibson, Mississippi

Chesley's Coconut Pie

¾ cup sugar   1 teaspoon vinegar
1 Tablespoon flour   1 cup coconut
2 eggs   1 cup water
¼ cup butter, melted   1 teaspoon vanilla extract
Pinch of salt   1 (9-inch) unbaked pie shell

In a large bowl thoroughly cream together sugar, flour, and eggs. Add to this mixture melted butter, salt, and vinegar; stir well. To this same mixture stir in coconut, water and vanilla. Pour this mixture into unbaked pie shell. Bake for 1 hour at 350°. Yield: 8 servings.

Chesley Armstrong Sadler

Fresh Coconut Cream Pie

Pie Filling

2 cups milk	1 teaspoon water
½ cup sugar	½ cup grated fresh coconut
Pinch of salt	1 Tablespoon butter
3 Tablespoons cornstarch	½ teaspoon vanilla extract
4 egg yolks	1 (9-inch) baked pie shell

Combine milk, sugar, and salt in a double boiler and bring to a near boil. Blend cornstarch, egg yolks, water, and add to milk mixture. Add coconut. Cook over hot water until custard thickens. Add butter and vanilla. Cool. Top with meringue or whipped cream.

Meringue

4 egg whites	¼ cup sugar
¼ teaspoon cream of tartar	½ cup grated fresh coconut
¼ teaspoon salt	

Beat egg whites with cream of tartar and salt until soft peaks are formed. Gradually add sugar, beating constantly. When meringue is fairly stiff, pile lightly onto filled pie. Be sure to seal edges. Sprinkle coconut on top. Bake at 400° for 10 minutes or until lightly browned. Yield: 8 servings.

This is a recipe from a native Hawaiian.

Mrs. Glover Warner
(Peggy Holder)

Heavenly Pie

1 (8-ounce) package cream cheese, softened	1 (9-ounce) carton frozen whipped topping, thawed
1 (14-ounce) can sweetened condensed milk	½ cup chopped pecans
⅓ cup lemon juice	1 cup drained fruit (pineapple, peaches, or mandarin oranges)
	2 (9-inch) graham cracker pie shells

Combine cream cheese, condensed milk, and lemon juice; beat until smooth. Fold in whipped topping. Stir in pecans and drained fruit; pour into pie shells and refrigerate for several hours. Yield: 2 pies.

Mrs. Herbert H. Wilkinson
(Faye Daniels)

Buttermilk Cream Pie

1 cup sugar minus 2 Tablespoons
¼ cup flour plus 2 Tablespoons
1 (5-ounce) can evaporated milk
1⅓ cups buttermilk

3 egg yolks
1 teaspoon vanilla extract
1 (9-inch) pie shell

Mix sugar and flour and add evaporated milk, buttermilk, and egg yolks. Stir until smooth. Place in medium-size saucepan over medium heat and stir constantly until it thickens and begins to boil. Remove from heat, let cool, and add vanilla. Pour into baked 9-inch pie shell.

Meringue

3 egg whites
6 Tablespoons sugar

¼ teaspoon baking powder

Beat egg whites until stiff. Add sugar gradually. Beat well and fold in baking powder. Place on top of pie filling and bake at 325° for 15 minutes. Yield: 6 to 8 servings.

Mrs. Robert Peters
(Sandra Kelly)

Sweet Potato Pecan Pie

½ cup butter
1 cup chopped pecans
1 small sweet potato, baked or
   boiled and peeled
1 cup sugar
½ teaspoon lemon juice

1 teaspoon vanilla extract
1 cup light corn syrup
3 large eggs, beaten
Dash of salt
1 (8 or 9-inch) pie shell

Brown butter and pecans in a saucepan until butter is golden brown, not burned. Add mashed, cooked sweet potato. In a separate bowl, add sugar, lemon juice, vanilla, corn syrup, eggs and salt, and stir. Combine with browned butter mixture and pour into unbaked pie shell. Bake at 425° for 10 minutes; lower heat to 325° for 40 to 60 minutes. Yield: 6 to 8 servings.

Mrs. Bob Coleman
(Cissy Wagner)

If you have stored a fruit pie in the refrigerator, the crust will taste better if you remove the pie 20 minutes before serving and warm it for a few minutes at 325°.

Old Time Lemon Pie

1½ cups sugar
7 Tablespoons cornstarch
Dash of salt
1½ cups water
3 beaten egg yolks
1 teaspoon grated lemon peel

2 Tablespoons butter
½ cup plus 1 teaspoon lemon juice,
    divided
1 (9-inch) pastry shell, baked
3 egg whites
6 Tablespoons sugar

Combine sugar, cornstarch, and salt in saucepan. Stir in water. Bring to a boil over medium heat and cook, stirring constantly until thick, about 3 to 5 minutes. Remove from heat; stir small amount of hot mixture into egg yolks, then return to remaining mixture in pan. Bring to a boil and cook 1 minute, stirring constantly. Remove from heat. Add lemon peel and butter. Slowly stir in ½ cup lemon juice. Cool to lukewarm. Pour into cooled baked pastry shell. Beat egg whites with 1 teaspoon lemon juice until soft peaks form. Gradually add sugar, beating until stiff. Spread meringue over filling sealing to edges of pastry to avoid shrinking. Bake in moderate oven at 350° for 12 to 15 minutes or until brown. Yield: 6 to 8 servings.

Mrs. Lewis Miller
(Carrie Paul)

Pumpkin Pie

1½ cups sugar
½ cup brown sugar
1 heaping Tablespoon flour
1 cup margarine, melted
3 eggs
1 cup cooked, mashed pumpkin
1 teaspoon lemon extract
½ teaspoon grated lemon rind
¼ cup evaporated milk

½ teaspoon nutmeg
½ teaspoon ginger
¼ teaspoon ground cloves
¼ teaspoon cinnamon
¼ teaspoon allspice
¼ teaspoon salt
1 (10-inch) unbaked pastry shell
Pecans (optional)

Mix sugars and flour. Add margarine and mix well. Add eggs 1 at a time, beating well after each. Add pumpkin, lemon extract, lemon rind, milk, spices, and salt. Mix well. Pour into pastry shell. Bake at 300° for 1 hour. Decorate top with pecans if desired. 2 smaller pies can also be made from this. Yield: 8 to 10 servings.

Mrs. Daniel Johnson
(Sue Buckner)

Lemon Chess Pie

1 Tablespoon flour
1 Tablespoon corn meal
2 cups sugar
4 eggs
¼ cup butter or margarine, melted

¼ cup fresh lemon juice
1 Tablespoon grated lemon rind
¼ cup milk
1 (9-inch) unbaked pie shell

Sift flour and meal into sugar. Beat eggs slightly and add to sugar mixture. Mix well. Add butter, lemon juice, lemon rind, and milk; combine thoroughly. Pour into unbaked pie shell. Bake at 350° for 45 to 60 minutes or until pie is firm. Yield: 6 to 8 servings.

This recipe is from the Kappa Delta House at Ole Miss.

Mrs. Joseph P. Harris
(Susan Gunn)

Mock Orange Chiffon Pie

1 (14-ounce) can condensed milk
1 pint sour cream
1 (9-ounce) container non-dairy
   whipped topping
¼ cup powdered orange breakfast
   drink

1 (9-inch) prepared graham cracker
   crust or baked pastry shell
1 (11-ounce) can mandarin oranges
   (optional)

Mix first 4 ingredients thoroughly and pour into prepared graham cracker crust or pastry shell. Chill well before serving. Mandarin oranges can be used for garnishing.

Mrs. D. B. Larr
(Bessie Maggio)

Fruit Cobbler

½ cup butter
1 cup self-rising flour
1 cup sugar
1 cup milk

1 (20-ounce) can fruit pie filling
   (apple, peach, blueberry, etc.)
1 teaspoon cinnamon
1 teaspoon nutmeg

Melt butter in an 8-inch square pan. Mix flour and sugar in a bowl. Slowly add milk and stir. Pour over melted butter; do not stir. Add fruit, cinnamon and nutmeg. Bake 1 hour at 300°. If using any filling other than peach or apple, omit spices.

Mrs. Charles Toney
(Lillian Hadad)

Black Bottom Pie

Chocolate Wafer Crust

¼ cup margarine   18 chocolate wafers, crushed

Melt margarine in an 8 or 9-inch pie plate. Add crushed wafers and mix well. Press into bottom of pie plate. Bake at 350° for 5 to 8 minutes or until crust becomes firm. Let cool completely.

Custard

1½ cups milk
1½ cups sugar
1 Tablespoon flour
3 eggs, separated
1 envelope unflavored gelatin
2 to 3 Tablespoons cold water

1½ squares unsweetened chocolate
½ teaspoon vanilla extract
1 (8-ounce) carton heavy cream,
  whipped
Shaved chocolate (optional)

Make a boiled custard out of milk, sugar, flour, and egg yolks. Boil in double boiler until spoon is lightly coated or until custard comes to an easy boil. Soak gelatin in cold water. Combine with boiled custard after removing custard from heat. Mix well and set aside. Melt chocolate and combine with ⅓ boiled custard. Add vanilla to chocolate mixture and pour into pie crust. Beat egg whites until stiff. Fold remainder of boiled custard into egg whites. Pour onto top of chocolate crust and refrigerate overnight. Before serving, top with sweetened whipped cream. Shave chocolate on top of whipped cream if desired. Yield: 8 to 10 servings.

Mrs. David I. Bridgers
(Dot Barranco)

Egg Pastry

3 cups sifted flour
1½ teaspoons salt
1 cup shortening

1 egg
1 teaspoon vinegar
½ cup ice water

Sift together flour and salt; cut in shortening until mixture looks like corn meal. Beat egg slightly; add vinegar and water. Gradually add egg mixture to dry ingredients. Mix just enough to hold dough together. Wrap and refrigerate. Pastry will keep about a week in refrigerator and will freeze indefinitely. Bake at 425° for 10 to 15 minutes. Yield: 3 single shells.

Harriet Sims

Fruit Cracker Pie

3 egg whites
½ teaspoon baking powder
1 teaspoon almond or vanilla
  extract
1 cup sugar

10 saltine crackers, crushed
½ cup chopped pecans
1 to 2 cups fruit (optional)
1 cup heavy cream, whipped
  (optional)

Beat egg whites in large bowl until fluffy. Continue to beat while adding baking powder and almond extract. Add sugar gradually and beat until stiff. Fold in crackers and pecans. Spread in a 9-inch pie plate which has been sprayed with vegetable cooking spray. Shape with outside edge higher than center. Bake at 325° for 25 minutes. Allow to cool completely and chill. If desired, top with fruit and whipped cream when ready to serve. Yield: 6 servings.

May be served with ice cream and shaved chocolate. Whipped cream may be mixed with 1 (16-ounce) can coconut or 2 cups sliced fresh sweetened strawberries for topping.

Mrs. William Larson
(Louise Moore)

Mary Opal's Pie

3 egg whites
¼ teaspoon cream of tartar
Pinch of salt
1 cup sugar
1 teaspoon vanilla extract

¾ cup crushed chocolate wafers
½ cup chopped pecans
Whipped cream or non-dairy
  whipped topping (optional)

With electric mixer beat egg whites, cream of tartar, and salt until stiff. Fold sugar into egg white mixture. Add vanilla, chocolate wafers, and pecans. Stir and pour into a 9-inch greased pie pan. Bake at 325° for 30 minutes. Cool. If desired, top with whipped cream or non-dairy whipped topping. Yield: 8 servings.

For a different flavor, graham cracker crumbs may be substituted for crushed chocolate wafers.

Mrs. Walter Johnston
(Maxine Irby)

To prevent crumb crusts from sticking to pan when serving, wrap a hot, wet towel around bottom and sides of pie plate.

Coffee Chiffon Pie

1 envelope unflavored gelatin
1 cup sugar, divided
⅛ teaspoon salt
3 eggs, separated
¾ cup brewed and cooled coffee
   with chicory

1 teaspoon coffee liqueur or vanilla
   extract
¾ cup heavy cream, whipped
1 (9-inch) graham cracker pie crust

Mix together gelatin, ½ cup sugar, and salt in top of double boiler. Beat together egg yolks and coffee. Stir into gelatin mixture. Cook over boiling water, stirring constantly, until dissolved. Remove from heat and stir in coffee liqueur or vanilla. Chill until it is consistency of unbeaten egg whites. Beat egg whites until soft peaks form. Gradually add ½ cup sugar, beating until stiff and dry. Fold in gelatin mixture and whipped cream. Turn into pie crust and chill until firm. Yield: 6 to 8 servings.

Mrs. Henry Faser
(Hester Ferris)

Grasshopper Pie

1½ cups chocolate wafer crumbs,
   divided
⅓ cup melted butter
⅔ cup milk
24 large marshmallows

¼ cup green crème de menthe
2 Tablespoons white crème de cacao
1 cup heavy cream, whipped
Chocolate wafer crumbs

Combine 1¼ cups crumbs and butter; press into an 8-inch pie pan and chill well. Combine milk and marshmallows in a heavy saucepan; cook over low heat, stirring often until marshmallows melt. Cool to room temperature. Fold liqueurs and whipped cream into marshmallow mixture. Spoon into pie shell; garnish with ¼ cup chocolate wafer crumbs. Freeze 4 to 6 hours. Yield: 6 to 8 servings.

Mrs. Herbert H. Wilkinson
(Faye Daniels)

 Cold ingredients will make a better pie crust. Even flour may be chilled.

Down in Dixie Bourbon Pie

1 box chocolate wafers, crushed
¼ cup butter or margarine, melted
21 marshmallows

1 cup evaporated milk
1 cup heavy cream
3 Tablespoons bourbon

Mix chocolate wafer crumbs and melted butter. Pat into bottom and sides of a 9-inch pie pan. Bake at 350° until set about 15 minutes. In saucepan, heat marshmallows and milk until marshmallows melt and mixture is smooth. Do not boil. Remove from heat. Whip cream until stiff. Fold into marshmallow mixture. Add bourbon and pour into cooled chocolate crumb crust. Refrigerate 4 hours or until set. Additional whipped cream and chocolate crumbs or chocolate curls make an attractive garnish. Yield: 6 to 8 servings.

Mary McKay and Warren Asher

Frozen Brandy Alexander Pie

1 (14-ounce) can sweetened
  condensed milk
1 cup heavy cream, whipped
2 Tablespoons crème de cacao

2 Tablespoons brandy
1 (9-inch) graham cracker crumb
  crust
Shaved sweet chocolate for garnish

Combine sweetened condensed milk, whipped cream, crème de cacao, and brandy. Pour into prepared crust. Freeze 4 to 6 hours until firm. Garnish with shaved chocolate before serving. Yield: 8 servings.

This may also be topped with Chocolate Sauce, whipped cream, or chocolate curls.

Mrs. Robert H. Weatherly
(Dannie Compton)

Chocolate Sauce

½ cup sugar
1½ Tablespoons cornstarch
Pinch of salt
½ cup boiling water

1 (1-ounce) square unsweetened
  chocolate, melted
1½ Tablespoons butter
1 teaspoon vanilla extract

Mix sugar, cornstarch, salt, water, and chocolate. Cook until thickened. Remove from heat. Add butter and vanilla. Serve over cake or ice cream. Yield: 1½ cups.

Mrs. Dan Waring
(Janice Gerache)

Frozen Peppermint Pie

2 ounces milk chocolate, melted
½ cup butter
2 cups powdered sugar
2 eggs, separated
1 (12-ounce) box vanilla wafers,
  crushed and divided

½ cup pecans, chopped
1 quart peppermint ice cream,
  softened

Melt chocolate with butter in top of double boiler. Remove from heat and stir in powdered sugar. Add slightly beaten egg yolks. Beat ingredients together. Beat egg whites until stiff and fold into chocolate mixture. Spread ½ vanilla wafer crumbs onto bottom of 9 x 13-inch pan. Sprinkle ½ pecans over wafers. Drizzle ½ cup chocolate sauce over pecans. Spread ice cream on crust. Top with remaining chocolate sauce. Top with remaining crumbs and pecans. Freeze at least 12 hours. Remove from freezer 5 minutes before cutting. Yield: 12 servings.

If peppermint ice cream is not available, substitute with 1 quart vanilla ice cream mixed with 1 cup crushed peppermint.

Mrs. James Penley
(Betty Prewitt)

Mississippi Mud Pie

½ (8½-ounce) package chocolate
  wafers
½ cup butter, melted
1 quart coffee ice cream, softened

1½ cups fudge sauce or chocolate
  fudge ice cream topping
Whipped cream, sliced almonds, or
  chocolate curls for garnish
  (optional)

Crush chocolate wafers and set aside. Melt butter in large frying pan over low heat. Add crushed wafers and toss in butter to coat well. Press crumb mixture into a 9-inch pie plate and allow to cool. Soften ice cream and spoon onto wafer crust. Freeze until firm. Top with cold fudge sauce. Store in freezer about 8 to 10 hours. To serve, top with whipped cream and sliced almonds or chocolate curls. Remove from freezer and allow to stand 5 to 10 minutes before serving. Yield: 6 to 8 servings.

Mrs. Kenneth Kussmann
New Orleans, Louisiana

Cookies

Mama's Gingersnap Cookies

¾ cup shortening
1 cup sugar
1 egg, slightly beaten
¼ cup molasses
2 cups sifted flour

1 Tablespoon ginger
2 teaspoons soda
1 Tablespoon cinnamon
½ teaspoon salt

Cream together shortening and sugar; add egg and molasses. Sift together flour, ginger, soda, cinnamon, and salt. Combine all ingredients and mix well. It is best to chill the cookie dough several hours before shaping into 1-inch balls. Place the cookies 2 inches apart on an ungreased cookie sheet. Bake cookies at 325° for 12 to 15 minutes. Let cool several minutes before removing from cookie sheet. Yield: 4 to 5 dozen.

Cookie dough may be rolled in granulated sugar before baking. This recipe dates back to 1885.

Mrs. J. T. McNeely
Oxford, Mississippi

Chocolate Krinkles

4 squares unsweetened chocolate
½ cup butter or margarine
2 cups sugar
4 eggs
½ teaspoon salt

2 teaspoons baking powder
2 cups flour
2 teaspoons vanilla extract
1 cup powdered sugar

Melt chocolate squares over very low heat in heavy saucepan. When almost melted, add butter. Stir until melted. Place sugar in large mixing bowl. Pour chocolate and butter mixture over sugar and mix well. Add eggs, 1 at a time, beating well after each. Sift together the dry ingredients and gradually add to other mixture. Add vanilla and beat well. Refrigerate for at least 5 hours or overnight. Heat oven to 350°. Roll a bite-size ball of dough in powdered sugar. Place on ungreased cookie sheet 2 inches apart. Bake 10 to 12 minutes. Let stand 1 minute before removing. Store in cookie jar or tins. Yield: 4 to 5 dozen.

Mrs. Kirk Fordice
(Pat Owens)

Chocolate Cream Cheese Cookies

½ cup butter or margarine
½ cup shortening
1 (3-ounce) package cream cheese
1½ cups sugar
1 egg
½ teaspoon salt
2 Tablespoons milk

1 teaspoon vanilla extract
2 ounces unsweetened chocolate, melted
2¼ cups flour
1½ teaspoons baking powder
⅔ cup chopped pecans

Cream butter, shortening, cream cheese, and sugar together. Add egg, salt, milk and vanilla; mix well. Stir in melted chocolate. Sift flour with baking powder and add to batter a little at a time, mixing well. Stir in nuts. Drop by teaspoonfuls onto cookie sheet. Bake at 350° for 15 minutes. Yield: 5 dozen.

Mrs. Shouphie Habeeb
(Norma Daquilla)

Arabian Macaroons

1⅓ cups coconut
½ cup finely chopped dates
½ cup chopped walnuts
½ cup sugar

⅛ teaspoon salt
1 egg, well beaten
½ teaspoon vanilla extract

Combine coconut, dates, walnuts, sugar and salt; mix well. Blend in egg and vanilla. Let stand 5 minutes; drop from teaspoon onto greased baking sheet. Bake at 350° for 15 minutes or until golden brown. Remove at once from baking sheet. Yield: 1 to 1½ dozen.

Mrs. George E. Abraham
(Mabel Ellis)

Praline Cookies

Honey graham crackers
1 cup margarine
1 cup light brown sugar, packed

1½ cups chopped pecans or slivered almonds

Cover a cookie sheet with whole graham crackers, placing them as close together as possible. Bring margarine and brown sugar to a boil; let boil for 2 minutes, stirring constantly. Add pecans and spread mixture evenly over graham crackers. Bake at 350° for 20 minutes. Cut and separate immediately. Let cool. Yield: 3 dozen.

Miss Enez Bourdon

Chocolate Oatmeal Cookies

½ cup margarine
2 cups sugar
½ cup milk
2 teaspoons vanilla extract

2 Tablespoons cocoa
½ cup peanut butter
2 cups oatmeal
1 cup chopped pecans (optional)

Melt margarine in saucepan and combine sugar, milk, vanilla, and cocoa. Boil for 1½ minutes. Take off heat and add peanut butter, oatmeal, and pecans; beat until blended. Drop onto waxed paper and let cool to harden. Yield: 2 to 3 dozen.

Mrs. Stan Terry, Jr.
(Sallie Bingham)

Lacy Oatmeal Cookies

2 eggs, well beaten
1 cup sugar
¼ cup melted butter
Pinch of salt

2 teaspoons baking powder
½ cup flour
1 teaspoon vanilla extract
2 cups raw oatmeal

Mix all ingredients together, adding oatmeal last. Blend. Drop onto greased cookie sheet and bake 10 minutes at 350°. Remove from cookie sheet immediately and let cool until crisp. Yield: 2 to 3 dozen.

Mrs. Dick Foster
Cleveland, Mississippi

Butterscotch Oaties

1 (6-ounce) package butterscotch
   morsels
¾ cup butter or margarine
2 Tablespoons boiling water
1 teaspoon baking soda

2 cups old-fashioned oatmeal
1 cup sifted flour
¾ cup sugar
Dash of salt

Preheat oven to 350°. Combine butterscotch morsels and butter; melt in double boiler. Remove from heat. Mix boiling water with baking soda and add to butterscotch mixture. Gradually blend in remaining ingredients. Roll into small balls. Place on ungreased cookie sheet. Bake at 350° for 10 minutes. Yield: 5 dozen.

Mrs. Dan Waring
(Janice Gerache)

The Best Cocoons

2 cups sifted flour
1/4 cup sugar
1/2 teaspoon salt
1 cup butter, softened

2 teaspoons vanilla extract
1 teaspoon almond extract
1 1/2 cups finely chopped pecans
Powdered sugar

Sift together flour, sugar, and salt in a large bowl. Add butter, vanilla, and almond extract. Mash lumps well with a fork; add pecans and stir well. Take a 1-inch ball of mixture and roll between hands to shape into a cocoon, about 3 inches long and 1 inch wide. Place on ungreased cookie sheet and bake at 325° until golden brown around edges, approximately 10 to 15 minutes. Do not overcook. Sift powdered sugar over cocoons while still warm. Yield: 3 dozen.

Mrs. Glenn Taylor
(Liz Smith)

Scotch Shortbread

1 cup butter
2 cups flour

3/4 cup cornstarch
1/2 cup sugar

Melt butter and add remaining ingredients. Press into a 9-inch round pan. Bake at 350° for 45 minutes. Cut into pieces immediately after removing from oven. Sprinkle with granulated sugar. Yield: 10 to 12 wedges.

Colored sugar sprinkles may be used for topping at holiday time. The dough may also be rolled out and cut into crescent shapes. Bake about 20 to 25 minutes, but do not let brown.

Mrs. George Rogers, Jr.
Washington, D.C.

Lemon Cookies

1 cup butter
1 cup vegetable oil
1 cup sugar
1 cup powdered sugar
2 teaspoons lemon extract

2 eggs
4 cups flour
1 teaspoon cream of tartar
1 teaspoon salt
1 teaspoon soda

Combine first 4 ingredients. Add lemon extract and eggs. Beat 1 minute. Add remaining ingredients, which have been mixed together. Drop by teaspoonfuls onto ungreased cookie sheet. Bake at 375° about 10 to 12 minutes. Yield: 75 small cookies.

Mrs. Robert O. Bailess
(Ruby Wilshire)

Meringues

2 egg whites	¾ cup sugar
⅛ teaspoon salt	1 (6-ounce) package chocolate chips
¼ teaspoon cream of tartar	1 teaspoon vanilla extract

Preheat oven to 350° for 15 minutes. Beat egg whites, salt, and cream of tartar until frothy. Gradually add sugar and continue to beat for 15 minutes. Fold in chocolate chips and vanilla. Turn off oven. Drop by spoonfuls onto ungreased cookie sheet. Place in oven for 1½ hours. Do not open oven door during cooking time. Peppermint flavoring may be substituted for vanilla and food coloring may be added. Yield: 4 dozen.

Mrs. Albert Dornbusch
(Gloria Abraham)

Hebrew Cookies

1 pound butter	1 quart pecans
1½ cups sugar	1 quart flour
3 eggs, beaten	8 ounces powdered sugar
1 cup whiskey	2 teaspoons cinnamon

Cream butter and sugar. Add beaten eggs. Add whiskey very slowly, stirring constantly. Add pecans and flour. This makes a very soft dough. Roll out on floured board, keeping dough as soft as possible. Cut in small squares with knife. Bake on cookie sheet at 375° to 400 °. Roll in sugar and cinnamon sifted together. Yield: 8 dozen.

Mrs. D. P. Waring, Jr.
(Betty Jeanne Williams)

Thumbprint Cookies

½ cup margarine	1 teaspoon vanilla extract
½ cup shortening	2 cups flour
½ cup brown sugar, packed	½ teaspoon salt
1 egg	

Heat oven to 350°. Mix margarine, shortening, brown sugar, egg, and vanilla thoroughly. Blend flour and salt; stir in. Roll 1 teaspoon dough into balls. Place 1 inch apart on ungreased baking sheet; press thumb gently into centers. Bake 10 to 12 minutes. Cool. Fill centers with jelly or tinted powdered sugar icing. Yield: 5 dozen cookies.

Mrs. Jerry Dykes
(Tina Hazzlerigg)

Mama's Teacakes

⅓ cup shortening
⅓ cup butter or margarine
1⅓ cups sugar
2 eggs
2 teaspoons cream of tartar

¼ teaspoon salt
1 teaspoon soda
3½ cups flour
1 teaspoon vanilla extract
1 Tablespoon milk

In a mixing bowl cream shortening, butter and sugar until smooth and light; add eggs, 1 at a time, mixing after each. Add sifted dry ingredients and mix well; add vanilla and milk; mix well. On a floured surface roll out dough approximately to ⅛-inch thickness or more, if desired. Cut into desired shapes and bake 10 minutes at 350°. Cookies may be sprinkled with sugar before baking or iced after cooling. Cookies may be frozen after baking. Yield: 3 to 4 dozen.

Mrs. Bucky Buckner
(Melvia Riddell)

Bourbon Balls

2 (12-ounce) boxes vanilla wafers
1 cup chopped nuts
1 cup sifted powdered sugar

3 Tablespoons light corn syrup
½ cup bourbon
Powdered sugar

Crush vanilla wafers. Mix wafers, nuts, and sugar in a large bowl. Add corn syrup and bourbon. Form balls and roll in powdered sugar. Yield: 75 appetizers.

Mrs. Dick Peterson
(Josephine Coker)

Orange Balls

½ cup margarine, softened
1 (16-ounce) box powdered sugar
1 (6-ounce) can frozen orange juice, thawed

1 (12-ounce) box vanilla wafers, crushed
1 (6-ounce) package coconut
1 cup pecans, finely chopped

Mix all ingredients, except pecans. Shape into small balls and roll immediately in finely chopped pecans. Let stand in refrigerator for 3 hours. Store in airtight container in refrigerator. Freezes well. Yield: 60 orange balls.

Mrs. Bill Pierce
(Pat Hand)

Christmas Puffs

½ cup butter
½ cup sifted powdered sugar
1 egg, separated
½ teaspoon vanilla extract

1½ cups sifted flour
¼ teaspoon salt
2 Tablespoons sugar
Candied cherries

Cream butter and powdered sugar together. Beat in egg yolk and vanilla. Add sifted flour and salt. Form into balls, using about 1 teaspoon of dough for each. With end of wooden spoon or with thumb, make a well in the center of each. Refrigerate in covered container until completely chilled or overnight. Place on very lightly greased cookie sheet. Bake at 350° for 12 to 15 minutes or until very lightly browned. Remove from oven. While cookies are baking, beat egg white until stiff; gradually add sugar. After removing the cookies from the oven, place a small dab of beaten egg white in the center and return cookies to oven to brown meringue, about 5 minutes. While they are still very warm, place a candied cherry on meringue. Cool and store in covered tin. Doubles easily. Yield: 3 dozen.

Mrs. George Jabour, Jr.
(Miriam Penton)

Pecan Crisps

1½ cups flour, sifted
1¼ cups sugar, divided
¾ teaspoon salt
½ cup margarine, softened
1 egg, separated

3 Tablespoons milk
1 teaspoon vanilla extract
¼ cup vegetable oil
1 cup pecans, finely chopped

In a medium mixing bowl put flour, 1 cup sugar, and salt. With a fork mix thoroughly the margarine, egg yolk, milk and vanilla. Combine 2 mixtures. Roll into bite-size balls. Place on ungreased baking sheet. Press flat (¹⁄₁₆-inch thick) with the bottom of a glass dipped in oil and remaining sugar. Brush with slightly beaten egg white. Sprinkle with pecans. Bake at 375° for 8 to 10 minutes. Do not overbake. Yield: 5 dozen.

Mrs. Jerry Mayfield
(Pam Jabour)

 Cake layers or cookies left in the pans too long can be loosened by returning to a 350° oven for 2 minutes. Remove immediately from pan.

Almond Cookies

½ cup real butter
1 cup shortening
1½ cups sugar
2 eggs
2½ Tablespoons almond extract

3¾ cups flour
2½ teaspoons baking soda
¾ teaspoon salt
36 whole almonds

Preheat oven to 350°. Cream butter, shortening and sugar until fluffy. Add eggs, 1 at a time, and continue beating until smooth. Add almond extract. Sift flour, baking powder, and salt together; stir into butter mixture. Knead a bit to make a stiff, smooth dough. Form dough into 1½-inch balls and place 2 to 3 inches apart on a greased baking sheet. Flatten slightly with hand; center a whole almond on each cookie. Bake 10 to 12 minutes; cookies should be lightly browned on bottom but very pale on top. Cool on racks before storing in cookie tins. Yield: 4 to 5 dozen.

Mrs. Albert Dornbusch
(Gloria Abraham)

Mary Pickford Cookies

1 cup sugar
1 cup brown sugar
1 cup butter or margarine
3 eggs
1 teaspoon vanilla extract
4 cups flour

1 teaspoon soda
Pinch of salt
½ teaspoon cinnamon
¼ teaspoon nutmeg
¼ teaspoon cloves

Mix above ingredients. Roll on flat surface. Cut into desired shapes. Bake at 350° for 10 to 15 minutes or until browned. Frost with sugar crystals. Yield: 5 dozen.

These make excellent holiday cookies by cutting into Christmas shapes frosted with red or green sugar crystals.

Mrs. Gordon Carr, Jr.
(Rainy Loe)

 When making rolled cookies, a mixture of 1 part sugar to 2 parts flour to dust the pastry cloth will make rolling and cutting easier.

Deluxe Peanut Butter Cups

½ cup butter or margarine, softened
½ cup crunchy peanut butter
½ cup sugar
½ cup firmly packed brown sugar
1 egg
½ teaspoon vanilla extract

1¼ cups flour
¾ teaspoon baking soda
½ teaspoon salt
48 miniature REESE'S peanut
*   butter cups*

In a large mixing bowl, cream butter and peanut butter. Gradually add sugars, beating until light and fluffy. Add egg and vanilla, beating well. Combine flour, soda, and salt; add to creamed mixture, mixing thoroughly. Chill dough 1 hour. Shape dough into 48 (1-inch) balls. Place in lightly greased 1¾-inch muffin pans, shaping each into a shell. Bake at 350° for about 10 minutes. During baking time, unwrap peanut butter cups. Remove pans from oven and immediately press 1 peanut butter cup into each hot crust. Cool completely before removing from pan. "REESE'S" is a registered trademark of Hershey Foods Corporation and used with permission. Yield: 48 pieces.

Mrs. John Hadad, III
(Susan Phillips)

Cookie Press Cookies

1½ cups butter, softened
1 cup sugar
2 eggs, separated
3¾ cups flour
¼ teaspoon salt

1 Tablespoon plus 1 teaspoon
*   vanilla extract*
2 Tablespoons water
Colored sugar and candy
*   decorations*

Cream butter and sugar until very light and fluffy. Add egg yolks, flour, salt, and vanilla; mix well. Put dough into cookie press and press cookies onto ungreased cookie sheet. Brush cookies with egg whites beaten slightly with water. Sprinkle decorations on each one. Bake at 400° until golden brown, 5 to 6 minutes for thin cookies and 8 to 15 minutes for thick ones. Cool slightly and remove from sheet with spatula. These can be frozen after baking. Yield: 9 to 10 dozen.

Mrs. Fred Farrell
(Kay McCorkle)

Cookies bake more slowly on a shiny pan than on a darker one.

Fruit Cake Cookies

½ cup butter or margarine, softened
½ cup firmly packed light brown
  sugar
2 eggs, beaten
¼ cup buttermilk
1½ cups self-rising flour
½ teaspoon soda

½ teaspoon ground allspice
½ teaspoon ground cinnamon
1 cup chopped candied cherries
1 cup chopped candied pineapple
1 cup chopped dates
1 (8-ounce) package raisins
2 cups chopped pecans

Combine butter and sugar, creaming until light and fluffy. Add eggs, buttermilk, flour, soda, and spices. Mix well. Stir in remaining ingredients. Drop by teaspoonfuls onto greased baking sheets. Bake at 300° for 25 minutes. Yield: 6 dozen.

Mrs. Jerry M. Hall
(Carolyn Buckner)

Hunter's Cookies

1 cup shortening
2 cups sugar
1½ cups brown sugar, packed
2 eggs
2 teaspoons vanilla extract
1 cup cherries
2 cups flour

2 teaspoons baking powder
2 teaspoons baking soda
1 teaspoon salt
½ teaspoon nutmeg
1 teaspoon cinnamon
2 cups oatmeal
2 cups corn flakes

Mix shortening with sugars. Add eggs, vanilla, and cherries. Combine flour, baking powder, baking soda, salt, nutmeg, and cinnamon. Add these dry ingredients to shortening mixture. Stir in oatmeal and corn flakes. Drop by Tablespoon onto greased cookie sheet. Bake at 350° for 10 to 15 minutes. Nuts, raisins or prunes may be substituted for cherries. Yield: 4 dozen.

Mrs. Jack Palmer
(Sandy Holliday)

Brown quick-cooking oats in a little butter or margarine and use as a substitute for chopped nuts in cookie recipes.

Pecan Tarts

6 Tablespoons butter or margarine   1 cup flour
1 (3-ounce) package cream cheese,
   softened

Cream butter and cheese. Add flour and blend well. Form into 1 large ball
of dough. Divide dough into 24 equal balls. Flatten each ball into circle in
palm of hand. Fit circles into miniature muffin tins to form tart shells.
(Balls of dough may be placed in muffin tins and pressed with tart tamper
to form tart shells.) Spoon in filling and bake for 20 minutes at 350°. Yield:
2 dozen.

Filling

2 Tablespoons butter or margarine   ½ to ¾ cup chopped pecans
¾ cup light brown sugar   1 teaspoon vanilla extract
1 egg, beaten

Cream butter and sugar. Add egg, pecans, and vanilla and mix well. Drop
by spoon into each shell.

*Tart shells may also be baked without filling. (Prick shells before baking.) Then fill
with your favorite pie filling: chocolate, lemon, cherry, strawberry, or coconut, and
top with whipped cream or meringue. Filling for a 9-inch pie should fill 3½ to 4
dozen tart shells.*

Mrs. E. A. Buckner, Jr.
(Ruth Vicknair)

Date Tarts

1 (8-ounce) package dates   1 egg
1 cup boiling water   1 cup flour
1 teaspoon soda   1 cup chopped nuts
1 cup sugar   Whipped cream (optional)

Place dates in bowl; add water and soda; cover. When cool, mash well and
mix in sugar, egg, flour, and nuts. Bake at 350° in greased miniature muffin tins for 15 to 20 minutes. Serve with whipped cream, if desired. Yield:
4 dozen.

Mrs. E. A. Buckner
Tallulah, Louisiana

Tom Thumb Cookie Bars

½ cup butter or margarine
½ teaspoon salt
1½ cups firmly packed dark brown
sugar, divided
1 cup plus 2 Tablespoons sifted
flour

1 teaspoon vanilla extract
2 eggs, beaten
½ teaspoon baking powder
1½ cups coconut
1 cup chopped pecans

Combine butter with salt. Add ½ cup brown sugar and cream thoroughly.
Add 1 cup flour and blend. Pat mixture into 8 x 12-inch floured, greased
pan. Bake in moderately slow oven approximately 325° for 15 minutes or
until delicately browned. Add remaining brown sugar and vanilla to eggs,
beating until thick and foamy. Add 2 Tablespoons flour, baking powder,
coconut, and nuts. Blend. Spread over baked mixture. Return to oven and
bake for 20 minutes. Yield: 16 (2-inch) squares.

Mrs. John Corey
Paducah, Kentucky

Lemon Squares

Layer I

2 cups flour
½ cup powdered sugar

1 cup margarine

Cut and mix together flour, powdered sugar, and margarine. Pat into ungreased 9 x 13-inch baking pan. Bake 20 minutes at 325° or until slightly
browned at edges.

Layer II

4 eggs, beaten
½ cup fresh lemon juice
2 cups sugar

¼ teaspoon salt
4 Tablespoons flour
Powdered sugar

Mix eggs, lemon juice, sugar, salt, and flour and pour onto first layer. Bake
25 minutes more at 325° or until firm. While warm, sprinkle with powdered sugar. Does *not* store well. Yield: 24 squares.

Mrs. H. Charles Justus
(Beth Gaudet)

Story's Fudge Ripple Bars

1 cup butter	*2 teaspoons vanilla extract*
2 cups sugar	*1½ cups sifted flour*
4 eggs	*1 teaspoon baking powder*
2 squares unsweetened chocolate,	*1 teaspoon salt*
melted	*1 cup chopped pecans*

Cream butter and sugar; add eggs. Blend in chocolate and vanilla. Add dry ingredients to creamed mixture and mix well. Stir in pecans and spread in a lightly greased and floured 13½ x 12½ x 1½-inch pan. Bake at 350° for 25 to 30 minutes, being careful not to overcook. Cool. Yield: 3 dozen.

Frosting

⅓ cup butter	*1 square unsweetened chocolate,*
3 cups sifted powdered sugar	*melted*
3 Tablespoons cream or milk	*1 Tablespoon melted butter*
½ teaspoon vanilla extract	*1 Tablespoon powdered sugar*

Melt ⅓ cup butter and blend in powdered sugar, cream and vanilla. Spread on baked mixture. Combine the chocolate, 1 Tablespoon melted butter and powdered sugar; drizzle over frosting, swirling the chocolate with a knife. Cut into bars when icing has hardened.

Mrs. Bruce Ebersole
(Story Stamm)

Butterscotch Bars

1 cup sifted flour	*1 cup firmly packed brown sugar*
1 teaspoon baking powder	*2 eggs*
¾ teaspoon salt	*½ teaspoon vanilla extract*
1 cup butterscotch morsels	*½ cup chopped walnuts or pecans*
¼ cup butter	

Sift together sifted flour, baking powder, and salt; set aside. Melt butterscotch morsels and butter in top of double boiler; remove from heat and stir in brown sugar; let cool 5 minutes. Add unbeaten eggs and vanilla and mix well. Blend in sifted dry ingredients and chopped nuts. Turn into greased 13 x 9 x 2-inch pan. Bake at 350° for 20 to 25 minutes. Cut into squares while warm. Yield: 24 bars.

Mrs. Jerry Dykes
(Tina Hazzlerigg)

Pecan Chewies

4 eggs, slightly beaten
1 (16-ounce) box brown sugar
1 teaspoon vanilla extract
2 cups sifted flour

1 teaspoon baking powder
½ teaspoon salt
1½ to 2 cups pecans, chopped
½ cup powdered sugar

In top of double boiler, cook eggs and sugar until slightly thickened, about 10 minutes. Add vanilla. Mix flour, baking powder, and salt. Add flour mixture to egg mixture. Mix well. Stir in pecans and pour into greased 9 x 13-inch pan. Bake at 350° for 25 to 30 minutes. When cooled, dust with powdered sugar. Cut into squares. Yield: 3 dozen.

Mrs. E. A. Buckner
Tallulah, Louisiana

Great Keepsake Brownies

4 squares unsweetened chocolate
1 cup butter or margarine
2 cups sugar
3 eggs, beaten

1 teaspoon vanilla extract
1 cup chopped nuts
1 cup sifted flour
¼ teaspoon salt

Melt chocolate and butter together over low heat or over hot water. Remove pan from heat; add sugar, eggs, and vanilla. Mix well and stir in nuts. Mix flour and salt. Add this to chocolate mixture gradually, mixing well. Pour into greased and floured 9-inch square pan. Bake at 350° for 40 to 45 minutes. Cool before cutting. Yield: 24 bars.

Mrs. James A. Dupuy
(Kathryn Roussel)

Brownie Icing

4 (1.45-ounces) HERSHEY bars
4 Tablespoons milk

2 Tablespoons butter
2 cups powdered sugar

Melt HERSHEY bars in milk and butter. Add powdered sugar. Mix well and spread over warm brownies. "HERSHEY'S" is a registered trademark of Hershey Foods Corporation and used with permission. Yield: 2½ cups.

Mrs. Ron Wilson
(Linda Weaver)

Butter Creme Brownies

1 square semisweet chocolate
¼ cup butter
1 egg

½ cup sugar
¼ cup flour
¼ cup pecans, finely chopped

Melt chocolate and butter together over hot water and cool slightly. Beat egg until frothy. Stir into chocolate mixture. Add sugar. Blend well. Add flour and nuts and stir until well blended. Pour into 8 x 8-inch pan. Bake 13 to 15 minutes at 350°. Cool and cover with butter creme filling. Yield: 2 dozen.

Butter Creme Filling

1 cup powdered sugar
2 Tablespoons butter, softened
¼ teaspoon vanilla extract

1 Tablespoon heavy cream or
evaporated milk

Cream together and spread over brownie layer. Put pan in refrigerator for 10 minutes. Remove and spread with glaze.

Glaze

2 Tablespoons butter

2 squares semisweet chocolate

Melt butter and chocolate together. Spread gently over filled brownie layer being careful not to disturb filling. Chill in refrigerator until glaze sets. Cut into small finger strips. Can be frozen.

Food coloring may be added to creme filling for different holidays and occasions.

Mrs. Earl Lundy
(Edith McWilliams)

Ice Cream and Candy

Fresh Strawberry Ice Cream

6 eggs
2 cups sugar, divided
1 quart milk
¼ teaspoon salt

1 quart heavy cream
2 teaspoons vanilla extract
4 cups fresh strawberries

Mix eggs thoroughly. Add 1½ cups sugar, milk, and salt. Cook in sauce-pan over medium heat, stirring constantly, just until bubbles appear. Cool slightly. Stir in cream and vanilla. Crush strawberries with ½ cup sugar. Add to custard and pour into ice cream freezer tub. Freeze using 6 parts ice to 1 part ice cream salt or according to freezer directions. Yield: 3 quarts.

For fresh peach ice cream, substitute 3 cups mashed peaches for strawberries.

Mrs. George Guider
(Annie Lee Faulk)

Raspberry Sorbet

2 cups water
1 cup sugar
1 (10-ounce) package frozen
    raspberries

⅓ cup lemon juice
Pinch of salt
1 to 2 Tablespoons Kirsch

Combine water and sugar in saucepan. Stir over high heat to dissolve the sugar. Bring to a boil; reduce heat and let boil for 5 minutes without stir-ring. Remove from heat and let cool at room temperature. Strain juice from berries to make ⅔ cup; discard berries. Stir in lemon juice and salt. Pour into a shallow 9-inch square metal pan. Place in freezer and freeze until firm throughout. Remove from freezer. Break up with a wooden spoon; beat with mixer or in food processor until free of lumps. Stir in Kirsch. Freeze until firm again. Yield: 6 servings.

Mrs. Bob Coleman
(Cissy Wagner)

Lime Sorbet

3 cups water
1¼ cups sugar
¾ cup light corn syrup

⅔ cup fresh lime juice (4 large or 6
   medium limes)
Lime wedges to garnish (optional)

Combine water with sugar and corn syrup in heavy saucepan. Stir over high heat to dissolve the sugar. Bring to a boil. Reduce heat to moderate temperature and let boil for 5 minutes without stirring. Remove from heat and let cool at room temperature. Stir in lime juice. Pour into metal mixing bowl and put in freezer until firm throughout. Place beaters in freezer to chill. Remove lime mixture from freezer. Break it up with wooden spoon. Beat on low speed until free of lumps. Return to freezer until firm again. Rebeat with chilled beaters. The sorbet will keep in the freezer at a smooth consistency for weeks. Lemon juice can be substituted for lime juice and green food coloring can be added. The clear, clean look of the lime sorbet without coloring with a garnish of lime wedges is beautiful. Yield: 4 to 6 servings.

This adds an elegant touch to a dinner party when served between courses to cleanse the palate. It can also be used as a light refreshing dessert.

Mrs. Robert R. Morrison, Jr.
(Twick Cooper)

Custard Ice Cream

6 cups whole milk
1 (13-ounce) can evaporated milk
   or 1 pint light cream
1 (12-ounce) can sweetened
   condensed milk

9 large eggs
¾ cup sugar
2 Tablespoons vanilla extract
½ teaspoon almond extract
   (optional)

Combine 3 milks and heat. Do not let boil. Beat eggs and sugar together and slowly add to hot milk, stirring constantly and cook until thickened, about 5 minutes. Strain, cool, and add flavorings. Freeze in ice cream freezer for ice cream or bake as a custard. To bake custard, place dish in pan of hot water. Bake in 350° oven for about 1 hour or until knife comes clean when inserted in center. Yield: 1 gallon.

Mrs. C. B. Patterson
(Sue Nelson)

Our Favorite Ice Cream

4 cups milk
8 eggs, well beaten
2 cups sugar

3 to 4 Tablespoons vanilla extract
¼ teaspoon salt
4 cups heavy cream

Scald milk in double boiler over hot water. Add eggs and cook until thick as boiled custard. Remove from heat; add sugar and stir until dissolved. Add vanilla, salt, and cream. Chill overnight in refrigerator. Freeze in ice cream maker. It is best served immediately, but remaining portion can be frozen. Yield: 1 gallon.

Mrs. Clyde C. Hughey, Sr.
Memphis, Tennessee

Ice Cream Variations

These variations may be added to "Our Favorite Ice Cream" recipe or any other custard recipe.

Praline Ice Cream

Crumble 6 pralines into custard mixture and freeze.

Coffee Ice Cream

Add 2 Tablespoons instant coffee powder to hot custard and freeze.

Peppermint Ice Cream

Crush ½ pound peppermint candy. Soak in milk for 2 hours and add to custard. Freeze.

The Editors

Lemon Ice Cream

5⅓ cups heavy cream
5⅓ cups milk
1¼ cups fresh or frozen lemon juice
    concentrate

4 cups sugar
2 teaspoons lemon extract
2 Tablespoons grated lemon rind

Mix all ingredients thoroughly. Chill overnight. Pour into ice cream freezer and freeze according to directions. Yield: 3½ quarts.

Mrs. Louis Field
(Marianna Robbins)

Pineapple Sherbet

Juice of 6 lemons
1 (20-ounce) can crushed pineapple
in own juice

1 scant cup sugar
1 quart milk
1 pint light cream

Pour lemon juice over pineapple and its juice. Stir in sugar. Refrigerate until chilled and ready to use. Mix milk and cream and place in ice cream freezer. Freeze 5 to 10 minutes to get milk thoroughly chilled. Carefully wipe top of freezer container with damp towel so no salt will get into milk when opened. Pour in pineapple mixture. Replace top. Continue to freeze until firm. Yield: Approximately 2 quarts.

Mrs. Charles Faulk
(Elizabeth Young)

Bing Cherry Parfait

1 (16-ounce) can bing cherries
½ cup bourbon
½ gallon vanilla ice cream,
softened

2 dozen almond macaroons
1 cup chopped pecans
½ pint heavy cream, whipped

Soak cherries in their juice and bourbon for 1 to 2 hours. Cut cherries in half. Add cherry juice mixture to softened ice cream. Crumble macaroons and work into ice cream mixture. Blend in pecans. Spoon into parfait glasses and freeze. Top with whipped cream before serving. Yield: 6 to 8 servings.

Mrs. Bobby Robinson
(Jan Harris)

Maple Parfait

½ cup pure maple syrup
2 eggs, separated

½ pint heavy cream, whipped
1 cup chopped pecans

Heat maple syrup. Pour over beaten egg yolks. Cook in a double boiler 15 minutes. Let cool and fold in stiffly beaten egg whites. Fold in whipped cream and pecans. Pour into parfait glasses and chill. Yield: 6 servings.

Mrs. B. J. Gunn
(Frances Kivett)

 Mix a half gallon of vanilla ice cream with 4 cups mashed figs to make fresh fig ice cream.

Crème de Menthe Parfait

1 quart vanilla ice cream, softened
1 pint lime sherbet, softened

1 (4½-ounce) carton frozen
whipped topping, thawed
¼ cup green crème de menthe

Combine all ingredients in container of electric blender; blend at medium speed until mixed. Freeze 3 to 4 hours in parfait glasses. Yield: 6 to 8 servings.

This makes a very colorful dessert served on a crystal plate with frosted brownies.

Mrs. Jimmy F. Vessell
(Ann Duncan)

Butterscotch Nut Sauce

½ cup light corn syrup
⅓ cup firmly packed brown sugar
3 Tablespoons butter or margarine
Dash of salt

2 Tablespoons evaporated milk
½ cup chopped pecans or walnuts
⅓ cup light rum

Combine corn syrup, sugar, butter, and salt in heavy saucepan. Bring to a boil, stirring constantly, until mixture reaches soft ball stage (234°). Cool about 5 to 8 minutes. Add milk, blending well. Add nuts and rum. Yield: 2 cups.

Mrs. George Guider
(Annie Lee Faulk)

Caramel Sauce

1 cup brown sugar
½ cup light corn syrup
¼ teaspoon salt

4 Tablespoons butter
¾ cup evaporated milk
1 teaspoon vanilla extract

In medium saucepan mix brown sugar, corn syrup, and salt. Bring to a boil and cook 10 minutes. Add butter. Remove from heat and add evaporated milk gradually. Let cool; add vanilla. Keeps well in sealed jar in refrigerator. When ready to use, set jar in warm water or put in microwave to heat. Serve over ice cream. Yield: 1½ to 2 cups sauce.

Mrs. Warner Biedenharn
(Jowilla Shaw)

Pineapple Candy

3 cups sugar
1 cup crushed pineapple with juice
24 marshmallows

Pinch of salt
1 teaspoon vanilla extract
2 cups broken pecans

Boil sugar with pineapple until it forms a hard ball in water (235°). Remove from heat and beat well. Add marshmallows, salt, and vanilla and beat until cool. Stir in nuts. Drop by teaspoons onto waxed paper. Yield: 4 to 5 dozen.

Sister Mary Perpetua, R.S.M.

Divinity

3 cups sugar, divided
1 cup water, divided
¾ cup light corn syrup
2 egg whites

1 teaspoon vanilla extract
1 cup chopped pecans
Candied cherries (optional)

Mix 1 cup sugar and ½ cup water. Boil until it spins a thread (234°). Mix 2 cups sugar, ½ cup water, and corn syrup. Boil until it forms a hard ball in cold water (260°). Beat egg whites until stiff. Pour first syrup in thin stream into egg whites, beating until creamy. Repeat process with second syrup. Add vanilla and nuts. Drop with spoon onto waxed paper. Garnish with cherries if desired. Yield: 3 to 4 dozen.

Mrs. Frank S. Hill
(Virginia Heggie)

Mississippi Millionaires

50 caramels
2 Tablespoons water
2 Tablespoons butter
3 cups halved pecans

10 ounces milk chocolate candy
bars
3 ounces paraffin

Melt caramels, water and butter in double boiler. Add pecans. Drop by teaspoonful onto foil-covered cookie sheet. Cool. Melt chocolate and paraffin together. Use ice pick to remove caramel-nut drops from foil and dip in warmed chocolate mixture. Return dipped candy to foil to cool. To reach desired firmness, more or less paraffin may be used. Yield: 3 to 4 dozen.

Mrs. Butch Bailess
(Ginner Kennedy)

Chewy Delights

2 cups sugar
2 Tablespoons cocoa
1 pint heavy cream
½ cup butter

1¾ cups light corn syrup
1 Tablespoon vanilla extract
3 cups chopped pecans

Mix sugar and cocoa. Add other ingredients in heavy pot. Cook at medium to medium-high until candy thermometer reaches 246°. Grease 9 x 13-inch pan with butter and pour in candy. Let cool and cut into squares. Wrap in plastic wrap. Yield: 2 to 3 dozen.

This is not a hard candy. It is chewy and absolutely divine.

Mrs. Harry Meyer
(Louise Angelo)

Caramels

2 cups sugar
2 cups light corn syrup
1 (12-ounce) can evaporated milk

½ cup butter
1 teaspoon vanilla extract
1 cup chopped nuts

Combine sugar and syrup. Cook to 248°. Add milk and butter. Cook to 248°. Remove from heat and add vanilla. Beat until thickened. Stir in nuts. Pour into a well greased 8 x 10-inch pan. When cooled, cut into squares. Wrap each piece in waxed paper. Yield: 5 dozen.

Sister Mary Matthew McCloskey, R.S.M.

Peanut Butter Cups

2 cups peanut butter, creamy or
  crunchy
½ cup plus 1 Tablespoon melted
  butter, divided

2¾ cups powdered sugar
1 (12-ounce) package chocolate
  chips

Stir together peanut butter, ½ cup melted butter, and powdered sugar. Press mixture into bottom of a 9-inch square pan. Melt chocolate pieces and stir together with remaining Tablespoon of melted butter. Spread on top. Refrigerate for 10 minutes to set chocolate. Cut into small squares. Store at room temperature. Mixture may also be pressed into small cups. Yield: 4 dozen squares.

Mrs. Robert W. Thompson
(Barbara Rollison)

Microwave Peanut Brittle

1 cup sugar
Pinch of salt
½ cup light corn syrup
1 cup raw peanuts

1 teaspoon vanilla extract
1 teaspoon margarine
1 teaspoon soda

Combine sugar, salt, corn syrup, and peanuts in large glass dish, such as a large measuring cup. Cook in microwave on high for 7 minutes. Remove; stir, and add vanilla and margarine. Cook in microwave on high for 2 minutes. Remove and add soda. Stir well and pour onto greased foil. Store in airtight container. Yield: 1 pound.

Mrs. L. C. Hand
Terry, Mississippi

Sallie's Brown Candy

3 pints white sugar, divided
1 pint light cream
¼ teaspoon soda

¼ pound butter
1 teaspoon vanilla extract
2 pounds pecans, finely chopped

Pour 1 pint sugar into heavy aluminum or iron skillet and place over low heat. Begin stirring with wooden spoon and keep sugar moving so it will not scorch. It will take over 30 minutes to completely melt this sugar and, at no time let it smoke or cook so fast that it turns dark. It should be about the color of light brown sugar syrup. As soon as sugar has started to heat in the skillet, pour remaining 2 pints of sugar together with cream into a deep heavy kettle and set it over low heat to cook along slowly while melting the sugar in skillet. As soon as all the sugar is melted, begin pouring it into kettle of boiling cream and sugar, keeping it on very slow heat and stirring constantly. The real secret of mixing these ingredients is to pour a stream no larger than a knitting needle and to stir across the bottom of the kettle at all times. Continue cooking and stirring until the mixture forms a firm ball when dropped into cold water. After this test is made, turn heat off and immediately add the soda, stirring vigorously as it foams up. As soon as the soda is mixed, add butter, allowing it to melt as stirred. Remove from stove for about 20 minutes; then add vanilla and begin heating. Use a wooden spoon and beat until the mixture is thick and heavy, having a dull appearance instead of a glossy sheen. Add the broken pecan meats and mix. Turn into tin boxes or into square pans where it may be cut into squares when cooled slightly. Easier if 2 cooks work together—one pours, one stirs. Yield: 4 dozen.

Mrs. E. A. Buckner
Tallulah, Louisiana

That's Good Candy

Boiling water
4 cups whole pecans

4 Tablespoons butter or margarine
2 (8-ounce) bars milk chocolate

Pour boiling water over nuts; drain immediately. Toast nuts and butter in iron skillet at 300° for 45 minutes stirring occasionally. Cool. Melt milk chocolate in double boiler. Stir in pecans. Drop by teaspoon onto waxed paper. This takes time to dry. Yield: 2 dozen pieces.

Mrs. William H. Bobb
(Mary Bell Wood)

Peanut Butter Fudge

3 cups sugar
¾ cup milk
Pinch of salt
3 Tablespoons light corn syrup

1 teaspoon vanilla extract
2⅔ Tablespoons margarine
½ cup peanut butter

Put sugar, milk, and salt in a heavy pot and bring to a boil. Stir occasionally; add corn syrup, and reduce heat to low. Cook to hard ball stage. Add vanilla and margarine and stir well. Remove from heat and add peanut butter. Beat by hand until creamy. Pour onto a platter greased with butter. Yield: 2½ pounds candy.

Phillip Vedros

Texas Millionaire Fudge

2 (6-ounce) packages semisweet
    chocolate chips
1 pint marshmallow cream
1 teaspoon vanilla extract

4½ cups sugar
1 large can evaporated milk
¼ pound margarine
1 pound chopped pecans

Place first 3 ingredients in a large mixing bowl. In a heavy saucepan put sugar, milk, and margarine. Bring to a boil and let boil 7 minutes, stirring constantly. Add this mixture to first part. Add pecans and mix until chocolate chips are melted. Pour mixture into a 14 x 8 x 2-inch greased pan. Let cool. Put in refrigerator to firm. Yield: 2 to 3 dozen.

Mrs. Murray Pinkston, Jr.
(Clara Parks Booth)

Chocolate Fudge

3 (1-ounce) squares unsweetened
  chocolate
3 cups sugar
½ cup light corn syrup

1 cup evaporated milk
3 Tablespoons margarine
1 teaspoon vanilla extract
1 cup chopped pecans

Melt chocolate in heavy saucepan. Add sugar, corn syrup, and milk. Cook over low heat, stirring constantly, until mixture comes to a boil. Cook to soft ball stage (238°). Remove from heat and add margarine. Cool until lukewarm and add vanilla. Beat until mixture is creamy and loses its gloss. Stir in pecans. Pour into buttered 8 x 8-inch pan. Cool and cut into squares. Yield: 2 to 3 dozen.

Mrs. George Guider
(Annie Lee Faulk)

Martha Washington Candy

2 (16-ounce) boxes powdered sugar
½ cup butter, melted
1 (14-ounce) can sweetened
  condensed milk
1 (3¼-ounce) can coconut

1 teaspoon vanilla extract
2 cups chopped pecans
1 (12-ounce) package semisweet
  chocolate chips
2 ounces paraffin

Mix sugar, butter, and milk. Add coconut, vanilla, and pecans. Stir well and roll into balls. Place on cookie sheet and freeze for 30 minutes. Melt chocolate chips and paraffin in a double boiler. Using toothpicks, dip balls into chocolate. Place on waxed paper to harden. Yield: 4 to 5 dozen.

Mrs. Albert Dornbusch
(Gloria Abraham)

Butter Mints

1 (3-ounce) package cream cheese,
  softened
2 teaspoons butter flavoring
¼ teaspoon oil of peppermint

1 (16-ounce) package powdered
  sugar
Yellow paste food coloring

Combine first 4 ingredients; beat at low speed on electric mixer until blended. Add a small amount of food coloring and mix until blended. Press mixture into mint molds or roll into small balls and flatten slightly. Yield: Approximately 7 dozen.

Mrs. Lawrence B. Pope
Collins, Mississippi

Chocolate Brittle

2 cups butter
2 cups sugar
¼ cup plus 2 Tablespoons water

12 (1.05-ounce) milk chocolate
candy bars
3 cups chopped pecans

Combine butter, sugar, and water in a Dutch oven; cook over low heat until candy thermometer registers 300°. Remove from heat and immediately pour into 2 buttered 12-inch pizza pans. Melt chocolate in top of a double boiler over hot water. Spread over brittle; sprinkle pecans evenly on top. Press pecans into chocolate. Let stand until chocolate is firm. Break candy into pieces. Yield: 4 pounds.

This candy is very good as gifts for teachers or friends. Just break up and put into ball jars or small canisters.

Mrs. Robert Dew
(Betty Jo Mood)

Old-Fashioned Hard Candy

2 cups sugar
1 cup water
⅔ cup light corn syrup
1 teaspoon oil flavoring (purchased
   at drugstore or baking supply
   shop)

Food coloring as desired
Powdered sugar

Mix sugar, water, and syrup until sugar is dissolved. Boil on medium heat to 300° or hard ball stage. Remove from heat. Add flavoring and food coloring and mix well. Odor will be extremely strong at this time so prepare in well ventilated kitchen. Pour in streams onto cookie sheet which has been very generously covered with powdered sugar. Make little ditches of powdered sugar so the candy does not spread too much. Sift more powdered sugar on top of candy streams. Cut with scissors into bite-size pieces as it begins to cool and outer edge will hold its shape. Do not wait until it is completely cooled, because it becomes hard and impossible to cut. Yield: 1 pound hard candy.

Makes a wonderful Christmas gift for friends and neighbors.

Mrs. Lambeth Woodward
(Carolyn Moore)

 On a hot humid day cook candy 2° higher than on a cold dry day.

Sis's Pralines

2 cups granulated brown sugar
1 cup sugar
⅛ teaspoon soda
2 Tablespoons light corn syrup
¾ (14-ounce) can sweetened
   condensed milk

½ cup tap water
12 marshmallows
1 quart pecan halves

Mix all ingredients except marshmallows and pecans and cook until a dab forms soft ball in water. Stir to prevent burning. Add marshmallows and continue cooking until marshmallows melt. Continue stirring. Remove from heat; add pecans, and beat until candy loses some of its gloss. Drop onto waxed paper with cloth underneath. Yield: 3 dozen.

Mrs. Jerry Silver
(Sis Waring Hughes)

Microwave Pralines

1½ cups packed brown sugar
⅔ cup cream
⅛ teaspoon salt

2 Tablespoons melted margarine
1½ cups pecans, chopped

Combine first 3 ingredients in a deep glass dish, mixing well. Blend in margarine. Microwave on high for 10 minutes, stirring once. Stir in pecans. Cool for 1 minute. Beat by hand until creamy and thickened, 4 to 4½ minutes. The mixture will lose some of its gloss. Drop by Tablespoonful onto waxed paper. Yield: 2 to 2½ dozen.

Kristi Abraham
Memphis, Tennessee

Date Roll

3 cups sugar
3 Tablespoons light corn syrup
1 cup evaporated milk

1 cup chopped dates
1 cup chopped pecans
Powdered sugar (optional)

Mix together sugar, syrup, milk, and dates. Cook until it forms a soft ball in cold water (238°). Beat until creamy. Stir in nuts. Pour onto waxed paper on damp cloth in a long strip. Roll up. Slice when cool. May be rolled in powdered sugar, if desired. Yield: 1 loaf.

Mrs. Frank S. Hill
(Virginia Heggie)

Lakemont

The ghost of Judge Lake's wife seems very real on late summer afternoons at Lakemont. Generations have reported strange incidents—a rustle in the yard or the swishing sound of petticoats, accompanied by a faint breeze wafting a trace of her perfume. The story persists that she still returns to mourn her husband's death which occured in 1861 under cottonwood trees across the Mississippi River as she watched from her upstairs gallery.

The Lakes were aristocrats. Judge William Lake, a lawyer originally from Virginia, had served as U.S. Congressman; then was elected a representative to the Confederate Assembly in 1861. Before he could take his seat, he became embroiled in a dispute with a political rival. In the manner of the times and according to the code of honor of the day, the antagonists would settle their differences with pistols at 20 paces on the cottonwood bar. Lake was killed instantly; his wife, watching from her balcony, retreated to her rooms and gardens. As the Civil War moved close to Vicksburg, she fled to Alabama to live with relatives. The home passed to other owners.

Many years later, the upper story was heavily damaged by fire and it was removed. Today there is no suggestion of the Lake duel, the Civil War or the fire. Lakemont, furnished in the elegance of Judge Lake's day, is a one-story structure with brick streets running alongside and in front. The original iron fence, damaged by Union shells during the Siege of Vicksburg, still guards the entrance.

It is an attraction on the Vicksburg Tour; and to this day residents persist in the story of Mrs. Lake's ghost.

After the Theatre Encore Menu pictured:
Toasted Pecans, Lemon Jelly Cake, Shrimp Party Sandwiches, Fruit 'n Crackers, Tomato Sandwiches, Party Pepperoni Canapés

Vicksburg Variety
Miss Mississippis' Favorites

Mary Ann's Fudge Brownies

2 cups margarine
4 squares unsweetened chocolate
2¼ cups sugar
5 eggs, beaten

2 teaspoons vanilla extract
1¾ cups sifted flour
1 teaspoon salt
1 cup nuts, coarsely chopped

Melt margarine and chocolate together over hot water. Beat sugar, eggs, and vanilla together. Slowly add melted chocolate and beat until well blended. Sift flour and salt together. Mix with nuts and add last. Pour into two 9 x 9-inch greased and floured pans or 1 large pan. Bake at 350° for about 35 minutes or until a toothpick comes out clean.

Fudge Icing

2 cups sugar
½ cup margarine
¼ cup light corn syrup

½ cup milk
Dash of salt
2 squares unsweetened chocolate

Mix together and cook slowly until all is melted. Bring to a boil rapidly 1 to 2 minutes. Beat until creamy and smooth. Yield: 9 servings.

Mary Ann Mobley Collins
Miss Mississippi 1958
Miss America 1959

Grandma's Old-Fashioned Egg Custard Pie

1⅓ cups sugar
1 Tablespoon flour
2⅔ Tablespoons butter or
   margarine

4 eggs
1 cup milk or cream
1 (9-inch) unbaked pie shell

Use fingers to mix sugar, flour, and butter in a bowl until it looks like coarse meal. Add eggs and mix well. Add milk and beat about 1 minute with mixer. Pour into unbaked pie shell. Bake at 400° for about 25 minutes or until firm. Yield: 8 servings.

Betty Jane Porter Hallberg
Miss Mississippi 1959

Spinach Pastry

4 (10-ounce) packages frozen
　spinach
1 large onion, chopped
2 Tablespoons butter
½ pound Monterey Jack cheese,
　shredded
2 eggs, well beaten

2 teaspoons nutmeg
1 teaspoon salt
Lemon pepper to taste
12 sheets phyllo pastry at room
　temperature
½ cup butter, melted

Heat spinach until thawed and hot. Sauté onion in butter and add to spinach. Add cheese, eggs, and spices. Set aside to cool. Brush melted butter on a 2-quart rectangular baking dish (sides and bottom). Place 2 sheets phyllo pastry over buttered dish and brush leaves with butter. Add 2 more sheets and brush well with melted butter. Repeat until 8 leaves have been placed lengthwise over dish. Add spinach mixture; spread out to fill entire dish. Fold over excess sheets of phyllo on top of spinach and brush with butter. Fold each of the 4 remaining phyllo sheets in half and place over top of spinach to make a top crust, brushing butter between each double sheet. Butter top and tuck in all pastry around sides. Bake at 375° for 30 to 45 minutes or until top is golden brown. Cut into squares and serve hot. Yield: 15 servings.

Lynda Lee Mead Shea
Miss Mississippi 1959
Miss America 1960

Chalie's Bread Pudding

½ cup butter or margarine
1½ cups sugar
3 eggs
1 (13-ounce) can evaporated milk
1 cup water

1 teaspoon vanilla extract
Pinch of salt
2 or 3 small loaves Earth Grain or
　Pepperidge Farms French Bread
Nutmeg

Using electric mixer, cream butter and sugar; add eggs 1 at a time. Add milk, water, vanilla, and salt. (It may look curdled.) Pour ½ liquid into an 8 x 8-inch baking dish. Break bread into small pieces and put in liquid in baking dish. When baking dish is full, pour in remaining liquid, making sure all bread is saturated. Sprinkle nutmeg on top. Bake for 30 minutes at 350°. Yield: 10 servings.

Recipe best served hot from the oven. Good with a bit of whipped cream or ice cream.

Chalie Carroll Ray
Miss Mississippi 1962

Jan's Casserole

¼ cup olive oil
⅓ cup minced onions
3 cloves garlic, crushed
½ cup diced carrots
3 ribs celery, diced
1 pound ground beef
1 (6-ounce) can tomato paste
2½ cups tomatoes
1 Tablespoon salt

½ teaspoon pepper
¼ pound thin noodles
1 (10-ounce) package frozen
  chopped spinach
½ cup buttered fresh bread crumbs
½ cup shredded processed
  American cheese
Grated Parmesan cheese

Heat oil in skillet and sauté onions, garlic, carrots, and celery until light brown. Add beef and cook until red color disappears. Simmer, uncovered, for 2 to 2½ hours. Add tomato paste, tomatoes, salt, and pepper. Cook noodles and spinach separately according to package directions. Drain well and add to sauce in a 1½-quart casserole. Sprinkle with bread crumbs and cheese. Bake 30 minutes at 350°. Serve with Parmesan cheese. Can be frozen, leaving off bread crumbs and cheese. Yield: 6 to 8 servings.

Jan Nave Barnes
Miss Mississippi 1963

Gingerbread

4 cups flour
2 cups sugar
½ teaspoon salt
2 teaspoons soda
1 teaspoon ginger
1 teaspoon nutmeg
½ teaspoon allspice

½ teaspoon cloves
2 teaspoons cinnamon
1 cup butter
½ cup molasses
2 cups buttermilk
2 eggs

Sift together all dry ingredients. Cut in butter to make crumb mixture. Take out 1 cup crumbs and set aside. Add molasses, buttermilk and eggs. Mix well and pour into a 9 x 13-inch pan. Sprinkle reserved crumb mixture on top. Bake 25 minutes at 350°.

This is delicious served warm and topped with Lemon Sauce (see Index). When using, omit crumb topping.

Joan Myers Bayer
Miss Mississippi 1967

Simono's Cheese Cake

Crust

2 cups graham cracker crumbs (for
    thicker crust, use more)

2 Tablespoons butter or margarine
1 teaspoon sugar (optional)

Mix together in a 10-inch springform pan and pat into bottom. Refrigerate 3 to 4 hours.

Cake

4 eggs, separated
1 cup sugar
3 (8-ounce) packages cream cheese,
    softened

Dash of cream of tartar

Beat egg yolks with sugar until lemon colored. Add cream cheese and mix well. Add cream of tartar to egg whites and beat until stiff. Fold into cheese mixture. Spoon mixture into springform pan and bake at 325° for 40 minutes. Carefully remove from oven. It will appear shaky and not done.

Topping

1 pint sour cream
½ cup sugar

1 teaspoon vanilla extract

Mix together. Pour over cake and bake 20 minutes at 250°. Let cool in pan before refrigerating and then refrigerate overnight before cutting. Yield: 16 to 20 servings.

Judy Simono Durff
Miss Mississippi 1964

Raw Vegetable Dip

1 pint mayonnaise
1 pint sour cream
3 teaspoons beau monde seasoning

3 teaspoons dill weed
3 Tablespoons dried onion
3 Tablespoons parsley

Stir all ingredients together and chill. Better if prepared a day ahead. Yield: 50 servings.

Robbie Robertson Pinkerton
Miss Mississippi 1966

Crabmeat Mold

3 envelopes unflavored gelatin
½ cup cold water
3 pounds lump crabmeat
½ to 1 teaspoon red pepper
1 quart mayonnaise

1 small onion, grated or chopped
 green onions
6 Tablespoons lemon juice
Melba rounds

Dissolve gelatin in water and heat until all particles are melted. Add all other ingredients and put in barely greased fish mold. When set, turn onto platter and serve with melba rounds. Yield: 12 to 16 servings.

Mary Donnelly Haskell
Miss Mississippi 1977

Tangy Cocktail Meatballs

2 slices bread
2 pounds ground chuck
1½ packages dry onion soup mix
Butter
1 cup ketchup
8 Tablespoons vinegar

1 cup apricot nectar
8 Tablespoons brown sugar
4 teaspoons prepared mustard
4 teaspoons horseradish
2 teaspoons Worcestershire sauce

Dampen bread with water and squeeze it out. Combine bread, ground chuck, and soup mix. Shape into small balls and brown in butter. Combine all remaining ingredients and simmer 10 minutes. Add meatballs and heat 10 minutes. Serve in chafing dish. Yield: 50 meatballs.

Joan Myers Bayer
Miss Mississippi 1967

Lemon Freeze

1 (12-ounce) can evaporated milk
1 cup sugar
¼ cup lemon juice

1 teaspoon vanilla extract
Graham cracker crumbs or slivered
 almonds

Pour milk in bowl. Place bowl and beater in freezer for 30 to 45 minutes. Whip milk with sugar with electric mixer until doubled in size. Add lemon juice and vanilla. Pour into loaf pan or 8 x 8-inch square glass dish. Top with graham crackers or almonds. Freeze. Yield: 6 to 8 servings.

Chris McClamroch Akern
Miss Mississippi 1970

Chinese Chicken Salad

½ *pound cooked chicken, shredded*
Soy sauce
Sugar
2 ounces rice sticks
Cooking oil

4 green onions, finely sliced
2 Tablespoons sliced almonds
2 Tablespoons sesame seed, toasted
1 head lettuce, shredded

Soak chicken in soy sauce and sugar to taste. Fry rice sticks in very hot oil. Combine ingredients and toss with dressing.

Dressing

2 Tablespoons sugar
1 teaspoon salt
¼ teaspoon pepper
¼ cup salad oil

1 Tablespoon sesame oil
3 Tablespoons vinegar
1 teaspoon ajinomoto (optional)

Mix all ingredients well. Yield: 4 to 6 servings.

Rice sticks will puff up as soon as they are put in hot oil, so remove as soon as this happens. This salad is also good without the rice sticks. Shrimp can be substituted for chicken.

Glenda Meadows Grubbs
Miss Mississippi 1972

Baked Cheese Tomatoes

6 medium tomatoes, ripened
2 ounces gourmet rice vinegar
1½ teaspoons salt, divided
1 cup shredded Cheddar cheese
1 cup soft bread crumbs

½ cup melted butter
1½ teaspoons basil leaves,
  crumbled
½ teaspoon ground red pepper

Cut each tomato in half and brush outer skin with vinegar. Place cut-side up in baking dish. Take 1 teaspoon salt and sprinkle cut surface of each tomato and set aside. In small bowl combine cheese, bread crumbs, melted butter, basil, red pepper and remaining ½ teaspoon salt. Blend. Spoon about 1 teaspoon cheese mixture on top of each tomato. Bake 350° for 10 to 12 minutes. Yield: 6 servings.

Jane Carol Foshee Kirkpatrick
Miss Mississippi 1969

Crabmeat Van Devender

½ cup butter
½ cup flour
¼ cup grated onion
⅛ cup chopped parsley
2 cups heavy cream
1 cup white wine
2½ ounces shredded Swiss cheese
½ cup chopped green onion
2 teaspoons salt

½ teaspoon cayenne pepper
½ teaspoon black pepper
2 (14-ounce) cans and 1 (6-ounce)
    jar artichoke hearts, chopped and
    drained
4 Tablespoons lemon juice
2 (4-ounce) cans sliced mushrooms
3 Tablespoons Romano cheese
1 pound lump crabmeat

Melt butter and stir in flour for 5 minutes. Add onion, stirring 2 more minutes. Stir in parsley and cream. Allow to get hot. Add wine and simmer. Add Swiss cheese and stir until melted. Turn off heat until lukewarm. Add all other ingredients and stir. Pour into a buttered 2-quart casserole dish. Bake at 350° until heated throughout. Yield: 8 servings.

Mollie Magee Van Devender
Miss Mississippi 1975

Mushroom Rolls

¾ pound fresh mushrooms, cleaned
    and finely chopped
½ cup butter
3 heaping Tablespoons flour
¼ teaspoon monosodium glutamate
½ teaspoon salt

Dash of black pepper
¾ cup cream
2 teaspoons chopped chives
1 teaspoon lemon juice
2 loaves fresh sandwich bread

Sauté mushrooms in butter about 5 minutes. Blend in flour, monosodium glutamate, salt, pepper, and cream and cook until thick. Add chives and lemon juice and stir until blended. Let cool. Remove crust from bread and roll thinly with rolling pin. Spread thinly with mushroom mixture and roll up. Cut into 2 pieces. Bake at 400° for 30 minutes or until brown. Freezes well. Yield: 70 to 80 rolls.

Mary Donnelly Haskell
Miss Mississippi 1977

Refrigerate candles 24 hours before using to prevent dripping.

Red Velvet Cake

½ cup butter
1½ cups sugar
1 teaspoon vanilla extract
2 eggs
2 heaping teaspoons cocoa
3 ounces red food coloring

2½ cups cake flour
1 teaspoon salt
1 cup buttermilk
1 teaspoon soda
1 Tablespoon vinegar

Cream butter, sugar, and vanilla. Add eggs, 1 at a time, and mix well. Make thin paste from cocoa and food coloring and add to creamed mixture. Sift flour and salt together. Add flour and buttermilk to creamed mixture 1 Tablespoon at a time, beginning and ending with flour. Mix soda and vinegar (it will bubble) and blend into mixture. Grease and flour two 8-inch pans and line bottom of pans with waxed paper. Bake at 350° for 20 to 30 minutes. Cool completely before icing.

Icing

4½ Tablespoons flour
1½ cups milk
1½ cups butter

1½ cups sugar
1½ teaspoons vanilla extract

Make thick paste of flour and milk, not adding all milk. Use wire whisk to beat mixture and gradually add remaining milk. Cook in double boiler, beating until thick. Cool. Cream butter, sugar, and vanilla. Beat until fluffy. Add cooled mixture and continue beating until consistency of whipped cream. Cool before using. Yield: 16 servings.

Sherye Simmons Green
Miss Mississippi 1979

Seven Layer Salad

1 head lettuce, shredded
½ cup chopped celery
½ cup chopped green pepper
½ cup chopped green onions
1 (10-ounce) package frozen green
  peas, cooked, drained, and salted

1 cup mayonnaise
3 teaspoons sugar
4 to 6 ounces shredded Cheddar or
  grated Parmesan cheese
8 strips bacon, fried and crumbled

Layer ingredients in large dish in above order. Cover tightly and refrigerate at least 8 hours before serving. Yield: 6 servings.

Cheri Brown Howle
Miss Mississippi 1978

Mexican Wastebasket Stew

½ onion, chopped
1 (10-ounce) can ROTEL Tomatoes
   and Green Chilies
½ (7-ounce) can chopped green
   chilies
½ (6-ounce) can SNAP-E-TOM®
   Tomato and Chile Cocktail
2 (16-ounce) cans pinto beans
1 (16-ounce) can whole kernel corn

1 package beefy onion soup mix
1 cup chopped celery
1 large zucchini, chopped
2 packages small smoky link
   sausages, sliced
1 (16-ounce) can lima beans
1 (16-ounce) can black olives, sliced
1 pound Monterey Jack cheese,
   cubed

Combine all ingredients except cheese in a large kettle and simmer for at least 1 hour, until all flavors are blended. Correct seasonings if needed. Pour over cubed cheese in bottom of bowl. Can be served with tortillas. SNAP-E-TOM is a registered trademark belonging to Del Monte Corporation and is used here by special permission. Yield: 15 cups.

Jennifer Jo Blair Bailey
Miss Mississippi 1971

Microwave Enchilada Casserole

1¾ pounds lean ground beef
1 large onion, finely chopped
2 cloves garlic, minced
1 (10-ounce) can ROTEL Tomatoes
   and Green Chilies, mashed

1 (1⅝-ounce) envelope taco
   seasoning mix
6 corn tortillas
3 cups shredded Cheddar cheese,
   divided

Crumble beef into a 2-quart glass container. Add onion and garlic and mix lightly. Place in microwave and cook on high for 3 minutes. Drain meat mixture; then stir. Microwave on high for 2 more minutes. Stir in ROTEL Tomatoes and Green Chilies and taco seasoning. Cook on high for 3 minutes and remove from microwave. In a 2-quart round microwave dish, place ½ tortillas, ½ beef mixture, and 1¼ cups cheese. Repeat layers. Cover and cook in microwave on high for 7 minutes. Sprinkle with remaining ½ cup cheese. Yield: 4 to 6 servings.

Diane Bounds Garner
Miss Mississippi 1974

 Clean coffee cans make good baking containers for gift breads.

Apple Pie

6 large apples, peeled, cored and
   sliced
Unbaked pastry for 2-crust pie
1 Tablespoon lemon juice
2 Tablespoons flour
½ cup sugar

½ cup brown sugar
¾ teaspoon cinnamon
¾ teaspoon ginger
¾ teaspoon nutmeg
⅛ teaspoon salt
3 Tablespoons butter or margarine

Place apples in unbaked pie shell. Sprinkle lemon juice over apples. Mix flour, sugars, and spices. Sprinkle flour mixture over apples. Dot with butter. Cover pie with top crust. Bake at 450° for 10 minutes. Reduce heat to 350° and bake for another 45 minutes. Yield: 6 to 8 servings.

Bobbye Wood Covalt
Miss Mississippi 1976

Chicken Quiche

2 (9-inch) pie shells
6 medium chicken breasts, boned
   and skinned
2 (10-ounce) packages frozen
   broccoli spears

Seasoned salt to taste
1 cup mozzarella cheese
1 cup shredded Cheddar cheese
6 eggs
2½ pints heavy cream

Brown pie shells. Brown and then boil chicken breasts until fork-tender with desired seasoning. Cut into bite-size pieces. Cook broccoli with seasoned salt as directed and cut into small pieces. Layer ½ chicken, broccoli, mozzarella cheese, and Cheddar cheese in each pie shell. Mix eggs with cream and pour ½ mixture on each quiche. Sprinkle tops with seasoned salt. Bake at 325° to 350° for 35 to 55 minutes depending on personal preference. Yield: 12 to 16 servings.

Wanda Gayle Geddie
Miss Mississippi 1983

Asparagus Chiller

1 (10½-ounce) can condensed cream
   of asparagus soup, undiluted
½ cup yogurt

1 soup can water
½ cup chopped cucumber
1 Tablespoon chopped red onion

Blend soup and yogurt; gradually stir in water. Add cucumber and onion. Chill 4 hours or more and serve in chilled bowls. Yield: 2 to 3 servings.

Karen Hopson
Miss Mississippi 1981

Chocolate-Chocolate Chip Cake

1 (18½-ounce) yellow cake mix
1 (4-ounce) package instant
  chocolate pudding mix
½ cup vegetable oil
½ cup water

4 eggs
1 pint sour cream
6 ounces semisweet chocolate chips
Flour

Mix first 6 ingredients. Lightly dust chocolate chips with flour and stir into batter. Pour into a bundt pan that has been greased and floured. Bake at 350° about 1 to 1½ hours. Yield: 12 to 15 servings.

Cheryl Prewitt
Miss Mississippi 1979
Miss America 1980

Southern Yeast Biscuits

5 cups flour
3 Tablespoons baking powder
3 Tablespoons sugar
1 teaspoon salt

1 package dry yeast
½ cup water
2 cups milk
⅔ cup cooking oil

In large mixing bowl, sift together all dry ingredients. Dissolve yeast in warm water. Add all liquid ingredients and mix well. Cover and let rise for about 30 minutes. Pinch off biscuits as needed. Keep remainder in refrigerator in an airtight container. Bake at 400° for about 15 minutes. Yield: 24 biscuits.

May be mixed a day or two ahead and used as needed. Will store several days.

Donna Pope
Miss Mississippi 1980

Monkey Bread

⅔ cup sugar
2 teaspoons cinnamon, divided
4 cans biscuits, individually
  quartered

1 cup chopped nuts
1 cup light brown sugar
½ cup butter or margarine

Combine sugar and 1 teaspoon cinnamon in a bag. Add biscuit pieces and shake. Drop biscuit pieces into greased tube pan and sprinkle with nuts. Combine brown sugar, 1 teaspoon cinnamon, and butter and bring to a boil over medium heat. Pour over cake. Bake at 350° for 40 to 45 minutes. Turn out and serve while warm. Yield: 12 to 16 servings.

Dianne Evans
Miss Mississippi 1982

Fettuccine Milano

1 pound mild Italian sausage
2 cups sliced mushrooms
2 cloves garlic
1 large bell pepper, seeded and
   chopped
1 cup chopped green onion
1 cup chopped parsley
1 teaspoon sweet basil, crumbled

½ teaspoon oregano, crumbled
¼ teaspoon rosemary, crumbled
½ cup olive oil
½ cup butter
12 ounces fettuccine, cooked
   according to package directions
Grated Parmesan cheese
Crusty French bread

Brown sausage and drain. Sauté mushrooms, garlic, bell pepper, onion, parsley, and seasonings in olive oil and butter until bell pepper is soft. Remove from heat and stir in sausage. Toss with hot fettuccine. Sprinkle generously with Parmesan cheese and serve with French bread. Yield: 6 to 8 servings.

Karen Hopson
Miss Mississippi 1981

Strawberry Dream Cake

1 (18½-ounce) package white cake
   mix
1 (6-ounce) package strawberry
   gelatin
2 Tablespoons flour

½ cup water
4 eggs
½ (10-ounce) box frozen sliced
   strawberries, thawed
¾ cup cooking oil

Combine cake mix, gelatin, flour, water, and eggs. Beat 2 minutes. Add strawberries with syrup to batter and beat 1 minute. Add oil and beat 1 minute. Pour into two (9-inch) pans. Bake at 350° for 25 to 35 minutes. When cooled, frost with Strawberry Frosting. Yield: 12 to 15 servings.

Strawberry Frosting

½ cup butter
1 (16-ounce) box powdered sugar

½ (10-ounce) box sliced
   strawberries with syrup
½ teaspoon vanilla extract

Beat butter until smooth. Add sugar alternating with strawberries and syrup until smooth. Add vanilla and if necessary thin with a little milk or cream to spreading consistency.

Kathy Manning
Miss Mississippi 1984

Cooking for Children

Pool Mix

1 (15-ounce) box raisins
1 (1-pound) package "M and M's"®
  Plain Chocolate Candies

1 (16-ounce) jar dry roasted peanuts

Mix all ingredients together. Store in airtight container. Good quick energy. "M & M's" are a registered trademark of Mars, Inc.

Mrs. Steve Harris
(Linda Walker)

Poppycock

2 cups light brown sugar, packed
1 cup margarine
½ cup light corn syrup
½ teaspoon cream of tartar

1 teaspoon soda
14 cups popped corn
8 ounces cashews or other favorite
  nuts

Combine first 4 ingredients and cook at high temperature, stirring constantly for 5 minutes. Add soda and remove from heat. Pour over popcorn and nuts and stir. Cook at 300° for 30 minutes, stirring after 15 minutes. Yield: 14 cups.

For a change in flavor use dark brown sugar and dark corn syrup.

Mrs. Harry Walton
(Sally Madison)

Apple Corn

½ cup butter
1¼ cups dried apples

½ cup brown sugar
4 quarts unsalted popped corn

Melt butter in saucepan. Add apples and sugar. Cook over low heat for 5 minutes, stirring frequently. Pour over popcorn and toss until evenly coated. Store in airtight container. Yield: 4 quarts.

Suzanne Harris

Doughnuts

Cooking oil   Powdered sugar
1 can refrigerator biscuits

Pour cooking oil in a medium skillet or heavy saucepan to a depth of 2 inches. Heat oil for deep frying to 375°. Press each biscuit flat in palm of hand and tear a hole in the center of each one to create doughnut shape. Drop into hot oil and fry until golden brown on each side. Remove and drain. Sprinkle generously with powdered sugar. Serve hot. Yield: 10 doughnuts.

Mrs. John Hadad, III
(Susan Phillips)

Bismarks

1 can refrigerator biscuits   Powdered sugar
Jelly or jam   Cinnamon (optional)
Vegetable oil

Flatten each biscuit. Place ½ teaspoon jelly in center of biscuit. Fold over and seal edges with fork. Fry in heated oil. Drain on paper towels and sprinkle with sugar and cinnamon, if desired. Yield: 10 biscuits.

Mrs. Wiltsie Haley
(Jeannie Crans)

Apple Crisp

4 cups sliced, peeled, cooking   1 teaspoon cinnamon
   apples   ½ teaspoon salt
¼ cup water   6 tablespoons butter
¾ cup flour   Ice cream
1 cup sugar

Place apples and water in a 10 x 6-inch baking dish. Sift flour, sugar, cinnamon, and salt in a bowl and add butter. Cream mixture until it is coarse. Sprinkle over apples. Bake at 350° for 45 minutes or until apples are tender. Serve with ice cream. Yield: 6 to 8 servings.

Mrs. Howard Waring
(Belynda Lyons)

 Cut ends of bread with a biscuit cutter. These make perfect "child size" hamburger buns.

Orange Dream Pops

½ cup orange juice
¼ cup sugar

1 cup whole milk

Mix all ingredients. Freeze in popsicle molds. May add yellow and red food coloring. Yield: 4 popsicles.

Nutritious and delicious.

Mrs. Al Sellers
(Brenda Hall)

Dreamsicles

1 (3-ounce) package orange or
   cherry flavored gelatin

1 cup hot water
1 pint vanilla ice cream, softened

Dissolve gelatin in 1 cup hot water in a medium-size bowl. Add ice cream. Pour into molds and freeze. Yield: 1 dozen.

Mrs. Kenneth E. Hicks
(Margaret Bonney)

Monster Cookies

½ cup margarine
2 cups sugar
1 (16-ounce) box brown sugar
6 eggs
1½ teaspoons light corn syrup
1½ pounds crunchy peanut butter
1 cup flour

1 tablespoon baking soda
9 cups uncooked oatmeal
6 ounces chocolate chips
6 ounces "M and M's"® Plain
   Chocolate Candies
6 ounces "M and M's"® Peanut
   Chocolate Candies

In a very large bowl, cream margarine and sugars. Add eggs and mix until fluffy. Stir in corn syrup and peanut butter. Add flour and soda. Add oatmeal and mix well. Stir in remaining ingredients. Using an ice cream scoop, drop onto greased cookie sheet, no more than 6 per sheet. Bake at 325° for 13 minutes. Yield: 2 to 3 dozen. "M & M's" are a registered trademark of Mars, Inc.

Mike Hall

Popcorn will pop better if left in the freezer for a full 24 hours before using.

Ice Cream Cone Cupcakes

1 (18½-ounce) box cake mix
24 to 28 flat-bottomed ice cream
   cones

Prepare batter according to directions on box. Fill cones ¾ full with batter.
To bake, place cones in muffin tins to prevent toppling. Cook 20 minutes
at 350°. Remove from oven and cool.

Frosting

1 box powdered sugar
½ cup shortening
1 teaspoon vanilla extract

1 teaspoon almond flavoring
   (optional)
¼ cup milk
Food coloring (optional)

Cream together all ingredients until frosting is smooth. Decorate cooled
cupcakes. Yield: 24 to 28 servings.

Jeff Harris

Gingerbread Man Cookies

⅔ cup shortening
½ cup brown sugar
2 teaspoons ginger
1 teaspoon cinnamon
¼ teaspoon cloves
1½ teaspoons salt
1 egg

¾ cup molasses
1½ cups flour
1½ cups whole wheat flour
1 teaspoon baking soda
½ teaspoon baking powder
Raisins

Cream together first 6 ingredients. Add egg and molasses and mix. Sift
together dry ingredients and stir into mixture. Chill. Roll out dough. Cut
into gingerbread man shape. Decorate with raisins. Bake on ungreased
cookie sheet 8 to 10 minutes at 375°. Yield: 3 dozen.

Mrs. Johnny Mims
(Susan Bailess)

Cut bread for children's sandwiches with animal cookie cutters.
Make a triple decker "Zoowich" that will stand up on the plate by
spreading 3 pieces of cut bread with a favorite filling, such as peanut
butter and jelly or egg salad.

Fried Ice Cream

½ cup caramel syrup
6 ounces corn flakes
½ gallon vanilla ice cream
Cooking oil (enough to cover ice
    cream balls)

1 (12-ounce) carton non-dairy
    whipped topping
12 cherries

Mix caramel with corn flakes until sticky. Scoop out ice cream and apply corn flake coating to cover ice cream. Store any leftover coating in refrigerator. Immerse ice cream ball in hot oil 15 to 20 seconds. Place in a dish; top with whipped topping and a cherry. Yield: 12 servings.

Great for teen parties. Adults love these, too!

Ginkade

Jason S. Bailess

4 cups boiling water
6 tea bags
1 (6-ounce) can frozen lemonade

1 (6-ounce) can frozen limeade
1½ cups sugar
12 cups water

Pour water over tea bags and let set 10 minutes. In a large container mix next 4 ingredients. Add tea and chill. Keep refrigerated.

There was always a pitcher of this in my grandmother's refrigerator. My cousins called her "Gink." Thus, "Ginkade" was named.

Mrs. Jimmy Gouras
(Peggy Mayfield)

Children's Party Punch

1 (3-ounce) package flavored gelatin
1 cup boiling water
1 cup sugar
1 (12-ounce) can frozen orange
    juice, thawed

1 (12-ounce) can frozen lemonade,
    thawed
1 (32-ounce) can pineapple juice
1 (32-ounce) bottle ginger ale
1 (6-ounce) bottle cherries

Mix gelatin with boiling water and sugar. Combine all juices and gelatin mixture. Add enough water to make 1 gallon. Put in plastic containers and freeze. Thaw slightly before serving and add ginger ale and cherries. Any color gelatin can be used or food coloring may be added. Yield: 30 servings.

Mrs. J. E. Blackburn, Jr.
(Jeane McNeel)

African Slush Punch

4 cups sugar
7 cups water, divided
4 bananas
1 (12-ounce) can frozen orange juice

1 (6-ounce) can frozen lemonade
1 (32-ounce) can unsweetened
    pineapple juice
3 quarts ginger ale

Boil sugar and 6 cups water in a saucepan for 3 minutes. Cool. Mash bananas in blender. In large container, mix bananas with fruit juices and 1 cup water. Add sugar water and blend well. Freeze for at least 24 hours. 1 hour before serving remove from freezer. Mash mixture to a pulp. Add ginger ale and mix. Yield: 5 to 6 quarts.

Mrs. Woody Brumitt
(Debbie Dottley)

Children's Favorite Orange Drink

1 (3-ounce) can frozen orange juice
½ cup milk
½ cup water

¼ cup sugar
½ teaspoon vanilla extract
Crushed ice

Mix first 5 ingredients together in blender. Add ice and blend until thick and icy. Can be stored in freezer. Yield: 6 small servings.

Mrs. Steve Harris
(Linda Walker)

Pear Bunny Salad

4 canned pear halves
4 lettuce leaves
8 whole almonds
8 raisins
4 maraschino cherry halves
16 (1½-inch) strips red licorice
    laces

4 heaping Tablespoons cottage
    cheese
4 Tablespoons processed cheese
    (optional)
4 sprigs parsley (optional)

Place pears core-side down on lettuce leaves. Use large end of pear for bunny's face. Gently push almonds into top of large end of pear to form ears. Use raisins for eyes, cherry for nose, and licorice strips for whiskers. At small end of pear, place a small mound of cottage cheese for tail. To garnish, form processed cheese into 4 small carrot shapes. Use parsley sprigs for carrot tops. Chill. Yield: 4 servings.

Mike Hall

Candle Salad

4 lettuce leaves
4 pineapple slices

2 bananas
4 maraschino cherries

On small plates, place lettuce leaves. Put 1 slice pineapple in center of each lettuce leaf. Cut bananas crosswise in half to make 4 equal pieces. Stand ½ each banana cut-side down in middle of pineapple ring. With a half of a toothpick, secure cherry on top of each banana. Yield: 4 servings.

Mrs. George Cupstid
(Mary Tullos)

Hattie's Spaghetti and Cheese

1 (3-ounce) package extra thin
  spaghetti, cooked
3 cups boiling water
1 egg

1½ cups milk
4 ounces cheese, divided
Salt and pepper to taste
8 Tablespoons butter

Add spaghetti to boiling water. Cook about 20 minutes. Drain spaghetti and put in a 1¾-quart casserole. In separate bowl combine egg, milk, ½ shredded cheese and a dash of salt and pepper. Pour these ingredients over spaghetti and stir. Slice remaining cheese and lay on top. Pat butter on top. Salt and pepper top. Cook at 450° for 20 minutes. Yield: 4 to 6 servings.

Mrs. John Prewitt
(Betty Marsalis)

Saucy Franks

3 slices bacon, diced
½ cup chopped onion
2 Tablespoons chopped green
  pepper
¾ cup unsweetened pineapple juice
½ cup ketchup

⅛ teaspoon chili powder
10 wieners, sliced into ½-inch
  pieces
10 hamburger buns
1 cup shredded cheese (optional)

Cook bacon until crispy. Add onion and green pepper; cook until limp. Add pineapple juice, ketchup, and chili powder. Add wiener slices; cover and bring to a boil. Lower heat and simmer 8 to 10 minutes. Spoon onto warm hamburger buns. Sprinkle with cheese if desired. Yield: 10 servings.

Mrs. George Jabour
(Miriam Penton)

Pizza Burgers

1 pound ground beef
8 English muffins
1 (14-ounce) jar pizza sauce
6 to 8 ounces mozzarella cheese,
  shredded

1 (4-ounce) can mushrooms
  (optional)
Pepperoni, olives, sausage, onions,
  etc. (optional)

Children 6 and older can prepare this. Brown ground beef. Some mothers would rather do this chore. Open buns and place them on a cookie sheet, cut-side up. Spread sauce on muffins and top with ground beef. Top with cheese. Add optional toppings if desired. Put into broiler of oven until the cheese melts. Yield: 8 burgers.

Mrs. Syd Johnston, II
(Dinnie Kelly)

Bologna Cups

6 round slices bologna, skin
  removed
1 (16-ounce) can pork and beans
½ teaspoon mustard

½ teaspoon ketchup
½ teaspoon steak sauce
1 onion, chopped

In ungreased oblong baking pan, place slices of bologna. Do not cut edges of bologna. In center of each round, place 1 Tablespoon pork and beans, mustard, ketchup, and steak sauce. Top with chopped onion, about 1 Tablespoonful or to taste. Run under broiler of oven until beans are heated and bologna forms a cup. This is a "happy meal" for children when served with French fries or chips and a brownie. Yield: 3 to 6 servings.

Nick Cassino

Peanut Butter Fondue

2 cups peanut butter
1 (5⅓-ounce) can evaporated milk
1 cup light brown sugar
¼ cup margarine
⅛ teaspoon salt
Apple wedges

Marshmallows
Graham cracker pieces
Sliced bananas
Cherries
Seedless grapes

Mix first 5 ingredients well. In heavy saucepan, cook over low heat until well blended and hot. Pour into fondue pot. Use remaining ingredients to dip.

Anna Stone

Condiments and Gift Ideas

Mother's Chili Sauce

8 medium onions
8 bell peppers
24 ripe medium tomatoes
4 Tablespoons salt
2½ cups sugar
6 cups white vinegar

4 teaspoons ground cloves
4 teaspoons ground cinnamon
4 teaspoons ground ginger
Red pepper or TABASCO brand
    pepper sauce to taste

Chop in food processor with steel blade onions, bell peppers, and tomatoes. Put in large pot. Add salt, sugar, vinegar, cloves, cinnamon, and ginger. Stir well. Put on low heat. Simmer, stirring occasionally, 6 to 8 hours. Add red pepper or TABASCO (2 to 4 dried whole red peppers, chopped, or 1 to 3 Tablespoons TABASCO, according to your personal taste). Pour into hot pint jars. Seal. Store in cool place. Refrigerate before serving and store opened jars in refrigerator. Serve with meats as a hot relish. Yield: Approximately 4 pints.

Mrs. Charles Faulk
(Elizabeth Young)

Green Tomato Relish

2 quarts green tomatoes, chopped
1 quart onions, chopped
½ cup salt
2 quarts cabbage, chopped
1 quart green pepper, chopped
2 hot peppers, chopped
1 medium head cauliflower,
    chopped

2 quarts vinegar
3 cups sugar
1 cup flour
¼ cup dry mustard
¼ cup turmeric
1 Tablespoon celery seed

Sprinkle tomatoes and onions with salt and let stand overnight. Drain above mixture and combine well with other vegetables. Add a little vinegar to dry ingredients to make a paste. Add remaining vinegar and paste to vegetables. In a large saucepan bring relish to a boil. Reduce heat and cook slowly for 1 hour. Put into sterilized jars and seal with a water bath.

Mrs. J. Carter Stamm, Sr.
(Dorothy Williams)

419

Hot Chocolate Mixture

2½ cups powdered sugar
1¾ cups instant chocolate

1½ cups coffee creamer
7½ cups powdered milk

Mix all ingredients in large mixing bowl. Use ½ cup mixture for every cup of boiling water. Store in large jar. Yield: 13 cups.

Mrs. James Ruggles
(Karen Psitzer)

Mother's Crisp Pickles

6 large sour or dill pickles
3 cups sugar
3 teaspoons pickling spice

3 Tablespoons vinegar
3 cloves garlic

Slice pickles into thick rounds and place in crock with lid. Add sugar on top of pickles, then rest of ingredients. Cover. Stir once a day, stirring from the bottom, for at least 1 week. After a week place pickles in clean jars. Cover with juices and put a clove of garlic in each jar. Cover and refrigerate until ready to serve. Yield: 3 pints.

A good gift idea.

Mrs. Charles Faulk
(Elizabeth Young)

Pickled Eggs

12 eggs
Water to cover
2 cups vinegar
3 Tablespoons sugar

1½ teaspoons salt
1 teaspoon dill seed
1 clove garlic

Place eggs in pan and cover with tap water. (If eggs have been refrigerated, let stand in water until they reach room temperature.) Bring to a boil, then turn off heat and let eggs stand in hot water for 20 minutes. Pour off hot water and rinse with cold to stop cooking process. Meanwhile, mix vinegar, sugar, and salt; simmer. Add dill and garlic; simmer 5 minutes longer. Crack and peel eggs and pack in a sterile jar. While eggs are still hot, pour vinegar mixture over eggs. Seal jars. Allow eggs to stand in refrigerator for 3 to 4 days before eating. Will keep almost indefinitely. Yield: 12 eggs.

Mrs. Edley Jones, Jr.
(Lucy Imig)

Sweet Cucumber Pickles

2 cups pickling lime	2 Tablespoons salt
2 gallons water	1 Tablespoon whole cloves
8 pounds cucumbers	1 Tablespoon whole allspice
10 cups sugar	1 Tablespoon celery seed
2 quarts plus 1 cup white vinegar	

Use plastic or crock container to soak cucumbers. Do not use aluminum. Dissolve pickling lime in water and put in cucumbers which have been cut in slices 1-inch thick. Let soak 24 hours. Remove cucumbers and wash well in 3 or 4 waters. Make a pickling solution of sugar, vinegar, salt, and each spice tied separately in a thin cloth bag. Heat just enough to dissolve sugar. Pour over pickles and let soak 30 minutes. Then boil 30 minutes. Put in sterilized jars and cover with pickling solution and seal. Yield: About 14 pints.

Mrs. John Kamman, Jr.
(Betty Blackburn)

Bread and Butter Pickles

25 to 30 medium cucumbers	5 cups sugar
8 large white onions	2 Tablespoons mustard seed
2 large sweet peppers	1 teaspoon turmeric
½ cup salt	½ teaspoon cloves
5 cups cider vinegar	

Wash cucumbers and slice as thin as desired or ⅛ to ¼-inch thick. Chop onions and peppers. Combine with cucumbers and salt; let stand 3 hours, then drain. Combine vinegar, sugar, and spices in large preserving kettle. Bring to a boil. Add drained cucumbers and heat thoroughly but do not boil. Pack while hot into sterilized jars and seal at once. Yield: Approximately 7 pints.

Mrs. Lucille Kennedy
Granite Shoals, Texas

Cucumbers used for pickles should be gathered no more than 24 hours before pickling.

Squash Pickles

8 cups sliced small yellow squash
2 cups onions, sliced into rings and
  separated
2 green bell peppers, coarsely
  chopped
2 red bell peppers, coarsely chopped

2 Tablespoons salt
3 cups sugar
2 cups red vinegar
2 teaspoons mustard seed
2 teaspoons celery seed

Cover squash, onions, and peppers with salt. Let stand 1 hour. Drain. Combine sugar, vinegar, mustard seed, and celery seed in large saucepan. Bring to a boil and add squash, peppers, and onions. Boil 1 minute. Pack into sterilized jars and seal. Yield: 4 pints.

Mrs. Lindsey Blackledge
Laurel, Mississippi

Dilled Beans

5 pounds green beans
⅛ teaspoon red pepper
1 clove garlic
1 head dill or dill seed

2 cups vinegar
3 cups water (or more)
¼ to ½ cup salt (to taste)

Remove stems on beans and leave whole. Cook beans until barely tender, approximately 10 minutes. Place pepper, garlic, and dill in jars with beans. Heat vinegar, water, and salt to boiling; pour over beans and seal. This may be used as an appetizer. Yield: 5 to 6 quarts.

Mrs. Molly Dever
Granite Shoals, Texas

"MOTTS"

¼ cup marjoram
¼ cup oregano

½ cup thyme
¼ cup savory

Put all ingredients into a food processor and blend as well as possible. Store in airtight jar. MOTTS is so called because of the proportions: 1 part each of marjoram, oregano, and savory and 2 parts thyme. It is delicious when served generously with chicken, duck, turkey, rabbit and lamb, with vegetable dishes, and in tomato sauce. Yield: 1¼ cups.

Mrs. Tony Benjamin
New Orleans, Louisiana

Cossar's Pickled Green Tomatoes

2 pints tiny green tomatoes
1⅓ cups vinegar
⅔ cup water
2 Tablespoons dill seed

2 Tablespoons salt
6 to 8 cloves garlic, peeled
4 to 6 small hot peppers

Fill 2 sterilized pint jars with green tomatoes that have been washed. Bring water and vinegar to a boil. Add spices, garlic, and peppers to jars. Pour vinegar and water over tomatoes. Seal jars in water bath. Let jars stand upside down for about 24 hours. After about 7 to 10 days, they are ready to serve. Yield: 2 pints.

If tiny whole tomatoes are not available, large tomatoes cut in wedges may be substituted.

Mrs. Elizabeth Cossar

Fig Preserves

4 pounds ripe figs
2 teaspoons baking soda

2 cups water
4 pounds sugar

Wash figs in mixture of baking soda and water. Rinse in clear water. Place figs in heavy saucepan or Dutch oven. Pour sugar over all figs and let stand 2 hours or until syrup begins to form. Cook fig mixture over medium heat until figs are brown in color and syrup thickens. Stir occasionally at start of cooking process and as preserves begin to thicken. Pack into hot sterilized jars and seal. Yield: 5 pints.

Mrs. Oren D. Bailess, Sr.
(Betty Dement)

For best results when pickling, be sure that the liquid for pickling and the food to be pickled are hot. The food absorbs the flavor more quickly.

Dilled Okra

3 to 4 quarts tiny okra
6 tiny whole red peppers
6 tiny whole green peppers
6 cloves garlic, peeled
6 stems fresh dill or 1 Tablespoon
   dill seed

2 Tablespoons celery salt
1 quart water
1 pint vinegar
½ cup salt

Wash and remove stems of okra pods. Do not trim too closely as they will bleed. Place in sterile jars. In each jar, place 1 green and 1 red pepper, 1 clove garlic, 1 stem or ½ teaspoon dill, and 1 teaspoon celery salt. Mix together water, vinegar, and salt. Cook for 5 minutes. Pour over okra. Seal with a water bath. Let stand 2 to 3 days before eating. Yield: 6 pints.

Mrs. Eustace Conway
(Stella Colhoun)

Brandied Peaches

3 cups sugar
1 cup water
2 quarts peeled peach halves

¾ cup brandy (apricot or peach),
   divided

Combine sugar and water in a large saucepan. Bring to boiling point over medium heat. Reduce heat; simmer for 10 minutes. Add peach halves to sugar and water syrup; simmer for 10 minutes or until peaches are tender. Remove saucepan from heat. Place 1 Tablespoon brandy in 4 sterilized hot pint jars. Fill jars with remaining peaches. Add 1 Tablespoon more brandy. Cover with hot syrup. Seal jars immediately. Yield: 4 pints.

Mrs. John Newton
(Cathie Bailess)

Plum Jelly

4 pounds plums
1 cup water

6½ cups sugar
1 package fruit pectin

Place washed plums in saucepan or Dutch oven. Add water and cook until soft about 20 minutes, stirring occasionally. Mash fruit with potato masher and place in old pillow case or similar bag to drip. Measure 4 cups juice; add sugar and mix well. Bring to boil, stirring constantly. Stir in pectin and bring to boil. Boil hard 1 minute, stirring constantly. Remove from heat; skim off foam. Pour into hot sterilized jars and seal.

Mrs. Oren D. Bailess, Sr.
(Betty Dement)

Potpourri

3 cups dried flowers and leaves
1 Tablespoon allspice
1 Tablespoon orris root
Citrus peel of 3 oranges, 3 limes,
    and 3 lemons

6 drops rose oil
6 drops gardenia oil
Cinnamon sticks (optional)

To dry flowers spread on newspaper and dry at least 1 week. They should be dry to touch, but not crumbly. Add remaining ingredients when dry and store in a large covered container 6 to 8 weeks. Shake weekly. Makes a lovely gift. NOT EDIBLE.

Mrs. William W. Ramsey
(Carolyn Sasser)

Creole Seasoning

26 ounces salt
1½ ounces ground black pepper
2 ounces ground red pepper

1 ounce garlic powder
1 ounce chili powder
1 ounce monosodium glutamate

Mix well. Store in airtight containers with a shaker top. Good seasoning for salads, meats, and vegetables. Additional salt may be added if it is too hot for children.

Mrs. Bill Pierce
(Pat Hand)

Pepper Jelly

3/4 *cup finely chopped bell peppers*
1/4 *cup finely chopped red hot*
  peppers
1½ *cups vinegar*
6½ *cups sugar*

1 *teaspoon salt*
1 *(6-ounce) bottle fruit pectin*
2 *to 3 drops red or green food*
  coloring, optional

Put peppers into blender with vinegar. Mix pepper mixture with sugar and salt in large pan. Bring to a full boil; boil 2 to 3 minutes. Remove from heat and add fruit pectin and food coloring, stirring constantly. Let stand 2 minutes then skim off foam. Put into sterilized jars and seal while hot. Yield: 5 (8-ounce) jars.

Excellent over cream cheese and crackers. Also good served with meats.

Mrs. Oren Bailess, Sr.
(Betty Dement)

Blackberry Fig Preserves

7 *to 8 cups mashed ripe figs*
5 *cups sugar*
1 *(6-ounce) box blackberry gelatin*
  (or strawberry or raspberry)

1 *(1¾-ounce) package powdered*
  fruit pectin

Mix ingredients in a large pot. Bring to a boil, stirring occasionally, and then let simmer for 20 minutes. Spoon into clean, sterile canning jars. Put tops on and tighten lids. Place in a deep pan; cover with water about an inch over the lids. Bring to a boil and boil gently for 5 minutes. Remove from water bath. The tops will pop when seal is complete. If preserves are not sealed, keep in refrigerator.

Mrs. James B. Steen
(Dot Segrest)

Kahlúa

1 *to 1½ cups water*
3½ *cups sugar*
1 *(2-ounce) jar instant coffee (take*
  out 1½ to 2 Tablespoons)

1 *fifth vodka (100 proof)*
2 *to 3 Tablespoons vanilla extract*

Bring water to boil in large saucepan. Add sugar and coffee to water. Stir well and let cool. Add vodka and vanilla. Vapor will be strong. Yield: Approximately 1 gallon.

Mrs. Stan Terry, Jr.
(Sallie Bingham)

Peach and Raisin Conserve

4 pounds peaches, skinned and
   pitted
3 cups water

6 cups sugar
2 cups seedless raisins
1½ cups chopped pecans

Place peaches in pot. Add water and sugar. Cook for 15 minutes. Add raisins and cook until mixture thickens. Add pecans and cool 15 minutes more. Pour into hot, sterilized jars and seal. Serve with pork. Yield: 8 pints.

Mrs. Robert A. Harbison
Jackson, Mississippi

Brandied Fruit

1 (16-ounce) can pineapple
1 (16-ounce) can peach halves
1 (20-ounce) can crushed pineapple
1 (11-ounce) can mandarin orange
   slices

1 (10-ounce) jar maraschino cherries
Brandy or bourbon

Let fruit drain for 12 hours. For every cup of drained fruit add ½ cup sugar. Let stand 12 hours. Add 1 cup brandy or bourbon. Put in jars and store in refrigerator. Ready to serve in 3 weeks. Delicious over vanilla ice cream. Makes pretty Christmas gifts. Yield: Barely ½ gallon.

This is an old recipe dating before use of brandied fruit made with "starter."

Mrs. Robert C. Odom
(Idamae Ellzey)

Holiday Aroma

1 quart pineapple juice
1 quart water
1 quart apple cider
4 pieces ginger

2 Tablespoons ground cinnamon
2 Tablespoons ground allspice
2 Tablespoons whole cloves
2 Tablespoons pickling spice

Combine all ingredients in large pot and bring to a boil. Boil for several minutes. Reduce heat and simmer. Add more liquid if needed. This can be kept in the refrigerator in a plastic carton.

This gives your house a wonderful aroma for a festive party. DO NOT DRINK.

Mrs. Jerry M. Hall
(Carolyn Buckner)

Garnishes

Vegetable Garnishes

Artichoke Cup: Cut off stem so that artichoke will sit level. Snip tips of leaves off artichoke. Steam until tender about 45 minutes. Drain and chill. Hollow out inside of artichoke. Place a small glass or bowl inside cavity. Fill with dip and place in center of tray. Place crackers, vegetables, etc. to be dipped around artichoke.

Cabbage Container: Select a red or green cabbage that still has large outer leaves. Carefully curl back outer leaves. Cut so cabbage will sit flat. Cut a cavity out of center. Place a small glass or bowl in cavity. Fill with dip. Surround with fresh vegetables or boiled shrimp.

Carrot Curls: With a swivel vegetable peeler, cut long strips of carrot pushing peeler away from body. Roll up strips and secure with toothpicks. Drop in ice water and chill for several hours. Remove toothpicks when ready to serve.

Stuffed Celery: Use 2 ribs of celery approximately the same size. Cut off leaves and tough end. Fill each with your favorite cheese spread. Place 1 celery rib on top of other. Tie ribs together at each end. Refrigerate. When ready to serve, remove string and cut crosswise into small slices. Serve with sandwiches or on relish trays.

Cucumber Pinwheels and Twists: Using fork or citrus stripper, score cucumber lengthwise all the way around. Cut in thin slices to form pinwheel. Use as a garnish for meat trays, for relish trays, or for salads. To form a twist, cut from center of cucumber slice through outside edge. Gently twist to form an "S" shape. Chill in ice water to set.

Cucumber or Turnip Lily: Cut 2 thin cucumber circles. Carefully curl 1 circle into a cone shape. Wrap the other cucumber circle in opposite direction around cone shape. Secure base with toothpick. Use a small strip of carrot in center of lily for stamen. Chill in ice water until serving time. The same method may be used with turnip slices.

Cucumber Tulip: Cut a 2-inch piece off end of cucumber. Cut 6 triangular sections down from cut edge evenly around cucumber to make tulip petals. Scoop seeds and some pulp out of center. Push a small circle of carrot into cavity to form center of flower. Chill in ice water.

Green Onion Fans: Cut root off thick green onion. Cut again to make a 2 to 3-inch length piece. With the point of a small knife, starting ¼ of the way from stem end, cut into center and down to root end. Continue to make cuts around onion, keeping cuts as close together as possible. Chill in ice water to make onion curl. A few drops of food coloring may be put in ice water to tint onion.

Onion Mums: Choose a medium-sized, well-rounded white onion. Do not use onions with a double growth inside. Remove skin and cut off any roots leaving root end intact. Use a small sharp knife and start cutting at top of onion through center towards root end. Do not cut all the way through. Stop ½-inch from root end. Continue making cuts all the way around onion. Place onion in hot water for 5 minutes. Then chill in ice water until time to serve. To tint, add food coloring to ice water.

Parsley Wreath: Cover a small, green florist's wreath with parsley sprigs, using wire florist picks to secure parsley. Decorate wreath with broccoli and cauliflower florets, fluted mushrooms, celery fans, radish roses, carrot curls, and boiled shrimp, if desired. Use toothpicks to secure these decorations. Place bowl of vegetable dip in center of wreath.

Pepper Cups: Use large green, red, or yellow peppers that will sit flat. Cut stem end off peppers and remove seeds. Fill with mustard and mayonnaise and place on meat trays or fill with vegetables or relishes.

Pumpkin Bowl: Cut top off pumpkin and remove seeds. Place a bowl inside pumpkin. Use as a container to serve fresh fruit, vegetables, or punch.

Radish Mum: Cut root and stem off a well rounded radish. Starting at root end, make parallel cuts almost through stem end. Turn radish ¼ turn and make another series of parallel cuts at right angle to other cuts. Chill in ice water to open petals.

Radish or Pickle Fan: Cut root and stem off a long oval radish with a small knife. Make crosswise cuts in accordion fashion almost through radish. Keep cuts as close together and as even as possible. Chill in ice water to open into fan shape. Small pickles may be used, also.

Radish Rose: Cut root and stem off a well-rounded radish. Starting halfway down radish, make a downward cut in red skin parallel to side of radish, stopping ¼-inch from end of radish to make petal. Repeat evenly around radish making 4 cuts. Turn radish ¼ turn. Starting further toward center, make 4 more downward cuts around radish, stopping at top of first row of cuts. Hollow out center. Push a small circle of carrot into cavity to form center. Chill in ice water to make petals open.

Tomato Rose: Choose a firm tomato. Start at bottom of tomato and peel in a 1-inch wide continuous spiral slightly scalloping edge. Be careful not to break spiral. Coil spiral skin-side out to form rose bloom. Secure with toothpick, if necessary. Place rose on small lettuce leaf or bed of parsley to garnish. The same process can be used with lemons and oranges.

Turnip Flowers: Cut thin slices of turnips. Use flower-shaped canapé cutters to cut flower shapes out of turnip slices or cut flower shapes with small, sharp knife. Cut small circles out of carrots or turnips. Place circles in middle of flowers. Secure with toothpick. Flowers may be tinted by soaking in water colored with food coloring. A stem may be added by slipping tops of green onions over toothpicks. Use without stem to garnish molds. Fill an orange or grapefruit cup with turnip flowers with stems and parsley or curly leaf lettuce to make a small flower arrangement to be used in center of tray.

Fruit Garnishes

Citrus Bows: With a citrus stripper or mushroom fluter, cut around lemon, lime, or orange making 1 continuous thin strip at least 8 inches long. Tie strip in a bow or use as a curlicue to garnish seafood, vegetables, salads, or desserts.

Citrus or Melon Crowns: Slice off stem ends of lemon or other citrus fruit. Holding fruit on its side, make a diagonal cut into core. Continue making cuts in a zigzag fashion all the way around center of fruit. Make sure each cut goes all the way into core and that first and last cuts will meet evenly. Gently twist halves and pull apart. Place a sprig of parsley, cherry, or olive slice in center of crown. Cut melons in the same manner. Scoop out seeds and fill with melon balls, cottage cheese, chicken salad, etc.

Citrus Twists: Use a citrus stripper to score fruit lengthwise at regular intervals. Slice the fruit ¼-inch thick. Cut from center of fruit through outer edge at 1 of scored spaces. Gently twist into "S" shape. Use to garnish food or beverages. For extra color, dip a cotton swab in food coloring and paint the scored spaces in either same or alternating colors.

Cranberry Garlands: With needle and thread, string fresh cranberries. Use to garnish turkey or some other meat trays at holiday time.

Cranberry Cut Outs: Slice canned jellied cranberry sauce ¼-inch thick. Cut into shapes with cookie cutters. Place on orange slices and use to garnish meat or seafood.

Sugared Grapes: Wash and dry grapes. Break into smaller clusters. Bring to a boil ½ cup water and 1 cup sugar. Simmer about 5 minutes. Dip each cluster into sugar syrup. Let excess syrup drip off and immediately sprinkle with additional sugar. Place on waxed paper to harden. Do not refrigerate. Use to garnish cheese boards, sandwich and dessert trays or cakes. Other small fruit may be sugared in same manner.

Grapefruit or Orange Baskets: Use a thick skinned fruit. With stem down, cut away a wedge on each side of center leaving a ½ to ¾-inch wide strip to form handle. If desired, zigzag or scallop around sides of basket. Carefully scoop out fruit pulp. A grapefruit spoon is helpful for this. Fill basket with sugared grapes, fresh flowers and greenery, or flowers made from vegetables.

Pineapple Boats: Slice a large pineapple in half lengthwise. Scoop out fruit. Fill halves with fresh fruit, chicken or shrimp salad. Pineapple may also be cut in quarters. Then cut fruit away from skin in 1 piece. Leaving the fruit in the skin, remove core and cut into bite-size pieces. (Leave core whole.) Place a maraschino cherry on top of each pineapple piece and secure each with a toothpick. This makes a beautiful as well as delicious garnish.

Strawberry Fan: Leave stem on strawberry. Turn strawberry stem-side down. Make 5 or 6 parallel, vertical cuts through bottom of strawberry almost to stem.

Beverage Garnishes

Ice Bowl: Fill a large bowl ¾ to 1 inch deep with water and freeze. Place another bowl (of similar shape but 2 inches smaller) inside larger bowl. Secure bowls with masking tape and place a weight, such as a heavy can, inside smaller bowl. Place citrus slices or fresh flowers and greenery around insides of larger bowl; fill with water and freeze at least 24 hours. To unmold, let stand until bowls come loose. Place ice bowl on tray. Surround with greenery and fill with cold beverage. Bowl may also be lined with plastic wrap or a clear plastic bowl and used as a container for boiled seafood or melon balls.

Ice Ring: Fill a metal ring mold with water. Pour this water into a bowl. Let this water sit 10 to 15 minutes, stirring water 4 or 5 times. This process expels the air bubbles. Pour ¼ to ⅓ water back into mold. Place mold in freezer and refrigerate remaining water to chill. When water in mold is slushy, remove and add a wreath of fruit, flowers, and greenery. Holly is attractive at Christmas time. Pour cold water just to top of decorations. Freeze until firm. Pour over another layer of cold water to fill mold. Freeze. To unmold, wrap a hot, wet towel around mold. Float ring in punch bowl.

Garnishes by the Glass: (1) Cut a slit in citrus slices to garnish rim of glasses. (2) Garnish a red wine glass with a small cluster of red grapes and white wine glass with green grapes. (3) Cut a small piece from a ring of pineapple and place over rim of a glass of fruit drink. (4) Garnish the rim of a glass of sangria with a wedge of apple dipped in lemon juice. (5) Float a strawberry in a glass of champagne. (6) Cut a slit in a strawberry and place it on the rim of a glass of strawberry daiquiri. (7) Make a fruit kabob for fruit drinks by placing a cherry, a pineapple chunk, and a small orange wedge on a toothpick. (8) Garnish a bloody mary with a carrot stick or a small celery rib. (9) Float a lemon or orange slice studded with whole cloves in hot spiced cider or tea. (10) Garnish hot chocolate with a cinnamon stick, a cinnamon candy stick, or peppermint stick. (11) Place a long sprig of mint in ice tea.

Miscellaneous Garnishes

Bacon Curls: Fry bacon nearly crisp, pressing bacon flat as it cooks. Immediately upon removing from skillet, roll into coil. As bacon cools, it will hold the shape. Use as a garnish for egg dishes or quiches.

Bread Baskets: Hollow out center of large round, rectangular, or oval bread leaving a ¾-inch shell. Fill with dip and use bread pieces for dipping, if desired. A rectangular bread can be used as a container for finger sandwiches. The bread can also be cut with a sharp knife to make a basket with a handle.

Butter Balls and Curls: Dip a melon ball scoop in hot water for a few minutes; then scoop out butter. Drop butter balls into ice water. Refrigerate until time to serve. To make butter curls, place butter curler in hot water. Pull curler lightly across top of a firm, but not too cold, stick of butter. Drop curls into ice water. Refrigerate. To serve butter balls or curls, drain and serve piled in a pyramid on a dish of cracked ice.

Chocolate Curls: Warm slightly the blade of a vegetable peeler. Hold a wrapped chunk or bar of chocolate in hand to warm. Pull blade across chocolate to make curls. Use a toothpick to pick up curls and place on dessert.

Chocolate Cutouts: Melt 6 ounces semisweet chocolate over low heat. When slightly cooled, pour chocolate onto a cookie sheet covered with foil. Spread over pan until chocolate is smooth and about ⅛ to ¼ inch thick. When chocolate is almost set, cut firmly with cookie cutters. Lift with spatula when firm. Cover and store in refrigerator.

Chocolate Web: Spoon 2 ounces melted and partially cooled semisweet chocolate in a decorating bag with a number 2 tip. Pipe concentric circles ½ to ¾ inch apart on top of a cake that has been smoothly iced. Pull a toothpick through circles across diameter of cake from edge through center. Lines should be equally spaced.

Crystallized Violets: Pick violets while still dewy and let dry on paper towels. Beat an egg white with 1 to 2 teaspoons cold water. With a small, soft brush paint flowers with egg white. Dust with granulated sugar. Dry and store in a tightly closed container. Mint leaves and grapes may also be crystallized in same manner.

Substitutions

2 large eggs	*3 small eggs*
1 cup fresh milk	*½ cup evaporated milk plus ½ cup water*
1 cup sour or buttermilk	*1 Tablespoon vinegar or lemon juice plus sweet milk to make 1 cup*
1 cup sour cream	*1 Tablespoon lemon juice plus evaporated milk to equal 1 cup*
1 cup all purpose flour	*1 cup plus 2 Tablespoons cake flour*
1 cup self-rising flour	*1 cup all purpose flour plus 1 teaspoon baking powder and ½ teaspoon salt*
1 cup cake flour	*1 cup minus 2 Tablespoons all purpose flour*
1 teaspoon baking powder	*½ teaspoon cream of tartar plus ¼ teaspoon soda*
1 Tablespoon cornstarch	*2 Tablespoons all purpose flour*
1 pound fresh mushrooms	*6 ounces canned mushrooms*
1 clove fresh garlic	*1 teaspoon garlic salt or ⅛ teaspoon garlic powder*
1 Tablespoon fresh herbs	*1 teaspoon dried herbs or ¼ teaspoon powdered herbs*
1 ounce unsweetened chocolate	*3 Tablespoons cocoa plus 1 Tablespoon butter or margarine*
1 small fresh onion, minced	*1 Tablespoon instant minced onion*

433

Table of Equivalents

3 teaspoons = 1 Tablespoon
4 Tablespoons = ¼ cup
5 Tablespoons plus 1 teaspoon = ⅓ cup
8 Tablespoons = ½ cup
16 Tablespoons = 1 cup
2 Tablespoons = 1 fluid ounce
1 cup = 8 fluid ounces
1 cup = ½ pint
2 cups = 1 pint
4 cups = 1 quart
2 pints = 1 quart
4 quarts = 1 gallon
8 quarts = 1 peck
4 pecks = 1 bushel
1 dash = less than ⅛ teaspoon
1 pinch = as much as can be taken between tip of finger and thumb
1 ounce = 28.35 grams
1 gram = .035 ounces
1 quart = 946.4 mililiters
1 liter = 1.06 quarts
1 square chocolate = 1 ounce
1 pound butter = 2 cups or 4 sticks
2 Tablespoons butter = 1 ounce
28 saltines = 1 cup crumbs
22 vanilla wafers = 1 cup crumbs
1 slice bread = ¼ cup dry bread crumbs
14 square graham crackers = 1 cup crumbs
⅓ cup raw rice = 1 cup cooked rice
7 ounces spaghetti = 4 cups cooked spaghetti
4 ounces macaroni = 2¼ cups cooked macaroni
Juice of 1 lemon = 3 Tablespoons
1 medium onion, chopped = ½ cup
1 cup heavy cream = 2 cups whipped cream
½ pound Cheddar cheese, shredded = 2 cups
2 to 2½ pounds shrimp in shell = 2 cups shelled, cooked shrimp

Gold Patrons

Judge and Mrs. Oscar P. LaBarre
Mr. and Mrs. Earl W. Lundy
Mr. and Mrs. Robert L. Pickett

Ramsey, Andrews & Sorey, P.A.
Wheeless, Beanland, Shappley &
Bailess

Patrons

Raymond Abraham Construction
  Company
Dr. and Mrs. Robert M. Abraham
Mr. and Mrs. Oren Bailess, Sr.
Boolos, Hawkins & Richardson
Cassino's Florist
Mr. and Mrs. E. A. Buckner, Jr.
The Bug's Ear Gift Shop
The Cherry Street Cottage,
  Mr. and Mrs. Don Barnes
The Collection of Vicksburg, Inc.
Dr. and Mrs. James W. Cook
Bill Dalrymple Ford, Inc.
Mrs. Robert Lowry Dent
Deposit Guaranty National Bank
Mr. and Mrs. Albert Dornbusch
Falco Lime, Inc.
Mr. and Mrs. Fred Farrell
First National Bank,
  Vicksburg, Mississippi
Dr. and Mrs. James P. Guerriero
Mr. and Mrs. Shouphie Habeeb
Bill Harris Real Estate
Mr. and Mrs. Donnie W. Harris
Mrs. Tom Harris, Jr.
Jitney Jungle #4
Mr. and Mrs. Sydney K. Johnston, II
Just Us Kids
Dr. Herman Kellum
Koury's Children's Shop, Inc.
Mr. and Mrs. C. Hays Latham
Lions Club of Vicksburg
Mr. and Mrs. Frank Myers Maxwell
May and Company
Mr. and Mrs. Raymond B. May
Mr. and Mrs. Robert McConnell
Dr. and Mrs. Lamar T. McMillin

Dr. and Mrs. Frank T. McPherson
Merchants National Bank,
  Vicksburg, Mississippi
Miller Ready Mix Company, Inc.
Mr. and Mrs. Don S. Miller, Jr.
Monsour's Restaurant
Mr. and Mrs. Robert Morrison, Jr.
Moss Construction Company
Neill Butane, Inc.
Mr. and Mrs. Robert C. Odom
Dr. and Mrs. Bill Pierce
Dr. Wayne M. Pitre
Dr. and Mrs. W. K. Purks
Mr. and Mrs. Bobby D. Robinson
Mr. and Mrs. Allen D. Rooke
Dr. and Mrs. Robert Sadler
Mrs. Gorman Schaffer
Dr. and Mrs. Kurt R. Schrock
Dr. Patricia Dornbusch Sistrunk
Dr. Deborah Smith
Taylor-Jones/American International
Teller, Chaney & Rector, Attorneys at Law
Mr. and Mrs. Joseph Stanford Terry, Sr.
Mr. and Mrs. Ernest Thomas
United Cleaners
U.S. Rubber Reclaiming Company—
  Division of Genstar
Mr. and Mrs. Joe E. Varner
Varner, Parker & Sessums
Vicksburg Evening Post/Vicksburg
  Sunday Post
Vicksburg Medical Center
Vicksburg-Warren County
  Tourist Commission
The Vision Clinic
Mr. and Mrs. Emmett Ward
Mr. and Mrs. D. P. Waring, Jr.

We sincerely thank these individuals and businesses for their generous contributions.

Index

Index

Index

Index

Index

Index

Index

Index

Index

Index

Index

Vintage Vicksburg

P.O. Box 86
Vicksburg, Mississippi 39181-0086
601-634-1084
cookbooks@javicksburg.org

Please send me ___ copies of *VINTAGE VICKSBURG!* @ $24.95 each $ _____

Mississippi residents add 7.00% sales tax @ $ 1.75 each $ _____

Postage and handling @ $ 3.00 each $ _____

Gift Wrapping @ $ 1.00 each $ _____

Total enclosed $ _____

Name _____

Street _____

City _____ State _____ Zip Code _____

Charge to: ☐ MasterCard ☐ Visa

Account Number _____ Expiration Date _____

Phone Number _____

Make checks payable to: *JAV Publications*. All proceeds from the sale of *VINTAGE VICKSBURG* will be used to finance community service projects of the Junior Auxiliary of Vicksburg, Inc.
Visit our website: **www.javicksburg.org** to place orders or learn more about the charities of the Junior Auxiliary of Vicksburg.

AMBROSIA

P.O. Box 86
Vicksburg, Mississippi 39181-0086
601-634-1084
cookbooks@javicksburg.org

Please send me ___ copies of *AMBROSIA!* @ $29.95 each $ _____

Mississippi residents add 7.00% sales tax @ $ 2.10 each $ _____

Postage and handling @ $ 3.00 each $ _____

Gift Wrapping @ $ 1.00 each $ _____

Total enclosed $ _____

Name _____

Street _____

City _____ State _____ Zip Code _____

Charge to: ☐ MasterCard ☐ Visa

Account Number _____ Expiration Date _____

Phone Number _____

Make checks payable to: *JAV Publications*. All proceeds from the sale of *AMBROSIA* will be used to finance community service projects of the Junior Auxiliary of Vicksburg, Inc.
Visit our website: **www.javicksburg.org** to place orders or learn more about the charities of the Junior Auxiliary of Vicksburg.

Reorder Additional Copies